Personal and Archetypal Dynamics in the Analytical Relationship

Proceedings of
The Eleventh International Congress
For Analytical Psychology,
Paris, 1989

Mary Ann Mattoon
Editor

DAIMON
VERLAG

Personal and Archetypal Dynamics in the Analytical Relationship
edited by Mary Ann Mattoon.
The translators of individual papers are given on the final page of each translation.

Cover design: meta4 – Jeanne Fountain and Joel T. Miskin
Cover art: Ilisha Helfman; "Another World View", 1989.
Paper construction, 4.75 x 4.75 in., private collection.

ISBN 3-85630-524-6

Contents

Analytical Psychology and Inter-Cultural Experience

Jung and Anti-Semitism (Workshop)

Alphabetical List of Authors

Editor's Preface

The setting of the XIth International Congress for Analytical Psychology in September 1989 was historic, in a special sense: Paris, in the 200th anniversary year of the beginning of the French Revolution. This Congress also marked, with a one-year delay (the Congress intended for 1961 was held in 1962), the 30th anniversary of the first Congress – 1958, in Zurich.

These Congresses, and the nine between, have been the triennial meetings of the International Association for Analytical Psychology (known as "the International" or "IAAP"), the professional organization of Jungian analysts, founded in 1955. (A person must be a member of the IAAP to use the title "Jungian analyst.") At the time of the first Congress, the 40 founding members of the IAAP had increased to 150, in eight member groups. New groups were admitted at nearly every conference until, by the end of the Paris Congress, the groups numbered 28, the members 1455. Attendance at the Congresses has increased from about 150 in 1965 to over 700 in 1989. (Figures are not available for 1958 and 1962.) The number of presentations has grown from about 25 in 1962 to nearly 60 in 1989. The increase is due largely to the addition of afternoon lectures and workshops to the traditional, lengthier morning papers.

* * *

The theme "Personal and Archetypal Dynamics in the Analytical Relationship" is, as Hans Dieckmann mentioned in his closing presidential address, an outgrowth of the accumulated experience of past Congresses. Varying and controversial emphases between "clinical" issues and "archetypal" considerations have given way to a synthesis. Over the years it has become increasingly clear that Jungians' emphasis on the archetypal level of the psyche is well advised, because it provides a depth of understanding of personal and social problems not otherwise available. Indeed, this emphasis is the genius of the Jungian approach to psychology. At the same time, the archetypal, symbolic approach must take into account individual experience.

The new synthesis has provided, also, an awareness of the common ground among subgroups of Jungian psychology, often identified as classical, developmental and archetypal. When we focus on the analytic relationship, it becomes clear that we must understand its component parts, transference and countertransference, and their interrelation. As the papers from this Congress reflect, sometimes this understanding comes through awareness of specific images, such as God images; sometimes through specific problems, such as neonatal loss; sometimes through seeing an old therapeutic problem in a new light, such as resistance to change; and sometimes through looking at the total process from a fresh perspective, perhaps suggested by an alchemical image. This list is by no means exhaustive.

Although some papers in this book focus on specific therapeutic issues, such as erotic transference or depression, very little attention has been given to diagnostic categories. This restraint is characteristically Jungian. Jungian psychotherapy is guided by the subjective experience of the analysand, not the observable behavior that defines diagnostic categories. The de-emphasis on behavior is an aspect of the Jungian truism that the "medical model" is usually not helpful in the therapy of the psyche – sometimes described as the "cure of souls." Jungians find that souls are not healed by diagnosis and treatment of specific symptoms or behaviors. Rather, healing occurs most effectively by attention to an individual's suffering, an accepting environment, and the discovery of meaning in the person's immediate situation and life in general.

* * *

Presentations at the Congress took the form of longer morning papers, followed by relatively brief responses; and afternoon lectures and workshops, with multiple presenters and sometimes multiple sessions. The "workshops" are so designated; the accompanying discussions are not recorded here.

All presenters/authors are Jungian analysts. Each is identified by the place of practice and by group membership. If a presenter is a member of more than one IAAP group, the local organization mentioned is the one through which that person holds a vote in the IAAP. (In a few instances, an IAAP member practices in one place and retains voting membership in another city or even another country.) The Society of Analytical Psychology is the oldest of four member groups in London, England.

Many presenters delivered longer papers than appear here. A few presented excerpts from much longer written works.

* * *

A book comprising papers by many individuals inevitably includes disparate writing styles, contents, and points of view. The goal of the editing has been to retain the individuality, while clarifying and enhancing each author's contribution.

Jung's works are indicated in the text, wherever possible, by CW (*Collected Works*), volume number, and paragraph number. Other Jung references include MDR (*Memories, Dreams, Reflections*), Let-1 and Let-2 (Jung's *Letters*, Vols. 1 & 2). Freud's works are indicated as SE (*Standard Edition*) and their volume number. These works of Jung and Freud are not listed in the end-of-paper references. Biblical references are from the Revised Standard Version.

Other textual citations follow the format of the *Publication Manual* of the American Psychological Association. Thus, they indicate author and date, keyed to the reference at the end of the paper. Each reference is in the language cited by the author.

American punctuation and spelling have been used, according to the University of Chicago *Manual of Style*. Non-English words in the texts have been translated into English, unless they are terms – such as those from alchemy – that are well-known to Jungians, or are available in a standard English dictionary. Names of archetypes are capitalized when it is necessary to distinguish them from often-used words, such as Great Mother. "Self" (capitalized) refers to Jung's concept of the center, totality and integrating factor of the psyche; "self" (not capitalized) carries a variety of other meanings. Dream texts are in italics.

If a paper was delivered in a language other than English, the name of the translator appears at the end of the paper. Sabine Osvatic was assisted in her translations by Dagmar Henle-Dieckmann. Jennette Cook Jones assisted the editor with refining some translations from Italian. Manuscripts were typed on computer disks by Shirley Whiting, Beverly Cicchese, and William Jones. Final proof-reading of all the papers was done by Bonnie L. Marsh, as well as by the Editor.

Mary Ann Mattoon
Minneapolis, Minnesota, USA
July 1990

Introductory Remarks

Thomas Kirsch
San Francisco, California, USA
First Vice-President, IAAP

It is my great honor and pleasure to open the scientific portion of our Eleventh International Congress. Much work has been done by the Program Committee, under the direction of Rosemary Gordon, and by the Organizing Committee, under the direction of Jean Clausse, to provide a memorable experience for all of us.

In my welcoming remarks at our 1986 Congress in Berlin, I focused on *place* and the meaning it had for us as analysts. Now, here in Paris, *time* seems to be the crucial factor. First, it is the 200th anniversary of the French Revolution; its celebration has been a world-wide event. Time also has a special meaning for us as Analytical Psychologists. Starting from a very small group of under one hundred analysts in 1955, the membership of IAAP has grown to over 1400 analysts, with an almost equal number of candidates in training. In the early days Jung was still alive, most analysts still had contact with him, and each member knew almost all of the others. Early Congresses were very much in line with Jung's own thinking, and the influence of first generation analysts was dominant. Our Association grew slowly for many years, and a Congress was a relatively cozy affair. Yes, there were the conflicts between the "Zurich school" and the "London school," but the organization still felt like family. Being part of a family meant that there were fights.

In the last ten or fifteen years there has been an enormous growth in our organization. Numbers of analysts and professional societies have expanded at an enormous rate. The Congresses have lost their coziness. As an extraverted feeling type, I have difficulty with this loss; I like to know everyone. Now that we have become a large and mature professional organization, what does it mean for each of us to be "Jungian" in today's world? How does it feel for each of us to be labeled as a "Jungian analyst?" Would you prefer to be called a psychoanalyst? As we look at the titles of the papers at recent Congresses, we see how much the tenor of our psychology has changed. Gone are papers on the amplification of particular symbols; rather, papers tend to focus on clinical issues, and there is much more cross-fertilization with other psychological theories and techniques.

On the whole, these have been creative developments. I sometimes wonder if we may become too narrowly focused on clinical issues, and lose the broader cultural perspective that Jung gave us. Obviously, these tensions are played out in analytical societies. The particular blend in each depends upon many factors: who the founders were, the cultural context, the size of the group, and the national character. In contrast to the French Revolution, we have guillotined no one; there has been an evolution in our field rather than revolution.

Time has become important in another way. Almost none of the founders of the original societies will be present at this meeting. Many have died, to our great loss, and others no longer travel. In any case, they have ceased to be immediate influences in Jungian thinking.

We who follow owe them a great debt; it was not easy to be a Jungian analyst in those early days. Many of them were treated derisively, just as accusations were leveled against Jung. Although accusations persist, it is to a lesser degree. As entirely new generations of analysts have emerged, our discipline has evolved; it is no longer the work of one man. Jung the person becomes more removed, more legendary, and we see various lines of development in Jungian theory. I can still remember the day when one could keep up with all the Jungian literature. Now it is absolutely impossible, with 27 different journals in the field of Analytical Psychology alone.

These are some of my thoughts and impressions as we enter this Congress. I am eager to launch into the scientific program, so will refrain from further remarks, except to hope that we enjoy ourselves, renew old friendships, and make new ones.

The Dynamics of Transference and Countertransference: A Model of Inner Dialogue and Parallel Processing

Harry Wilmer
Salado, Texas
Inter-Regional Society of Jungian Analysts

> Mathematical principles in particular are not imposed on existence or on nature *ab extra*, but are found in and abstracted from the subject-matter and march of experience....The mind in shaping its barbarous prosody somewhat more closely to the nature of things, learns to note and to abstract form that so strikingly defines them. These forms reveal their dialectic.
>
> George Santayana

Inner dialogue is the creative precursor of speech and rhetoric. This paper presents a model for processing inner dialogue at the moment it is happening in analysis. Clarity of outer dialogue rests on conscious understanding of the nature of language and silence as well as on psychology. I use the theory of parallel processing to illustrate how parenthetical thoughts are amplified and then reconstructed for outer dialogue.

Rothenberg (1988) proposed two creative thinking processes of psychotherapy. The first is Janusian thinking: actively conceiving two or more opposites simultaneously as a key to flashes of insight and paradox. Janusian thinking also explains the thinking of unusually gifted people and geniuses.

Rothenberg's second process is the homospacial process, actively conceptualizing two or more discrete entities occupying the same space and leading to articulations of new identities.

The model that I propose does not conceptualize simultaneous opposites or discrete entities in the same space, but ties together rational thinking with metaphoric expression. This model embodies Jung's (CW5) concept of two kinds of thinking. One is logical thinking in words with directed attention; the other is dreaming: non-directed thinking or fantasy thinking.

My model is based on dialogue, the dialectic process of analysis. The word *dialogue* means: a conversation between two or more persons, a literary work in the form of conversation with two or more persons, or a musical composition for two or more voices. All three of these apply figuratively to psychological analysis.

The word *dialectic* means the theory or practice of weighing and reconciling juxtaposed or contradictory arguments for the purpose of arriving at truth, especially through discussion and debate. In Socratic philosophy, dialectic is the discussion and reasoning by dialogue as a method of intellectual investigation.

Consciousness of the analyst's inner dialogue in the immediacy of therapy is a key to brief and sagacious comments and interpretations. The model that I propose applies to the inner dialogue of both analyst and analysand. This model is a geometry of the psyche, based on the torus image of topology and computer concepts of parallel distributed processing. I shall return to the model following some examples of inner dialogue.

The Double

The analyst's inner dialogue compares to a discourse between ego and alter ego or *doppelgänger*. Auschwitz survivor Primo Levi, in a book published shortly before his suicide, wrote:

It is obvious that perfectly lucid writing (or speaking) presupposes a totally conscious writer, and this does not correspond to reality.... Therefore, we are condemned to carry from crib to grave a doppelgänger, a mute and faceless brother who nevertheless is co-responsible for our actions, and so for all of our pages.

It is known that no author deeply understands what he has written, and all authors have the opportunity of being astonished by the beautiful and awful things that the critics have found in their works and that they did not know they had put there.

It is up to the author to make himself understood by those who wish to understand him. (Levi, 1980, p. 1)

If the doppelgänger becomes identical with the ego, a dangerous situation occurs because there is no polarity; the matrix of inner dialogue is the polarity and tension between doppelgänger and ego. Our doppelgänger, our inner reader or listener, becomes the catalyst or tormentor who drives us to refine and clarify inner dialogue, as in a rehearsal for speaking.

There is an ancient and widespread belief in the existence of a doppelgänger, or spirit double, an exact but usually invisible replica of every person, bird or beast. Such a figure occurs in the dialogues of Fyodor Dostoyevsky's *The Double*, Josef Conrad's *The Secret Sharer*, E. T. A. Hoffman's *The Devil's Elixir* and Samuel Beckett's last work, *Stirrings Still.* In Beckett's short prose piece, a character who resembles the author sits alone in a cell-like room until he sees his double appear – and disappear. Accompanied by "time and grief and self so-called," he finds himself "stirring still" to the end. Otto Rank (1971) quoted the 19th century French writer Musset:

> Wherever you go, I shall be there always,
> Up to the very last one of your days,
> When I shall go to sit on your stone. (p. 6)

"Inner talking" came to scientific attention in 1884 with William James' theory of stream of consciousness. A similar trend in literature began in 1887 with Edouard Dujardin's *Les Lauriers Sont Coupes*, translated as *We'll to the Woods No More*, in which the protagonists' inner thoughts were expressed directly. This literary device characterizes an entire genre of fiction and drama.

Being Grounded

Intellectual and conceptual formulations for the analytic dialectic are meaningless unless the therapist is grounded on the earth (see Wilmer, 1987b). Jung wrote,

Anyone who wants to know the human psyche will learn next to nothing from experimental psychology. He would be better advised to put away his scholar's gown, bid farewell to his study, and wander with human heart through the world. There, in the horrors of prisons, lunatic asylums and hospitals, in drab suburban pubs, in brothels and gambling-halls, in the salons of the elegant, the stock exchanges, the socialist meetings, churches, revivalist gatherings.... Through love and hate, through the experience of passion in every form in his own body, he would reap richer stores of knowledge than textbooks a foot thick could give him, and he will know how to doctor to the sick with real knowledge of the human soul (CW7, par. 409).

I have worked with people in these places, and have written about them: prisoners (Wilmer, 1965), schizophrenics (Wilmer, 1976), Korean War casualties (Wilmer, 1958), young drug and sexual casualties in Haight-Ashbury in San Francisco (Wilmer, 1968), Vietnam combat veterans (Wilmer, 1986) and AIDS patients (Wilmer, 1987a). As one of my inmate patients at San Quentin Prison, California, said to me in a group therapy session many years ago, "Look, Harry, I've been around the block a few times. What about you?" Some analysts and psychotherapists have not been around the block, or even if they have, they have retreated into the insular cave of their consulting rooms.

George Steiner (1981) said, from a literary point of view:

That the page in front of you, or the poem you have learned by heart, or the play you've seen comes to possess you more than any order of experience. That living things seem unreal compared to the intensity of imaginative experience. I think that's the most exciting thing that can happen. [Then] why do I say it's dangerous?

Because like many other people addicted to literature, I've often noticed in myself that the cry in the street seems mysteriously less powerful, less important, than the cry in the book, in the story.

And that the tears that come over the great tragic scene have a bitter despair which after all should be elicited by what is happening in the city around us. So this is a danger.

An imagination too utterly absorbed and fascinated by great art and literature [and mythology] can become autistic [and whirl] within its own very closed world. On the other hand, great art is probably our one constant, constant window on something much larger than ourselves.

Inner Dialogue of Analysand and Analyst

A young woman saw a therapist for depression when she was in her teens. While she recognized her need for professional help, she also struggled with the need to "be normal" and fought with the stigma of being "mentally unbalanced." During the therapy, she wrote a poem about her feelings of being in therapy, with parenthetical thoughts about the therapy and the therapist. These parenthetical thoughts are the residue of parallel processing.

Why must it be kept quiet when
        (Don't leave the cage-door open, the monkeys)
I'm not the only one who
        (like to run out but they don't)
Feels this way?
        (always like to come back.)
So I talk to professionals
        (The zoologists want to observe this)
In another attempt to refine
        (rare species, because their traits)
My ideas. Sometimes it
        (are peculiar to this climate, and)
Works, sometimes it doesn't but
        (these monkeys aren't quite as intelligent)
Most of the time I feel like
        (as we'd like them to be.)
I'm not communicating.

(I think they understand us)
Do you understand?
(so, don't leave the cage-door open.)

The creative inner dialogue of the analysand more or less mirrors the inner dialogue of the analyst. The analyst's failure to understand this leads to resistance by the analysand. When he or she does not challenge the analyst so as to make inner dialogue conscious, the analyst is likely to view his or her inner dialogue in an inflated Gongoresque light.

A young depressed woman attempted suicide in the course of her analysis with me. During the two months after the suicide attempt, as her depression lifted, she reported a series of sequential nightly epic dreams (see Wilmer, 1977) that unfolded an archetypal journey. These dreams were enthralling to her and she remembered them in precise detail without writing them down, but at first I made no interpretation. However, unwilling to remain silent for long periods of time, one day I interpreted a dream. She listened attentively and then went on as if I had said nothing. That night she dreamed *she was standing alone on a promontory by the sea, when suddenly a flock of large golden birds flew at her eyes. She struggled to ward them off, but they seemed intent on blinding her*. It was a different kind of dream, an interlude in the epic dream. She awoke frightened.

As she related this dream my dialogue with my inner doppelgänger instantly told me the unwelcome meaning of the dream. This transference dream was not about me specifically. The birds were not my words, but probably were symbolic ambivalent images representing my interpretation: golden, for value; birds, for spirit. Intent on interfering with her vision, they were potentially destructive. I made no interpretation of the golden bird dream, nor any interpretation of her dreams for a long time. It was as if a bird had told me.

The dream of another analysand presents images of unconscious dialogue. This woman was extraverted, creative and successful in the world of art, but on the verge of utter failure. Before she was referred to me because of intractable depression, she had received a variety of treatments: traditional psychotherapy, drugs, shock and hospitalizations. In my estimation the drugs were counterproductive and hospitalization contraindicated. During analysis her depression receded, dreams helped guide her and, as she recovered, her art work flourished. She developed a strong positive transference, often with a panicky feeling that her survival depended on me; she feared that I would disappear or die. This fear progressively diminished and, after coping with negative transference, she continued her analytic work with an unflagging positive rapport until her depression was gone.

Recently, for the first time in years, her depression returned, along with panic, when her child was hospitalized with a serious illness. This recurrence of depression, again treated by analysis without drugs, subsided just before our most recent session, when she told me this dream:

There is a world-famous expert who is known for his ability to rescue astronauts in space. I see a huge, shining silvery spaceship, sleek and beautiful in the dark sky of outer space. The crew of seven astronauts are flying in small pods, circling their spaceship. At last the crew leader radios the six other men that since they cannot find the damage, they must return to the mother ship.

As they approach it, a man, alone, dressed in ordinary street clothes, comes walking through space, and just before the crew arrives he enters the spaceship. At that instant the craft convulses in flames, turns into molten metal, erupts and becomes a fiery sky dragon.

The seven astronauts, suspended helplessly in space, feel that their situation is hopeless. But the leader radios the famous astronaut rescuer who responds in a calm, confident manner, reassuring them that he will get them.

He begins slowly and carefully to plan the life-saving mission. He receives a second emergency call from a spaceship whose crew consists of a mother and her daughter.

This second spaceship had been launched in a perfect trajectory when something went wrong and they were now flying beyond their orbit. In a firm, cool-headed way the rescuer tells them that he will save them.

At the same time, he receives a third desperate call from a spaceship with a single astronaut as the crew. The rescuer now sets out to save the crews of the three spaceships in an amazing mission.

At that instant, I realize that the woman he loves will be a crew member on the next space launch, and I know that he is afraid that there will be a fourth accident.

Now the dream changes and I am in my home. I open the front door and discover that the house is surrounded by a circle of cherry trees with fragile pink blossoms glowing in the morning sun. At a distance stands a single cherry tree with delicate blue flowers and one branch of pink blossoms.

It seemed that, in the dream, the patient was projecting onto me a savior in the form of a superhuman astronaut to bring her down to earth. But instead of identifying myself to her as the rescuer I asked her, "Who is the astronaut rescuer?"

She replied as if the answer were self-evident. "Oh, of course, that is the me who is calm and not the excitable flighty girl I used to be. You know, I think that in spite of all the problems I have, I will survive, no sweat."

She said that the woman whom the rescuer loved was herself, bravely going on about her plans and journey. When questioned, she reflected on herself in the dream as "Aphrodite." I responded, "Yes, but put it more simply." She answered, "Oh, that part of me that says, 'Please like me' – when I strike a pose like this." She smiled, stood up, and postured in a coquettish, charming manner that seemed electric.

Had I spoken of the rescuer as Dr. Wilmer, as my inner dialogue first tempted me, I thought that it would have been self-centered, self-pleasing and diminishing her own heroic animus. She projects her dream hero onto me, but I do not project myself onto her dream hero. The analyst is often not as important a figure in the dream life of analysands as is commonly thought. To see oneself in each and every figure resembling us in our analysands' dreams is a narcissistic intrusion that can cripple the psyches of both analyst and analysand. Not every figure that resembles the analyst is the actual analyst.

When I appear as myself in the analysand's dream, that is another matter. Key dream characters who resemble the therapist are that part of the dreamer's psyche that is the precursor of projection. When I see a resemblance of the analysand's fantasy of me in a dream figure, my inner dialogue moves through multiple working hypotheses (see Chamberlain, 1965) in the sorting of the data of parallel processing.

Let us return to the dream and the ordinary man in the business suit who walks in space, her other heroic animus who dies like a martyr in the inferno of the spaceship that he detonates to save the crew from death. In the end, there is the flowery enclosing circle of feminine pink with a dash of blue. Her mythological reference to Aphrodite, while significant, is not as important as the cry in the street, "Please like me," from which she had saved herself and finally come down to earth. It was as if her heroic masculine archetype had blended into the feminine fertile and calming earth.

The Torus Model

Imagine an object in the form of a cylinder formed into a circle, like a donut (Figure 1). Consider logical thought as the central core contained within the outer circumference. This vi-

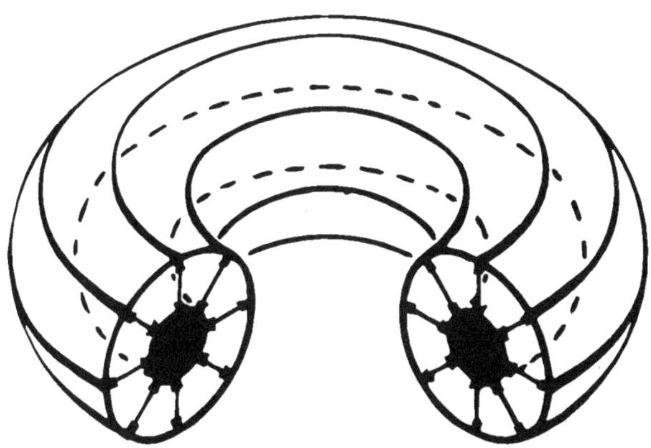

Figure 1: Representation of Three-Dimensional Torus

sual image is called a "torus" in the science of topology, which is the geometry of transformations and connectivity (see Courant & Robbins, 1956).

The torus diagram is cut to show its interior. The space between central core and circumference represents thought processes, amplifications and associations – our customary conscious working field. The lines on the circumference suggest the parallel processing that runs in various directions. This abstract model allows us to conceptualize the realms of inner dialogue.

Now let us look at the outer surface of the torus (Figure 2). A circle perpendicular to the "donut" circles the outer rim and is called a first-factor circle. A circle parallel to the "donut" is called the second-factor circle (see McCarty, 1968). At the intersection or coincidence of these two circles, the radiating arrows from the central core to the circumference (Figure 1) indicate the point of entry into the interpenetrating networks of the parallel processing.

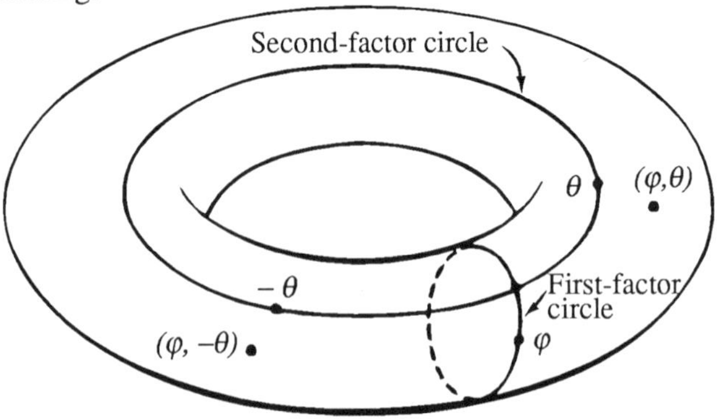

Figure 2

Parallel Processing

My model of parallel processing resembles a computer concept of parallel distributed processing – but it involves feelings and value judgments. McClelland and Rumelhart (1968) discussed parallel and serial processing of mental contents. Parallel processing simplifies overwhelming complexities of parenthetical thoughts. It resembles the cybernetic principle of feedback, reducing the uncertainty among the set of alternatives available.

Jung was using parallel processing when he learned to split stones in the Bollingen quarries for his tower and said that "one of the motives was the workableness of matter to compensate for the airiness of psychology. The historical form had to be there in order to give the ancestral souls an abode pleasing to them" (Let-I, p. 168). His experience is an illustration of the interconnectedness of *theoria* and *practica*, between the archetypal depths of the soul and the physical world of walls, windows and doors – between physical creative labor and mental creative labor. To dwell exclusively in the house of the mystical world of the collective unconscious is the refuge of those who do not want to split the stones and build their home on the earth.

Parallel processing – evoked by parenthetical thoughts, sounds (Wilmer, 1951) and narrative fantasy (Wilmer 1964, 1975) – is not merely foreground and background information, but is a far-reaching, self-propelling, self-regulating system. These thought processes occur at "lightning" speed. Though they may appear simultaneous they cannot be, but they are almost instantaneous in real time. The process is discontinuous and progressive.

Parallel processing is as if psyche's doors open to countless inner world dictionaries, encyclopedias, libraries and museums, archives and the reaches of human history and prehistory. It also offers ways to dig ditches and cut stones. It is an avenue to empathy and compassion in both spoken and silent dialogue.

Solving a problem by computer can involve millions of parallel systems. And yet, without the human mind – brain and psyche – attached to the system, parallel processing becomes autistic. It is necessary to make value judgments, to sort, to see patterns and rhythms, to know which thoughts to ignore and which to select among the seemingly endless possibilities. Here, a conscious multiple working hypothesis comes into play.

Another example of parallel processing occurred during the writing of this paper. After the first few drafts, I was unable to get my ideas in suitable form and completed a number of unacceptable drafts. But thinking about the subject went on in my mind. I used a dictionary to help find the right words relating to transference and countertransference, closeness and distance. Suddenly I found the need to write a dictionary on closeness, taking related words from the two-volume Fourth International Merriam Webster Dictionary. Then, with the collaboration of Merriam Webster and the Institute for the Humanities at Salado, the dictionary (Wilmer, 1989) was published. When the galley proofs came back, this paper took satisfactory shape. When the published book arrived, I was able to complete this paper.

Summary

Models of creative thinking take many forms. The proposed model of the torus with linear thinking and parallel processing manifests in reflective deep thought. Progressive, non-simultaneous and discontinuous, it relates the logic of directed thinking to the dream/fantasy of non-directed thinking and has the potential of unending creative thinking. This study of the interactive nature of dialogue suggests new ways for self-supervision in the immediacy of clinical work, and the understanding of transference and countertransference.

I have presented words and images illustrating the inner dialogue of analyst and analysand within the dialectic of analysis. Inner dialogue prepares us for clear, imaginative and brief responses, explanations and interpretations, and diminishes tendencies to pretentiousness. The aim is to speak clearly, simply and with merciful brevity.

Using the model of parallel processing and the topology image of the torus, I have explained how inner dialogue works in preparation for outer dialogue or rehearsal and silence. Moreover, I postulate that the inner dialogue can be imagined as dialogue between ego and alter-ego or doppelgänger, and that this life-long companion of our inner world speaks to us in creative inner dialogue in therapy and in dreams, and at odd moments when what we are doing seems unrelated to what we are thinking. In such ways discoveries sometimes are made.

For more than two years I have labored, trying to express these ideas in an understandable form and language. They seem clear and even self-evident to me as a clinician. But the innumerable drafts of this paper and my struggle to find the right words and images attest to the fact that my own inner dialogue is part of the process. It is difficult to describe with objectivity a process of which I am the major part. Perhaps the formulations I have made are more like a poem and a painting of a scientific hypothesis than ordinary sense.

> Some say that my teaching is nonsense.
> Others call it lofty but impractical –
> But to those who have looked inside themselves,
> This nonsense makes perfect nonsense,
> And to those who have put it in practice,
> This loftiness has roots that go deep.
>
> Tao Te Ching

REFERENCES

Chamberlain, T.C. (1965). The method of multiple working hypotheses. *Science*, *148*, 754-60. (Reprinted from *Science,* 1890.)

Courant, R. & Robbins, H. (1956). Topology. In J. Newman (Ed.), *World of Mathematics*. New York: Simon and Schuster.

Levi, P. (1980, November 20). This above all: Be clear. *New York Times Book Review*, p. 1.

McCarty, George (1988). *Topology*. (reprint of 1967). New York: Dover.

McClelland, J. & Rumelhart, D. (1968). *Parallel Distributed Processing: Explorations in the Microstructure of Cognition*. Vol. 2: *Psychological and Biological Models*. Cambridge, MA: Massachusetts Institute of Technology Press.

Rank, Otto (1971). *The Double: A Psychoanalytic Study*. Chapel Hill, NC: University of North Carolina Press.

Rothenberg, A. (1988). *The Creative Process of Psychotherapy*. New York: W.W. Norton.

Steiner, G. (1981, May 2). Literature, language, and culture. Transcript of *Bill Moyers' Journal, PBS*. New York: WNET/Thirteen.

Wilmer, Harry (1951). An auditory sound association technique. *Science*, *114*, 621-22.

Wilmer, Harry (1958). *Social Psychiatry in Action, A Therapeutic Community*. Springfield, IL: Charles C. Thomas.

Wilmer, Harry (1964). Odyssey of a psychotherapist. *Science*, *145*, 902-903.

Wilmer, Harry. (1965). The role of the rat in prison. *Federal Probation*, *29*, 44-49.

Wilmer, Harry (1968). Drugs, hippies, and doctors. *Journal American Medical Association*, *206*, 1271-75.

Wilmer, Harry (1975). Symbolism and creativity. *Perspectives in Biology and Medicine*, *18*, 353-62.

Wilmer, Harry (1976). Origins of a Jungian-oriented therapeutic community for schizophrenic patients. *Hospital and Community Psychiatry*, *27*, 338-42.

Wilmer, Harry (1977). Epic dreams and heroic ego. *Spring*, 46-61.

Wilmer, Harry (1986). The healing nightmare: A study of the war dreams of Vietnam combat veterans. *Quadrant*, 47-61.

Wilmer, Harry (1987a). The Neglected Inner World of AIDS. Office of Educational Resources, University of Texas Health Science Center at San Antonio. Four teaching videotapes and published manual.

Wilmer, Harry (1987b). *Practical Jung: Nuts and Bolts of Jungian Psychotherapy*. Wilmette, IL: Chiron Publications.

Wilmer, Harry, (1989). *Closeness: A Dictionary of Ideas*, Vol. I. Salado, TX: Institute for the Humanities at Salado.

Response

Randolph S. Charlton
Palo Alto, California, USA
Society of Jungian Analysts
of Northern California

Those unfamiliar with the breadth of Analytical Psychology might think that Wilmer's notions of the practical and the Jungian do not go together easily. Yet any contradiction in these terms is more apparent than real. Practical Jung expresses a tension of opposites – opposites that are necessary for the success of any analytical endeavor. The practical refers to everyday experiences which transpire on the earth; Jung refers to those symbolic events which occur both above and below the surface of our conscious experience. Together they combine to form a more complete picture of reality than does either one alone.

On the most obvious level, Wilmer presents us with a model of the inner dialogue in the mind of an analyst preparatory to the formation of understandable and communicable thoughts and feelings. Wilmer suggests that this dialogue is similar to the interplay of transference and countertransference.

The expressed values of his model are clarity, precision, and practicality. Analysts are asked to say what we mean and mean what we say, to make plain talk about what is going on right here, right now. This is a cogent and valid request; analytic language can become an abstruse code for the initiated. The convoluted turns of psychological discourse are all too often used to glorify and falsify. One picture can be worth a thousand words, but in the everyday work of analysis, a few clear words can be worth a thousand pictures.

Wilmer warns us about the fiery danger of ungrounded imagination precisely because it is in our fascination with the reality of the psyche that we run the risk of becoming lost in smoky clouds of mistaken intuition and defensive inflation. Wilmer would add to this list of risks, I think, the archetype, the mythologem and the nonscience of alchemy when they are disconnected from the nuts and bolts of life.

In the best of times analysts would balance securely on the tightrope of psychic equilibrium. We would speak succinctly, value precision and discipline and compensate for our airy theories with an earthy knowledge of the slings and arrows of life's outrageous fortune. Our own foibles would not lead us to overbalance toward mundane reality or transformative symbols. But in the real world all analysts eventually do slip and fall. If our inflation is not too great and our fall not too far, the very humanness of our failures can contribute to the progress of an analysand's self-inquiry.

Wilmer's common sense approach to analysis maintains that psychological relevance comes only marginally from theory and only partially from the personality of the analyst. Fertilized by a unique form of dyadic relationship, analytic meaning is born in the womb of the analysand's psyche. It is the analyst's job to provide a safe and contained birthplace in which nascent awareness is not destroyed by self-interest, impetuous action and rampant unconsciousness. Supportive curiosity, cogent amplifications, observations, and a few concise interpretations are the overt contributions of the analyst.

Wilmer calls his model of analytic dialogue parallel processing, and he relates it to the capacities of modern computer technology. He tells us that the thought processes work via intuition and feeling to amplify and balance the thinking and sensation orientation of the dialectic process. He describes these processes as almost instantaneous – but not simultaneous – blending richness, immediacy and eternity. In computer terminology, parallel processing would be an ingenious and incomprehensibly complex process in which multiple loops of parenthetical information are sorted into a totally relational field. In our Jungian terminology this may fall under the rubric of what we call the reflective and compensatory functions of the psyche.

Given Wilmer's philosophy we might expect a direct, rational, and pragmatic analysis of this process. However, there are so many metaphors, powerful symbolic images, evocative dreams and ambiguous dilemmas in his paper that it is much more than a simple and clear-cut presentation. Remember the disturbingly vivid admonition to Close the Door? Certainly a pragmatic and effective warning about the dangers of a house fire. What a wealth of disturbing feelings and burning images come to mind if we apply this announcement to the analytic setting!

Wilmer's presentation goes beyond its pragmatic, rational content. It is psychologically onomatopoetic. That is, his discussion of the inner dialogue within the mind of the analyst is itself an inner dialogue in the mind of an analyst. Wilmer tells us about the dialogue of transference and countertransference and simultaneously illustrates it in the structure and content of his presentation. He has offered us a window into his own inner dialogue as he struggles to make our Jungian psychology more understandable and pragmatically useful.

In order to accomplish this task, he now has to come to terms with Jung. I think it accurate to say that all of us with an allegiance to Analytical Psychology have transferences to Jung – symbolic relationships which profoundly influence our way of understanding the psyche and working with analysands. The inner dialogues with Jung as the wounded healer, the wise philosopher, and the creative and iconoclastic youth are central to our search for an analytic identity.

In the far-reaching dialogue presented by Wilmer, we have heard Jung's words used to assure us that there is room for a simple and understandable form of Analytical Psychology, that one who wishes to know human nature will not stay in the consulting room but venture into the world, and that the practical work of splitting stones is as much a part of an analytic identity as are mysterious and arcane symbols. These messages are compensatory for those of us who feel the pull of imagination most strongly, and perhaps irritating to those of us who most wish to move away from the muddy and sometimes trivial pursuits of everyday life.

Analysts of all persuasions struggle to be clear and comprehensible, but in the impossible work of analysis there is an inevitable and sometimes painful limit to our ability to accomplish these aims. Lacan (1979) has stated: "Analytic experience is not definitively objectifiable. It always implies within itself the emergence of a truth that cannot be said, since what constitutes truth is speech, and then you would have in some way to say speech itself which is exactly what cannot be said in its function as speech" (p. 406).

Language limits itself. And yet, ironically, a major part of all analytic work is done at the very limit of language. The closer we approach the edge of language, the more overdetermined experience becomes. Words cease to be clear and precise. Multiplicity flourishes, language melts, and unconscious enactments, images and symbols are born.

This knotty truth is anything but an argument to become lax in our efforts to be clear. In fact, it is the opposite. As Wilmer has told us, it is precisely when we are dealing with vividly evocative material, with tragically conflicted aims and emotions, with our human inability to make sense of the psyche, that we must be most careful to keep one foot on the ground, remember the practical side of life, and speak as clearly as possible.

The leitmotif that holds Wilmer's many images together is the repeated presentation of the tension underlying our efforts to wrestle with the unknown. He is amplifying our attempts to unite the practical with the symbolic, the inner with the outer. His idea of parallel processing includes the concepts of multiple determination of psychic events and multiple meaning of psychological experience. It is one way of speaking about the work of association in the service of the self-directed process of analysis.

By repeatedly presenting evocative and symbolic images and counterposing them with clear and earthy wisdom, Wilmer has offered us a spiraling expression of the transcendent function. Braving the border between clarity and confusion, conscious and unconscious, we stand on the threshold of many potential worlds.

It is the analytic calling to discover meaningful worlds and to work to open doors between them.

REFERENCE

Lacan, J. (1979). The neurotic individual myth. *The Psychoanalytic Quarterly*, *48*-3, 405-425.

The Changing Person and the Unchanging Archetype

Judith Hubback
London, England
Society of Analytical Psychology

Thousands of books and professional papers, in many languages, present studies of change from every conceivable angle. Each of us can read only a small fraction of them. In addition to the inspired, change-seeking scriptures of religions and sects, countless works of likely interest to us as Analytical Psychologists are produced by members of other specialties: philosophers, theologians, historians, physicists, biologists, environmentalists and even plumbing engineers. But before this paper follows many others into the sewer of oblivion (perhaps it will become, symbolically, organic and transformative manure for someone's garden), I call your attention to one area of interest. How is it that persons seeking psychotherapy – in the broad Jungian sense of the term – seem to want change, yet so often cannot achieve it, and find themselves time and again in a malign web of defensive maneuvers? Do repetitions have an archetypal quality? If so, what does such a formulation add to our understanding and to our clinical work? I am not going so far as to propose a new archetype, although I think that Strauss's (1964) suggestion of the archetype of separation is a valid one.

I include in this paper only short sketches of clinical material, out of respect for confidentiality in the analyses on which the material is based. My focus is on a theoretical, perhaps cool, exposition. The people whose experiences have generated or validated the theories are in the background, in contrast to their primary place in the course of daily consulting room work.

As analysts we seek to bring about results that are more profound than symptom removal or behavior modification. The essential thrust of our work is to use our own combined consciousness and unconsciousness – that hard-won *coniunctio* – to penetrate, and to help the analysand to penetrate, into the places in his or her psyche where trouble festers and change is postponed.

A dream sequence illustrates the repetition that may be a necessary preliminary to an effective analytic penetration. It seemed that the analysand needed to dream many variants of the same image before she could understand their meaning. In addition, it had to become clear that she was obsessionally redreaming them, to get through to the analyst, whose defensive uncertainties interfered with her receiving the dream messages. Thus, the dreams were part of the interactive transference/countertransference.

The dreams in the sequence were about *a room – usually a bedroom, and sometimes a whole wing of her house – which she had not realized was there. She had the urge, or the task, of opening the room and getting it into use. Sometimes it had been walled off and plastered over, seemingly hermetically sealed.* In one dream *it could be reached only through a series of cobwebby attics.* In other dreams *she knew there were more rooms, but also believed firmly that they were occupied by other people, who considered the rooms theirs.*

The dreams came at times when she was ready, with varying amounts of pain and difficulty, to allow repressions to be discovered and analyzed, to get rid of an attitude of complacency, to admit consciously that she was under-functioning and that she had defensively split off and projected necessary parts of herself. Still, imagining that she could control not-yet-conscious processes, she felt guilty each time unconscious omnipotence of thought was revealed through the repetitions. Jung, in "Answer to Job," called attention to a similar need in Yahweh: to listen to "an obscure intimation of something that questions his omnipotence" (CW11, par. 587). Jung saw Job as sensing that Yahweh, when he relied on might rather than right, was doing violence to the fullness of his own nature: "Job had never doubted God's might, but had hoped for right as well" (CW11, par. 586). The analyst seeks a similar result: achieving the right kind of penetration, probably combining thinking and feeling, at the right pace and at the most favorable moment for the awareness to be received and accepted.

My analysand bemoaned the fact that she had had the dream so many times and was so often defeated by it; she felt that it was of no use to her and stronger than she was. Such strength is the hallmark of archetypal possession. I remember feeling that I must not be caught up in those defeatist old sayings, such as, "The more things change, the more they stay the same" and "You cannot change human nature." Human nature does present people with what Lambert (1981) once called the perennial problem of resisting the experience we long for. Analyzing, melting and dispelling resistances to increased consciousness are essential in therapeutic analysis. Also essential is depotentiating the compulsive and projective repetitions that hold us back from valid individuation. Analysts must have at least some faith in the possibility of internal change, to keep going week after week. But it is well to keep in mind that faith must not be ruined by an omnipotent idealization – which could be introjected by the analysand – that we can work transformative miracles. My concern here is the amount of change that we can work for – validly – in the variety of analysands who come, with different pathologies. Marvelous metamorphosis is very unlikely for human beings; we are neither tadpoles becoming frogs, nor chrysalises turning into butterflies.

I interpose here a reference to the *Tao Te Ching*. Many passages in it illustrate early Chinese philosophical and psychological wisdom with regard to change. An example is the well-known opening sentence, similar to some of Jung's descriptions of the Self and its archetypal character:

> The Tao that can be expressed is not the Unchanging Tao;
> The name that can be named is not the Unchanging Name.
> The Unnameable is that from which Heaven and Earth
> derived, leaving itself unchanged.

> Thinking of it as having a name, let it be called the
> Mother of all things.

And another, stranger passage:

> Can you sponge away the dust from the surface of the
> Mysterious Mirror, leaving nothing obscure?
>
> (Lao-tzu, 1946).

The translator suggests in a footnote that "the Mysterious Mirror is the imaginary line which divides the conscious from the ... unconscious" (p. 24). This statement is a comment on analysts' and analysands' attempts to use the improved clarity of understanding, which follows the integration of previously unconscious elements in themselves. Anyone who tries to keep an actual mirror really clean for more than a short time can appreciate the vivid image Lao Tzu offers of the need to persevere with our repetitive analytic efforts – for as long as possible.

An analyst may have to face the question, from time to time, whether to bring a treatment to an end because of repeated unsuccessful efforts to resolve a basic structural defect or an intractable delusional transference/countertransference conflict. In that kind of ending, which Fordham (1989) has discussed, a great deal of psychotherapy may have been achieved, but the core anxiety or defect has not been resolved. A similar experience occurs when an analysand leaves because of not wanting or not being able to go further. It may not be possible at the time to discover just what was the blocking factor.

In one instance, early in my career, the meaning of an analysand's terminating without warning could be seen later as his repeating in reverse the major childhood trauma and unconsciously retaliating against parent figures. He had been sent away from home during the Second World War to save him from almost certain death. He could not remember having been given any explanation and he never saw or heard from his family again. The people who adopted him gave him a new name. Our work did not constellate any good personal or archetypal images, nor did it revive in him the withered dynamism of the Self. I realized at the time that I did not feel warm enough toward him and could not offer him *agape*. I must have introjected the coldness of the total loss of the parents. I think now that at that time there had not been enough internal changes in me, his analyst. Not yet enough integration of split-off parts of myself, for him to be able to reach in toward his potential for healing and for movement to be activated in a life-enhancing direction. Death was in the transference/countertransference.

The concept of change is neutral. It may be forward or backward, for better or for worse. The assumption is that we are working with a view to change for the better – whatever is meant by "better." Such change may be good for the person who is changing, perhaps taking rapid and important steps toward individuation. But it may result in the disruption of a marriage; the other one in the partnership may regard the disruption, at least for a while, as unbearably painful. In such a case change may have been too fast for the one who is left, even if it felt right to the one who was changing.

It can happen also that, when an analysand is resisting change, the resistance may be an indication that he or she has introjected the anxiety aroused in others but is unconscious of that introjection. The analysand may experience the resistance in the form of depression – angry depression, absorbed from others. Through analysis of that introjection, the paradox of wanting and fearing change may become meaningful, rather than remaining stuck in defensive confusion, where ambivalence reigns. If the analyst can understand and use what appears to be simple resistance, acceptance of the pace of change may be integrated into the analysand's ego. The quality of the individuation process may be improved, because the analysand will have discovered that it is possible to respect the needs of others while attending to his or her own needs.

Even if, as analysts, we hold that change should not be a simplistically held value, it is still a fact that analysts are interested in change. We may be careful not to force it or organize it, but we tend to become anxious if the analysand seems to be completely stuck. Then we catch, or introject, the analysand's block. An analogy occurs in physical birth when the mother is pushing and believes that the baby is pushing also.

Whichever kind of Analytical Psychology we favor – classical, archetypal or developmental – it is more or less certain that our *Weltanschauung* contains a basic component of desire to tap dynamic systems in ourselves and our analysands. And they probably sense that in us, however much we try to avoid value judgments. If we become anxious about no change, we have to guard against our unconscious manipulations designed to bring about what we want. If such manipulations occur, it is the analyst who needs to change before the analysand can. Franz (1969) wrote about a case of his which had run into difficulties. He decided it required that he concentrate on his own psychic development. He did this by returning to "active therapy" (p. 146).

The subject of the part the analyst can play is, of course, not news. Many of us have studied unconscious countertransferences widely, deeply and experimentally (e.g. Hubback, 1988). Our knowledge helps us to discover more and more subtleties – and often distortions – in our unconscious projections into the interactions with the analysand.

Countertransference as well as transference can be stuck in repetitiveness. On one occasion Jung used the rather exciting phrase, "the violence of unconscious dynamism" (CW5, par. 524). The phrase is important in connection with a more measured passage: "The conscious can know the unconscious only so far as it has become conscious. We have only a very hazy idea of the changes an unconscious content undergoes in the process of becoming conscious, but no certain knowledge" (CW10, par. 779).

We try to clarify that "very hazy idea" by the same means as the apparently anti-therapeutic mechanism of the repetition compulsion. One of the many benefits of reading the books and papers of our forebears and of our contemporaries is to think more clearly and more incisively, thereby to work through our resistance to radical change. Laboratory scientists, who are often intuitive people, repeat experiments until they and other scientists are convinced of the validity, or the doubtfulness, of the proposition they are putting forward. Archetypal images are very repetitious in their nature, even though they are not so in their content. Hence there is value in studying constantly how they operate and what they may mean to each analysand.

The theme I am developing may appear to be painfully circular. Yet I do not want to present a picture of the problem of change in analysis as one where the transference/countertransference relationship becomes a kind of dual solipsism, or one where there is no exit from the circle – sometimes called the vicious circle. I am less convinced than I used to be by the argument, or rather the oft-repeated counter-image, that we are not stuck in circles but that we deal in spirals. The question remains: What changes a circle into a spiral? What is the dynamism that shakes up and disrupts the previous structure?

In the 1970s and 1980s some American mathematicians and physicists developed "Chaos Theory" (Gleick, 1987). At first simplistic questions arose in the mind of the research meteorologist, Edward Lorenz, and other scientists. They studied physical disorder, disruption, chance, turbulence, improbability and the unexpected; all of these feature in analytical psychotherapy. Some of these scientists worried lest asking simple – and today as yet unanswered – questions about often-observed phenomena was eccentric, perhaps rather mad. Yet the Fool in Shakespeare is a Wise Child and poets who seek and hold to their own center are often considered eccentric.

Jung's "Answer to Job" (CW11) speaks to us quite particularly through its paradoxical features: Yahweh, who should know everything, is presented by Jung as being far from the center of Job's awful experiences, both material and psychological. Sophisticated modern theologians are still working, I understand, on the problem of the sources of disruptive evil and suffering. They, like analysts, prefer not to resort to either predestination or chance. It would be simplistic to see change and determinism as contradictory opposites. Perhaps chaos is somewhere between? How does turbulence give way to a new pattern? Concepts or visualizations from other disciplines (e.g., physics or geology) sometimes help in the process of thinking through problems in our own specialty. Some depressions feel chaotic. The analysand is in turbulent agitation, having lost much ego-functioning and the usual sense of time, yet wakes up one morning feeling lighter and clearer-minded; the geological "plate tectonics of the deeper levels" have moved while he or she was asleep. The ego is returning. Thinking becomes possible again. The analyst knows that it is not due to chance.

There is no hard and fast distinction between clinical experience, images, concepts and theories. They are interactive; they help each other. During acute times in an analytic therapy both parties may be caught in turbulence, in the heaviness of depression, or in chaotic projections and introjections. Either or both of them may resort to splitting, to extricate themselves from the chaos.

As long ago as 1960 Murray Jackson, who was at that time still an Analytical Psychologist, described a case of his where there were stressful syntonic happenings in the transference/countertransference. They were worked through successfully and the analysand achieved a new integration. Jackson (1960) discussed the various ways of conceptualizing how the depth of the shared experience between analyst and analysand could be named and described. He decided that "the imagery of the archetypal model" was the most helpful; it gave "a theoretical basis to [the] shared experience, indicating that the 'sharing' may be a good deal more profound than can be accounted for by the analyst's skill, experience and benevolent neutrality" (p. 92). Jackson considered that the new integration had been set in motion at the archetypal rather than at the ego level.

It is impossible to express any of these concepts in non-imagery terms, since the evidence for the existence of archetypes comes from experiencing images. It is in the imaginal inner world or at the archetypal level ("world" and "level" are both images) that dynamism waits to be activated. Since integration of previously unconscious elements, during analysis, is best explained in terms of the force of archetypal imagery experienced between two people, it is worth while to consider blocks and resistances as possibly archetypal. Among the characteristics that imagery has to have in order to qualify as archetypal are the following: 1) it occurs generally, perhaps universally; 2) it repeats a specific recognizable pattern or form; 3) it is purposive, integrative; 4) the affect is very powerful, sometimes numinous; and 5) it is associated with bodily, instinctive levels of experience. In analytic practice I find that the main resistance to change, known as the repetition compulsion, has all those characteristics.

The term repetition compulsion was coined by Freud in an essay entitled, "The 'Uncanny'" (SE17), a word from – I believe – ancient Scottish referring to the mysterious, what we do not know or do not yet know. Freud wrote:

> It is possible to recognize the dominance in the unconscious mind of a "compulsion to repeat" proceeding from the instinctual impulses and probably inherent in the very nature of the instincts – a compulsion powerful enough to overrule the pleasure principle, lending to certain aspects of the mind their demonic character." (p. 238)

Freud saw the compulsion to repeat as "an ungovernable process originating in the unconscious" (Laplanche & Pontalis, 1973, p. 78), an autonomous factor that we Jungians can associate readily with the theory of complexes. As has been pointed out often, the instincts are inherently conservative and repetitive. They can be seen also as valid protective forces, rather than undesirable defenses against the anxiety that is generated when one needs to think freshly about old things. Instincts are the mainly physical version of archetypal purposive factors.

The concepts of destiny and fate are contiguous and essential components of early Freudian thinking about the repetition compulsion. According to the *Oxford English Dictionary*, destiny conveys the sense of divine pre-ordination, and fate is "that which has been spoken by the gods, ... an unalterable sentence." Analytic work describes and defines, but it also teases out the usable meanings and aims of destiny and fate, which carry so much weight in the popular mind. In collective psychology ideas about the repetitiveness and predictability of instincts often resemble ideas about determinism and Calvinistic predestination.

To consider repetition first, there is the obvious connection with the factors from their earlier lives that analysands project into the analysis: the fully documented transferences of parental and sibling images, and the assumptions about familial interactions. The analysis throws light, however, onto the analysand's entire psychological world, both past and present. Of most experiential importance is the pain that supervenes in the process of unraveling strands from the past that have become mixed in with present-day relationships, usually to their detriment. Through the focus of transference/countertransference and new pain, there is the possibility of freeing the analysand from the malignancy of old pain, which may be a generalized, overall misery.

An analysand that I remember as having been in psychological pain virtually all the time that I knew her, over six years of analysis, wept throughout the first session. Weeping then became typical of her response to whatever I was able to offer. It was a whining kind of weeping; she never managed to let go and really howl. She often spoke about the nagging misery of many psychosomatic illnesses from infancy onward. Although I was able to empathize with her from my reality position, the transference onto me was a difficult one, stemming from her mother's telling her that the mother had not wanted a baby. When I felt particularly useless and at my wit's end, I found myself wishing that I had been much more careful before taking her on; I had introjected and thereby "become" the unwelcoming mother who had wished that the infant had not been conceived.

Her internal life seemed a shallow one. It had been formed and colored by the aggressive information of an original rejection, compounded by her certainty that her father had wanted a son. Thus, she felt that she satisfied neither parent. Her whole tone was miserable; so was the analysis. She maintained that none of it was of her doing, let alone her fault; other people had conceived her and made her the sex she was. She was living the shadow. At the end of the analysis she was still miserable, but not quite as much as six years before.

Compulsion plays a part in the repetitive block against change; indeed, archetypes and compulsiveness go together. When Freud spoke of the "demonic character" of "certain aspects of the mind" (SE17, p. 238) he was referring to the powerful figure of the daemon who is both the evil Devil of medieval Christianity and the dynamic Satan or *diabolos* who, in Kenneth Lambert's words, "symbolises the shadow ... that works unbeknown to ego-consciousness – a factor unsubject to space and time, unrelated and often operating under the guise of goodness" (1977, p. 165). Some analysands become caught in an obsessive-compulsive reaction to their inability to control diabolic fragmentation episodes, and they lose contact with the cohesive Self. They are caught in an archetypal and – to them – devilish, timeless repetition of the central besetting difficulty of their particular pathology. For some it is manifested as the trap of unconscious omnipotence; for others, the extreme of abandonment; for still others the terror of ultimate hate or expulsion. No wonder the poet John Milton, who in *Paradise Lost* was tackling the problem of evil via the Genesis myth, draws our attention to the ultimate unequalled power of God to expel humankind from paradise and to the human confrontation with the power of Satan – the dark side of God. In "Answer to Job" (CW11) Jung put forth the hypothesis that God, Satan and Job all represent, or symbolize, the various parts of humanity, which means each of us.

It is often possible to understand analysands' compulsive and repetitive regressions in the transference in terms of their aim, value and possible benefit. Then the analyst can track retrospectively the compulsion's grip on the analysand. Time and again it emerges that these compulsive repetitions happen under the power of the illusory wish to recreate the original, archetypal, idealized object: the totality of the first parent, the mother. Regression facilitates the analysis of the contents of the idealization. The transference idealization is heavy and troublesome but makes it possible to feel one's way into the internal idealization – which may have a fantasied quality or nature – and to shift it. The original idealized object was contained in a total – which implies archetypal – experience or unconscious fantasy of infant bliss and ecstasy at the breast in the mother's arms. The totality factor may have obstructed the painful but necessary experience of frustration that is part of emergence from infancy.

When the transference idealization is being analyzed and linked to very internal material, the imago of the mother-infant *coniunctio* can be re-experienced in the consulting room. But with some analysands there erupt into consciousness, between sessions, "little nasty thoughts," as they were once described to me, such as envy and attacks on me.

Or a death – a catastrophic loss – may occur, as the psychoanalyst, Wilfred Bion, has studied so closely. Bion fought on the atrocious Western Front in the First World War. His later fascination with catastrophic losses may have grown out of that. The years before that war were idealized, by many people more naive than Bion, as trouble-free. For other people, birth was the first catastrophic change, like the expulsion from the Biblical Paradise – even earlier than the loss of the mother's arms, which are equivalent to the hedges round the mythical Garden of Eden. Devils, even if seemingly small familiar ones, and cataclysms with their terrifying finality, are the archetypal representations we need to appreciate in order to achieve a satisfying understanding of the repetition compulsion and the valid analytic hope for change.

Before moving into the final part of this paper, it is important to mention the psychological value of rituals and anniversaries. Individually, arriving for a session and leaving it are ritualized by most analysands. Collectively, the annual religious and national holidays contain both valuable and dangerous repetitions. In the course of analysis in England, at least, Christmas is often more dreaded, since it is potentially so numinous, than are the other interruptions to analytic regularity. The repetitious nature of rituals, together with most analysands' intense dislike of anything that disturbs them, seem to show how symbolically they reproduce aspects of the infant-mother relationship. Inside each of us the reliable rhythm of the heart felt in the pulse in many parts of the body has a quality of ultimate reassurance. An analysand of mine who was recovering his balance after a most disturbing, stormy experience – one of many traumatic stages in his analysis – turned over onto his front, lay still for a few minutes, then said quietly, "I can feel my heart beating on the firmness of the couch. It has been beating all the days of my life. It's me, and it's looking after me."

In normal health we rely implicitly on the heart. It is not necessary to keep consciously in touch with it. There is not a split between the psychological core, the Self, and the body core, the heart; there is mutual reliance. The heart pulses repetitively so that the person can emerge from repetition. In a much less well-calibrated way it is the schizoid defensive mechanism that stultifies change. It keeps different parts of the ego separate from each other and the person lives with one part unavailable for conscious interactions. The most frequent example is that of the attacking or destructive impulse being out of reach, isolated there out of fear for the safety of both the ego and the object. That way of filling out what is subsumed under the term schizoid presupposes that there is an ego which is not using all its parts – non-integrated or disintegrated – as when an analysand has the experience of having collapsed or gone to pieces after a disastrous loss in outer life or a traumatic reliving, in the transference relationship, of such loss.

On a longer-term basis, an analysand who presents as needing to keep his or her life very patterned, owing to an inner world where archetypal structures predominate, gives a false impression of living impersonally. The person seems secretive, or deeply private, and fearful of revealing affect and of regression. There is a split between the personal and the archetypal in such a man or woman.

A different defense, one that is also difficult to get to, occurs when the most internal, early, integrated Self holds together – in a mysterious way – too tenaciously. Jungian analyst Michael Fordham observed both children and adults. In each individual the integrated Self – in health – deintegrated in the process and the service of ego development. In autistic illness, the Self failed to deintegrate. These observations have provided us with an important way of thinking about early states and defenses. For

Fordham, deintegration of the Self is set in motion spontaneously.

Integrative, or Self-experiences, follow deintegrations, during which the different parts of the Self had been distinct. In adult life these parts feel dangerously separated, divorced. There is a link to be made between that theory of the original integrated Self and the use Jung made of the imagery of the internal alchemical marriage, the *coniunctio*. In ordinary sexual acts, *coniunctio* is preceded and followed by distinctiveness. That coming together happens after the established existence of two separate people, because the two basic but contrasted components of the Self – namely, love and attack – both need to become and to be kept conscious. By analogy it would seem that, in therapeutic analysis, within the personal Self of each of the partners there are two conjoined elements. And they both have to be available for effective movement to occur. At such times, the numinous is real.

The proposition I am putting forward is that the spontaneous nature of the internal dynamism of the Self – which produces deintegration and reintegration movements – can be seen as archetypal. The lively, or creative, quality of this archetypal spontaneity can be described in the image of the spark. The sculptor, Barbara Hepworth, once asked: "What are the deep impulses to create? Some sort of clash, and sparks buried deep down, conflicts and torments and extremes" (quoted in Gardiner, 1988, p. 170). Physical sparks are caused by two flints, or matches, or electricity. In analytic therapy the person who wants to change comes into contact and conflict with an analyst who is aware, even if only dimly, of the very internal cohesiveness of the Self. That cohesiveness has all the characteristics that I detailed earlier as necessary for archetypal imagery – universality, pattern and form, purpose, numinous affect and body base. The embodied psyche – the person – does change, through activating and using the complementary unchanging archetypal nature of the cohesive Self.

In conclusion, I have developed my thoughts from states and experiences in which the analysand may be in much pain. Pain is likely in all analytic therapy that penetrates sensitive areas, but it is also true that, as Fordham wrote, pain "is a sign that the patient is struggling, and of his will to live" (1974, p. 197). It is often hard in clinical work to hold fast to one's convictions that it is worth while to continue to believe steadily in oneself – in one's Self, which includes so much – to go on being that strange hybrid creature, an analytic therapist. This belief is far less one-sided than the analysand perhaps imagines during painful persecutory phases of the analysis. The analysand's suffering may seem to be a defense against the analyst's perseverance, and pain can contain a certain defensive element, but it is also a necessary stage of healing and later recovery. For the analyst, respect for the analysand's potential for wholeness is essential, keeping in mind the repetitive need to work on what feels like the same internal material. If the problem recurs, there is more to be done about becoming whole. And the content of archetypal relationships, expressed in whatever changeable individual way, goes on being general, patterned, purposive, powerful, and experienced in the body. People and images are fluid and protean; the potential for archetypal cohesiveness is constant. Analysand and analyst both need to reach out, and in, toward it.

REFERENCES

Fordham, M. (1974). Defenses of the Self. *Journal of Analytical Psychology*, *19*-2, 192-99.

Fordham, M. (1989). On terminating analysis. In M. Fordham et al. (Eds.), *Technique in Jungian Analysis*. London: Karnac.

Franz, K. (1969). The analyst's own involvement with the process and the patient. *Journal of Analytical Psychology*, *14*-2, 143-51.

Gardiner, M. (1988). *A Scatter of Memories*. London: Free Association Books.

Gleick, J. (1987). *Chaos: Making a New Science*. New York: Viking.

Hubback, J. (1988). *People Who Do Things to Each Other*. Wilmette, Il: Chiron.

Jackson, M. (1960). Jung's "archetype": Clarity or confusion? *British Journal of Medical Psychology*, *33*-2, 83-94.

Lambert, K. (1977). Analytical Psychology and historical development in western consciousness. *Journal of Analytical Psychology*, *22-2*, 158-74.

Lambert, K. (1981). *Analysis, Repair and Individuation*. London: Karnac.

Lao-tzu (1946). *Tao Te Ching* (H. Ould, Trans.). London: Dakers.

Laplanche, J. & Pontalis, J.-B. (1973). *The Language of Psycho-Analysis*. London: Hogarth.

Strauss, R. (1964). The archetype of separation. In A. Guggenbühl-Craig, (Ed.), *The Archetype*. Basel, Switzerland: S. Karger.

Response

Warren Steinberg
New York, New York, USA
New York Association for
Analytical Psychology

Jungian psychology has overemphasized the integrative, upward-striving, progressive aspect of the unconscious. We tend to view the unconscious as the creative will of life which unfurls and which – if properly understood and integrated – will direct us toward development and the future. After all, inherent in the symbols we so love to interpret is a developmental directive: the path toward individuation, toward wholeness. Implicit is the assumption that, so long as the path toward psychological growth is clearly evident in the symbols produced by the unconscious, the inherent need for individuation will cause the individual to choose that way. Technically, the analyst's job is to make evident the analysand's developmental path by interpreting symbols, becoming aligned with the creative forces of the unconscious, and encouraging the analysand's integration of the disparate parts of his or her personality.

Hubback's focus on factors that inhibit psychological change serves as a necessary compensation to the usual focus of Jungian psychology. She raises the question: Why do people whose ostensible motive for entering therapy is change, so often not achieve it? One answer to this question is that something in the analysand works against therapeutic progress.

I first became interested in resistance that people have to psychological change when I noticed, as did Hubback, that the psychological condition of a number of my analysands did not improve when there was every expectation that it would. As a matter of fact, it was at the moment when improvement was most expected, when there had been some important insight or deepening of the therapeutic relationship, that these analysands seemed to get worse. They became depressed and anxiously denied progress in their development or regressed in the face of it.

In analyzing this problem, Hubback concludes that a key impediment to change is the repetition compulsion and that this compulsion has an archetypal quality. What is repeated in these instances, she suggests, are the contents of a childhood conflict or a defense. For example, the person who prematurely left therapy did so as a reenactment, in reverse, of her abandonment by her parents.

Often it is not the childhood conflict that is the problem, but the pain the person expects as a consequence of working successfully through the conflict. Change is associated with negative consequences such as separation, depression, guilt and envy. Individuals who fear their own growth experience intense unconscious fear of the analyst and maintain the unconscious fantasy that the analyst opposes their analytic progress, despite evidence to the contrary.

Hubback's comments on the analyst's countertransference are most interesting, but I feel do not go far enough. She rightly points out the analyst's investment in therapeutic progress and the anxiety the analyst develops when an analysis becomes stuck. But is there not a shadow side to our investment in the analysand's development?

Hubback notes that a person's resistance to change may be due to the anxiety introjected from others in their environment who would be frightened by their development. Is it not possible that one of the "others" who fears the analysand's growth is the analyst? I am not talking just about induced countertransference reactions now. If the resistance to change is archetypal and universal, do not we as analysts also participate in it and fear our analysand's development? I suggest that the analyst's fears are often the same as the analysand's: one's own separation anxiety, depression and envy, all resulting from the analysand's growth.

Self-exploration, discussion with colleagues and supervision of other professionals has led me to the conclusion that there exists in the analyst's unconscious an identification with the devouring aspect of the Great Mother that corresponds to the analysand's fear of therapeutic growth. This identification is experienced by the analyst as hostility toward the analysand's development, an impulse to interfere with therapeutic progress. Such impulses are usually repressed as the analyst seeks to identify with the nourishing, growth-encouraging aspect of the Great Mother. Identification with growth is accompanied by the desire to devour, which exerts its effect unconsciously.

Margaret Mahler's research on children and Erich Neumann's mythological studies indicate that psychological birth does not coincide with biological birth. For a time after physical birth the child remains merged in a psychological union with the mother. The process of separating from the mother creates anxiety in the child.

Many mothers, too, experience conflict over separation, due to their own separation anxiety. Such mothers so enjoy their children's dependence that they discourage the children's groping for independent functioning, thus failing to promote gradual separation. A mother may suffer so much separation anxiety that she is unable to bear it. When her young child reaches the separation stage of development, such a mother finds the anxiety intolerable and defensively withdraws. The child, lacking the secure feeling that mother is there, hesitates to separate for fear that there will be no one to return to. Fearing annihilation, the young child clings to the mother. When the child is afraid and clinging, the mother's separation anxiety is eased and she rewards the child with love. Soon the child infers that any sign of independence, self-assertion or initiative will lead to abandonment; weakness, clinging or failure will be rewarded.

People with severe separation anxiety may experience, in the analytic relationship, conflicts in relation to psychological development. Therapeutic progress may result in projection on the analyst of the anxious, withdrawing aspect of the mother. The analysand may then relate to the projected negative mother with weakness and failure. The analyst who identifies with the negative mother projection may feel separation anxiety and withdraw defensively.

Conversely, when the analysand becomes aware of psychological growth, the positive feelings of accomplishment may be projected onto the analyst. The analysand may then identify with the withdrawing mother and threaten to leave the analysis in order to make the analyst feel insecure and needy. An analyst who identifies with the projection of the analysand's abandoned ego may feel afraid of losing the analysand. This fear can lead to the analyst's clinging, depression or retaliatory aggression.

For example, a colleague asked me to consult on a case that was causing him difficulty. Due to countertransference problems, he had become identified with and was acting out his analysand's projection of her withdrawing mother. Whenever the analysand felt successful in her personal life or about the progress she was making in analysis, the analyst worried that she would no longer need him and would leave the analysis. To defend against his separation anxiety, the analyst unconsciously withdrew and caused the analysand to feel insecure and to react by clinging. The analysand experienced the analyst's emotional unavailability as terrifying.

When I interpreted the analyst's unconscious behavior, he became frightened of the desire to undermine his patient and overcompensated by encouraging her growth. The analysand's dreams and associations indicated that she misunderstood the analyst's excessive encouragement as an attempt to be rid of her. As part of her clinging defense, she then asked if a friendship would be possible once the analysis was successfully completed. The analyst's defensive acquiescence calmed the analysand but her dreams showed despair. While consciously she had been reassured, she had realized unconsciously that her separation anxiety would never be analyzed because she had been told, implicitly, that separation would never occur.

Therapeutically, I agree with Hubback's emphasis on the regressive phase of analysis and the analysis of transference/countertransference issues. I differ in that I do not find it useful to rework the content of the childhood conflicts until after progress has been made in analyzing the fear of development.

Symbol Formation in the Analytic Relationship

Ingrid Riedel
Konstanz, Germany
Schweizerische Gesellschaft
für Analytische Psychologie

Jungians often treat symbol formation, which is so important for therapy, as mysterious; we do not ask ourselves how symbols come into being, as if they always emerged spontaneously from a more or less indeterminate unconscious. When we observe the therapeutic process, however, we notice that symbols do not emerge by chance; they come into being at critical points in the analytical process. Symbol formation can be blocked by situations in the relationship which neither party understands: for example, when an analysand's complex, still completely unconscious, is projected onto the analytic relationship and can be experienced only in that context.

With a series of pictures from the analysis of a 34-year-old social worker I shall show how, in the analytical relationship, personal and archetypal powers constellate and change. I shall refer to focal situations in the analytical relationship in their connection to symbol formation.

Before our therapeutic work began, Marga had participated in a painting group where she could be choose her subjects freely. She had painted a number of collective symbols, but she could say little about them because she could not connect them with her personal life. Among them were spheres, which often fell into water and sank. Marga got the impression that the director of the painting group, who did not understand this recurring symbol, was displeased with such a stereotyped image. She seemed to ask why Marga did not just stop painting such spheres.

Marga was hurt deeply by the impatience of this director. As the daughter of a rejecting mother, her self-esteem was shaken easily. The motif persevered just because it was not accepted and understood, as depicting a complex or as a symbol. Experience shows that stereotypes dissolve and symbol formation occurs whenever the constellation that underlies a complex is received emotionally and understood.

Figure 1

During our first therapeutic session Marga showed me pictures of spheres (e.g., Figure 1) and told me about the impatience of the painting group director. Together we tried to find the possible significance of the sphere motif. They somehow reminded me of fairy tale images: heroines, golden spheres or balls which – as in the "Frog Prince" of the Grimm brothers – fall into a well and leave the princess inconsolable. It is her juvenile wholeness, her Self, that falls into the well. The fairy tale shows how precious this object is by presenting it as a golden sphere. Marga's sphere is light blue, almost glassy and transparent and fragile. In this symbol, which she formed time and again, her relation to her Self is at stake. This symbol glides away and seems to disappear in the depth of the water, of the unconscious. Her vital search for herself symbolized in this sphere had not been

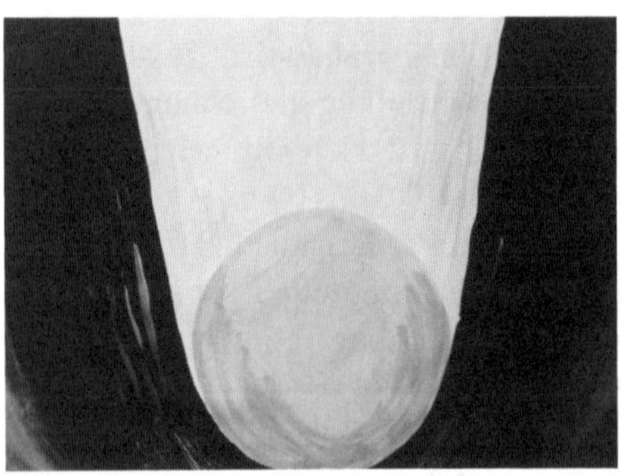

Figure 2

understood by others up to this moment; the ball she threw was not caught by the other person and so it fell into emptiness. But it seemed that in our first talk I had somehow succeeded in catching the ball.

Figure 3

Figure 4

After the first session Marga painted some pictures in which the motif of the sphere turned into a golden ball that fell, not into the water but onto solid ground (Figure 2). Then this golden ball started to take root; her search for herself started to take root in our therapy. As the roots were more and more penetrating the ball finally burst open (Figure 3). For the first time it released a concrete symbol which Marga could connect to her own life: the image of a mother holding a child who is thrashing about on her lap (Figure 4). The parts of the broken sphere can be seen swirling around the image of the mother with the child.

It is an archetypal image: the Great Mother with the child under the tree of life. In contrast to the sphere motif Marga could recognize here the main topic of her life: feeling secure with mother, with life itself. This was her basic problem and it also was to become the problem of our therapeutic relationship.

Marga's process had clear turning-points. Each of them was characterized by the formation of symbols to which she gave artistic form. She painted them spontaneously, out of an inner need; I did not ask her to do it. The formation of new symbols can be seen in a series of more than 100 pictures from which I include here only the most important ones.

I have found helpful a thesis of Verena Kast (1989), that symbol formation starts from the complexes:

> The complexes reflect the relationship patterns of our childhood as well as the affects and the stereotyped patterns of behavior which are linked to them. As long as these complexes are unconscious they determine the analytical relationship: quite often in a complex-like, collusive transference-countertransference situation. Only when this complex constellation in the relationship is understood emotionally and when the persons who participate in the relationship can be experienced as an inner Gestalt, can the complex completely "fantasize itself" and can new symbol formations be experienced. (p. 166)

Thus, everything depends on creating conditions where the complex can take the form of fantasy.

First it is necessary to understand the transference / countertransference situation with regard to the complex that is hidden in it. In most cases the persons to whom the analysand had related in childhood will become visible and will come to be experienced as an inner Gestalt. The experiences Marga had in childhood with her mother underlay her negative mother complex. It, in turn, affected our therapeutic relationship.

Marga was the fourth unwanted child of a family characterized by alcoholism. She felt constant disapproval and rejection from her mother, who was overburdened and in poor health. In order to provide for the family, the mother worked in a restaurant where she served alcohol and sometimes got drunk. It was terrible for Marga when her mother, in such a state, seemed to look through her and failed to recognize her. This "not being seen" was the basic experience of her childhood and had hindered her from building a stable self-esteem. Mother depreciated this child, unjustly regarding her as awkward and untalented. Before others, mother never stood by Marga. Whenever something was missing or broken in the household, Marga was the first to be suspected.

Because of this continuous tension and fear Marga occasionally suffered from bed-wetting until she was 18, hence was filled with enormous shame. When someone made completely well-meaning overtures to her, she feared being disappointed again, of being unwanted, and of behaving inadequately.

In accordance with this situation of her childhood she hoped for motherliness from me and at the same time was afraid of being disappointed. This fear showed in her withdrawal whenever we came a little closer to each other. In such situations she said that she was terribly afraid of me: of asking too much of me, of disappointing me, of being let down by me, and of not being allowed to remain in therapy because she was getting on my nerves and not talented enough. After a session in which there had emerged some warmth between us the contact was often cut off and she suddenly lost her feeling of connection with me. This was her way of forestalling my possible withdrawal.

She often spoke of her fear of becoming dependent on me which, of course, corresponded to the strong wish to be dependent and to have a sense of belonging. This longing and fear of becoming dependent had been a vital topic of her childhood. As she expressed it: "Throughout my whole childhood I had been busy being nice to women who by some little feature promised to give warmth and love. My heart was terribly hungry for that."

From the beginning I had strong motherly feelings in my countertransference for this poor creature to whom life had been so unkind. My continuous effort to warm her emotionally and to assure her of my confidence in her capacity for positive development were answered by her with mistrust and with the fear of being rejected and left alone as soon as I would know her better. She said she did not deserve such care.

All this was a trial of patience for me; in my willingness to accept her and in my emotional commitment to her I felt continually underestimated and frustrated. The situation matched what Kast (1989) described: a complex-like collusive transference/countertransference situation in which usually "the behavior of the analyst is determined – mostly in a polarizing manner – by the behavior of the analysand. Even when the analyst becomes conscious of this process the behavior cannot be changed immediately. A relationship pattern repeats itself in a stereotyped manner" (p. 166). The complex which at first appears insoluble can be unlocked only when analyst and analysand understand it deeply – emotionally – in its nature and also in its genesis from the relationship patterns of childhood. According to Jung a complex is known to emerge from "the clash between reality and the individual's constitutional inability to meet the demands it makes on him" (CW 6, par. 927).

This complex-producing procedure where the demand for adaptation meets an inadequacy of the individual can be understood at the same time as a relational procedure; the demand for adaptation must have come from persons to whom the analysand had close relationships in childhood. Therefore the complex produced by this clash is a clue not only to the person's disposition but also to the childhood relationships, which could offer another starting point to unravel the complex. In the history of infantile relationships the child and another person faced each other. As long as the underlying complex is not understood, it may happen that the analyst behaves like a person from childhood – who demands adaptation – and the analysand behaves like the child. But it can be reversed: the analyst resembles the child and the analysand resembles the demanding adult person. If this happens, the collusive transference/countertransference situation becomes even more difficult to comprehend.

What was it like with Marga? On the one hand she was the unappeased, demanding child who was prepared to be disappointed; I was the overtaxed mother who tried to do everything right but just could not come up to Marga's excessive expectations. On the other hand I was the child myself, the one who wanted to be understood and accepted by Marga in all my efforts; she was the cold, rejecting mother-person who didn't have a high opinion of me, treated me as she had been treated by her mother and was able to make me sad and angry. Only bit by bit did I – and finally did Marga – come to realize that our collusive, opposed roles had to be understood as coming from the story of her childhood. She projected onto both of us her childhood relation-

Figure 5

Figure 6

ship with her mother. After nine months of analysis she painted a mother who abandoned her in the desert bound in a sack (Figure 5), "Mrs. Octopus" who devoured her (Figure 6), and finally a mother who let her fall into an abyss when she confidently held out her hands to her (Figure 7).

In these pictures Marga recognized that the feeling of abandonment, fear, and anger which she felt toward me corresponded to the affects of her childhood. They surged up in her time and again because her mother had refused to give herself to Marga. She slowly started to see that she as well as I was attacking and refusing. She started to understand how she tried to forestall disappointments with this behavior, that she was the first to withdraw whenever we started to come a little closer to each other and that she herself constellated her feeling of abandonment. She started to understand how often she pulled

Figure 7

Figure 8

Figure 9

away from me. In one of her pictures she actively sprang off a precipice where a monster bared his teeth and opened wide his mouth to devour her (Figure 8). This picture made her ask herself whether this monster, like the one who sprang, was a part of herself.

We can identify several essential steps of this process and the new symbols that indicated these steps. By "new symbols" I mean those which, up to that point, could not be experienced and through which new emotions, ways of behavior and hopes could be gained. In the course of the therapeutic process thus far I have noticed six such turning-points.

The first turning-point was Marga's overcoming of the stereotypy of the abstract, collective ball motif at the beginning of our analysis. Following our mutual acceptance of this motif, a new symbol emerged: the concrete mother-child symbol which has served a guiding function for me in the diagnosis and prognosis.

The second turning-point was the transition from the infant-like symbiosis which, for about nine months, had characterized our therapeutic relationship: the ball as symbol of being captured in the negative mother complex still lurking at the left side, toward the unconscious (Figure 9). A new symbol emerges, of wandering together (Figure 10); the mother grasps the positive element of this therapeutic stage, the blooming blue flowers. This picture is not a static and archetypally exalted picture of the Madonna, like the previous one, but it is a picture of their wandering, expressed in the similar profiles of mother and daughter. The whole picture is directed toward the right side and emphasizes the shoes, that is, the mother's ability to wander. The small child is still carried in a rucksack. This transition had become possible when Marga, in spite of her ambivalence, became able to accept her longing for a mother – of which she had been ashamed before – and when she could feel understood by me in this longing. For Marga, whose only pride was the fact that she had become independent at a very early age, it was especially difficult to accept her wish to surrender and her longing for regression – wishes that were necessary for her ego development.

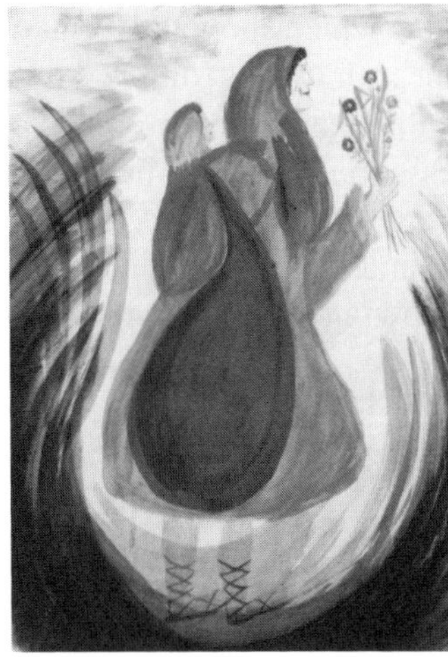

Figure 10

The third turning-point occurred when Marga was able to look back at the abandonment she had suffered in her childhood. It had become conscious now and she could recognize its reflection in our relationship. During this phase she produced a longer series of drawings. Simultaneously the pressure on the therapeutic relationship decreased. This series of drawings, in connection with which she had written part of her life-story as a sort of fairy tale, includes the already-mentioned drawings of being abandoned and devoured, along with other draw-

Figure 11

ings which show the formation of new positive symbols. Each of these drawings followed one of our talks about the other pictures, an indication that we had succeeded in touching emotionally the essential points. After her first picture about being abandoned, which prompted us to talk about her continuing fear of being abandoned in our relationship, came the drawing of a little plant growing between two ravens who perhaps symbolize her parents (Figure 11). This image unifies opposites, reflecting a budding hope that – in spite of everything – emerges time and again, regarding our therapeutic relationship.

Figure 12

This drawing is followed by one (Figure 12) that shows the tree-mother into which the little plant could develop and a first green leaf that appears in the branches between the two ravens. The child holds toward the tree-mother the transitional object, the bear, from the time when she had felt abandoned. With the symbol of the tree-mother, which includes the therapeutic mother, she rediscovered the symbol of the archetypal mother which is vital for her. She had already portrayed her recurrent fear of being devoured in "Mrs. Octopus" (Figure 6), a negative aspect of the Great Mother and of the unconscious in whose womb she is cradled but against which she kicks. I assured her that I could understand very well her kicking against being locked in, and that I supported her kicking.

Figure 13

For the next session she drew a picture (Figure 13) which showed her taken by a strong wind – a creative idea. It carried her out of the symbiotic state in the "Mrs. Octopus" picture and took her to the openness of the desert. But this unexpected freedom made her feel abandoned again.

Figure 14

The cave (Figure 14) to which she turned for shelter has a view, a perspective, even though after painting it she felt that she had lost her bearings. She wrote: "Still I feel empty and alone. I don't know any longer how to go on, and I have no idea where I am, either." There she was again, rescued but lonely. But the perspective had become wider, reaching into the depth of the picture. The awareness of space in a picture is a sign of a growing consciousness. In spite of Marga's statement that she doesn't know how to go on there is a path in this picture. There is also a sun painted in a vivid golden yellow, a color which had not occurred previously in this series. With the symbol of the cave she expressed her acceptance of a shelter and her ability to stand her fear of being locked in. In this picture she is not devoured, as she was in "Mrs. Octopus," but a window with a perspective remains open.

Figure 15

In the last picture of this series (Figure 15) there is even a little mischief; the situation is not as hopeless as she tried to make me believe. The very day she painted the picture with the cave (Figure 14) she also painted (Figure 15) a mother-figure with a large, inviting coat from behind which Marga, again as a child, peeps out. This was the first time Marga's humor showed in one of her pictures, a humor referring to her own typical behavior which she was beginning to see through.

The new symbols of this sequence offered her new ways to deal with the old fears. These symbols depicted the continuous growth of the child, despite some set-backs. At the same time, the image of the mother became visible for Marga as an inner image, as her own chance to trust in life. She could build this trust because of her growing trust in me. The depictions of mother and daughter are conspicuously similar; evidently Marga found herself in both.

In the fourth turning-point it became more obvious for Marga how much she tended to call in question the trusting relationship we had gained and to fall back on the negative mother-complex. At the same time this insight threatened to become another obstacle for us as Marga experienced herself as "evil" when she called our relationship into question. She thought that she was unbearable then and that, consequently, I would terminate therapy. Time and again I tried to show her that she questioned our relationship because her relationship to her mother had always been uncertain. Her behavior toward me could be explained by her fear of not being seen and of being let down by me for the smallest mistake. To accept her own shadow was very difficult for Marga. But more and more she succeeded in recognizing her mother's shadow in her own; she noticed it also in her own behavior and took responsibility for it.

Her declarations of mistrust toward me were echoed in her behavior toward her friends and in particular toward a female friend with whom she lived and who at that time was the only person to whom she was really close. She strained this friendship with her continuous fear that her friend would leave her. Simultaneously she felt this mistrust to be contemptible whenever she became aware of it and reacted with self-hate.

A picture which I named "Teddy-devil" (Figure 16) and at which we looked with more and more humor shows that she experienced her shadow still in an archaic, infantile and inflated

Figure 16

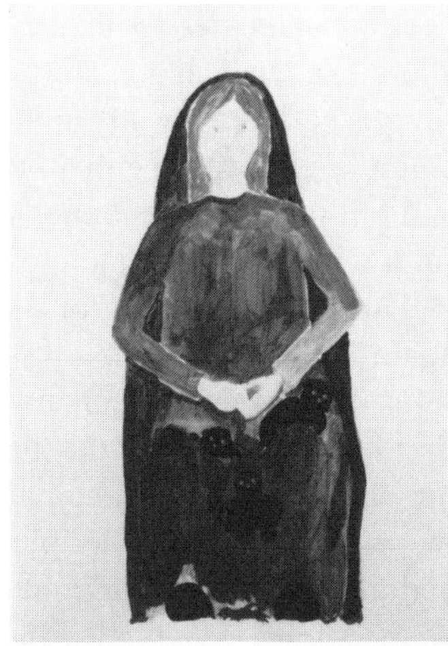

Figure 17

manner. Her next picture (Figure 17) shows a mother – me as the therapist and herself in her motherly qualities – on whose lap little devils crawl around like children who belong there. It shows that she no longer considered her shadow parts as contemptible but saw them as belonging to her life-story.

The fifth turning-point became the time of her deepest crisis. It had always been a big problem for Marga when a therapeutic session had to be cancelled or even postponed. On one occasion I could not manage to give her an extra appointment. She wanted it very much but did not tell me why it was so urgent for her. In spite of all the trust that had grown between us her negative mother-complex was activated again. Marga felt totally abandoned by me. In a picture (Figure 18) from this period she steps into space while crossing a gorge. I didn't want to realize the content of these pictures. I considered them exag-

Figure 18

gerated compared with the situation which had brought them about. Hence, I underestimated the existential crisis from which Marga suffered by my not giving her the appointment, and I could not react to it empathically. She plunged into her complex and fell into the jaws of her self-torture which kept her in its grip for a whole series of pictures.

Until the beginning of my summer vacation, when I left her again for some weeks, we struggled for an understanding of my refusal's producing such an enormous reaction in her. We found that it was caused by the abandonment she had suffered during her childhood and throughout her life. The crosses in the body of the monster in an earlier picture (Figure 8) symbolize the anger and abandonment Marga had felt when her father had died two years before. He had died from suffocation. She had experienced his death as extremely cruel – even though he was an alcoholic, had abandoned her, and she had emotionally rejected him.

Eventually the spell was gone; she felt understood by me in her terrible feeling of abandonment. I had remembered her mother's having looked through her and not recognized her. Only when really seeing her, taking her seriously in the abandonment she felt and expressing this to her could I reach her again. Marga was now determined to bear the loneliness of my vacation. She dreamed: "*I am painting in a group. When I show my picture to Ingrid, my therapist, she is very astonished how I have changed the picture at the end. She gives me more attention and that feels so good. She says she is astonished how I can always change and transform the picture. She gets pleasure from my picture.*" This dream shows that she felt seen and accepted by me. The fact that she could really change the situation made her paint a picture (Figure 19) where a girl kneels in a desert, lonely but

Figure 19

full of expectation and directed toward the light as if praying.

The sixth turning-point followed my return from vacation. Marga told me that my absence over such a long time and my leaving her had still been quite "a hammer blow" to her. There even is a hammer in one of her pictures, in a sequence of five which she had painted during my vacation. The first picture (Figure 20) shows again a ball falling into the water, similar to those she had painted time and again in the beginning. But in this picture the spurting waves are connected with the ball almost as if they were wings. Inside this ball, which looks like an amniotic sac, there is a black shadowy human being similar to a homunculus. Thus, at the beginning of my vacation Marga had returned into the amniotic sac, a regressive but hopeful situation.

Figure 20

But when she looked into the mirror (Figure 21) – where nobody except herself mirrored her, as I was not there – suddenly a part of her started to plunge backward down into the suction of the "mother's corner." But at the same time there is courageous passion in this movement, like diving backward from a springboard. She plunged into the depths of her mother-complex; she did it actively and confronted herself with it. The lines that show the direction of this fall are painted with a tremendous dynamism. Marga not only had gained completely new symbols but also a new, more generous technique. On her

Figure 21

right side a third face emerged, a lion's head, a sign that out of the midst of her despair a lion-like, sun-like energy was set off inside her: pride, anger, a feeling of strength. Altogether the picture gives the impression of a triple face – the steadfast, the jumper and the lion. It is like an explosion of energy; red and yellow flames and in between the black that shoots up like a volcano.

Figure 22

In the next picture (Figure 22) the mother – who seems to be also the therapist – is painted like a witch, angry and endowed with an enormous energy. Her robe is red like fire, like that of the standing and falling person of the preceding picture. At the same time it is the therapist in herself who has become angry but full of energy; this energy can become healing. It makes her glow, but the sun above her is black. The next picture (Figure 23) shows the hammer – the heavy blow, the abandonment my vacation had meant for her. But something had happened. Naked and sitting on the crescent moon as in a small boat she faces the hammer, with the flowing lion-like fiery hair which had appeared in the previous picture (Figure 21). A spot of this red, which characterized the falling angel as well as the witch, flaps in front of her like a red bullfighter's cape which she holds out toward the hammer. Thus, she holds her lion-like energy and witch's anger toward the hammer which would have destroyed her earlier. But her stable basis is the lunar symbol, of a regained

Figure 23

femininity, which now carries her like a small boat over the depth of the unconscious, over the black-blue waters.

Figure 24

Two weeks later she painted the last picture (Figure 24) of this series. It shows her no longer in the boat but swimming and gliding in the water – a grown-up naked shape, a strong female body. There is an obvious difference from the misshapen little homunculus in the amniotic sac. She has gained calm strength. The light blue semicircle which is around the woman's head promises shelter and protection. It recalls a rainbow, the Biblical sign for reconciliation. The black no longer is at the bottom of the picture; it no longer points to insecure depths. It is much lighter in this picture and only visible above the rainbow which seems to be pushing it back like the black of a withdrawing thunderstorm.

What had happened? During the time of my vacation she had kept the insight into the psychodynamics of her feeling of abandonment, which she had gained in the sessions before I went away. After her regression into the amniotic sac fear emerged which vented itself in her painting of a person who falls backward (Figure 21).

But there were also anger, pride, and strength, lion-like energies which formed a counterbalance to the suction of the fall. The therapist who left her time and again turned into a witch. This experience activated, of course, the energies of a witch inside herself. The anger of the witch, the courage of the falling and jumping person, and the fiery energy of the lion all connected inside her and gave her the strength to face the hammer. Simultaneously her lunar vehicle had given her stability against the depth of the unconscious, the security that she can rely on her femininity. In the first session after my vacation she returned to me almost astonished by herself and proud of the pictures that she could bring along in spite of the "hammer blow" I had given her. She said with some respect for herself: "I was so mad at you, but could still keep in touch with you." This attitude was new.

This last series of pictures, in which her abandonment complex could be fully fantasized until completely new symbols and energies emerged, proved that before my vacation Marga had felt understood by me in all her fear of being abandoned. She had recognized her mother's cold and rejecting side in the witch and the hammer and could now dissociate it from me. She had also recognized – which was almost more precious – that she no longer had to project the symbols of the hammer and of the witch, neither onto her mother nor onto me, but that she could regain the positive forces these symbols contain.

Translated from German
by Sabine Osvatic

REFERENCE

Kast, V. (1989). Turning points in analysis: Transference / countertransference and new symbol formation. *Zeitschrift für Analytische Psychologie*, *20*-3, 165-79.

Response

Rosemarie Ahlert
Stuttgart, Germany
Deutsche Gesellschaft
für Analytische Psychologie

When I had read Ingrid Riedel's paper I asked myself: but what about the patient's father? This question is the theme of my paper: where is the father? Or: what is the father-image of the woman Riedel is describing?

I have noticed that women between 20 and 30 decompensate in a depressive – sometimes psychotic – manner. They may plan or even attempt suicide. In their anamneses I find disturbed relationships between their parents. The daughter may have been born out of wedlock, the father may have died very early, or he may have appeared in a bad light because he was an alcoholic – a failure – and therefore the mother avoided him after the parents' divorce. These women get into crises when they are at the threshold of becoming self-determining. They have only one foot on the ground, the "maternal foot," and stumble along with difficulty. They don't have the "paternal foot" at their disposal. Metaphorically, it was amputated. Similar to the phantom limb pain which, after an amputation, gives the impression that the limb is still there, these women feel the pain long after the loss. (The loss of the mother would have similar dynamics.) In the life stories I have observed, the pain from the loss of the father usually was repressed; it is of vital significance for the child to preserve the mother's benevolence and reliability.

In some cases the daughter takes over the part of the father and even feels important. But she loses her childhood. The role becomes a burden for her. Usually she has the part not of the beloved and respected, but of the scorned and devalued, husband. Thus, the self-image must orient to the mother. The wish for the father's presence must be repressed. This denial of the paternal side and the repression of its negative aspects leads to a deficiency in the self-image and in the sense of being an independent individual.

Riedel reports that the analysand's father had died two years earlier and that he was an alcoholic. Evidently the father had not been available to her for a long time. Consequently, avoided him and – as it often happens – was ashamed of her father. We do not know what she experienced as so cruel in her father's death. But perhaps we can comprehend that she may have wished for a long time that her father would die because she wanted to avoid the confrontation with this negative side of herself.

Probably the mother had devalued her husband and the daughter had supported the mother's attitude in order to escape total abandonment. It was vital for her to secure for herself her mother's care and appreciation. The daughter pays for this betrayal of the father with a lack of power, fire, and consciousness. She doesn't know her own value; her whole being sinks into her mother's being, intra-psychically, into the unconscious. Thus, the negative father complex binds her energies so that she is not able to stand firm against the sinking, the regression, of the libido. Her first drawings show this in an impressive manner. Jung described this difficulty in his essay, "The Etiology of Neurosis" (CW4): The libido regresses when the ego doubts that it can master a conflict.

With the help of self-deception a fact gets a different interpretation. Jung used the example of a mountaineer who declares that a mountain cannot be climbed just because he thinks he is not capable of climbing it. Similarly, Riedel's analysand thinks that it is impossible to deal with this father; all the negative qualities are combined in him. She thinks that his death had solved this problem.

That the father problem is not solved may be seen from the fact that, only two years after his death, she starts analysis. She is on her way to fill with energy this paternal part of herself which was declared dead. In order to achieve this she must come, first, to good terms with the mother, that is, with the therapist. To be abandoned by both parents, as expressed in the symbol of the ravens – bad parents – would mean a complete lack of security and a breakdown.

Let us look at the family dynamics and realize the role of the father. It is his task to lead the child out of the narrowness of her exclusive bond to the mother. He can lead the child into the world, give her security and strength, and encourage her to master external conflicts. After having seen the first drawings of this analysand we must ask: Where had the father been, when his daughter fell over the precipice? Was too much asked of the analysand when she was a child and her mother assigned her a task which the mother should have solved? When we transfer the outward conditions of the parents' relationship into the intra-psychic situation of the analysand's mother we can assume that the mother was not able to integrate masculine aspects into her self-image. Rather, she relegated them to a destructive sphere ruled by inebriation and not by consciousness.

The task of releasing the father falls on the daughter. Externally she must liven up his image; intra-psychically she must make use of its hidden energies. She can then add the paternal half to her self-image and have both feet on the ground again, without pain.

In the positive relationship to the therapist the patient succeeds in mobilizing those energies which she integrates as anger and strength in the image of the lion. Because of the security she feels in the therapeutic relationship the solar symbols such as sun and lion appear, indicating the beginning of a process of releasing the father image. Only then will it be possible to deal with this father. To use Jung's metaphor: the mountaineer becomes aware of his lack of strength and takes a mountain guide. This woman takes a mountain guide – the analyst – who helps her to climb this mountain – the negative father-complex – in a better and less dangerous way.

The symbol of the hammer points to a similar male and

paternal direction as we are reminded of Hephaestos, the blacksmith, who is known to us from Greek mythology as the lame, deformed one. There are many stories that tell about his creative abilities when dealing with a problem. He forged objects in the fire, transforming them. He had the strength and the courage to make use of the fire and to reshape hard material, metal. These energies, which are hidden in the hammer, could also be at the analysand's disposal. We sometimes wish that someone would thump on the table with his or her fist in order to solve the situation when there is a lasting insoluble conflict in the family. In the same manner we can expect the hammer to help in clarifying the therapeutic relationship by bringing fire and strength – the energies that can become effective and usable in the transformation of the self-image. The analysand can become more aware of her own value by mastering the archetypal powers of the hammer and the fire. From the unification of mother-image and father-image she can draw on her own strength.

For today's women and men it may not be as necessary as some decades earlier to increase their own value by devaluing the other sex, either on a relational level or intra-psychically. For many centuries women thought that they were less valuable than men. Women devaluing men is a helpless effort to increase our own value. Such devaluations damage one's self-image.

Translated from German
by Sabine Osvatic

The Yellowing of the Work

James Hillman
Thompson, Connecticut, USA
Inter-Regional Society
of Jungian Analysts

A statement of Jung's in *Psychology and Alchemy* launches this paper on its course. Jung wrote:

> Four stages [of the alchemical opus] are distinguished, characterized by the original colours mentioned in Heraclitus: *melanosis* (blackening), *leukosis* (whitening), *xanthosis* (yellowing), and *iosis* (reddening).... Later, about the fifteenth or sixteenth century, the colours were reduced to three, and the *xanthosis*, otherwise called the *citrinitas*, gradually fell into disuse or was but seldom mentioned.... There were only three colours: black, white, and red.
>
> The first main goal of the process,... highly prized by many alchemists ... is the silver or moon condition, which has still to be raised to the sun condition. The *albedo* [whitening] is, so to speak, the daybreak, but not till the *rubedo* is it sunrise. The transition to the *rubedo* is formed by the *citrinitas* [yellowing], though this, as we have said, was omitted later. (CW12, pars. 333-34)

Some questions that arise from Jung's statements are: What is the nature of the omitted yellow? What are the specific qualitative consequences of this omission beyond the ominous reversion from a fourfold symbol-system to a trinitarian one? Since the color yellow continues to appear in the material of contemporary alchemy – analytic work, as an opus of imaginative sophistication – can this work shed light on the nature of yellow, and vice versa?

Because the alchemical craft supposedly developed from handworkers' arts, the alchemical mind perceived changes in color in the material at hand to be changes of essential nature. A bit of iron changes color when fired and when cooling. A cotton cloth dipped in blue tint irreversibly alters its plain white state. Dyeing, as bathing or dipping – the Greek word is *baptizein* – affects essence. The unbleached muslin now colored blue has been baptized; its soul has been changed.

Our usual view of colors is derived from Western philosophy – for example, Newton, Locke, Berkeley and Kant – who considered colors to be not inherent in things, but only secondary qualities residing in our subjective eyesight. But the philosophers' proposition is contradicted by the way we live in the world. Colors of the sky, sea, sunset portend the coming storm. As a fruit sweetens on the stem its color changes. As a patient sickens we see pallor, jaundiced skin, cyanotic lips, brown urine, empurpled nose, raspberry tongue, red rashes, white exudates, black stools. The human eye's distinguishing 20,000 varieties of hue helps us read the inherent intelligibility of the world.

Yellow signifies a particular kind of change, usually for the worse: withering leaves, aging pages and long-stored linen, old teeth and toenails, liver spots, peeling skin, indelible stains of food and semen. The process of time shows as a yellowing. The alchemists spoke of it as "putrefaction" and "corruption."

English and American common speech continues to use yellow in a manner that is, as the Oxford English Dictionary says, "often disparaging." Cowardice is yellow; so is jealousy. A yellow dog is craven and a canary informs on friends. The yellow press and a yellow-back novel are cheap and lurid. The yellow star pinned on Jews reflects the jaundiced eye of prejudice. The yellow peril raised engulfing fears. The yellow flag of quarantine is the international sign for dangerously contagious disease.

Yet yellow has a host of cheerfully sunny implications, from the etymological link of yellow with yolk to the metaphorical association with ripening grains, spring flowers, honey, sunlight and the apotropaic use of lemons to ward off death. The German *gelb* and the Latin *galbus* and *galbinus* derive from roots meaning radiant and shining, like gold; so the Homeric Achilles and Apollo are yellow-haired, blond, fair and sunlit. In addition, the most luminous of all hues (least saturated) is yellow and the yellow spot in the middle of the retina is where vision is most acute.

Thus, it would be easy to neglect Freud's insight into the contrary meanings inherent in the basic terms of language, and instead to look at yellow via Jung's lens of opposites. Then we would oppose yellow with purple as in our kindergarten color wheels, or with blue as did Goethe, or with green as did Jung himself in opposing yellow – for intuition, with green – sensation (CW9-I, pars. 582, 588n). Definition by opposition, however, restricts the meaning of a phenomenon to that face to which it is opposed. If purple means mysterious depth, then yellow must be crass and blatant. If green means growth and concrete nature, then yellow must be mental and loftily abstract. If blue is cold, withdrawn, deep and sober; then yellow must be hot, active, shallow and crazy.

The opinion that yellow is crazy floats through the arts – yellow (gold) was Edgar Allan Poe's favorite color, as well as van Gogh's – leading Ellis (1896) and Birren (1962) to state that yellow frequently appeals to troubled minds. Kandinsky (1977) wrote that yellow "may be paralleled in human nature with madness,… with violent, raving lunacy" (p. 33).

The lens of opposites tends to ignore the context in which a yellow appears, its precise hue, and the words that describe it (butter, primrose, sulfur, chrome, cadmium, mustard, amber, straw, etc.), its relation with other hues in the same image, and the personal myths perceived in the experience. For van Gogh, for instance, yellow was the color of love, as it was in Gauguin's painting "Yellow Christ." For Kandinsky (1977), yellow was aggressive, trumpet-like, acidic, eccentric. The most we gain by imagining in terms of opposites is seeing clearly a divine, gold-like, incorruptible yellow on the one hand and on the other, corruption and decay.

Here I need to intersperse some supposed facts from anthropological research. By compiling lists of the words for different colors from languages the world over, Berman and Kay (1969) state the following conclusions: all languages have terms for bright and dark, that is, white and black; if a language has a third color term, it is always red; if a fourth term, yellow or green; and if a fifth, either green or yellow. If we imagine colors along a scale from simple to sophisticated, then yellow-green – the hue the Greeks called *chloris* – becomes the essential bridge between black-white-red and the color terms that follow: blue, brown, purple, pink, orange, and gray; in that order, more or less universally. Isaac Newton's chromatic prism, curiously, locates green-yellow in the center of its spectrum and Leonardo da Vinci's six primary colors (black, white, red, yellow, green, blue) also give yellow a median position.

To draw a first conclusion: neither by translating yellow into a symbolic meaning nor by dividing it into positive and negative poles can we uncover its significance for an alchemical psychology. Rather, we must find answers to our questions within the context of alchemical relations, in which yellow appears as a specific transitional quality in a temporal process.

An Excursion On Sulfur

In the oft-quoted passage from Mary the Jewess, to whom is attributed one of the earliest alchemical formulations of the transitions in the process, we find this sentence: "When one yellows three becomes four, for one yellows with yellow sulphur" (Hopkins, 1967, p. 99). Albertus Magnus (1967) says: "The yellow colour in metals is caused by the Sulphur, which colours them." (III-ii).

Raw sulfur, heated with lime, results in calcium sulfide, which, when added to water, results in the gas hydrogen sulfide. Hydrogen sulfide – spirit of sulfur – stinks. By introducing this gas into solutions of a variety of metals, various colors appear, as they do on the surface of metals. The alchemical mind regards these changes perceived by the nose and eye as evidence of the dictum, "By means of rot essential change takes place." The organic process of putrefaction is fortified by sulfur. Sulfur hastens nature toward its decay and thus toward its next season, and so, when things stink, when they yellow with decay, something important is going on, and what is going on is sulfuric.

Since the texts so often warn that the sulfur of which they speak is a "sophic" material and not your common or vulgar sulfur, we need to translate the term "sophic" into "metaphoric" or "psychic." We are speaking, therefore, of psychic change, which appears as "something going wrong," and going wrong in two particular ways. First, when things corrupt, rot, decay; second, when they become physically hyperactive because sulfur is defined as the principle of "combustibility" – flaring up, "easily kindled to violence or passion" (Oxford English Dictionary), "tumult" (Random House Dictionary) and the "principle which hinders perfection in all its works" (CW14, par. 138) – because sulfur hinders sublimation. Sublimation, as Ruland's 1612 alchemical dictionary says, "is effected by means of Distance" (1962), p. 303). The yellowing caused by sulfur therefore impedes detachment and distancing.

"Sophic" best translates as "not natural" – sulfur mediated by *sophia*, sulfur as having an esthetic and reflective interiority beyond its crude compulsion. Sendivogius (1556-1636) gives a hint of this hidden potential within sulfur in his parable of wounded sulfur bleeding as "pure milk-white water" (1953). Within my hot greed for the fatness of life, my desirous reach into the world – what analysis long condemns as manic defense, projective identification, and acting-out – there lies an anima, a soul significance. Sensationalism, consumerism and compulsions have other than common or vulgar significance. They have a *suksma* aspect, a sophic interiority beyond sheerly appetitive goals. This interior intention disguises itself in the vivid object of desire, but sulfur's desire is its own true intention, that leonine heat, that "earthy feculence" (CW14, par. 138) without which the opus has no life and the *lapis* cannot redden. In each hunger there lies the whiteness of anima, which is revealed in the wounds suffered by sulfur.

Similarly, when things go wrong as rot – my job stinks, my marriage stinks, this analysis stinks, I stink – this stench signifies sulfur making changes. These changes, however, do not have to appear as the result of a process, as a clearer reflective consciousness *after* the putrefaction. No. The feeling of putrefaction is itself an awareness; the feeling bad and wrong is already sulfur experiencing its own wound.

To say it again: combustion and decay are the two ways sulfur sophisticates. Sulfur becomes aware of itself violently. Hence, some alchemists said sulfur could not be worked with until it had first been calcined, that is, had been dried of its moisture or abstracted from its propensity for emotional attachment. They were afraid of its eruptive inflammability. We too are afraid, most of us still enchanted by Anna Freud's dictum that the patient who acts out cannot be analyzed; most of us are afraid of an analysis going wrong, beginning to stink.

Jung devoted a chapter to sulfur in the *Mysterium Coniunctionis* (CW14): not many pages, but wondrously condensed information and interpretation. He considered sulfur to be the active principle in the opus and thus of human life. He equated sulfur with what psychology calls the motive factor: on the one hand the conscious will, on the other unconscious compulsion.

The extreme language to which alchemy resorts to describe sulfur indicates to Jung that sulfur has affinities with the Devil – as corrupter and compeller – and with Christ, giver of warmth and life. In either direction, Devil or Christ, sulfur is usually imagined as male, hot, of an obdurate earthly body, fat and oily, desirous as a dragon or lion. Though it is the urgent agent of change, sulfur at the same time not only resists sublimation but is that very component of the psyche, as Jung said, "responsible for our resistance to psychology in general" (CW14, par. 152).

The innate *extraversum* (CW14, par. 134) or turning outward of sulfur (despite its milk-white interior) corresponds with the place of yellow in Japanese medical color symbolism, where yellow and red are outside, black and white inside. According to this four-color set, black is inside and cold; white, inside and chill or tepid; yellow is outside and warm; red, outside and hot. The transition then, from white to yellow would show both as an increase in warmth and a conversion from inside to outside.

Warm and outside: like the games we played as children, where clues to the hidden are given by temperature. The closer you get, the warmer you are, as if drawn outward and toward the object by its *calor inclusus*, its innate sulfur, that hidden warmth concealed in the world.

"Outside" – that is our clue for the relation between the yellowing and sulfur. "In what substance is this Sulphur to be found" asks the alchemical inquirer (Sendivogius, 1953). "In all substances," is the reply. "All things in the world – metals, herbs, trees, animals, stones, are its ore" (p. 154). Outside: wherever interest is kindled, wherever the active attention turns away from itself to things, things lighting up to be consumed, the "I" (which we call "ego" but which may well be the sulfuric element in personality) is called forth by its counterpart, the sulfuric element in the world which calls the soul from the chill lunar reflection of the *albedo* into a combustible fusion with the warm-bodied objects of desire. As things light up and catch fire, we get burned by the sulfur lurking in each tree, lurking from behind every stone, like the devil tempting us into the body of the world.

Between White and Red

So far we have been explicating yellow *per se*. Our main concern, however, is with yellow*ing* as transitional process in which something is yellowed. The "something" yellowed is the *albedo*, that lunar style of consciousness when the anima or soul infuses the work with its whiteness.

This *albedo* whiteness, achieved after the soul's long exile in *nigredo*, must be distinguished from the primary white of the *materia prima*, the *candida* of unmarked and unremarking innocence. In analysis, this *albedo* whiteness refers to feelings of positive syntonic transference, of things going easily and smoothly, a gentle sweet safety in the vessel, insights rising, synchronistic connections, resonances and echoes, the dead alive on the moon as ancestors who speak with internal voices of the activated imagination – all leading to the invulnerable conviction of the primacy of psychic reality as another world apart from this world, life lived in psychological faith. In this tepid and shadowless lunar light, everything seems to fit. As Jung said, this is the first main goal of the process and many alchemists were satisfied to stop here, bringing the opus to rest in peace.

This condition does not want more light, more heat. Like the lyric cry of the lunatic, the lover or the poet, it asks for asylum, poetic reveries, and love. "One night of love" – a forever lunar night that would be spoiled by dawn. Having absorbed and unified all hues into the one white, the mirror of silvered subjectivity expands to reflect all things at the expense of differentiation of itself. For it takes something outside subjectivity to see into oneself. Hence, Jung's insistence on "the other" for individuation. This other, however, does *not* have to be confined to the other person in the analytic situation. Rather, "the other" refers to anywhere that the different appears, anything outside subjective reflection, any moment that intrudes upon white consciousness's love of its own lunar illumination which is precisely where its blindness lies (Hillman, 1986).

As Figulus (1963) says, "Matter, when brought to whiteness, refuses to be corrupted" (p. 287). The white refuses to be yellowed. It seems a spoiling. Yellowing rots the perfection. It is hot, smelly, earthy, male, active; to use an alchemical simile, the yellowing of the white is like milk becoming cheese. The white coagulates, takes on body, flavor, fatness. White resists this physical substantiation, for it feels like a regression to the vulgar drivenness of earlier moments in the work – *materia prima* and *nigredo* – which the arduous hours of analytic reflection have finally sophisticated and pacified.

Yet Figulus also says that whiteness remains imperfect unless it be brought to highest redness and, in fact, remains "dead" until that occurs. Other authors agree that the yellowing brings life, calling the yellowing a "resurrection." "*Citrinatio est resuscitatio*" (Johnson's *Dictionary*, p. 57). To achieve this resuscitation, as another treatise (*Collectanea Chemica, 1963*) says, the artifex "goes on increasing his fire till it assumes a yellow, then an orange or a citron colour" (p. 116; see also Fabricius, p. 143). The increasing yellow is imagined as growing within the belly of the white, its lunar mother and, as Hopkins (1967) says, "What was silver on the outside, was yellow on the inside; at the same time you whiten on the outside, you yellow on the inside" (p. 96).

Clearly then, the yellowing is more than a spoiling of the white. It is also its brighter illumination, clarifying vision. This clarification is particularly intellectual. The alchemical writer, Gerardus Dorn, on whom Jung relied for many insights, made this explicit: "The form, which is the intellect, is the beginning, middle and end of the procedure; and this form is made clear by the saffron colour" (CW12, par. 366). This should come as no surprise. Since the yellowing follows directly upon the *unio mentalis*, it would have to be a transmutation of the mind, a change in intellect. "Birds play a prominent part in the citrinitas" (Fabricius, 1976, p. 146).

"The growing light of solar illumination helps [one] discern more clearly the imperfections of the lunar sphere" (Fabricius, 1976, p. 143). Therefore, one may expect a growing, though hidden, critical discernment of analyzing itself; for "yellow observes whiteness" (Klossowski de Rola, 1973). The yellow flowers of celandine (chelidonia) mentioned by Dorn at this juncture of the transition become a "precious ingredient" because chelidonia "cures eye disease and is particularly good for night blindness" (CW14, par. 687). Paracelsus gives similar prominence to the *cheyri* or four-petaled yellow wallflower, both an abortive (out of the belly) and restorative (*resuscitatio*; CW13, par. 171 & 171n). "When the *citrinitas (xanthosis*, "yellowing") appears, there is formed the collyrium (eyewash) of the philosophers" (CW9-II, par. 195). Many eyes appear in the *cauda pavonis*, and these peacocks' tails are yellow (Klossowski de Rola, 1973, figure 61), heralding a new yellow ground of seeing. Where white unifies all colors into a monotheism of subjective reflection, the yellow clarification is also a dawning of multiple vision, seeing each thing as it is, beyond subjectivity, and thus bridging to the *rubedo's* sanguine tincturing of the world out there.

The intellect too goes through changes; not only the heart, the body and the imagination. "Thinking and being are the same" according to Plotinus (III, 8, 8), a position shared by Gnostics and

Zen teachers as well as alchemists. Alchemy (and analysis) clarifies the mind and sophisticates its thought since thought derives from psyche. During early phases of the work alchemy speaks of clouds, haze and fog, of the *massa confusa*, of white smoke, metaphors equally viable for the mind at beginning moments in analysis – and beginning moments occur not only at the literal beginning. They recur all through the work. The mind in *nigredo* shows characteristics of downward and backward thinking, an intellect caught in reductive and depressive reasonings and figurings out: past history, materialized fantasies and concretistic explanations. The *nigredo* psyche knows itself as victimized, traumatized, dependent, and limited by circumstantiality and substantiality. The *nigredo* psyche is *eo ipso* substance-abused. The mind in *albedo* more likely dreams. Receptive, impressionable, imagistic, self-reflective and perhaps comfortably magical. "But in this state of 'whiteness' one does not *live* ... it is a sort of abstract, ideal state" (Jung, 1977, p. 228). No problems, except the vast generalized abstractions of spirit – for spirit and soul are unified.

Dorn's intellectual account of the yellowing as an aurora of the moon becoming sun does not describe adequately the nature of the yellowed intellect. It is not the continued expansion of white consciousness, an increase of reflective capacity. It is more than aware, more than enlightened. It must be hot and male, beginning with the light yellow or dirty brown of Mars (Fabricius, 1976, p. 143) and even putrid, if it is to spring the mirrored prison of reflection. Since sulfur with all its corruption, intensity and feculence has been instrumental in its change, this mind "burns" with its own bitter bile, yellow *choler* (Klibansky et al., 1964, p. 53). "The yellowing phase in Senior is expressed by an arch of armed eagles ... [which] adds yet another image to the cutting swords, splitting arrows, cleaving serpents, and piercing rays of the citrinitas" (Fabricius, 1976, p. 147). Brighter, more coagulated and more combustible, the yellowed intellect is complicated with emotions, as one is indeed aware and alive in jealousy, cowardice, fear, prejudice, aging and decay. It is like an instinctual smoky light shining through reflections from within –

no longer mere mirroring, but responsive outward, the mind like a smoldering yellow effusion staining with intellect whatever it meets. "The yellowness of the sulphur has brought out all the hidden yellow of the metal and changed it into a kind of gold in which yellow was abundant and overflowing" (Hopkins, 1967, p. 97).

This is not the usual intellect, dried with concepts, abstracted – pulled away; this is the fat intellect, physical, concrete, emotional, fermenting with instinctual interiority, an unctuous passion. Having first been whitened, its desire is not simple and driven, but desire aware of itself through intellectual fervor – an *intellectus agens* – dawnings of the winged mind, sure as gold. No longer that separation between mercury and sulfur, between fantasy flights and dense emotional body. In the carcass of the lion a new sweetness, thick and yellow and sticking to all things, like honey, like oil, flowing like wax and gilding as it touches. So does *citrinitas* lead to the reddening, in which often the image of the king dominates.

The *rubedo* as a purple-red is also called in Greek terms the *iosis*, which means poisoning. So it would seem that the *rubedo* deconstructs the very matter from which the King arises. "All corruption of matter is marked by deadly poison" (Figulus, 1963, p. 287). The uroboros, that can also indicate the *rubedo*, at this red juncture signifies a final dissolution of sunlit consciousness and all distinctions; that is, all the stages, phases, operations, and colors. It is a moment of the *rotatio*, a turning and turning like the cosmos itself, requiring endless numbers of eyes to see with, like the King seeing and being seen by each one in the realm. The work is over; we no longer work at consciousness, develop ourselves, or possess a distinct grid by means of which we recognize where we are, how we are, maybe even who we are. "The dissolution of Sol should be effected by Nature, not by handiwork," concludes Figulus (1963, p. 296). Psyche is life, life psyche.

A Case

Turning now to a case for further amplification and using alchemy as grid for conceiving the psychology of analysis, I confess myself a Jungian rather than of another school that relies on other basic metaphors such as infancy, typology, chronological development, mythical Gods, diagnoses, transference. I take Jung seriously, even literalistically, when he claims that alchemical metaphors best provide understanding for what the psyche goes through in deep, long-term analysis (see Holt, 1973). I also confess myself a Jungian by introducing a case as further amplification of the metaphors and figures. "Instead of deriving these figures from our psychic conditions, [we] must derive our psychic conditions from these figures" (CW13, par. 299).

The analysand: a woman in her forties, professional, married though not closely, childless, intensely introverted, yet adapted. After a second bout of analysis lasting two years, she was required to return to her home country on a fixed date. Although she often had dreamt of colors, at this juncture with the departure date firm in our calendars, her dreams began to yellow, as follows and in brief:

January 18: A cat dozing on and off; yellow and white stripes.
January 20: Yellow cloth with letters on it.
January 24: White lustrous letters.
January 24: Yellow legal-size note-pads.
January 27: "I remember I had a baby; baby is wrapped in a yellow robe."
January 27: A yellow book opened to where it says, "end Chapter One; beginning Chapter Two."
January 28: Big eye on the wall. Eye looking through a hole in a curtain. "I said the word 'origin' in English."
[Origin comes from *orire* = to arise, from which orient, east, sunrise.]
February 1: Big rooster, Black, "but some part had a different color."
February 2: "It became daylight."
Later in February: Bright light even with eyeshades (dark glasses) on.

Themes in this material correspond with the *citrinitas*: alternating yellow and white in the striped cat's dozing on and off; the logos clarifications in letters, words and books; eyesight; awakening; daylight; new life. The yellowing of her dreams also corresponds with the phases of the analysis itself: ending to return to her obligations in the world.

Hers had been a very white analysis: two or three times a week; many dreams each session which she worked on assiduously; hours of solitude; reading, reflection, reverie, imagination, memory, nature; few relationships; eating alone; isolation owing to language difficulties; feelings and fantasies focused on the analysis and on me, the analyst.

Now she was planning her work for the next months at home: arranging schedules, letters and phone calls, parting ceremonies, shopping, and imagining further activities such as dancing, cooking, friends, and translating.

She suggested translating one of my books into her language. Then, we found a white interpretation for this suggestion. We understood translation as a way of remaining in the work by maintaining the relationship, abstract and distanced as exigencies had decreed.

Since then, I see that this turn to words in her dreams and plans accords with the yellowing, not only as solar clarification described in the "Ninth Key" of *The Golden Tripod* (Sendivogius, 1953), where "Grammar, bearing a yellow banner" precedes the Sun in the parade of planets and the virtues and arts associated with them. Dorn's emphasis on the activation of intellect during the *citrinitas* seems borne out in this case. So now I have a more yellowed and sulfuric interpretation for her suggestion to translate. It did not merely represent a backward move to retain the transference; it was also a move outward into publication, a *multiplicatio* and *proiectio*, her embodied mind entering the world. Besides, isn't translation a copulation, a meeting of tongues in linguistic intercourse?

Perhaps I have not made clear that her yellowing differs from another sort I have seen. Just as all whites are not the *albedo* – since the primary material can be *candida* rather than *falbus*

(Hillman, 1980), white as innocence rather than white as reflection – so there is sometimes a primitive yellow-orange of raw and burning activity, a pleasure principle of id fire, the uncooked sulfur of manic brightness. This figures in dreams as a boy with orange hair or a yellow shirt, a bright yellow car going like mad, a construction worker with yellow hard-hat on a high-voltage line, a lion escaped or a yellow dog, a yellow propellered plane crashing into mud. These examples of sulfuric intensity do not result from white as interior to it, like butter from milk, but require whitening the yellow as anterior to it. Again: colors have no single meaning; they must be placed with image, mood, time, context.

Despite the preparations for departure, the yellowing was mainly internal, where Fabricius' (1976) "yellow death" (p. 140) was taking place, as symbolic with aging and ending of life. "Fallen into the sear, the yellow leaf," as Macbeth says (V, 3), herself no longer the girl, her safety in whiteness no longer assured. How would her husband react? There occurred fear of losing what had happened; jealousy over others who did not have to leave, smoldering anger over what was not accomplished; that is, what was not fulfilled concretely in the martial urge toward me. Remember: "Yellow is a true sign of Copulation of our Man and Woman together" (Philalethes, in Klossowski de Rola, 1973, p. 27). Sometimes, a bitter look, a curled lip, a lapse into suppressive silence. A killing was also going on.

Looking back, I ask where was the smelly, oily, fat sulfur that brings richness, lightness and waxy impressionability to the *lapis* as *rubedo*, the ease and joy and capacity to float along? I remember feeling that an underlying depression had not all lifted and an acidic bitterness had not all sweetened; I was myself then disconsolate by what I felt had cut short the work. Our rapport had become complicated – she seemed suddenly so dense – by the increasing presence of indelible emotions that seemed bent on destroying the harmony and illuminating insights that nevertheless still kept coming. Then, I rationalized these perceptions by attending mainly to what we were achieving. Today, looking back through my yellow-tinted lens, I believe that what was also being achieved – besides the evident yellow illumination – was actually a thorough spoiling of the white harmony which her emotions and my perceptions were clearly indicating, a spoiling which my own analytic whiteness resisted and tried to smooth over. We had left the white and not entered the red; a poisonous, acidic "residuum of yellow powder" had not been "washed away" (*Golden Tripod*, 1953, p. 343). Yet the dawn had come, and clarity of understanding and expression permeated our hours and her new life.

The Analyst Too Is Yellowed

Jung said alchemy has two aims: "the rescue of the human soul and the salvation of the cosmos" (Jung, 1977, p. 228). Yellowing rescues the soul from the whiteness of psychological reflection and insight. For, to repeat what Jung said, "in this state of 'whiteness' one does not *live*.... In order to... come alive it must have 'blood'... the rubedo, the 'redness' of life.... then the opus magnum is finished" (Jung, 1977, p. 229).

I understand this rescue operation to apply to psychology itself. Let me explain: as the alchemical opus rescues the soul of the individual, so this opus can rescue the psyche of psychology conceived only in terms of the individual human. From the alchemical perspective the human individual may be a necessary but cannot be a sufficient focus; the rescue of the cosmos is equally important. Neither can take place without the other. Soul and world are inseparable: *anima mundi*. It is precisely this fact that the yellowing makes apparent and restores, a fact which the white state of mind cannot recognize because that mind has unified into itself the world, all things psychologized.

If psychological practice neglects its yellowing, it can never leave off psychologizing, never redden into the world out there, never be alive to the cosmos – from which today come our actual psychological disorders. Remember: sulfur is found in all things and out there; the yellow turns *outward*. The inwardness habit of psychologizing follows consequently from the *albedo* condition which, as an "undivided purity" (Burckhardt, 1967, p. 188), loses distinctions among the opposites it has united. Therefore, the *albedo* seeks mental integrations of the disturbing yellowing emotions of transference by means of psychological grids. Yet each new analytic refinement – object relations theory, Kohut, Langs, Lacan – continue to polish further the *albedo* mirror so that we may see more clearly, but what we see is still the human face and what we hear is still human language. Getting out there requires the yellow death, that poisoning *iosis* prepared by a putrefaction of the *unio mentalis* that is analytic consciousness.

This poisoning awakens. The *pharmakon* kills as it cures. Our eyes open to the narcissistic corruption (see Hillman, 1989) inherent to our theory, our diagnoses, treatment and training. We begin to see the addictive co-dependency of analyst and analysand disguised and glorified by theories of transference/countertransference which intensify the mirror's gleam to the world's neglect.

As analyst I too am yellowed; I cannot escape the opus since the artifex is myself, the material worked on. I therefore feel a fermenting discomfort of interior doubt, that yellowing inside the white which treacherously observes it from within. We feel ourselves betraying what we were, the realizations we believed, our very psychological faith and its achievements, even our former pain and the scars of identity it gave. For pain too changes color. As the *nigredo* has its inconsolable wounds that lift into the whitened suffering of aesthetic sensitivity, so the yellow brings the pain of knowledge, the eagles and arrows of seeing sharp and true, together with the fire and fear of seeing destructively the cowardice, jealousy, choler and decay that taints both opus and artifex.

To evade the death by yellowing, that is, going straight from white to red, soul to world, is not what alchemy recommends. The texts warn against the reddening coming too fast, warn against direct flame, warn that if a red oil floats on the surface the work has been spoiled. Without the yellow, the whitened mind converts directly to red, enantiodromia, moving straight forward by converting psychic insights into literal programs, red bricks without straw. We reflect the world in the mirror of psychology, reducing its political conflicts to shadow projections, its exploitation of the earth to body problems, the destruction of nature to repression of our interior unconscious wilderness. We prescribe more of "the feminine," more anima, more lunar consciousness – though the yellowing is a time of Mars where the "male is on top of the female" (Burckhardt, 1967, pp. 90-91). We believe magically that self-transformation trickles down (multiples and projects) into the world. As our learned colleague Edinger, who does not mention yellow in his major work on alchemical symbolism in psychotherapy, wrote (1985): "*Multiplicatio* gives us a hint as to how psychotherapy may work... the consciousness of an individual who is related to the Self seems to be contagious and tends to multiply itself in others" (p. 228). This approach psychologizes the world instead of mundifying the psyche.

Yet alchemy itself tempts away from the yellow which gives an inherent reason for its eventual neglect and our urge to jump over it. Because the last operations are so extraverted, the heat of the spirit so high, the King constellated in the *rubedo*, there is an exalted mission to multiply psychic projects in the world. Go forth and multiply. Mercurius as *multi flores* (many flowers) "tempts us out into the world of sense," says Jung, and his habitation is "in the vein swollen with blood" (CW13, par. 299). This blood, identified in the secular unconscious with the redemptive and missionary blood of Christ (cf. CW13, par. 383-91), urges ever forward to spread by conversion of the heathen (those "in need of psychology"). Our large-scale Jungian film-showings, summer institutes, public events, even our training programs may be driven by the exaltation of sudden reddening, which may also account for the conservative counter-moves to slow the *multiplicatio* by lengthening training. No wonder we are sometimes seen as latter-day Rosicrucians.

We began by recalling that the yellowing phase faded from the alchemical schema after the 16th century, which is precisely when alchemy itself began to fade partly into the Rosicrucian movement, or coagulating into either mountebank goldmaking for temporal princes, or into spiritual directions for esoteric Christian redemption, or into experimental physical techniques.

Against this scientific coagulation, the alchemists were ever on guard. "Beware of the physical in the material" was a basic caution. "Those who, in place of liquid Mercury, use sublimate, or calcined powder, or precipitate, are deceived, and err greatly" (Figulus, 1963, p. 293). There is an ever-present danger in regarding psychic materials by means of dry (calcined) metaphysical abstractions or from the naturalistic perspective of physical literalism (right-brain/left-brain, concrete holistic medicine, information theory, etc.). "The highest mystery of the whole Work is the Physical Dissolution into Mercury" (Figulus, 1963, p. 295). Keep the metaphors fluid.

Can we not draw a lesson from history? If the practice of Jungian psychology continues the alchemical tradition, then we too – unless we are fully yellow – simply repeat its fate, falling prey to either physical scientism, spiritual esotericism, or the business of professionalism as princes of this world – or all three mixed. For our work to approach its cosmic purpose, for it to reach the world, it must spoil itself. "The withering away of the state" (Karl Marx). "Displacing the subject" by deconstructing its own consciousness (French philosopher Jacques Derrida). Self-destruct as damage control. Kill the Buddha. Apocalyptic via negativa. Catastrophe theory. *Shevirath Ha-Kelim* or Breaking the Vessels.

If we washed our vision in the yellow collyrium we would be able to observe the whiteness of psychology with a fully jaundiced eye. We might then recognize that the issues plaguing professional psychology – sexual misbehavior, ethical rules, lawsuits, insurance payments, licensing laws, training regulations, regional and international organizations – expose the fermenting corruption breaking the white psyche out of its self-enclosure, which it defends by intensely, narcissistically, focusing on countertransference, training supervision, childhood, and the Self. The fermenting corruptions, which seem diversions from the main job of therapy, may actually be how the psyche is yellowing into the cosmos. If so, there will be more psychology actually going on, more soul actually to be made, in the ferment of these corruptions than in the enlightened discussions of cases and theories. The esoteric is always in the outcast area; today, the stone the builders reject is the building itself.

Furthermore, those analysands who turn on us, turn on analysis, who condemn, sue, expose, violate the trust, may actually be angels of the yellow road to the emerald city, angels in the salvation of the cosmos from the psyche closed long enough into individualism, sulfuric angels pointing the way at the end of this analytic century to an end of analysis that omits the world. What I hoped to do in this paper I feel is done: to disclose the yellow light within a process we ourselves are in and to leave on it an indelible yellow stain.

Finally this, inasmuch as every objective exposition is also a subjective confession and inasmuch as I have said that thought derives from psyche, what one thinks reflects where one is, the coloring of the *intellectus agens* as it filters through imagination. Let me bear empirical witness to these assumptions and to the *citrinitas* in my own case. I have, in part, been yellowed. Like Albrecht Dürer's self-portrait, I point to my own yellow spot.

Nine months ago I ceased practicing private analysis. I continue to practice psychology with large groups, in public speaking and teaching, publishing and writing. These activities are permeated with the same sulfuric fumes that have characterized this paper and others corrosive to the white psychology which other parts of me have long championed. In the white mirror I see myself as having simply walked out and closed the door on the consulting room of transference entanglements, too yellow-bellied and too withering in age to refine my skills further and so instead I am acting out my countertransference on analysis itself, globally, with the destructive vision of prophetic inflation, convinced that what takes place in the depths of one's soul is taking place as well in other souls, in the cosmic soul of the world. I attribute this conviction to a predominance of sulfur in conjunction with mercury. What else to say save that for me the white moon is down even if the red is not risen, and my choler not sanguine.

REFERENCES

Berman, B. & Kay, P. (1969). *Color Terms: Their Universality and Evolution*. Berkeley: University of California Press.

Birren, F. (1962). *Color in Your World*. New York: Collier Books.

Burckhardt, W. (1967). *Alchemy*. London: Vincent Stuart.

Collectanea Chemica (1963). London: Vincent Stuart.

Edinger, E. (1985). *Anatomy of the Psyche*. La Salle, IL: Open Court.

Ellis, H. (1989, Jan./June). The colour-sense in literature. *The Contemporary Review*, LXIX.

Fabricius, J. (1976). *Alchemy*. Copenhagen: Rosenkilde & Bagger.

Figulus, B. (1963). *A Golden and Blessed Casket of Nature's Marvels*. London: Vincent Stuart.

Hillman, J. (1980). Silver and the white earth. *Spring*, 21-48.

Hillman, J. (1986). Notes on white supremacy. *Spring*, 29-58.

Hillman, J. (1989). From mirror to window: Curing Psychoanalysis of its narcissism. *Spring*, 62-75.

Holt, D. (1973). Jung and Marx. *Spring*, 52-53.

Hopkins, A. (1967). *Alchemy: Child of Greek Philosophy*. New York: AMS Press.

Jung, C.G. (1977). Interview with Eliade. In W. McGuire & R.F.C. Hull (Eds.), *C.G. Jung Speaking*. Princeton, NJ: Princeton University Press. Bollingen Series XCVII.

Kandinsky, W. (1977). *Concerning the Spiritual in Art*. New York: Dover.

Klibansky, R. et al. (1964). *Saturn and Melancholy*. London: Thomas Nelson.

Klossowski de Rola, S. (1973). *Saturn and Melancholy*. London: Thames & Hudson.

Magnus, A. (1967). *Books of Minerals*. (D. Wyckoff, trans.). Oxford: Clarendon Press.

Ruland, M. (1962). *A Lexicon of Alchemy*. London: John Watkins.

Sendivogius, M. (1953). *Hermetic Museum*, Vols. I & II. London: John Watkins.

Response

Andrew Samuels
London, England
Society of Analytical Psychology

I am responding by speaking directly to James Hillman. Jim, having given up conventional analytical practice, you find the words to clarify the analytical attitude: not wanting, not even hoping; not clean, but sullied; not focused on things going well, but on things that stink. Not against thought, but aware that what the analyst thinks affects what he or she does. You point out the greed attached to an exclusively interior perspective and expose our attempts to resolve our profession's inferiority complex – whether by a moralistic demand for a "religious attitude to the psyche" or a mechanistic demand for "here-and-now transference interpretation."

Turning now to your case material, I am interested in your experience of what, coming from my tradition, I call countertransference. You described yourself as "disconsolate," sensing your analysand as "dense" and the relationship as complicated. Could it be that you were also embodying her depressive despair both at losing you and ending the analysis, and her depressive guilt at the "killing" that was going on? If so, your countertransference at the time was already plugged in imaginally to that yellowing – long before your conscious realization.

Two persons – analyst and analysand – are in a relationship wherein it is possible for the experiences of the one to be relevant for the other. Not only because of projective identifications – which assume a gap of empty space between the two – but also because, within the analytical container, both of them acquire access to the *mundus imaginalis* (imaginal world). They are both contained in the same imagery, both nourished by the same rhizome. The analytical relationship in and of itself has archetypal properties and archetypal dynamics and, paradoxically, these impersonal properties come to life just because there are two ordinary persons present. The personal and the impersonal facilitate each other (see Samuels, 1989, pp. 143-74).

Keeping in mind the persons present in analysis: I think there is a specter stalking your work just now, Jim, threatening to subvert it. That specter is the human subject (*le sujet*). Your psychology has now to deal with a return of the human subject, claiming ontological priority: prior to body, prior to society, prior to word, prior to image. All these depend on the human subject. Most, if not all, Jungians would agree with you that "the soul has inhuman reaches" (Hillman, 1975, p. 173) and that there's more to psychology than the individual human being. But the human subject who appears in your work, in this paper, only to be dismissed from it, isn't the human subject at all, but rather a distortion of the human subject. You seem to equate the human subject with sentimental, humanistic, ahistorical trumpeting of the supremacy of the so-called individual. This equation leads, among analysts, to the elevation of the analysand in a myopic, clinical triumphalism.

This unthinking and reactionary version does not grasp the nature of *le sujet*. The human being who is waiting in the wings is not like that, not "white" at all, not a romantic cliche, not a humanistic idea, not the unified being of orthodox psychology, not Jungian Self nor Freudian ego. Did that pristine creature, which both of us have attacked, ever exist? Was it perhaps part of our transference onto analysis? No. The subject who is returning to the culture is already a yellowed subject, characterized by lack, somewhat faded as well as jaded, jerky, marginalized, alienated, split, guilty, empty, imaginary. Post-Klein, post-Lacan – yes, and post-Hillman, too – we recognize this anti-heroic, yellowed, plural human subject. If we don't count this human subject "in," then all the rest – soul, world, cosmos – won't inform our psychology either.

What has happened to the human subject in your work? Why is he or she mocked as "personalistic"? Why do you make so slight a place for the human subject? Is the so-called "psychology of the individual" really so powerful and threatening that it calls forth such iron-hard defenses? Why ignore the anthropomorphic movements of the alchemical imagination itself? Why does the psyche *person*ify? Yes, all these are metaphors, all must be seen through. But at the core of any metaphor there is something that is not part of the metaphor. It is used in the metaphor but it is not the metaphor. The psyche needs its *prima materia.* But the psyche cannot just switch off or disregard the material with which it is suffused. When the psyche empowers images of humans, it cannot stop the literal human subject from shining through. The literalism of the human subject infects the metaphor. The idea of the human subject has left an indelible mark. The human subject is an integral part of psyche's discourse, even when his or her presence is no longer discernible (see Samuels, 1989, pp. 24-25, 48-65). Metaphor is undermined because metaphor cannot divorce itself from its *prima materia.* You allow for the literalism of alchemy, but not for the literalism of the human subject.

What shall we do with this de-idealized, decayed, putrefied, violent and marvelously rebellious human subject? This is the crunch point. The yellowed, human subject is the means to mundify the psyche, not the obstacle to it. The means, not the obstacle. The yellowing in which you are interested turns out to be co-terminous with the human subject in whom you are not. The human subject does not require what you call a "counterpart" in the world; he or she makes and is made by that world in a ceaseless, generative struggle. As they discovered here in Paris in the year 1789, but had lost sight of by 1792, we can change the world that is changing us. Just as the state has not withered away, *le sujet* has not been deconstructed out of sight.

Le sujet is where we find discriminations and conjunctions and bridges: inner and outer, physical and mental, body and soul, mind and spirit, world and psyche. The human subject is Agent Yellow. Thus, for me, this is where reacting to your latest courageous and confessional work has led: the re-invention of the human subject. Maybe now, for the first time in a hundred years of our strange profession, archetypal psychology and human psychology could become the same thing.

Now I turn to discuss alchemy and something you say about it that is directly relevant to the theme of our Congress. You confess yourself a Jungian in your usage of the alchemical metaphor for analysis and you mention and dismiss other metaphors such as infancy or the gods. Now, I would not say that it is possible for analysts to feel equally at home with alchemy, infancy and the gods. But it may be possible to feel unequally at home with all these metaphors for analysis. Does locating oneself within a single metaphor mean that the only possible attitude to the others is ignorance shading into contempt? It is very seductive to argue, first, that these metaphors are radically different from each other, and, second, that only a single metaphor, in which the analyst has passionate conviction or faith, will do the trick. Do those two arguments hold up?

The problem is to find an approach, a vision, a form of words, which respects the deep and specific differences among the metaphors while, at exactly the same time, apperceiving them as linked. After all, the different metaphors do the same, almost impossible job of tracking the typical psychological movements of an analysis. (Citing "infancy" as a metaphor is an important statement and one with which many developmentally-oriented analysts would agree.)

I believe that it helps to turn to William James here, and to pluralism. Pluralism isn't the same as "multiplicity" or "the Many." Rather, it is a study of how "the One" and "the Many" interact. James says that "each part of the world is in some ways connected, ... [and] in other ways not connected with its other parts." The key word is "some" and, as James says, "pluralism stands for the legitimacy of the notion of *some*" (1909, pp. 40-41). Alchemy, infancy and the gods, are different metaphors but they are connected in some ways.

If we could agree that there are some connections among these various warring metaphors for analysis, then we can start to see what kind of dialogue might take place – or see what kind of dialogue is already going on – for, in this paper, as in much of your writing, you are in an implicit dialogue, or "interview," with something or somebody you have created. A pluralistic dialogue isn't quite so solipsistic; it is full of competitive aggression and tricksterish bargaining, full of power struggles, as each analyst or group of analysts strives to annihilate the other. But the warring analysts and the warring metaphors cannot simply shake off their contact with each other. The opponent, like the human subject, won't just go away. Annihilation is a delusion. The omnipresence and integrity of one's opponent, resisting the false ways in which we all (not just you) try to describe him or her, is what yellows the dialogue. Certainly, you can describe the opponent as narcissistic, transference-bound, religiose. But he or she will bounce back, rejecting that distortion and returning to the argument. Like it or not, the dialogue and confrontation go on, as they always have in depth psychology. And, amidst the seemingly ridiculous institutional splits, a kind of exchange is constantly being crafted.

I think that this exchange – and let us recall that Hermes is the god of trade – has reached the point where we have to look, yet again, at what is meant by "Jungian analysis." My view is that, already for quite some time, Jungian analysis has been pluralistic, employing many diverse metaphors such as alchemy, infancy, and the gods, remaining one discernible enterprise.

But our thinking may not have caught up with what we do, or can do. Yellowing, just as you depict it, is a part of Jungian analysis. So, too, are object relations, Aphrodite, Hermes and the others. If a Jungian analyst seeks to place so-called "Jungian analysis" and so-called "object relations" in eternal opposition, then our history is passing him or her by.

What I have called the "schools" of Analytical Psychology (Samuels, 1985, pp. 1-22) are themselves metaphors, for they are also within each of us, within each Jungian analyst. Your recognition of your analysand's personal transference to you shows that you, too, are in the developmental – or, more exactly, that the developmental is in you.

I hope you don't hear me as arbitrating among the metaphors, or as advocating synthesis or eclecticism. Nor is this a dry perspective; passion abides in dialogue and tolerance as much as it does in monologue and fanaticism. I am saying that the differing metaphors for analysis are simultaneously diverse *and*, in some way part of a unified phenomenon called Analytical Psychology. A whole set of monotheistic, integrative and elitist concerns talk with a whole set of polytheistic, interactive and democratic concerns; Analytical Psychology has become plurivocal.

I agree that it is gross inflation to use the insights of the consulting room as if they were recipes for curing the world. It can also be embarrassing, to say the least, this "pan-psychism." But I wonder: does being an analyst in one way rule out being an analyst in another way? Wouldn't that be too monotheistic a ruling? I think it is possible to dwell and work in psyche and city in a spirit of (in Walter Bagehot's words) "animated moderation."

REFERENCES

Hillman, J. (1975). *Revisioning Psychology*. New York: Harper & Row.

James, W. (1909), *A Pluralistic Universe*. London: Longmans, Green.

Samuels, A. (1985), *Jung and the Post-Jungians*. London & Boston: Routledge & Kegan Paul.

Samuels, A. (1989), *The Plural Psyche: Personality, Morality and the Father*. London & New York: Routledge.

The Dark Self: Death as a Transferential Factor

Peter Mudd
Chicago, Illinois
Chicago Society of Jungian Analysts

Expressions such as, "It won't kill you," "Do or die," "dead serious," "scared to death," "death and taxes," "a matter of life and death," each refer to our shrouded awareness of the omnipresence, decisiveness and ultimate nature of death. Our commonplace, everyday anxieties concerning any form of risk, failure, need or limitation – all of which inhabit the darker reaches of the psyche – ultimately can be traced to the ego's most dreaded fantasy: its own extinction. We can glimpse in these expressions, which invade our daily conversations, just how powerful an influence death exerts on our everyday lives. Yet our awareness of this inevitable fact of the human condition is fragmented and obscured by the illusions that attend the self-preservational drive, which Freud aptly called "ego instincts."

Despite the ego's horror in the face of its own mortality, death has tremendous psychological utility. It is the primary catalyst for individuation and offers us an opportunity to enter our own destinies by passing through the ego's illusions into the ineffable essence of human life.

> O Young folk (the Zen master says)
> if you fear death,
> die now!
> Having died once,
> You won't die again.
> (Hakuin, 1986, p. 6)

The wisdom of this advice challenges us to surrender to inevitable fate and embrace the dark Self in order to gain true Selfhood. It exhorts us, long before physical death, to undergo a process that will release the ego from the slavery of the self-preservational instinct into a far fuller life.

The model I propose represents a synthesis of aspects of the work of many psychoanalytic theorists and some original work of my own. My greatest debt is to C.G. Jung, whose pregnant offhand sentence in his book, *Symbols of Transformation* (CW5), began a process of consolidation of my own wandering ideas. That sentence reads, "The neurotic who cannot leave his mother has good reasons for not doing so: ultimately, it is the fear of death that holds him there" (par. 415). Jung wrote this sentence but did not pursue it with a specific or detailed analysis; he was satisfied with the essential correctness of the statement and left it at that.

Intuitively I agreed with what Jung said, but my relentless thinking function demanded more detailed analytic explanations. What is the relationship between the parental image and self-preservation? That was the central question that demanded examination and led me to Freud's concept of the superego, where the parental image is enshrined for better or for worse, and to the further question of why the superego had such a compelling and numinous character. Jung's essay, "A Psychological View of Conscience" (CW10), provided an illuminating distinction between Freud's superego, as a constructed conventional conscience derived from personally conditioned experience, and the Self as an inborn natural conscience with inherent authority. I was taken by the obvious validity of both concepts and wanted to understand the processes whereby the one is created and the other discerned. This led directly and inevitably to parent/child relations and even further into the foundations of all human relations.

Consider the child *in utero*, an image ripe for the speculation and projection of all humanity, an image so powerful and fascinating that it occupies a central position in nearly every mythological and religious system. It serves as one of the most poignant symbols of human potential and hope and as the starting point for my own theory-building efforts.

As a kind of caveat: the words, ideas and diagrams that follow are presented as a general paradigm for conceptualizing experience. I concede, indeed, I insist that infinite variations are both possible and probable because each individuation process is by definition unique. Yet I also contend that individuation unfolds within an archetypal context that inherently assigns a quality of fundamental sameness to all such processes.

The pattern I shall outline takes place, as I imagine it, within the normal range of pregnancy, birth, and developmental experience – all of which is entirely natural and non-pathological. I am offering my description of the interior detailed workings of Jung's general remark about the fear of death.

The theoretical model I propose suggests that the fear of death or the self-preservational drive is the prime mover in object relations, that field where the internal and external worlds penetrate each other and intermingle to create the psychological structures and the sustaining illusions that govern our lives. Identity – what Jungians call persona – and its fraternal twin, the shadow, as well as the constructed conscience that Freud termed the superego are all spawned by the ego's struggle with the paradoxical nature of the Self, the light and dark of life and death.

The death experience is propulsive, catalytic and continual. Most often it operates from the unconscious depths and influences our every action, but it must be allowed to break the surface of consciousness if life is to unfold in some approximation of its completeness. Mortality underlies relations with the Self and with others and facilitates, often quite unpleasantly, the psyche's compensatory/self-regulating process which reaches its pinnacle in the capacity that Jung termed the "transcendent function."

I propose to you that the transcendent function is built on the prototypical experience of living through the threat of physical death and is nothing short of the ego's achieved capacity to die repeatedly an ongoing series of conscious voluntary psychological deaths in the service of individuation. Further, I propose that it is human relationship that provides the sacred space within which we learn to die and which enables the transcendent function to evolve into an operational psychological reality. Nowhere is this more true than in the analytic relationship. An archetypal pattern promotes and contains this process, as I shall explain.

Intrauterine State

Figure 1 depicts the interpersonal and intrapsychic dimensions of intrauterine existence which form mirror images of one another; the relation of the fetus to the mother is analogous to the relation of the ego to the Self. My premise is that ego development begins *in utero* and I ask you to accept that premise as a way into the model. In the intrauterine condition, a symbiotic state of fusion and interpenetration exists between ego and Self with only the vaguest sense of any differentiation. This interpenetration is represented by the dotted line which defines the hazy boundaries of the ego. This stage of ego life is characterized by qualities of relative blissfulness, effortlessness and omnipotence because the distinction between ego and Self is nearly nonexistent. Feeding, holding and waste management are all totally automatic processes provided by the mother, and their automatic character creates the paradisiacal nature of the womb as the garden of Eden.

Figure 1

Progress of Pregnancy

Figure 2 depicts the changes in this state as pregnancy progresses. The steadily shrinking amount of space in relation to the growing fetus, the increasing development of the child's physical, sensory and mental capacities, and the normal impingements of maternal stress interact and steadily narrow the "symbiotic openings" in the boundary of the pre-natal ego. As these openings close, the process gradually creates a dim but growing sense of separation. That is, the ego progressively feels acted upon; this feeling implies otherness, separateness and potential independence as well.

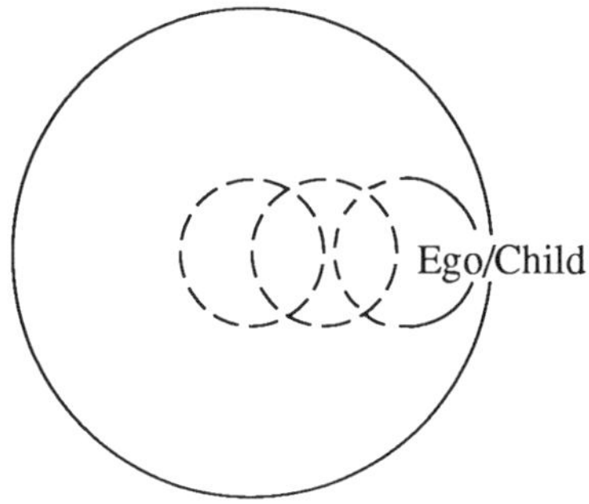

Figure 2

Birth/Death/Separation.

Figure 3 depicts, much too non-dramatically, the birth process. During that process, the slowly decreasing state of cosmic unity is shattered. Blissfulness becomes threatening panic and anxiety, effortlessness becomes an intense struggle for survival, and omnipotence is challenged by a new sense of fragile vulnerability. Mother and child, ego and Self, are propelled apart. The first basic splitting process, prepared during intrauterine life, explodes into a new intensity, and the fundamental pairs of opposites are activated. Among these are life and death, pleasure and pain, hope and despair, and perhaps even good and evil. Birth is the first death experience.

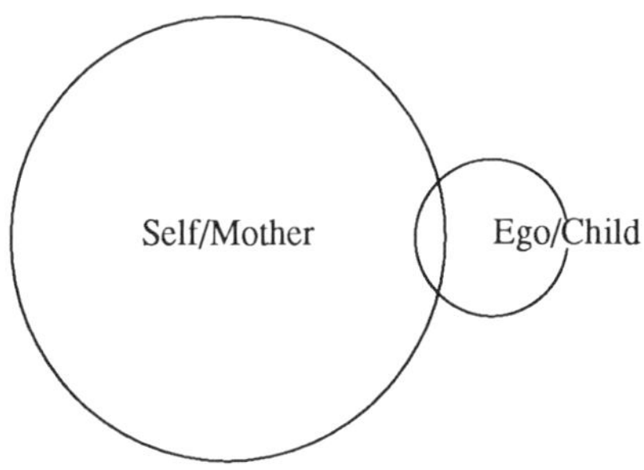

Figure 3

The encounter, at birth, with death as a physical process of extinction is the prototypical experience of ego relativization which will become psychologized and "remembered" as the central emotional feature of the transcendent function. The capacity gained at birth or at other critical points in the life cycle to face and survive the physical threat of death underlies the ability to let go, to meet destiny.

The birth process calls to mind Plato's image of the first humans as described by the character of Aristophanes in *The Symposium*. These humans were round creatures with two heads and two sets of limbs who were so content within themselves that they felt no need for the favor of the gods, and so neglected their obligation to make proper sacrifice. The gods in their narcissistic rage wanted to destroy them for their arrogance, but Zeus saw a more advantageous solution and decided instead to split them in half. According to Plato (1969) the result was:

When the work of bisection was complete it left each half with a desperate yearning for the other, and they ran together and flung their arms around each other's necks and asked for nothing better than to be rolled into one. So much so that they began to die of hunger and general inertia for neither would do anything without the other. (pp. 543-44)

These images could depict just as easily birth trauma and anaclitic and post-partum depressions, where traumatic separation is the key feature. Remembering that the intrauterine experience has been hypothesized to be a relatively blissful but gradually diminishing fusion state between ego and Self, I suggest that the unconscious and predominantly somatic recollection of that immortal state is the underlying experience which structures all subsequent images of goal-oriented striving. Thus, we are programmed by the combination of having occupied this state and then losing it, perpetually to seek re-entry into its conditions as a restoration of a sense of immortality.

Relative Simulation of Intrauterine Life

Figure 4 depicts the partial, simulated return to the intrauterine state through an experience of what can be termed the "externalized environmental womb." In a kind of yoyo-like motion, the ego and Self separate, retouch and even intersect, especially at times of satisfying need-fulfillment, but with a crucial difference: processes that were once automatic (feeding, holding, waste management) are now fulfilled according to the level of attention offered by the parents or other caregivers. For better or for worse, the nature of the parent-child relationship will determine the stability and efficiency of the developmental process. In normal development, what has been termed the facilitating or average expectable environment, the good-enough parent, or the process of optimal frustration now begins to simulate intrauterine conditions to an adequate degree while simultaneously "teasing" the child/ego into greater consolidation of its unit status by "failing" to duplicate exactly those same conditions. Each so-called "failure" interrupts the ego's persistent omnipotent fantasy of fusion with the Self and the parents as part of that Self. This developmentally necessary failure exposes the child/ego to the same set of responses – fear, vulnerability and helplessness – which occasioned birth, but in significantly smaller and less intense doses.

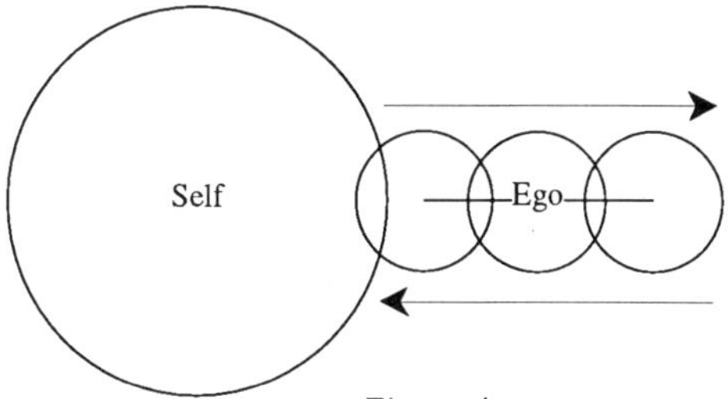

Figure 4

Perhaps a less abstract image will help to communicate my point. In the movie "Jaws" the initial appearance of the shark is especially disturbing. A playful, attractive young woman, cavorting with her lover, swims out into the ocean at night only to be brutally mauled and killed by the demonic great white shark. This experience is analogous to the birth experience, with a critical difference that in birth the infant survives. In the film, when the shark is nearby but unseen, an ominous musical theme is played on a cello. This music never fails to evoke the memory of that first horrible attack and whenever we hear it we are immediately apprehensive. The music is directly analogous to the smaller doses of affect associated with birth or reminders of death's presence created by the environmental failures that I am describing.

The ego re-experiences the presence of death through a process I call "somatic intuition," a bodily awareness of the presence and possibility of death that promotes an ever-increasing awareness of separation between ego and Self and between child and parent. The euphemism "to know it in your bones" captures this concept well. This oscillating process of the arousal of death-fears through delays in need fulfillment followed by "good-enough" gratification is paralleled by a steadily developing ego strength. These parallel processes eventually lead from primary reliance on somatic intuitive perception and the activation of primitive affective flooding responses to a predominance of cognitive mental perception and the development of psychological structures which can begin to cope with the powerful affects. Consciousness can be said to be "clearing up."

The Birth of Clarified Consciousness

Figure 5 depicts the state eventually achieved by this process, which reaches a critical point four to eight months into post-natal development. The steady dosing of death-fears and their subsequent mitigation, accompanied by significant increases in ego functioning, has enforced a creeping sense of separation between child and parent, ego and Self. Imagine a scale that represents the ego's relationship to the Self. *In utero* the scale is tipped in favor of merger with the Self and a sense of omnipotence. Birth puts a significant weight on the other side, followed by very small but consistently mounting weights added through the so-called "failures" to duplicate intrauterine conditions exactly. It takes four to eight months before the scale tips toward the side of ego / Self separation.

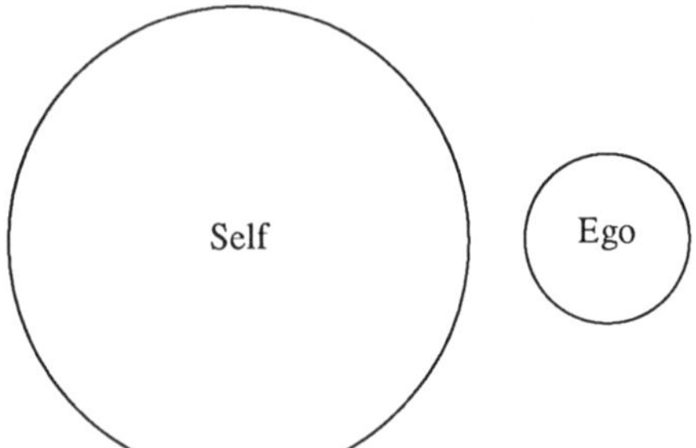

Figure 5

As the scale tips, a profound realization thrusts itself upon the ego, the realization that it is in fact not identical with the Self and that the parent is not an aspect of that Self but an entirely separate being on whom the ego is utterly dependent. This is a psychological event of the greatest imaginable magnitude; the prior eroding fantasy of omnipotence is shattered. The death-fears erupt into a new level of clarified consciousness and the ego is split away from its identity with the Self as in birth, but with a qualitatively different awareness. Ego consciousness has attained a consolidated, clarified mental capacity that results in the firm establishment of I/Other relations. The intense anxiety induced by the ego-Self division sets off a fundamental archetypal process that encompasses a new level of identity formation, complex building, persona/shadow differentiation, and superego construction.

Sacrificial Projection of the Self

Figure 6 suggests the loss of identity with the Self. This loss is experienced when the individual discovers the I/Other nature of relationship. The discovery creates something of a panic and leads the ego to seek the security of that omnipotent lost Self in order to re-establish the balance of the pre-split period. Since the ego has realized that the now separate other is far more powerful, the omnipotent aspect of the Self is assigned to that other by projection. Thus, the ego's lost sense of numinous/omnipotent identity with the Self is now "out there."

The parents are essentially deified by virtue of this sacrificial projection of the Self. The projection oscillates but is "out there" more often than it is "in here." The deification of the parents and the ego's new, frightening non-numinous dependent state lead to the child's need to accommodate to the

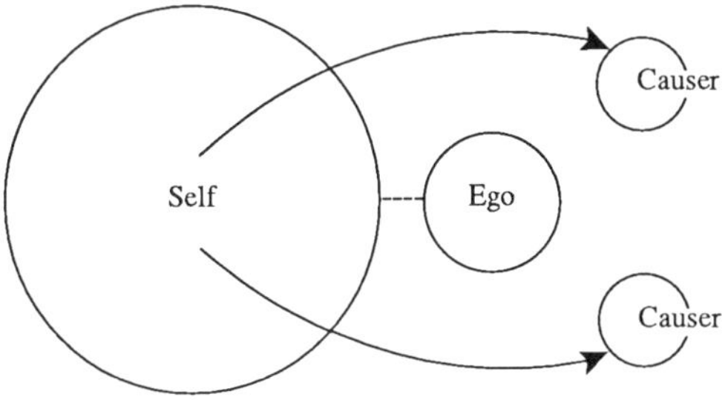

Figure 6

will of these new gods in the interest of survival.

These accommodations are internalized or introjected and, through repetitive effectiveness, lead to the construction of the superego and other complexes. The numinosity of the Self which is projected into the parents, who are then introjected, "contaminates" their imagos with a psychological "radioactivity" that lasts most lifetimes and imparts an enormous sense of authority to those imagos. These internalized parental deities, which Freud called the superego, and what I call "the causers," then preside over the development of the persona and shadow and determine in great measure the contents and feeling tones of the complexes. These processes are essentially simultaneous and create what I call "the caused personality." Thus, parental direction becomes "divine law" and carries with it the threat of death as a consequence for disobedience.

The child, affected by the loss of identity with the omnipotent Self and its relocation in the parents, becomes a supplicant offering sacrifice to the supreme beings who govern the child's fate. The laws of the gods are carved into the psyche of the child, whose obedient conformity becomes manifest in the persona while disavowed impulses are relegated to the shadow. This act of propitiation "buys" the benevolence of the gods and with it the illusion of a share of their immortal status.

The reality of death, by virtue of this self-sacrifice, is pushed deep into the shadow and is overlaid with self-preservational structures that promise protection from death. This consignment of death to unconscious status is entirely appropriate because it enables the ego to thrive through achieving a state of confidence in a protective god. A typical feature of this process of Self-projection that I have encountered many times in my practice is that of "orbiting." The numinosity/ omnipotence/immortality of the Self lifts off from the gravitational field of the ego-complex and attaches to the parent around whom the ego then orbits. The stability of this orbit and the sense of security it provides are determined by the psychological proximity and empathic concern of the caregivers. I term this state "de-gravitated affiliation" because it describes the interim nature of the ego/Self relationship at this stage of development. It is neither here nor there, or is both here and there. This "space" between ego and Self is the space that is inhabited involuntarily and fearfully in borderline states and is precisely that which is entered voluntarily and traversed when the transcendent function is active. If we hold this image and examine the etymology of the word "transcendent" – "to climb across" – we can begin to see the vital importance of this aspect of individuation. Herein lies the potential for consolidation of imaginative capacities or the agony of being unable to move through transitional spaces into newly evolving stable spaces.

Stable Dosing Response

Figure 7 depicts the response to the process of sacrificial projection which facilitates socialization, ego consolidation, and the establishment of adequate defenses. It also provides the basis for solid interpersonal relations, but it contains a serious danger. The sacrificial projection of the Self can intoxicate a parent when that parent identifies with the numinous/omnipotent aspect of the projection, usually because of inadequate resolution of this phase of the parent's development. The result can be a destructive limitation of the child's developing personality when the parent does not return the Self adequately through the process of mirroring, supporting and containing the developing child. This process, which I have termed the "stable dosing response" means a consistent, continual re-installation of the projected Self into the child.

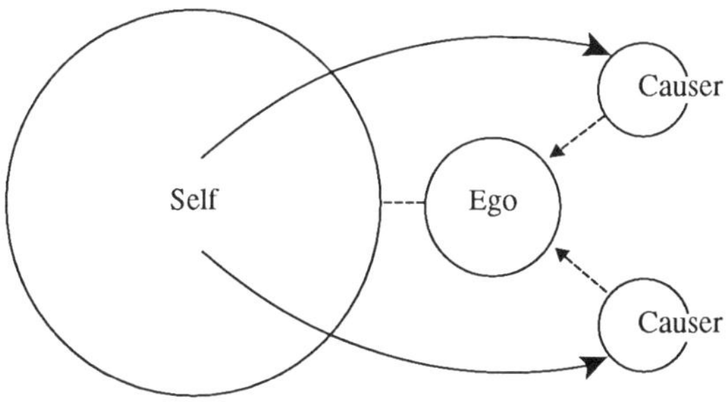

Figure 7

The key here is to gauge the dose properly. The parent who fails to re-install the Self becomes a vampire-like glutton who feeds on the idealization process and cannot tolerate its appropriate gradual reduction. The vampire parent or analyst undermines the development of a coherent internal organizing center of the personality by refusing to relinquish the claim to be the source of life and death. A crippling addictive dependency on a projected externalized center is thus set in motion. This denies the ego access to the Self and usurps the Self's innate right and ability to activate and direct the unique individuation of this particular child or analysand. The parent who feasts on the Self projection engenders conflict and inner division because the true Self of the child is obscured by the controls of the inflated parental image. The Self's regulatory function of compensation will attack the false gods internally and constellate rebellion through an energized shadow. The ego is led to a bewildering multitude of conflicting impulses and responses which undermine genuine stability and hamper the efficiency of adaptation.

This process is likely to produce a rigidified clinging to the persona, whose enactment is demanded by the self-preservational instinct, and to an inappropriate reinforcement of the defenses protecting it. The defenses are aroused by the shadow contents and impulses that are activated by the Self's compensating function and associated with death. They revive the powerful, terrifying affects that reside in the shadow. A vicious circle is set in motion that stunts the movement of individuation and produces a one-dimensional personality bound by a rigid ideology. In these cases, as Jung repeatedly warned us, the source of this tragic process is the unconscious, unlived lives of the parents which are projected into their children for fulfillment.

This vicious circle is what I like to call "individuation by proxy" or "individuation by annexation." The child is essentially appropriated as a psychological surrogate who lives out some aspect of the parental Self. These unlived lives almost always are elements of the parental Self which were consigned to the shadow by the same dynamics that are now visited upon their children's psyches. As the Bible says, "The fathers have eaten sour grapes, and the children's teeth are set on edge" (Ezekiel 18:12). Parents rely less on this dictator style of child-rearing by annexation when they assume an attitude that I characterize as "custodial." This means the development of a less perfect child in favor of a more complete child. It eventually means a more imaginative, self-reliant person instead of a precisely trained, compliant individual whose soulfulness is buried under the defensive structures of self-preservation.

The relationship with the vampire or false god results from the mishandling of the stage of orbiting. Instead of being re-integrated by stable dosing, the Self is withheld by the causer for narcissistic reasons and the ego feels drained, empty and lifeless. Often the image of bleeding or blood transfusion appears in the dreams and fantasies of persons who have suffered this fate.

The experience appears in the analytic transference as symbiotic dependency, idealization, deification, or – negatively – as profound hatred, fear or resistance, often mediated through issues concerning the fee and availability of the analyst. Intense feelings of panic, despair and longing for merger often occasion the end of a session and are particularly pronounced at times of extended separation such as vacations. The analysand is experiencing the fear of the lethal aspect of the Self: death, constellated by the absence of the Self object. Fantasies and dreams of uncontrolled floating, being in orbit in outer space with no means of re-entry to earth's gravity, and the emergence of time disorders often herald the dreaded arrival of the dark Self. These imaginings attempt to portray to the ego its own situation but, because the ego does not possess a developed symbolic capacity, it is merely terrorized by the images.

There is a correlation between the quality of the causers and the nature of the caused personality. This relationship is nowhere more crucial than in the development of the transcendent function, which underlies the capacity to imagine and yield to new forms and so fully enter the destiny of the Self. The transcendent function is the capacity to die, because it requires the suspension of the exclusivity of structures that come into existence carrying the promise of self-preservation. If the nature of the causers is overly authoritarian and one-dimensional, the caused personality will resist suspension of this primacy and the transcendent function will remain latent. Without the transcendent function as an operational psychological reality, the fear of death or the dark Self will persist as the ruling principle mediated through the superego or causers. The true Self is met with opposition because it does not conform to the causers' rules and the personality is impoverished.

The nature and tasks of the analytic relationship begin to be obvious, I believe. The Self projection, recapitulated as the central feature of the transference, sets up the analyst in the role of the causer and views the analytic relationship as a matter of life and death. The analyst's fundamental task then is to keep the analysand "alive" while simultaneously helping him or her learn how to die. This means that a steady reduction of the authority of the causers, leading to the revival of death fears which the analysand then can be helped to cope with more productively. Herein lies the possibility of the emergence of the transcendent function and with it the hope of personal authenticity. This process is nearly always mediated through the transference/countertransference relationship whose most essential element is the living example of the analyst. In simple terms, the analyst must know how to die, demonstrate that capacity to the analysand, and provide a new image for internalization.

The core aspect of the process is the acceptance of the sacrificial projection of the Self and its being worked through via a stable dosing response, but there are often preliminary steps preceding the entry into the heart of the matter. Though we could say with some confidence that the mere request for analysis is an implicit Self-projection because the analyst is already imagined to be a "causer," I view the projection as a trial attempt at locating a suitable object. For the projection to take root as a viable transference the analyst must demonstrate, not by doing but by being, the ability to carry the projection and so constellate hope in the analysand. If hope is constellated the essential condition for the work is present and a conflict in the analysand will be set in motion between the old causers and the new potential Self object of the analyst with the analysand's soul as the battleground. The analyst must survive this trial by combat and earn the problematic prize of the Self-projection. The establishment of this transference acts like a psychological heart-lung machine and enables the patient to "hook up" to a life sustaining source while psychic organs are healed, strengthened, and stabilized.

This combat between the old causers and the analyst is most often conducted through the factor of resistance, which is a manifestation of the self-preservational drive. It is served through the compulsive compliance of the ego to the caused personality. To overthrow the causers is to invite death. An essential aspect of this battle with the causers is what Jung referred to as the reductive personal analysis. Almost without exception, the material presented by the analysand derives from the structural effects of the relationship to the causers. These are the elements most likely to appear in the transference at this time in analysis. Differentiation of the analyst from the causers is the primary verbal/intellectual task of the therapeutic work and it is very important for providing a conceptual space within which the analysand can begin to imagine different forms of being, but it is of secondary importance overall.

The most essential task is simply "being" as the transactions of analysis proceed. I characterize this being as the custodial attitude of countertransference that honors the primacy of the Self and actively witnesses how that Self is unfolding in the absolute present of the encounter. The combination of active differentiation and simple being is the key to the defeat of the causers and the relocation of the Self projection. Frequently a profound period of disorientation ensues, but carries with it the hope of establishing a flexible balance and ultimately the transcendent function.

The transference now takes on archetypal proportions; the analyst, fused with the Self, becomes the new causer. The nature of this causer's being and doing can now assist in the rebirth and restructuring of the caused personality but should act only as a midwife might when she leaves as much as possible to nature. This process of transference/countertransference becomes the stable dosing response and should be governed by the analyst's awareness of his or her own mortality. This means a tacit acceptance of the divine status of the causer role, accompanied by a continual conscious awareness that it is a necessary temporary therapeutic illusion. Further, it is to be diminished in direct proportion to the analysand's increasing development of a stable ego/Self axis.

In essence, then, the countertransference is a living embodiment of the conscious capacity to die which, in my opinion, is synonymous with the central dynamic feature of the transcendent function. As Jung stated, "In actual practice, therefore, the suitably trained analyst mediates the transcendent function for the patient, i.e., helps him to bring conscious and unconscious together and so arrive at a new attitude. In this function of the analyst lies one of the meanings of the *transference*" (CW8, par. 146). This process of holding – through the acceptance of the Self projection, stable dosing response and therapeutic dying – leads from transference pathology to the eventual emergence of kinship libido, which can be re-imagined as the recognition of the common fate of mortality and the empathy that results from that shared recognition. In death we can recognize our utter equality.

REFERENCES

Hakuin (1986). *Japanese Death Poems*. Y. Hoffman (Ed.). Rutland, VT and Tokyo: Charles E. Tuttle.

Plato (1969). The Symposium. In E. Hamilton & H. Cairns (Eds.), *Collected Dialogues*. Princeton, NJ: Princeton University Press.

Response

David Tresan
San Francisco, California, USA
Society of Jungian Analysts
of Northern California Society

I first came to this paper with my feelings and later with my thinking. Responding to the theme of the paper, that death dominates life, my feelings were outraged and critical. Later, my thinking discovered the plot: that death creates psychic structure. This I found interesting, stimulating, and even rather elegantly conceived.

My feelings were offended threefold. First, Mudd has written a highly theoretical paper about the most personal and intimate subject there is – my death and the ramifications of it while I am alive. This is a highly personal document for him also, but he gives me – us – no personal material against which to weigh our attempts to personalize his pronouncements about death. And so, like Inanna, it feels as if I (we) have had to descend to the underworld alone to find the meaning and truth of things.

When I was about eight years old, I used to lie awake in bed and play a game. I would imagine that one member of my family had to die and I had to decide, and wondered whom I would choose. Painfully, I would put myself in each person's shoes, once as the doomed one and once as mourner. It was an excruciating exercise, and I always ended by choosing myself. These are the kinds of thoughts that this paper has brought up, and like Inanna coming up from the underworld I have felt that I virtually dripped with death at times.

Second, I think that Mudd overvalues death. He wants it so

everpresent in our lives in a "natural and non-pathological" way that it "influences our every action." Others think this also. Otto Rank – for one – thought, as does Mudd, that the fear of death at birth is the source of all anxiety. For Rank in 1924 as for Mudd in 1989, life is a reaction to and abreaction of death. However, what Mudd says about death, that it is "propulsive, catalytic, and continual" can be said equally about life. In fact, it has been Jung's great gift to point us to the life-generating aspects of the numen, to suggest that no matter how severe the personal life, the spirit of the universe can heal us and drive us to some meaningful end. I think that even birth is not necessarily a primarily negative experience nor that moderated losses are adumbrations of death, and I think that death is not the natural sole determinant of life's course. Although it certainly figures in our destinies, there is a life force that animates us and drives us to consciousness as well. It is a matter of two opposites and of a glass both half full and half empty.

Third, I think that Mudd misrepresents death in affective tone. Even the term "Dark Self" in the title of his paper suggests something evil. Life is not naturally played in a minor key and dominated by fear. When it is, something has gone wrong in early life and/or there is a clear threat of death in the present. I feel that time and maturation bring a philosophy and substance against which death does not necessarily loom as inconceivable, intolerable, hopelessly fragmenting or as "the ego's most dreaded fantasy," and that optimistic and positive attitudes also have their counterpart in the natural instinctual integrity and elan of infancy and childhood. Life can be exciting in itself, and its own raison d'être.

In fairness, Mudd's paper is not just about death as the catalyst for life but also about death and the fear of it as an essential catalyst for the formation of psychic structures. He postulates a succession of losses of Self from birth on, losses that are intolerable and that he labels deaths and derivatives of death. These losses imply intolerable vacant spaces that induce the formation of a structure to fill that space or bridge it. This structure is the transcendent function. I have some difficulty with this formulation since it is not clear what the transcendent function is bridging for the psychically unformed infant. Even if labeled as "somatic intuition," what Mudd is postulating is a very early intact ego function.

This view stands in contrast to Michael Fordham's developmental schema, which postulates that no ego entity exists at such an early age. What Mudd says is a personal experience of loss or death is for Fordham the archetypal "deintegrations" of the original Self. For Fordham, only when deintegrates of the original Self connect to external factors do ego islands begin to form. These islands in time coalesce to create the ego. Only then is there truly a space between ego and Self to bridge and an ego to register the bridging.

This all comes together in practice; Peter's idea that for the analyst "the most essential task is simply 'being'" is absolutely correct. It is the same as the "stillness" of D.W. Winnicott's holding environment. It is the relative egolessness of the analyst qua parent. Some analysands find that this quiet being feels like deep and basic love. It may happen at the onset of analysis or require a great deal of work. It lasts an indefinite period of time, it recurs, and it persists as background. However, de- and re-integration cycles eventually commence in earnest; specific work gets done in relation to personal and relevant archetypal issues. This latter work is the shank of the analysis. Eventually, there comes a large coalescence of ego parts as in childhood, but this time with a thoroughness and deliberateness and a consciousness never before experienced. Here, for the first time – at the end of analysis, not at the beginning of it or at the beginning of life – comes a death experience that is natural and non-pathological and inherent in individuation. Now, for the first time, the ego can contemplate with fullness of affect what it will be like to lose one's hard gained life, not through the neglect of another, but because of one's very humanity.

I had such an experience as I sat in a movie theater with my children near the end of my analysis. I found I loved my life in a way I never had before, and then I became angry because it would all end. I had never quite minded before, not with passion at least.

But I accepted it without great difficulty in the movie, both the passion and the ending. It was all right. Who was my analyst to me in this experience? I flared at him briefly as if he had tricked me, but largely he was Tiresias looking on, the sphinx – and a friend who, like me, would die. I discovered later that Otto Rank knew all about this. At one time he had the idea of setting a date for termination early in each analysis in order to accelerate the experience.

As Mudd asks, can a person help this process along by actively espousing imaginal death? Maybe, but to be authentic the death experiences need to come as a timely part of the overall process of development. Like any technique it may or may not work or it may work sometimes. As for Mudd's overall theory, if we grant him the possibility that deintegration is a kind of death and has dysphoric affects which the ego will remember when it comes into existence, then his theory works and actually has an elegant coherence.

Speculation on the minute details of preverbal development is now perhaps the most interesting and exciting area of depth psychological inquiry. Although it is difficult, if not impossible, to use direct observation to prove what is subjectively true for the infant, it is of the greatest importance that theories be formulated so that we can attempt to understand baffling psychic states that come up in analysis. Moreover, each theory has its own treatment implications. Mudd's schema paints the picture of the analyst titrating the patient's frustrations, mirroring carefully, ever in danger of invoking the Dark Self in more than optimal measure but needing to allow it enough to promote psychological growth. On the other hand, Fordham's schema suggests a less tense dialogue in which both analysand and analyst participate more democratically and equally in the shaping of deintegrates. Analysands are all different; it is good to have more than one way of seeing.

Otto Rank changed his mind, or at least his emphasis. He decided that the life force, especially embodied in human creativity, propelled individuation instead of death's doing so. Like Jung he postulated a psychology of emergence and growth in contrast to the then prevalent Freudian model of consciousness rising as a by-product of conflict. For this, like Jung but 12 years later, Rank was ejected from Freudian circles. Both Jung and Rank, after writing books on how consciousness emerges, emerged themselves in significant ways. In the same vein, Mudd has written a paper about emergence of consciousness in which the dark is still very present. The tradition of Self-seeking through scholarship is well served by his paper. May it lead him to greater and greater light.

For helping me to find my bearings in much of this, I wish to acknowledge the work of and to thank Michael Fordham, Norah Moore, Mary Williams, Rosemary Gordon, Marie-Louise von Franz, and Verena Kast.

To Love and To Know: The Erotic Transference as Seen by Symbolic Psychology

Carlos Amadeu B. Byington
Sao Paulo, Brazil
Sociedade Brasileira de Psicologia Analitica

The development of consciousness is the center of psychology and its greatest mystery. The transference phenomenon expresses this mystery through a variety of interpersonal experiences. In some cases – by no means rare – transference is expressed through erotic love. Is this love merely infantile and pathological or can it be also mature and creative? I believe that the erotic transference constellates a fierce confrontation of archetypal defensive and creative forces in search of psychic totality within the Self. To demonstrate this view I shall consider some of Freud's and Jung's theoretical formulations of transference, incest and psychological development, and the limitations of these formulations. This paper expresses my personal ideas but also grew from the work of the Brazilian Society of Analytical Psychology and the Uruguayan Study Group of Analytical Psychology.

I take the view that the erotic transference can be understood and worked through only within an archetypal theory of development: individual and collective, pathological and normal. In order for the sacrifice of erotic love to take place, as part of the sacrifices inherent in the therapeutic relationship, the analysand needs extensive experience of psychic development and of the nature of psychic totality. This experience must include the confrontation of the pathological shadow and its neurotic and/or psychotic defensive structures, in the individual and in the cultural Self.

By sacrifice I mean the subordination of emotions to the knowledge of the Self, not the suppression or pasteurizing of those emotions. In the process of sacrifice, two great discoveries are fundamental. The first is the relationship of love and knowledge. Indeed, the erotic transference becomes fully conscious only when the erotic drive points toward knowledge of the Self. The second discovery is the role of the archetype of death in psychic development; to love and understand life we must grapple with death and its symbolic transforming power.

Modern psychology began with the case of "Anna O" (Bertha Pappenheim), a patient of Freud's colleague Joseph Breuer. This case opened the way to the study of the meaningful interrelation of the conscious/unconscious polarity in normal development and the symbolic understanding of symptoms. The discovery of the "talking cure," however, was accompanied by an erotic transference. Misunderstood and intensely rejected by Breuer, this transference produced a delusional childbirth, which catastrophically precipitated the end of the therapeutic relationship.

Jung's analysand Sabina Spielrein made a study of the creative interrelation of the life and death polarity in psychological development. This study was to play an important role in Freud's and Jung's theories. It revealed, also, a poorly understood erotic transference which included Spielrein's desire to have a child by her analyst. According to Carotenuto (1984), her experience led to the discovery of countertransference.

The personal myths of great persons and their creative work may bring about a significant expansion of consciousness in a culture. This occurrence can be understood symbolically within a historical context only when we relate it to the great myths of that culture. The psychological study of love and of creative knowledge in psychotherapy initiated by the pioneers of modern psychology would transcend individual problems in any culture. It does so especially in Western culture because its central – Judeo-Christian – myth is intimately related to both love and creative knowledge. Just as Delphi's oracular "know thyself" guided Greek culture, Christianity's search for totality was inspired by love. Consequently, awareness of the relationship of the transference phenomenon to the Christian myth is essential for archetypal understanding of the phenomenon, especially its erotic form, and for understanding the difficulties that the pioneers encountered when they first discovered the transference.

In the Old Testament, the temptation to eat from the tree of the knowledge of good and evil in the Garden of Eden is inseparable from Adam's and Eve's erotic relationship, so much so that the verb "to know" often indicates sexual intercourse, throughout the Bible. The fall from Eden is an image of an expansion of consciousness of the life and death polarity:

> Then the Lord God said, "Behold, the man has become like one of us, knowing good and evil; and now, lest he put forth his hand and take also of the tree of life, and eat, and live forever" – therefore the Lord God sent him forth from the garden of Eden to till the ground from which he was taken. He drove out the man; and at the east of the garden of Eden he placed the cherubim, and a flaming sword which turned every way, to guard the way of the tree of life. (Genesis 3:22-24)

The Judeo-Christian myth, continuing into the New Testament, comes from the east: from a rising sun, from a new archetypal pattern of consciousness through the eating from the tree of life. Indeed, the greatest "discoveries" of the myth of the incarnated divine Messiah were the receiving of grace and of resurrection into eternal life.

> Martha said to him, "I know that he will rise again in the resurrection at the last day." Jesus said to her, "I am the resurrection and the life; he who believes in me, though he die, yet shall he live, and whoever lives and believes in me shall never die." (John 11:24-26)

The wisdom that overcomes death is born through love that can confront, understand and integrate otherness, including sin and madness. Seen psychologically, the attitude of love toward the Other in the myth seeks the integration of the shadow through the acceptance of rejected, humble, oppressed and suffering parts of the individual and the cultural Self.

The expansion of consciousness occurs through two discoveries. The first is that the ego can confront intensely opposing forces, including the shadow – sin – without disintegration. The second is that, through dedication, shadow contents can become conscious again, in a symbolic process, the ritual of confession. The scientific law that "nothing is lost, everything is transformed" was a mythical reality almost two millennia before its formulation in scientific psychology.

Once more, a great discovery was associated with the man-woman relationship and the erotic dimension. Mary Magdalene, the follower of Jesus who carried the sin of sex and madness, was the one chosen to witness the resurrection. The meaning of the confrontation of conscious development with the archetype of death is situated here within the context of eternal life. Thus, the notion of psychic permanence is essential to the understanding of transformation.

> Now when he rose early on the first day of the week, he appeared first to Mary Magdalene, from whom he had cast out seven demons. She went and told those who had been with him, as they mourned and wept. But when they heard that he was alive and had been seen by her, they would not believe it. (Mark 16: 9-11)

This messianic redeeming love and respect for the Other was the Ariadne thread that led Western culture through the death cult and mourning of the Middle Ages into that age aptly called the Renaissance, a true cultural resurrection that brought love, truth and knowledge to create the natural sciences. The very intensity of the Renaissance experience – an archetypal one – led to its defensive maneuvering. A heroic messianic love message was expressed well in Augustine's ethical motto "love and do as you wish." It led collective consciousness toward the humanism of science and the modern social-democratic state. Parallel to the love message the patriarchal sword subdued and silenced the love message of the sacrificial cross, defensively substituting for it dissociation, power, economic and political injustice and hate.

We see an increasingly dissociated defensive expression of

patriarchal dynamism in the history of Christianity. The patriarchal pattern was not lived then, as it is normally is, in the name of conquest and power. Rather, that pattern was disguised in the name of that new pattern of love and salvation even while it practiced cultural plundering, genocide and slavery in the New World.

The Jesus-Mary Magdalene coniunctio pattern of relationship is the fundamental mythical amplification of the erotic transference in Western psychotherapy. For example, a woman analysand dominated by the erotic aspect of transference dreamt about a young carpenter who told her: "I want you to be the wood of my cross." The prospective meaning of the erotic transference is very difficult to understand both by analysands and analysts in our culture because our history has dissociated love from knowledge and life from death in the very myth that unites them.

The Inquisition was the longest and most viciously repressive movement history has ever known. It formed the immense pathological shadow of the devil or anti-Christ which included symbols of love – mainly erotic love – anger, creativity and many psychological structures such as envy, jealousy, joy and greed. These symbols and structures have been dissociated from the fixated, non-integrated Judeo-Christian myth. For a Christian, it is an immense moral effort to realize that the anti-Christ devil corresponds to an institutional shadow formed in response to the defensive reduction of the Christ symbol in religion and culture.

Jung's discovery of the anima/animus archetype opened the way for a still greater challenge to Christianity. He failed to undertake this challenge because he confused the anima with the mother archetype and the animus with the father archetype. The new challenge to modern Christianity is an outgrowth of the fact that the cult of Mary in the Middle Ages accompanied the increase of the devil symbolism and occurred at the expense of the Messiah's creative urge. Indeed, the incestuous reduction of the feminine to the mother image occurred together with the reduction of Christ to the child image. These reductions resulted in the repression of Mary Magdalene as the anima image and consequently in the castration of the coniunctio archetype.

Weakened through dissociation and incest, the hero came to be worshipped, predominantly, dead on the cross or in his mother's lap, thus either in after-life or as a child. Consequently, his cultural capacity for transformation through adult love was reduced greatly. It is not my intention to undervalue the symbols of the virgin mother, the miraculous child, the crucifixion and the resurrection; all of them are symbols of central importance in the myth. I intend to emphasize, however, their use as a defense to diminish the hero's adult significance and culture-transforming capacity.

The symbol of the redeemed-prostitute/mad-heroine as companion of the Savior in the anima/animus archetypal coniunctio is most significant for expressing this new pattern of consciousness. This symbol is significant because the anima and animus are delimited by patriarchal dynamism so that their structuring function becomes distorted individually and culturally, frequently appearing in the pathological shadow through symbols of corruption, madness and prostitution.

The transformation of the European cultural Self and its collective consciousness through the scientific and political revolution opened the way for the scientific discovery of the psyche through the pathological shadow, whose elaboration will be the work of many centuries to come. Significantly, the European psyche was discovered in the neurologist's consulting room, in the dimension of the individual Self, through Anna O's psychotic hysteria. The same psyche was discovered in the dimension of the pathological shadow of the cultural Self, in Philippe Pinel's freeing of the psychotics from the chains they shared with criminals in the Paris dungeons. This liberation of psychotics occurred during the transition of power from religion to science and from monarchy to democracy. We mark this transition in the bicentenary that we celebrate with our French colleagues in our present Congress. The liberation coincides meaningfully with the blood bath of the Reign of Terror, which expressed the psychotic cultural pathological shadow activated by the revolutionary constellation of the anima/animus archetypes in the French Revolution.

Such a psychotic volcanic explosion was controlled defensively by the return of patriarchal autocracy in the person of a self-crowned emperor, an impoverished defensive restoration of the monarchic persona. The use of the guillotine, symbolically seen within the cultural Self, was a synchronistic expression of this psychotic dissociation which overpowered collective consciousness during the birth of socialism. The cry for liberty, equality and fraternity – suffocated in Christianity by the Inquisition – was continued in the social-political quest of socialism but, again, was dissociated in the materialism of modern capitalism and communism.

We can realize today what fell on Breuer in an erotic transference: a very difficult clinical case with an individual psychotic shadow but also a millenary archetypal cultural problem which, in the late 19th century, turned its Medusa's eyes toward his brilliant career. We can understand Breuer's rejection of Anna O better when we remember that the date it happened – June 1882 – marked the 100th anniversary of the last decapitation of a hysterical woman in Glarus, Switzerland.

Amid this historical ambivalence of knowledge toward love, the erotic transference is an initiation into the transforming power of love. This initiation needs a theoretical stance to examine the pathology and the creative urge side by side, interrelating childhood and adult life within the four dimensions of the Self – individual, family, cultural and cosmic.

In spite of the enormous amount of research on the transference done during the century that followed Anna O.'s experience, any attempt to study the erotic transference becomes mutilating if it does not take into account the creative and pathological interaction of the pre-Oedipal and Oedipal dimensions – which correspond to matriarchal and patriarchal symbolism – with the anima/animus and coniunctio archetypes within the four dimensions of the Self.

In order to take these dimensions into account I invite you to imagine that the Self – the interaction of conscious and unconscious forces – is coordinated by an archetype that I call "central." An archetypal quaternio is formed by the great mother, great father, anima/animus and wisdom archetypes with the central archetype in the middle (Figure 1).

Collective and individual consciousness, the polarity ego/Other, the shadow and the persona are structures that operate permanently through this basic structure that I designate the "regent archetypal quaternio." Throughout life, psychological development is oriented by the central archetype, which coordinates symbolic elaboration and consciousness formation simultaneously in the individual and collective Self through the inter-

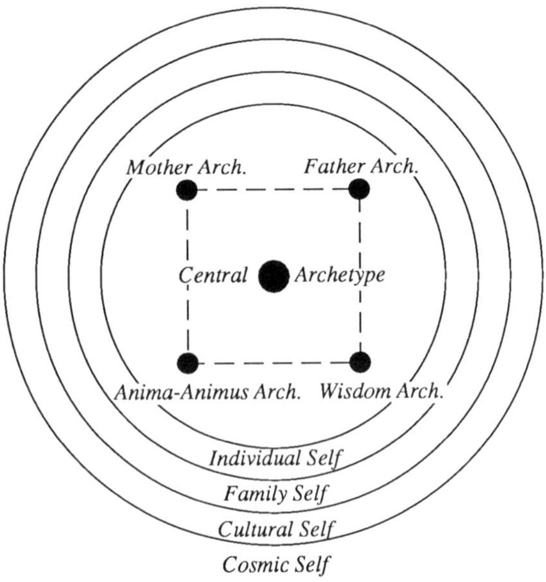

Figure 1: The Four Dimensions of the Self
The Regent Quarternio Archetype

action of this basic quaternio. Thus, every psychological event is both a symbol of the Self and a structuring symbol of consciousness: personal and archetypal, conscious and unconscious, subjective and objective. The event must be treated prospectively as well as reductively.

The concept of participation of the regent archetypal quaternio from the beginning of life in the structuring of consciousness and identity is the central contribution of this paper to developmental psychology and the theory of incest. The concept reformulates the developmental theories of Freud, Melanie Klein, Erich Neumann and Michael Fordham that were based exclusively on the relationship between baby and parents.

Mine is neither a psychology of the unconscious, nor depth psychology, nor Archetypal Psychology, but a psychology of the Self whose core is the symbol expressed in all psychic events. Therefore, its appropriate denomination is Symbolic Psychology. Because of its overall symbolic nature, which encompasses the objective dimension, Symbolic Psychology is conceptually different from Analytical Psychology.

Nevertheless, Symbolic Psychology's conceptual frame allows us to see that Jung's life example significantly surpassed his theoretical formulations. We can think, for instance, of his archetypal experiences during childhood and adolescence. From the perspective of the symbolic Self, the primary relationship of infant and mother is not seen as exclusively coordinated by the dominance of matriarchal dynamism. The Self of the primary relationship, although dominated by the great mother archetype, already operates within the regent archetypal quaternio for two reasons. First, because the mother's Self is intensely linked to the father's Self and, therefore, is permanently influenced by the anima/animus coniunctio. Second, because the Self of the primary relationship operates within the dimensions of the family and of the cultural and the cosmic Self coordinated by the regent archetypal quaternio.

Consciousness and the ego always operate within the Self. The limitation that I see both in Fordham's concept of deintegration and in Neumann's concept of the ego/Self axis is that they may create the illusion that the ego functions independently and even outside the Self.

The ongoing activity of the regent archetypal quaternio is of extraordinary importance and explains the profound influence that the anima and animus archetypes have on ego formation. These archetypes frequently are projected by the parents or society before the child is even conceived. This influence is also the archetypal basis for the thesis Dinnerstein (1976) presented: that unless the child experiences mutuality between the parents and their nurturing roles from the beginning, the child's relationship to the other sex may be deformed permanently.

The activity of the regent archetypal quaternio from the beginning of life must be correlated with the fact that the great mother, great father, anima/animus and wisdom archetypes coordinate symbolic elaboration and consciousness through four different typical patterns of I-Other relationship. Thus are formed four archetypal life cycles, each of which contains the history of that particular archetype in each individual, family, cultural and cosmic Self. This fact is essential for differentiating the specific archetypes and defenses involved in the transference.

Such a theory of consciousness and ego development from the beginning until the end of life enables us to see the competition of archetypal patterns to coordinate consciousness formation and orientation, especially between the anima/animus and the parental archetypes. Neumann (1986) began to describe this competition in one of his last works. These four archetypal patterns of conscious operation are so important that they justify changing the definitions of archetypes into a conscious and an unconscious pattern.

I have described these four archetypal patterns – matriarchal, patriarchal, alterity and cosmic – in many writings, three of them (1983, 1986, 1987) presented in our past Congresses. The matriarchal and patriarchal patterns are less difficult to understand than the alterity pattern of the anima/animus archetypes, because of Jung's cultural patriarchal bias. Although anima and animus are among his great discoveries, perhaps second only to that of the central archetype, the function of the anima and animus archetypes will be estimated properly only when we expand their conceptualizations with bi-gendership common to all other archetypes, and with the alterity cycle of consciousness.

The alterity pattern of consciousness is the underlying thought pattern of Taoism and the *I Ching*. Described in Buddhism as the middle path, it guided the political revolution of Gandhi. It was constellated in the Christian myth and, in spite of the Inquisition, continued through alchemy into modern science, the German philosopher Hegel's dialectics, socialism and Analytical Psychology. I have named it the alterity pattern because, unlike the parental patterns in which the I-Other pattern of relationship tends to be asymmetrical, here the ego tends to function in mutuality, symmetrically considering the Other as it does itself in a permanent relationship with wholeness.

The alterity pattern is the conscious pattern that allows us to perceive the equal importance of conflicting archetypes, ego and shadow and symbolic polarities, including analyst and analysand in psychotherapy. The alterity pattern of consciousness is the central contribution of alchemy to psychology and natural science. The alchemical *lapis* on the psychological level is the pattern of consciousness that is capable of perceiving all symbols as symbols and their polarities as manifestations of the Self – the symbolic equivalent of transmuting all metals into gold. And on the objective level is the concept of the common nature of matter.

Symbolic Psychology may include, therefore, the findings of Psychoanalysis within a developmental and archetypal perspective that avoids the conceptual patchwork now practiced between Analytical Psychology and Psychoanalysis. It conceives the personal as inseparable from the archetypal within normal and pathological development. Complementing Judith Hubback's paper (see Chapter 2 in this volume), I add from the perspective of Symbolic Psychology that, like all defensive structures, the repetition-compulsion defensive structure is a twin archetypal structure to the creative repetition structure. These structures are both archetypal but very different from each other. Whereas defensive structures maintain symbols in the shadow, preventing them from entering consciousness, creative structures foster symbols to structure consciousness. Creative and defensive structures are activated alternately by the Self, depending on existential conditions.

Perhaps the most important concept in understanding the erotic transference is that of incest. Freud's unawareness of the creative unconscious and of the anima and animus archetypes prevented his understanding of incest beyond the parental archetypes. If we accept the permanent presence of the regent archetypal quaternio in all symbolic elaboration, we become aware that the reductive and prospective understanding of the anima/animus archetypes in the parental complexes is indispensable for personality development. Thus, there is nothing wrong in being fascinated by mother or father as long as one realizes, differentiates and develops the symbolic structure of that fascination.

Jung's appraisal of Freud's treatment of incest as limited to a personal relationship is based on the assumption that the personal unconscious can be lived separately from the collective unconscious. This attitude overlooks the fact that the personal parents are among the most important archetypal symbols of human life and also overlooks the predominance of the patriarchal pattern in Freud's treatment of the Oedipus Complex.

Freud's reduction of the erotic transference to incest shows how much his psychology, through unawareness, left the anima/animus archetypes incestuously reduced to and thus imprisoned within the parental archetypes. Jung's reduction of symbolic incest to the *hieros gamos* incestuously confuses the anima/animus archetypes with the parental archetypes by leaving the parental archetypes out of the transference and out of the process of individuation. This prevented him from differentiating the anima/animus archetypes from matriarchal and patriarchal dynamisms and their characteristic defenses and shadows. It also made it difficult for him to see the necessity to elaborate every symbol reductively and prospectively, even more so when it is incestuous.

Thus, Psychoanalysis remained East of Eden, within a dichotomized theoretical frame which separated many polarities including Eros and Thanatos. Without the concepts of the anima and animus, Psychoanalysis never could conceive the dynamic bipolarity of symbols and the quaternary pattern of the Self as essential for the understanding of psychological development.

Jung's work also was affected fundamentally. His theory of archetypal symbolic incest exemplifies how much he confused the anima with the great mother archetype and the animus with the great father archetype. He exuberantly did this in several works (CW9-I, CW9-II, CW11, CW16) and, therefore, failed to see how much the anima/animus archetypes coordinate through synchronicity the symbolic quaternary post-parental I-Other and Other-Other patterns of relationship. It is my impression that Jung's confusion of the anima with the great mother archetype in the cultural dimension was influenced strongly by Layard's (1972) work, where the binary matriarchal pattern of moiety separation and incest regulation is identified, wrongly, with the anima/animus quaternary pattern.

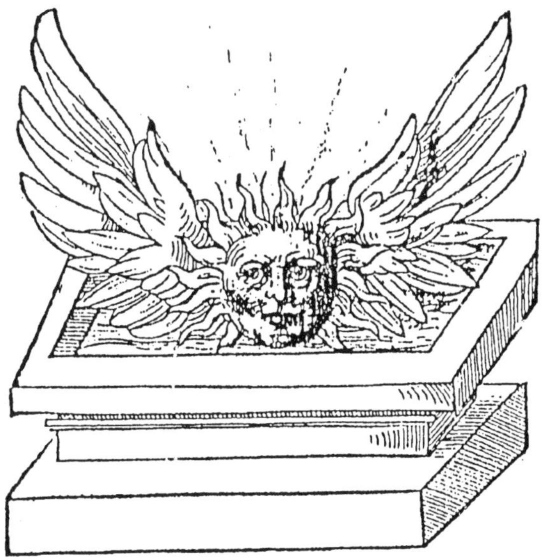

Figure 2: The Sun Bath

When one reads alchemy and its *Rosarium Philosophorum* from the perspective of symbolic development within the regent archetypal quaternio, one finds no reason to reduce the 22 images to 11 as Jung did in his *Psychology of the Transference* (CW16). Indeed, all 22 figures are most representative; the first 11 are more expressive of matriarchal and the last 11 of patriarchal symbolism. The figures of the dying sun (Figure 2) and of the

Figure 3: The green lion devouring the Sun

green lion devouring the sun (Figure 3), for instance, should not be left out; they are most expressive of patriarchal dynamism and of the father complex. The fact that both series contain the coniunctio is not sufficient basis to consider them repetitive. Both matriarchal and patriarchal dynamisms are bi-gender and have a typical coniunctio. The way toward the alterity pattern varies between matriarchal and patriarchal dominance. The matriarchal dominance is expressed better by the wingless coniunctio and the patriarchal by the winged images of the *Rosarium*. The different archetypal patterns of the coniunctio may explain Jung's ambivalence toward the hermaphrodite Rebis symbol (CW16, p. 305). Above all, the most important figure in the *Rosarium* relevant to the erotic transference is the final one of the risen Savior (Figure 4). It is a rare image in Christian iconography of the resurrected adult Messiah. The fact that he steps out of the tomb with his left foot forward could point to his revolutionary mission. This image exemplifies the hypothesis that alchemy was not a compensatory undercurrent to Christianity, but simultaneously its incarnation and the root of the natural sciences. Thus, alchemy expressed the

Figure 4: The victory of the stone represented by the resurrection of Christ

creative urge of the cultural Self to unite love and knowledge on the objective and subjective levels for the world's salvation. The present world- wide ecological awakening is an evidence of this hypothesis.

From such a perspective, alchemy was an undercurrent to the Inquisition and a direct expression of Christianity, including matter and its hidden dangers, which demanded alchemy's understanding and operation through love and knowledge. The rise of Christ at the end of the *Rosarium* expresses the *lapis philosophorum* (philosopher's stone), the ultimate result of the magnum opus, on the psychological and objective levels. The expression includes the redeeming alterity pattern of consciousness as the wisdom of the anima/animus quaternary coniunctio. The coniunctio allows us to understand reductively and prospectively the subjective and objective poles of symbols, by transmuting them continuously through love and knowledge into symbols of the Self.

I have been discussing the archetypal symbolic content of our quest for individual and cultural psychic developments, not how to go about it. Concretizing it depends on the honesty, dedication, patience and creativity of each therapeutic encounter, including the analyst as well as the analysand, as Jung so courageously showed us. Just as Western culture once saw a star which inspired its search, so every psychotherapist must pay attention to the horizon for the symbols that guide him or her on the difficult journey through the existential labyrinth.

REFERENCES

Byington, C. (1983). Symbolic psychotherapy, a post-patriarchal pattern in psychotherapy. In J. Beebe (Ed.), *Money, Food, Drink and Fashion and Analytic Training*. Fellbach, Germany: Bonz.

Byington, C. (1986). The concept of the pathological shadow and its relationship to the concept of defense mechanisms within a theory of symbolic psychopathology. In L. Zoja & R. Hinshaw (Eds.), *Symbolic and Clinical Approaches in Theory and Practice*. Zurich: Daimon.

Byington, C. (1987). The pathological shadow of the western cultural Self. In M. Mattoon (Ed.), *The Archetype of Shadow in a Split World*. Zurich: Daimon.

Carotenuto, A. (1984). *Diario de una secreta simetria*. Rio de Janeiro: Paz e Terra.

Dinnerstein, D. (1976). *The Mermaid and the Minotaur*. New York: Harper & Row.

Layard, J. (1972). *The Virgin Archetype*. Zurich: Spring Publications.

Neumann, E. (1986). The fear of the feminine. *Quadrant*, *19*-1, 7-30.

Response

Beverley Zabriskie
New York, New York, USA
New York Association
for Analytical Psychology

In 1880 Anna O – Bertha Pappenheim – was 21. Her father Siegmund, to whom she was devoted, was ill. As the family attended to Siegmund, Bertha became mentally and physically debilitated. Joseph Breuer was called in to attend to her while others cared for her father. As Byington says, the case of Anna O, as described by Breuer and Freud (1895), is pivotal in the history of Western depth psychology; the case challenged the cultural assumptions regarding hysteria, as embodying the dangerous irrationality of altered states, uncontrollable passions and suspicious forms of knowledge.

Freud convinced Breuer to co-publish a description and analysis of the case 13 years after it ended with, in Anna's words, "a talking cure"; in Breuer's words, "the final cure of hysteria" and establishing, in Freud's words, "the cornerstone of analysis." Breuer (1895) described the successful disappearance of Anna's multiple hysteric symptoms. Yet he also concluded his account with negative and dismissive remarks:

> Although I have suppressed a large number of interesting details this case history of Anna O has grown bulkier than would seem to be required for a hysterical illness that was not in itself of an unusual character.... In just the same way, the eggs of the echnoderm are important in embryology not because the sea-urchin is a particularly interesting animal but because the protoplasm of eggs is transparent and because what we observe in

> them thus throws light on the probable course of events in eggs whose protoplasm is opaque. (p. 96)

In their publication of this famous "cure" neither Breuer nor Freud mentioned some facts later reported to have been told by Freud – to Jung, Wilhelm Fliess, Ernest Jones, and James Strachey, and repeated by Ellenberger (1970) and Gay (1988). Shortly after termination, on a date set by Anna, the doctor was called back when his young patient had cramps. Bertha declared, "Now comes Dr. B.'s child." According to Goodheart (1984), the horrified Breuer withdrew from the case and referred Bertha to Ludwig Binswanger's psychiatric hospital at Kreuzlingen, where three months later she still had her initial symptoms. One year later she had relapses and, according to Gay (1988) was dealing with an addiction to morphine – which Breuer had prescribed. Gay, who opined that Bertha "reawakened all [Breuer's] dormant oedipal longings for his own mother, also called Bertha, who had died ... when he was three," tells us that Breuer "had come to see the case of Anna O as excessively demanding and downright embarrassing, ... a case he never forgot, but not a case from which he could ever really profit." He later (1895) recalled: "I vowed at the time I would never go through such an ordeal again" (p. 69).

One may not wish to fault the pioneering Breuer, a physician and hypnotist and not a psychoanalyst, for his lack of experience and symbolic understanding. Nonetheless, it is disturbing that, years later, he and Freud published an incomplete version of the events. It is sobering to remember on how muddy a cornerstone our profession rests: a misleading account of a savior-physician casting the devils from the possessed young woman, her personal agony misrepresented to promulgate theories and further careers. Lest we too lose the reality of Anna O and those who have come after, I must question some of Byington's formulations.

It is to be noted that each of his examples is of a female creature/disciple/patient and a male authority/savior/healer: Eve/God; Magdalene/Christ; psychotics/Pinel; Anna O/Breuer; Spielrein/Jung; female analysand/male analyst. These pairings restrict erotic transference to a hetero-erotic projection of the needier female onto a male image of power or rescue. Thus, the patriarchal bias, which Byington declares he abhors, nonetheless pervades his argument.

While correctly pointing out that a vector of the erotic transference is toward self-knowledge, Byington implies – incorrectly, I think – an equation between the erotic transference and love. If, as he states, the erotic transference may be both pre-Oedipal and Oedipal, both "infantile" and mature, may it not be also about appetite and lust? A wish to merge and the will to power? The need to play and to fantasize? To know demand and meet frustration? Within the analytic container, how can the erotic transference be love in the psychological sense? A love relationship posits knowledge of the other as other, not as a projective screen – a knowing of another as he or she is, not only in relation to oneself. Within the asymmetry and abstinence of the analytic stance, are not the analyst's longings to be known put aside? For the analysand to know the analyst as an individual posits a self-revelation that would intrude the analyst's person into the analysand's projective field.

Just as the deepest eros brings connection to an inner center, so too the eros of the erotic transference is wider and deeper than desire for the analyst. Anna O did not state that she wanted Breuer, the man and physician, as lover. Rather, she declared the date she had chosen to terminate their work to be a birth-day, when she would bring forth the fruits of their labors. Was she not declaring that she no longer needed him, that she was turning her attention away from the past, from the father and from Breuer as the instrumental and transitional man, toward immediate connection with new life emerging from within?

Eve of Genesis was expelled from Eden after having taken in the seed of knowledge, but outside its gates she gave birth, albeit in pain. The Magdalene to whom Byington refers as one from whom Christ had cast seven devils was first nearly stoned, and later disbelieved when she claimed to have seen the fallen hero in his risen form. The Inquisitors excommunicated and sentenced those they deemed witches. Bertha – Anna – was spurned when she spoke, both concretely and symbolically, of the seed received, borne and brought forth between her and Breuer. He sent her to psychiatrist Ludwig Binswanger at Kreuzlingen for treatment. There, some years later, psychiatrist Jung met inpatient Sabina Spielrein, who was greatly helped by him, until she was maligned for giving voice and scandalous image to her desire. She then sought help from Freud. Anna and Sabina managed to preserve and carry the potent and potential seminal energy from their miscarried therapies; after further treatment, they were able to claim individual lives of significant professional productivity, if not personal fulfillment.

One of Byington's central arguments is that "the Jesus / Mary Magdalene *coniunctio* pattern of relationship is the fundamental mythical amplification of the erotic transference in Western psychotherapy." This is a problematic paradigm for the therapeutic transference. How would this look in the analytic relationship? And who is in which role? Is Byington proposing a literal parallel, with the male analyst as savior-teacher and female analysand as bedeviled and prostituted, needing redemption? This paradigm is suspect, at best a transitional fantasy, and at worst regressive, insofar as the "solution" would exacerbate the hysteric's problem of loss of self.

Byington tells a dream of a woman analysand "dominated by the erotic aspect of transference" in which *a young carpenter said, "I want you to be the wood of my cross."* Understood subjectively, does the animus desire the woman to be the passive matter of a cross of his making, or the passive carrier of his crucifixion? Does the dream imply that the woman's animus will be fixed on a cross while her ego bears witness? In Christian myth, it is Christ crucified and Magdalene who suffers in her witnessing. If the Christ/Magdalene amplification is understood interpersonally and transferentially, is Byington imagining that the female analysand will bear witness to the analyst's experience, or that the analyst is crucified by the erotic transference? Such a crucifixion is the reverse of clinical reality for, in the erotic transference, is it not the analysand who is torn between the horizontal reach – of unfulfilled and frustrated longing for the analyst – and the vertical pull, into the depths of one's own being and "up" toward the unmediated Self? The analyst participates as compassionate companion and knowing witness to this crucial *agon*. Is Byington perhaps speaking about erotic *counter*transference? Or does he lead us to an archetypal crossing of anima and animus, within which it is the anima experience of the male analyst to feel prostituted in the offering of human availability for a price? Here we need clarification.

It is "important to recognize that the symbol of the redeemed-prostitute / mad-heroine as companion of the Savior in the anima-animus archetypal coniunctio is most significant to express [a] new pattern of consciousness," writes Byington. If the prostitute is recognized in the antique context, as one who places herself forward, with the religious connotation of one who offers sex as an act of worship to the temple deity, then the entrance and inclusion of Magdalene as convert, disciple, witness, and – in some traditions – a leader of the early Church, may be seen to connote the return and acceptance of the feminine in the new dispensation, from the exile outside Eden and the temples of the rejected goddesses of despised, foreign religions. She would indeed be the necessary and worthy companion of the hero. Byington believes that her presence grants vital masculinity to the adult Christ. However, in his schema of the four dimensions of the Self, with its regent archetypal quaternio, the child is oddly absent. Without this symbol, what carries the emerging ego consciousness forth from the matrix of the unconscious and the paternal structures of the established order?

While I agree that Jung's *poesis* in his configuring of anima becomes confused and confusing, it is not, I believe, primarily because it is contaminated with the mother. Rather, this intuitive concept became overly fused, through Jung's typological perspective, with his inferior function, and thus appears as if an embodiment of sensualized, sentimentalized, romanticized feeling.

I have no issue with Byington's outline of Symbolic Psychology, with its concerns for the synthetic and reductive, the dynamic and regressive, the linear and cyclic, the personal and historical, the individual and collective, structured by the interplay of various archetypal sources and patterns. What is not sufficiently convincing, however, is how and where Symbolic Psychology differs from the Jungian and post-Jungian models to which an alert contemporary clinician practicing within the tradition of Analytical Psychology attends. How, for example, is the regent archetype different from the concept of the Self? What is this system's singular contribution to our understanding of the point and counterpoint of death with life? To our theories regarding incest? And how does it add further meaning to the understanding of both female and male analysts, both male and female analysands who have known the agonies and ecstasies of fully-met and endured erotic transference and countertransference with all their challenging and crucial pre-Oedipal, incestuous and exogamous, infantile and transcendent energies? How might his approach have aided Breuer? And how might it have assisted in the birth traumas of Anna O?

REFERENCES

Breuer, J. (1895). Fräulein Anna O. In J. Breuer & S. Freud, *Studies on Hysteria*. New York: Penguin.

Ellenberger, H. (1970). *The Discovery of the Unconscious*. London: Penguin.

Gay, P. (1988). *Freud, A Life For Our Time*. New York: Norton.

Goodheart, W. (1984). Successful and unsuccessful interventions in Jungian analysis. *Chiron*, 89-117.

Narcissistic Restorations: Transference Dynamics

Genevieve Guy-Gillet
Paris, France
Société Française
de Psychologie Analytique

While rereading Jung's writings on psychotherapy (CW16) I was surprised to see how much his views anticipated current debates on the transference and, thus, how easily his ideas find their place at the heart of our reflections. When Jung stated that an instinct for relationship is at the center of the transference and – in the same breath – that each person is a stranger among strangers, does this contradiction not exemplify the drama of our times? How can one become an individual without cutting oneself off from others? Did Jung not echo in a strange way our present concerns when he observed the desperate efforts made by modern men and women to satisfy the need for kinship libido? They are estranged from it and it cannot be replaced by the collective substitutes that are abundantly available in our modern societies.

Jung presented the transference as a phenomenon that is fueled by the aim of kinship libido. His fundamental proposition was that only a relationship with another human being can satisfy this aim. How are we then to understand his contention that we are strangers to one another? In the loss of this desire for kinship libido? In the need to pull away from this desire for the sake of psychic differentiation, which is so necessary, but at the risk of severing all ties with others? We are confronted again with a proposition that is paradoxical, since neither kinship libido nor psychic differentiation can be foregone. Jung articulated the terms of this paradox: "Relationship to the self is at once relationship to our fellow man, and no one can be related to the latter until he is related to himself" (CW16, par. 446).

Stated in this way, the transference is basic to the method that we use in analysis. Everything that unfolds within the analytic frame and that we call the work of analysis – interventions, interpretations, and choice of appropriate techniques – is an expression of the transference, a creation between the two partners engaged in the analytic process.

In considering the other element of the transference, the Self, we have learned that all efforts to define it fail. Even if we are content to understand the Self intellectually as a concept of unity or of wholeness, the actual experience of it is a different matter. Clinical experience teaches us that the Self is active in the transference to such an extent that a specific approach to psychic healing emerges. We could call this approach a therapy of the Self, a therapy within which the experience of the transference puts the Self to the test. A test, because our presence can be for analysands a sign of hope that scattered psychic energy can be reoriented, to the extent that we agree to wander along with them and to search out their painful areas of meaninglessness.

Thus, we have before us the two key concepts that relate to the transference: kinship libido and the Self. I have chosen to demonstrate more particularly how a transference develops or is activated in those analyses that touch on a deficiency in the archaic relationship with the maternal figure. This kind of deficiency may appear in severe regressions at the very start of analysis or only later, after several "stints" in analysis.

The term narcissism, which comes up quite naturally in our discussion, is not – properly speaking – a Jungian term. But we can use it without compromising our allegiance to Jungian thought because the term evokes an experience intrinsic to current clinical practice. Indeed, it is our archetypal understanding of the Self that gives narcissism its dimensionality. In addition, we have our own concepts such as that of the primary Self, developed by Jungian analysts Michael Fordham and Erich Neumann, or that of kinship libido; both provide us with good theoretical tools.

The concept of kinship libido resonates with what a Freudian psychoanalyst, Grunberger (1971), also called "self" and which is, in a certain way, the "flowering" of Narcissus. This concept is indispensable for the organization of the drives because of its "narcissism-promoting" quality. Kinship libido appears as the eros quality that binds together different elements of object relations or that can account for the capacity to transfer libido from the mother, in whom it is invested entirely at first, to other love objects.

We refer frequently to Narcissus, undoubtedly because this image has come to us through the ages without losing either its searching or its enigmatic quality, and because analysts have learned to recognize the signs of its power in themselves as well as in their analysands. Still, although the image retains its seductive powers, we seem to be more sensitive nowadays to the suffering inflicted when its aim fails. We are more attuned to what lies hidden behind the shadow that ensnares Narcissus and more prudent before its archaic violence, which threatens to erupt and overwhelm the ego. Illustrative of what lies hidden is the case of a man who told me of a nightmare in which he felt irresistibly drawn to a "ghostly" door, behind which stood "Horror." Horror was the only word he could find to express the dread he experienced.

A few of our colleagues have taken up the story of Narcissus once again. I owe them a great deal. I am particularly indebted to Schwartz-Salant (1982) for his contributions. I shall limit myself here, however, to the study of what the transference teaches us on the subject. I speak of those analysands who, when we first meet them, put us on the alert as we glimpse their "lack-in-being," even if their narcissistic "fault" – in the geologic sense – is not yet visible. At times it is enough that this lack- in-being simply accompanies the analytic journey without activating the particular aspect of the transference that I am talking about.

As in all transferences, the relationship emerges from the interaction of the two protagonists in the analytic relationship. The transference relationship has an organization all its own, an organization reflecting the archetypal processes that are activated in the relational field. The focus of analysis and its outcome depends on our ability to make sense of these processes. Our exchanges, our way of interpreting and even our most profound psychic movements delineate its outline.

I find that the analytic transference is determined from the form of its representation. As Jung tells us, if form is meaning, then it is in attending to form that meaning can be discerned. The forms of the transference depend primarily on the psychic structure of our analysands and on the way that we become involved in that psychic structure. Experience teaches us that each analyst meets more frequently with one type of transference than with another.

Let us return to analysands who suffer from narcissistic deficiencies. An alchemical image selected from the *Rosarium Philosophorum* illustrates the form of the transference that these analysands evoke: the image that depicts the naked King and Queen taking a bath together (CW16, figure 4).

But, you may object, does not the entire series of images from the *Rosarium* apply to all forms of transferences? Why single out this particular image? My answer is that it is this image that presented itself to me when I began to think about this paper. Realizing how this image served as background to my reflections, I sought to understand its specific meaning.

For you to follow my exposition, I invite you to enter the image in a dream-like fashion to animate its content within yourself. I will explain then the reasons for choosing this image and the way that I think it operates in the transference. The image suggests first the unity of a closed space that contains, without enclosing, the naked bodies of King and Queen. The two are very close to each other in this basin, which is not round but hexagonal; within it they bathe, sharing the same water. The flowers they hold in their hands crisscross, while the dove between them joins its flower to theirs. This is the only contact that the King and Queen have with each other. The "two" and the "one" move back and forth in response to one another, avoiding both fusion and confusion.

If we examine this image from an archetypal perspective, we

see that it is highlighted by a twofold energetic movement that goes from the bottom to the top, then from the top down to the bottom. If we read the image structurally and symbolically from the bottom up, we can say that the water stands for the instinctual nature of libido. From it emerges the differentiation of the two creative principles, feminine and masculine. They are bound to the spiritual pole of the archetype, which in turn is represented by the dove.

Looking at the image from the top down, starting with the bird, we see that it is the movement as a whole that structures the meaning of the image. Everything here speaks of the Self and the way it works through the forms that express it. It is this idea that I will develop.

While giving the reasons that this image from the *Rosarium* seems to me to be illustrative of this type of transference, I find that I must see it as an image of the goal and at the same time attempt to grasp its underlying organization. Insofar as this scene from the *Rosarium* is an image of the goal, it brings to mind the distance that separates the beginning of the analytic journey from its final destination. It warns us of the temptation to see ourselves as King or Queen in the adventure, a temptation that mutual desires and narcissistic expectations elicit easily. Further, it teaches us not to confuse the goal with the process. If the living water of the bath is the energy source of the opus, the spiritual form of the "two and the one" must be sufficiently structured to give birth to differentiated forms; in this case to that of the King and the Queen. We know that this form is first inscribed in the psyche early in life and that it is intensified in the early phases of the mother-child relationship.

What can we do once we note serious deficiencies in the organization of this original form? Experience has taught us that here, as well as in the unfolding of the subject's personal history, the answer is to be found in relationship. As to the level of involvement in which the original form takes root, I find it best illustrated by the image of the King and the Queen in the bath.

I reached this conclusion because I was impressed with two characteristics of these royal personages, characteristics that shed light on the first lived moments of the transference. These characteristics are the proximity of the King's and the Queen's bodies to each other and their nudity.

When we are faced with narcissistic deficiencies in an analysand, something alerts the ego – and for good reason. We discover, as Jung warned us, that in certain cases, "A genuine participation, going right beyond professional routine, is absolutely imperative.... The doctor must go to the limits of his subjective possibilities" (CW16, par. 400).

In this instance, we are called upon to divest ourselves of all our clothing, a metaphorical expression, but a lived psychological experience. What compels us to strip bare is not what the other asks of us, in whatever ways that demand may be expressed. A certain amount of time may be necessary before we become aware that this need for psychological nudity emanates from the Self and, occasionally, even more time may be required before we are able to accept the echo of this need within ourselves.

The proximity of bodies that expresses the strength of this need may be converted at certain moments into resistances on both sides. Those resistances are not necessarily simultaneous but belong to the countertransference. Communication occurs even when an experience has not yet been expressed in words. This is the time for the analyst to develop the capacity to listen at a profound level. There, emotional experiences that are by turns explosive, contained, repressed or damaged are perceived by an empathy that can lead the way to feelings and to the words to express those feelings. Analysts who rely more on the introverted sensing function follow more easily by paying attention to somatic manifestations, thus facilitating the location of investments and defects in the body-self.

Although we are able sometimes to be readily empathic with certain analysands, with others we have to cross dark zones. Those zones include a state of mutual unconsciousness – hard to discern in these transferences – and hysterical defenses that mimic but do not replace empathic communication.

Resistances and defenses are as much on one side of the transference as on the other. These experiences in the transference relationship are organized, broadly speaking, along two very different lines of development that can appear at any time in the unfolding of an analysis. Whichever line of development the transference takes, its essential form remains the same.

In one line of development, the transference is oriented from the beginning toward a quest for totality as fusion where the "common bath" is seen as a promise to be realized. Here the demands of the Self appear to be confused with the strength of the desire; occasionally much time is needed before the menacing fear of leaving the primary "all" is confronted. The analyst is invested with formidable power and, after responding to this request for analysis, may be threatened with submersion by the release of a torrent of tumultuous waters. The analyst's ego will attempt to resist this onslaught, of course.

I recall the first transference of this kind I experienced with a woman analysand. I was her total love object, but she did not know how to possess me as she desired. One day she brought a dream in which she and I were on the "island of the dead;" we were the only living beings among the shades. She was very pleased with this dream because, she thought, there on that island I was all hers. She regretted that she could not keep me in that kingdom where, until then, she reigned all alone. I answered her, in a somewhat defensively humorous tone, that if she had any reason to rejoice, it was not so much because she had dragged me along to be among the dead but more because, thanks to me, a living being had finally managed to penetrate such a place. It took a long time before the distress she experienced in living was reversed into an Eros for life, a change that demanded of us enormous effort. Out of love for me, she agreed to find personal reasons to live, while I learned to come to terms with the power of this kinship libido, from which transpired both the Great Mother's omnipotence and the demands of the Self. This woman taught me a great deal and, although I was unable to recognize at the time the meaning of the transference in what we lived out together, I intuitively sensed that somehow an unconscious process had helped us in our efforts.

The other line of development that these transferences make

available takes us far away from the communal bath. The refusal, the fears of getting inside this transference, at times the ambivalence from the very start, become organized into tenacious resistances. Whereas some analysands plunge into the bath, others flee from it and demand of us that we not lose sight of them, while they measure in centimeters the distance we have to maintain from them. As an object that the analysand covets and also that provokes horror, the analyst becomes the focus for the analysand to relive anguishing moments relating to early deprivations. This dual movement of attraction-revulsion is betrayed in a man's words: "I feel at the same time like throwing myself in your arms and like strangling you." This statement reveals the strength of the instinct of the relationship bond that is awakened by the transference and the archaic violence provoked by the frustration of this instinct.

Those about whom I have just spoken showed their resistances actively and at the outset of analysis, but there are others whose resistances are more covert. Their analytic journey seems to follow the two lines of development I have just pointed to, but less obviously. The elaboration of the transference apparently follows a mid-course between fusion and flight from fusion; something seems to resist it in an obscure way. What is the nature of this resistance?

An example is a young woman whose narcissistic "fault" was compensated by an imaginary grandiose self. From it she seemed to have separated herself quite well. The transference, tinged with idealization, allowed her to repair to some extent her original wounds; nothing seemed to slow the integration of these archaic zones into consciousness. Yet somehow she always met the same obstacle in her relationships: an attitude of submission that she found horrifying but incomprehensible insofar as she played the role of good mother.

Nothing in the sessions yielded anything to which I could relate this conflict until one day, following an especially vivid account of her continued inability to free herself from this repetitive behavior, I felt a surge of rage take hold of me. I managed to shake off this rage, while asking myself: "What is it that is taking hold of me? This is ridiculous; besides it is completely ineffectual!" My analysand looked at me silently. It was then that I observed her expression, which was very different from the one she normally had in our sessions and, in amazement, I said: "You defy me!" Astounded, she nonetheless could recognize in herself the attitude I had pointed to. I added: "Toward whom did you have this attitude when you were a child?" She thought about it and all of a sudden found herself face-to-face with her father; when enraged he forbade her to go out and, silently to herself she defied him, although she would not have dared actually to disobey him.

This session opened the way out of our impasse. We came to understand that, under the auspices of the Self that continued to operate in our sessions and whose rightful progress I could recognize, a part of her remained possessed by the omnipotence of one of those images of the Great Mother that can lurk behind the radiance of the Self. She believed that she was seeing to her own personal projects when she devoted herself to her surroundings. In reality, however, she satisfied her revenge against the archaic image of the maternal figure that persecuted her in the guise of the confrontation with her father as well as her desire to remain possessed by that archaic image. These were conflicting desires; she could preserve the archaic bond to this mother only by protecting her against attacks from herself. The perversity of this unconscious maneuver took a long time to come to the surface because there was the immediate need to find another outlet for kinship libido. Only the depth of the relationship that we were able to live out together in the transference allowed this libido to be diverted and created the conditions that reoriented it toward individuation.

As I pursue further the reflections that this image of the transference has prompted in me, I am led to propose that we view this image from an additional level. If we approach, from an energetic point of view, the image of the immersion of the King and Queen into the bath, it takes on a double meaning. Certainly, this immersion spells the return to an original state, "the plunge into the amniotic fluid of the gravid uterus" (CW16, par. 454) with, as corollary, the risk of being swallowed up. We can see this immersion also as the work of sexual libido that floods the couple. In the transference the immersion can be seen as a lived experience that corresponds to sexual libido. If we speak, in alchemical terms, of the role played by chthonic and fiery Mercury in the analytic context, we are confronted with a lived experience ablaze with passion.

Analytic experience teaches us that sexual libido can be expressed between partners of the same sex. However, sexual differences structure the therapy of narcissistic restorations differently; the lived experiences of the transference point to divergent modes of treatment. I am expressing here my own experience as a woman analyst, but the ever-increasing opportunity to continue analyses that have been begun by other analysts – and the other way around – helps us to understand better a diversity of analytic approaches, as well as the ways that libidinal energy invests its objects in the transference.

In the relationship between analyst and analysand of opposite sexes, an erotic tension delimits the force field of the alchemical quarternity created by the King and the Queen and their projections upon sexual partners. Thus, when we must deal with structures whose basic narcissism is shaky, erotic tensions play a role in containing narcissism while acting as a safety valve against regressive tendencies. Sheltered by this transference love that protects the subject from attraction to the original source – the parents – the rise of kinship libido is filtered: libido and erotic drives merge, culminating in flaming passions. Once imaginary erotic pleasures have been sacrificed, these passions eventually find symbolic expression. Nonetheless, the analyst who is the object of the transference still has to live through a trying time.

It happens also that libidinal satisfaction obtained in the heterosexual relationship manages to satisfy the narcissistic demand and that nothing occurs to reactivate the archaic demand. At this point of the analysis, we frequently see analysands act out in lateral transferences, under the pretext of living out the sexual drive whose actual realization is forbidden by the law of analysis. Somehow what we think we had managed to avoid will be revealed, bringing to the light of day the object of conflict that we thought we had been spared. (I say "we" here because it is the analyst who has to monitor the countertransference.) This object does not always relate to transgression but, rather, may deal with the desire to keep the analyst in a state of fusion, sheltered from conflictual confrontations and narcissistic turbulences.

Finally, whatever the sex of the analyst, once uncertainty about sexual identity begins to resonate with the androgynous parts of the analyst, it can initiate phases – and times fixations – of an unconscious homosexuality. But we know of analysands for whom androgyny serves as a narcissistic refuge and a defense against intrusions. For some of them, the only heterosexual trait that is tolerable is the one relating to the analyst's own sexual embodiment – provided that it is not provocative but related to a quality in being. From here, we witness little by little the constitution of a primordial couple whose feminine pole is represented by the (female) analyst's body, while the masculine pole is represented by the analyst's animus. For this couple, the eros of relationship, guaranteeing the bond, is in the transference.

At this point I find it necessary to consider the image of the androgyne as a prefiguration of the Self that demands to be seen and recognized. Those who harbor this image may evolve only to the point of relating to their physical sexuality but not to the psychic androgyny that serves as original matrix. But if, for them, the King and the Queen never separate, at least the libido within which these two royal characters are immersed is united again to the life drive. And the analyst's acknowledgment of this image simultaneously restores its narcissistic value and supports the effort to bring it into the light of consciousness.

Let me speak now about the experience of women analysts with male analysands. Some men seek to use the transference as a way to fuse and ask the analyst to become the mother in whom they can lose themselves, because a psychological rebirth had been denied them at a critical time. A heterosexual approach offers a great deal in terms of energetic resources.

First, the animus of the woman is enormously attractive to an anima that is poorly differentiated from the archetype. For a woman analyst, the danger is certainly that of the animus' taking on a regal attitude that is far too authoritarian. But provided that analysts allow erotic tension to operate in the interplay of opposites in its own time, the anima of the male analytic partner gradually emerges. This emergence becomes evident in the sessions, especially in the fact that the desire to fuse ceases to predominate.

This propensity for fusion has been linked with the erotic drives and then expressed in the incestuous exchange. It can release its energy through dream representations and emotional experiences lived out in the sessions. It also becomes obvious in the transformation in our male analysands. Their masculinity is affirmed, in a spectacular fashion at times. An example is the man who always dressed in a "come-what-may" manner but who, one day, appeared at a session as a true dandy, even going to the trouble of asking me to observe the perfect coordination of his clothing. It is then that the recognition of a man's masculinity, of which he is reassured by the woman's gaze focused on him, contributes to restore the image of his masculine self that had been wounded so early in life. The more profound "faults," those contemporary to archaic experience, begin to emerge. Emotions that had been unrecognized emerge from the far away times when they first came to light, while images appear for the unmentionable and gradually tame the instinctual violence that had been given over to chaos.

Thus, the experiences of heterosexual transferences allow us to grasp better the differences of energies that operate between the woman analyst and her female analysands. With them, she enters the realm of the Mothers. If the analysand seeks her fulfillment there, it is in a body-to-body identification with the mother. This is a frightening experience, for it takes place without the protective cover of heterosexual erotic tensions. The battle waged with the archaic mother's omnipotence fails to break open the image of wholeness. This is a battle that shakes up the analyst and challenges even the defenses that her ego might have put up against the Terrible Mother. During this trying time an analyst must abandon the desire for power and even the narcissistic image of her own competence. Thanks to this abandonment the eros of the Self can function as organizer of relationship and the ego can be open to its effects. But it is also when the analyst can let go of power that the analysand can be free to discover her own power.

I return once more to the image of the "King and Queen in the Bath," in order to understand these feminine transferences that so profoundly engage the creative capacities of the two protagonists around the maternal space. The meaning of this image will reach its fulfillment when this space, which is destined to prepare for the "birth of the child of becoming," is reconstituted or when it is constituted for the first time.

In prologue to my conclusion, I give credit to Elie Humbert who, through his presence and his work, has enriched my clinical research. My reflections here afford me the opportunity to bear witness to his contribution and to his analytic approaches, which I share. Now let us see where our reflections have taken us.

As my beginning argument, I suggested that analysis which deals with narcissistic restorations structures a specific form of the transference. I have proposed, from the series of images drawn from the *Rosarium*, the image of the "Immersion in the Bath" in order to illustrate this form and to support my hypothesis.

I called also upon those of Jung's texts that lend support to the theory of the transference that I present. It is from Jung that I have taken the following quotations, both from the "Psychology of the Transference" (CW16): the Self "as union of opposites is never complete in an individual without a relationship with the other" and "the relationship between the 'I and the You' goes by way of the recognition of mutual projections of which the self is part" (par. 454). The alchemical image of the "King and Queen in the Bath" may help you to grasp the nature of projections that are placed upon us in the demands to restore narcissistic "faults" and in what kind of transference that restoration can occur. Thus, when a woman analysand told me: "You are my golden flower," her formulation expressed quite rightly the situation of the transference. She was letting me know what her mother had deprived her of and what she was hoping to obtain from me. She did not recognize at the beginning of her analysis that the golden flower was within herself; nonetheless she sensed its presence.

How can we tell when a particular form of a transference has run its course in an analysis? One sign of a depotentiated transference consists in recognizing that the energy that spearheaded the analytic push is spent. This does not mean that the analysis must stop at this point. In many cases, however, I have observed that this transference, through which narcissistic "faults" are restored, brings to a close that phase of analysis undertaken with that particular analyst. I think that most of those who leave analysis at this time, having gained access to psychic energy that nourishes the bond with the mother and animates the Self, want to keep the recovered image intact, even if they are ready to accept termination. Some will go no further in analysis; others will seek elsewhere and by other means the way of the father and an encounter with men.

Sometimes analysis continues with the same analyst, but with a displacement of energy to other forms of transference, after a break from analysis. In some instances, the patient expresses another need: "I would like to continue analysis, but in a different way."

It is not always possible to dissolve completely the narcissistic transference, but we can recognize its main components. We are dealing with the recognition of the self-image that is constituted in the eyes of the other. There may be a shift of the central image from the immersion in the bath to that of the King and the Queen facing each other, looking at one another in mutual recognition of differences and in an exchange of love.

At the beginning of an analysis, we are unable to know to what degree these narcissistic wounds can be healed. Jung reminded us that "Not everything can be healed, nor should everything be healed" (CW16, par. 463). Analysis may stop, at times tragically. As long as it continues, however, the hope that meaning will prevail over meaninglessness sustains the pursuit of the transference.

The essential quality that is most needed in these analyses is patience.

Translated from French
by Ronald Jalbert

REFERENCES

Grunberger, B. (1971). *Le Narcissisme*, Paris: Payot.

Schwartz-Salant, N. (1982). *Narcissism and Character Transformation*, Toronto: Inner City Books.

Response: Drowning in the Alchemical Bath

Guy Corneau
Outremont, Quebec, Canada
Inter-Regional Society
of Jungian Analysts

Being chosen as respondent for a paper at this prestigious conference flatters my narcissism. Unfortunately, as we say in English, "There is no such thing as a free lunch." And so I find myself faced with the task of producing some sensible reflections in order not to lose face before you. Lose face – that is, lose the reflection of my own idealized image in your eyes.

Genevieve Guy-Gillet's text presents us with several lines of thought; in them I discovered the author's creativity. At present I have in my practice several people who suffer from narcissistic wounding. They did not receive the "free lunch" of the first period of life. Several of them had taken their place at my table with voracious appetites.

One of them told me that, on the weekends, she had fantasies of eating my face and stomach to calm her anguish. Afterward she would beat me violently in order to get me out of her. Another such person saw himself eating the houses on the street in order to make for himself a normal inner family. A third person did not want to ingest anything I served her. She repeated to me many times that I told her only things she already knew and that I did not understand that she understood; this situation made her feel all the more misunderstood. She added that if I did not understand her it was because I disdained her.

Taking up the metaphor of the King and Queen in the Bath, I

cannot say that I was immersed in the waters of the alchemical bath with this third analysand. That would be a much too elegant way of describing my situation at that time. I was rather in the midst of drowning; I had sunk below the water line. I no longer saw my own reflection in the waters of the analytical pool. I had lost almost all sense of reflection.

My countertransference consisted in fighting against my analysand's transference. I felt like answering "Yes! That's it! You're right! I don't understand you and I disdain you! You bore me. I can't find anything wrong with you. Go see someone else."

I first read Guy-Gillet's paper just at this moment of my personal analytic and narcissistic adventure. Devoured by starving people, tired of being devoured, now it is I who devours the text. And miracle of all miracles, I immediately find in it my lost sense of direction; I gather courage from the text. I am so happy that someone is capable of recognizing forms in this tumult of raw archaic emotion that is drowning me. The paths Guy-Gillet follows thus appeared to me as so many life-buoys which helped me to lift my head out of the water and to breathe once again. I am grateful to her.

The first life-buoy that I grabbed hold of was called "the relational instinct." I am pleased to see Guy-Gillet remind us of Jung's words in reference to this instinct and that she places the task of narcissistic repair under this heading. Furthermore, she insists on the presence of a human tie in therapy. The matter is a simple one, but sometimes in conceptualizing these problems we emphasize too much Narcissus fascinated by his own image. We forget that, in these transferences, we are called upon not only to act as reflecting mirrors but also to be real people. Our capacity to have an authentic relationship is put to the test and our own frustrated relational needs are awakened by the needs of the other.

I grabbed hold of a second life-buoy. Guy-Gillet discusses the frequent activation of erotic desire that comes about in such transferences. I like the idea that someone finally allows herself to be moved by the fact that the image in the *Rosarium* of the philosophers shows the nudity of the King and the Queen and that this refers directly to sexuality. The author handles passionate experiences in therapy in an original way. She sees erotic desire as the motor of the venture of repair and also as the emergency brake for the regression to archaic dimensions of the wounded relational instinct. She helped me to understand those erotic fixations which at times become practically unshakeable. They serve as safety refuges for people faced with a horrifying past.

Guy-Gillet's warning not to take oneself for the King or Queen of the analysand's sexual desires reminded me of a romantic disillusionment I experienced when I realized one day in amazement the true nature of an analysand's desires. I responded to them with a countertransference equally marked by sexual drives. All of my interventions concerning an unresolved Oedipus complex missed the mark and were not confirmed by my analysand until one day I realized that it was her Self that she was projecting onto me and which she so ardently desired. I stood for her equilibrium and was the carrier of her illnesses as well as of her hidden treasures.

Thus, I was called upon to play a more important role than that of the handsome stallion; I was called upon to recognize the Self which organizes the therapeutic relationship, as Guy-Gillet puts it so well. From the moment that I realized this dimension and corrected my interpretations, everything seemed easier for my analysand; her anguish was calmed. For as much as she desired me, she also feared a sexual acting out on my part. She was afraid of losing me as the representative of her possible unity. In such a realization one rather becomes the servant of the King and one's narcissistic image suffers. All these experiences have to be lived and discovered as we go along; otherwise our analysands' desires for authentic relationship are not fulfilled.

Finally I caught hold of one more life-buoy. In her work with women Guy-Gillet shows us the image of an analyst battling with her analysands' archaic mothers, in a clinch with an inner mother who does not want to allow the Self to be constituted. I have spent a great deal of my time during the past years exploring the question of masculine identity. My book (1989) resulted from this work. In Guy-Gillet's conceptualization I have found the counterpart of what sometimes happens in narcissistic transferences from man to man.

In these cases, the subject is dealing with a tyrannical inner father whom one could describe as a Moses dictating his commandments from the top of the mountain and not permitting the analysand's Self to be constituted. The lack of a relationship with the personal father leads to the frustration of the relational need and does not permit the development of a positive father complex. The man fights against demands of perfection which suffocate him from the inside. He readily becomes the victim of conventional masculine stereotypes, for example, that we all have to be achievers to be real men. Guy-Gillet's paper helps me to understand the male version of the type of transference that she describes. For example, that the heroic over-adaptation of narcissistic people has to do not only with a deficiency in mothering, but also with a lack on the part of the father. The fight which then ensues is a fight with a primitive father who does not allow the subject's masculine identity to assert itself.

I thank Guy-Gillet for the timeliness of her paper. Not only was I able to draw courage from it, but I also was able to discover that for her the work of narcissistic repair is not confined to the surface.

Oral Presentation
Translated from French by Jan Bauer and Joanne Wieland-Burston

REFERENCES

Corneau, G. (1989). *Père Manquant, Fils Manqué: Que Sont les Hommes Devenus?* Montreal: Éditions de L'Homme.

Corneau, G. (1991). *Absent Fathers, Lost Sons.* Boston: Shambhala.

Finding Theory and Using It

Kurt Hoehfeld
Berlin, Germany
Deutsche Gesellschaft
für Analytische Psychologie

There are two reasons for my interest in the interrelation between theory and practice. The historical integration of our Berlin C.G. Jung Institute into a psychoanalytically-oriented comprehensive institute furnishes a "local" reason (see Von der Tann, 1989); the close cooperation with colleagues from another school requires exchange as well as delineation. It makes us Jungians ask ourselves: "What are we really doing?" – to use the title of a lecture by Plaut (1971).

A more general reason for my interest is the fact that, in the Federal Republic of Germany, analytic treatment is financed by health insurance. Thus, in Germany more than elsewhere, applied Analytical Psychology must take into account the aspect of rehabilitation; this fact affects our clinical orientation and requires accountability for our therapeutic activity.

In the interrelation between theory and practice, practice has a double function. It fosters the formation of new theories and it is the criterion testing the truth of a theory.

The dimensions of time and space enter into the theory of psychotherapy. With regard to time, the orientation of practice toward the future supplements the reconstructive quality which is oriented toward the past. Space is an element in the analytic setting; my willingness, knowledge, experience, and abilities form a space and a background for my analysands. I listen with sympathy and share their experience. The analytic setting becomes a stage, a space of mutual experience which makes it possible for my analysands to communicate and to act and react.

Alternating with the role I have described, I am also an observer and spectator. The word "theoria" is the Latinized form of the Greek word "theoros," the one who watches a spectacle – from "thea" (spectacle) and "horaein" (to watch). The term "finding theory," in my title means the formation of imaginative ideas, fantasies, hypotheses, and models from the behavior and the communications of analysands.

The finding of theory is a slow process of discovery. Rapaport (1973) said that the human gift for making discoveries consists of isolated events, each of them needing a long preparation, because the form of a thought has to meet with the corresponding form of nature and such coincidences are rare. If the correspondence is not specific and exact, if the individual is not prepared to recognize it or is unwilling to make use of it, the moment will be gone. Thus, it is not only the creative idea, the imagination and the event which have a significance. It is also their subsequent shaping that is decisive.

The willingness to make use of a cognition was described by Robert Mayer, a German medical doctor, in an 1844 letter that Jung quoted (CW7, par. 106). In the middle of the last century, while Mayer was on a sea voyage as a ship's doctor, the idea of the conservation of energy came to him. Since Mayer did not have a physics background, Jung used Mayer's discovery as a piece of evidence for the thesis of the autonomy of archetypal ideas.

Every analyst is a discoverer in the sense of pursuing ideas and thus participating in the formation of theory. At the least, one can reach a novel formulation of already discovered theories. New discovery of theories includes finding something one was not seeking or combining theories that had not been connected before.

As an example of such a combination I begin with Jung's constructive treatment of the unconscious. In my practice it has become necessary to combine this approach with the relationship model of Psychoanalysis.

What is the purpose of neurotic suffering? This question was revolutionary when Jung began to ask it, out of observation of his analysands. His thesis is that suffering is the expression of a tendency of the contents of the unconscious to compensate the one-sidedness of consciousness; the result is a conflict. According to Jung this conflict is caused by a dissociation or splitting between the conscious and unconscious attitudes. This splitting is bridged by the "transcendent function."

Treatment requires a concentration on the affect whose energy becomes available by spontaneous productions of the unconscious. Jung called this approach "constructive." The term "constructive treatment" of the unconscious reaches its full technical and meta-theoretical significance when it focuses on future possibilities of development as well as on present disorders in adaptation. The term also developed out of Jung's intensified therapeutic emphasis on environment and reality.

The definition of neurosis changed, too; Jung described it as an insufficient adaptation and a one-sided consciousness. We could call it an ego-psychological point of view similar to one developed later by one branch of Psychoanalysis.

Jung's understanding of transference, too, changed through this new understanding of neurosis. Transference is no longer understood in a reductive way as an "erotic infantile fantasy" but it is a "metaphorical expression of the not consciously realized need for help in a crisis." Thus, Jung demanded, "Do not look for an understanding of transference in its historical prerequisites but in its purpose" (CW8, par. 146).

Dealing with the constructive treatment of the unconscious means dealing with the practical use of theory, too. I mainly understand by it the necessary activities of the analyst, which include more than interventions and interpretations. I shall concentrate on two models.

The first derives from the term "constructive treatment of the unconscious" and the technique of active imagination which Jung developed from it. He introduced this technique in 1929 in his lecture, "The Purpose of Psychotherapy" (CW16). Much more than in 1916, Jung now emphasized the analyst's active participation in the mutual process, with his or her own ideas and fantasies.

In my practice I normally use two corollaries of the constructive treatment of the unconscious: imaginative countertransference and an imaginative attitude. By imaginative countertransference I understand daydream-like fantasies which can arise spontaneously in moments of deep relaxation. I find that hearing voices in such situations does not occur as often as Jung found. Along with the visual fantasies I have also experienced psychosomatic and sometimes kinesthetic reactions. At the beginning of a new treatment or at the beginning of a session the images are brief and fleeting. But in the course of a treatment the imaginative fantasies often become clear, impressive and similar to a dream. Sometimes they have a constructive diagnostic value.

I distinguish this imaginative countertransference from a more passive attitude toward the central image offered by the analysand. My imaginative attitude has a constructive effect in fostering empathy and stimulating unconscious possibilities of development.

In this psychoanalytic model the activity of the analyst aims at turning an intrapsychic conflict into an interpersonal one. The common aim of analyst and analysand is the "actualisation of the transference conflict" (Morgenthaler, 1978, p. 58). The analysand's fear of the conflict activates resistance – all that "in the activities and words of the analysand blocks the access to his or her unconscious" (Laplanche & Pontalis, 1973, p. 622).

An exclusive use of the constructive treatment of the unconscious seems to be justified when problems of autonomy and individuation are the main issue or, as Jung wrote, when the one-sidedness of consciousness needs to be compensated by the transcendent function. It seems wrong and short-sighted to use the constructive treatment when we work on forms of negative transference or conflicts in the transference which Psychoanalysis calls transference resistance. In such cases the use of the relationship and the conflict model seems to be appropriate.

In my experience relationship problems that must be worked through constructively or reconstructively, are always closely linked or alternate with each other. I think, therefore, that an appropriate combination of both models is recommended, taking the specific case into account. With some case examples, I shall show how I use Jung's model of the constructive treatment of the unconscious.

Case Examples

First is an example of imaginative countertransference: a 32-year-old analysand whom I have treated once a week in a sitting position. Her mother had a miscarriage between her own birth and the birth of her brother nine years later. Also, her mother had had another daughter six years before my analysand was born, but this daughter suffocated, for unknown reasons, at the age of two months.

During one session I am becoming very tired; I have difficulty in maintaining a sense of connection to the analysand. Suddenly the image of a black kitchen knife arises in my mind. The analysand falls silent, then talks about her current fantasies. She experiences fantasies of killing that are aimed at her boy friend, who had left her. It is disturbing and threatening for her that she experiences no distinction between her fantasies and their realization. She remembers that she once had such fantasies toward me; they had worried her a great deal but she had not told me. I am feeling the strangeness of her condition. It occurs to me that a short time earlier I had unsuccessfully encouraged her to lie down. I am surprised that my memory of her refusal coincides with my imaginal fantasy. I say, "I think you are afraid of being murdered if you lie down." To my surprise she answers, laughing: "It's top-secret, something you are not allowed to say. I don't know why, either. But now it has become unrealistic."

In the following sessions our relationship intensified. Repressed conflicts with the mother came up. The analysand did not want to establish a relationship, either to her actual mother or to the inner image of her. A short time later she dreamed the beginning of a lesbian relationship, evidently as an expression of a positive approach toward the image of the mother. Only because of the mainly positive transference and resilient working alliance is it possible for my analysand – who is often rigid and unrelated to experience her splitting tendencies into bad boy friend/good analyst and her destructive murderous impulses. Up to the present all her fantasies had been sadistic and masochistic. In the analytic situation I have described, her contact with reality was at least partly dissolved, as happens in borderline structures.

My spontaneous imaginative fantasy may appear a little schizoid or concretizing. Experienced even before the analysand communicated her aggressive fantasies, it enabled me to look inside the sado-masochistic father-daughter relationship whose roots had not been clear. When I asked her to lie down it was an expression of my unconscious tendency to get rid of the paralyzing closeness so that I could work better. The imaginative fantasy of the black kitchen knife was a compromise between my inhibited countertransference aggression and the projective identification with the aggression of the analysand. That situation led to the relatively quick interpretation of the anxiety which underlay her aggressive fantasies.

I could make this interpretation of her anxieties because of my positive countertransference and a good contact; the analysand felt that she was understood. Through the experience we had shared, the conflict had been successfully resolved. The possible increase of a transference resistance had been avoided and its root could be integrated. This case illustrates the necessity of combining work on the relationship conflict with the use of imaginative countertransference.

The imaginative attitude responds to the central image offered by the analysand. By central image I mean the initial dream, an essential recurrent fantasy, a significant metaphor, or a memory. Through the imaginative attitude this image supplies a point of reference which lies outside the actual process and to which we come back time and again during the analysis. Such an attitude developed in connection with the initial dream of 32-year-old student, Andreas:

> *Together with some others I am walking through a jungle. I guess it is South America. We are coming higher and higher and can already see the beautiful promised land. But first we have to pass through a cavern. We are moving backward, it is very narrow, I think I even had to be dragged through by my hips.*

This dream from one of the first sessions was followed by a dream in the 17th session:

> *I saw a pass somehow from above, I think I was floating above it. I knew this pass, I think it was in France. It was snow-covered, it was not passable at this moment but the most important thing for me was: the road is still there!*

The motif of the pass recurred in a dream from the 180th session:

> *I was on a pass, the scenery was rugged, woods and meadows all around, the colors were blue and green. The road was broad, I think it was in Alaska. I leave my car, I can't go on. My sister is skiing, going higher.*

The dream broke off and I encouraged the dreamer to do active imagination, thinking that he might succeed in getting over the pass on foot. But he could not do that in his fantasy. It was only later that I understood my failure. During the following sessions he reacted with dreams whose contents seemed psychotic.

A short time later he expressed for the first time his wish to get out of his masochistic impotence fantasies. He then had a dream in which a man preached in a church. This man was a well-known figure in the religious history of my analysand's home country. In contrast to a similar dream three months earlier, the church did not cave in nor was there a big flood by tidal wave. In the 188th session he had a dream that contained the solution of his problems regarding the mountain pass:

I was in Colorado, there was a train on a pass, going full speed down to the valley. The train was very modern. I was in the dining car with my girl friend and her mother. I looked out of the window. I saw castles outside, and one below me, down in the valley. With admiration my girl friend's mother said to a third person: "It's amazing what he can see!"

In the subsequent time period a great deal of water appeared in his dreams and the landscape became flatter. Instead of the group in his initial dream he was now traveling with one friend. About the 240th session, near the end of the analysis and before his mother (who had come to visit him) left, he dreamed:

I am in a cavern. Inside there is warm water, a well. I can swim very easily. I let myself be carried out by the current.
My stepfather is swimming in front of me. Then I land on an embankment.

Without my being sufficiently aware of it, from the beginning the motif of the pass had been for me a leading theme in this analysis. Presumably it was the good end that had been anticipated by the analysand himself in his initial dream and which helped me to accompany this analysis in a helpful manner.

Seven years after the end of the analysis I met Andreas by chance. To my surprise he considered his analysis, in retrospect, as being more successful than I had believed.

Another case example shows how the constructive and the reconstructive approach overlap and why their combined use seems to be necessary. The analysand quickly developed a father or brother transference, characterized by his Oedipal feelings of rivalry. At our first meeting, for example, he sat on my chair.

The father or brother transference also referred to a woman colleague of mine, of whose family the analysand was a friend. His wish to feel relaxed was disturbed by the analysand's strong feelings of competition and envy which interfered with the success of our work.

Along with this partly disturbing therapeutic reaction he showed the following clinical symptoms: dysfunction at work, depression, an almost paranoid jealousy of his girl friend with whom he lived, and a fear of traveling through East Germany. At the same time he liked to make long journeys; there soon developed a disagreement about how to deal with cancellations of sessions.

Physically he suffered from recurrent hemorrhoidal bleeding, apparent swelling of the mucous membranes, and tenseness of the muscles, all of which kept him, at times, from leaving his bed. He was compulsive but experienced this characteristic as ego-syntonic, not as a symptom.

His girl friend had had an analysis some years before; its success had helped motivate him to look for a therapist. From his studies of philosophy he had some theoretical knowledge. With this background he tended to an intellectualizing and rationalizing defense which, to my surprise, he could drop from time to time as if he wanted to assure himself of our undisturbed cooperation.

My strongest countertransference feeling was that I liked him somehow. At the same time I often had a feeling of incompetence toward him. I experienced him as a special analysand; it was quite late in the analysis that I realized that this feeling may have been connected with my omnipotence fantasies. Their countertransference nature had remained unconscious and presumably caused my poor application of active imagination. These difficulties made way for an explosion of his omnipotence fantasies, marking a culmination point in his analysis.

Just as in crossing a real pass, from that point on the analysis went down again, toward the sea. Thus, he reached his "promised land." In the end he gained a new relationship to his actual mother through a fantasy of symbolic birth and rebirth.

Critique and Conclusion

The clinical material illustrates my thesis that only the combination of constructive and reconstructive approaches results in appropriate analytic treatment. I turn now to some theoretical statements that apply to both models and to the understanding of neurosis.

In the center is the conflict which the ego must manage outside, in the environment; and inside, in the unconscious. According to Jung, successful dealing with the outer world results in an adaptation of the ego, which corresponds to the Freudian "reality competence of the ego." In Analytical Psychology the inner conflict is caused by the prospective tendency of the unconscious – the principle of individuation. Psychoanalysis speaks of a conflict of the ego with the needs of the id and the demands of the superego. The results of the ego's successful dealing with the demands of the inner world are known as the autonomous development of the personality or individuation in Jungian psychology, and as the well-known capacity to work and to love in the Freudian school.

From Freud's point of view the neurosis, as a result of the ego's inability to cope with conflicts, is the expression of intrapsychic dynamics whose play of powers is determined by repression; it became the main content of his observations and the starting point of analysis.

Jung's definition of neurosis as poor adaptation and one-sidedness of consciousness or as dissociation of the personality seems static to me. The dynamic Jungian view lies in the concept of the compensatory or complementary function of the unconscious, which led to the concept of finality, formulated in "The Transcendent Function" (CW16). Freud, however, denied the existence of the prospective tendency of the unconscious. This difference between Jung's view and Freud's is understandable from their varying theoretical views, which I have mentioned.

Both approaches focus on the conflict, while the ways of treatment differ. In Psychoanalysis the affect serves as an organizational core for the transfer of the intrapsychic conflict to an interpersonal one, which – in the form of a transference neurosis – becomes available for analysis. In Analytical Psychology Jung proposed to transfer the energy of the affect to the active experiment of an encounter with the Self. He developed this procedure mainly from his own experience with encountering the Self. As I read the relevant passages (CW16, par. 167) it was not clear to me whether Jung described an actual therapy situation. I was not surprised that Jung discarded free association at that point; an analytic process needs a dialogue partner who creates an atmosphere of constant attention.

In the modern definition of Psychoanalysis the contrast that I had assumed between the "active" Jung and the "passive" Freud does not exist. Beyond the adherence to different schools, analytic practice is characterized by a focal principle and, as Meltzer put it, "The analyst is the chairman in the unfolding of the process" (1988, p. 211).

The analyst's performance as chairperson depends on presuppositions. This is especially true for the founders of schools; in the face of similar clinical findings they came to different theoretical judgements and as a result to different practical consequences.

No matter which approach is applied, however, there are certain preconditions that are necessary for a successful analytic treatment. These are:

1. Positive transference of analysand on procedure and analyst;

2. A special clientele. Jung described his clientele of 1929: two-thirds were in the second half of life, one third did not suffer from a neurosis which could be classified clinically, there were hardly any acute cases, many of his analysands had undergone previous therapies. The majority of them were Protestants who had become estranged from their churches; only a few were Jews or practicing Catholics. Most of Jung's analysands were socially adapted and, in their daily life, very efficient.

From the latest developments in the psychology of neurosis today we would speak of character neuroses, narcissistic neuroses and compulsive structures. Particularly with this clientele Jung could do without a determined observance of the transference resistance in favor of the constructive method of treatment or of active imagination. He could not be blamed for using a purely suggestive way of overcoming the resistance. But it would be short-sighted to use constructive treatment or active imagination apart from the conditions mentioned.

To judge Jung's practice we also need to clarify to what degree the theorist Jung and the practitioner Jung differ from each other. I find that the practitioner is sometimes much ahead of the theorist.

Translated from German
by Sabine Osvatic

REFERENCES

Laplanche, J. & Pontalis, J.-B. (1973). *Das Vokabular der Psychoanalyse*, Zweiter Band. Frankfurt am Main: Suhrkamp.

Meltzer, D. (1988). *Traumleben: Eine Überprüfung der Psychoanalytischen Theorie und Technik.* Munich: Verlag Internationale Psychoanalyse.

Morgenthaler, F. (1978). *Technik: Zur Dialektik der Psychoanalytischen Praxis.* Frankfurt am Main: Syndikat Autoren und Verlagsgesellschaft.

Plaut, A. (1971). Was tun wir wirklich? Wir lernen aus Erfahrung! *Zeitschrift für Analytische Psychologie*, 2-4, 231-43.

Rapaport, D. (1973). *Die Struktur der Psychoanalytischen Theorie.* Stuttgart: Klett.

Von der Tann, M. (1989). A Jungian perspective on the Berlin Institute for Psychotherapy: A basis for mourning. *The San Francisco Institute Library Journal*, *8*-4, 43-73.

Response

Dirk Evers
Zurich, Switzerland
Schweizerische Gesellschaft
für Analytische Psychologie

Facts and theories are reciprocal contents that are reflected in the world, which is objective and at the same time interpreted. Theory, application and production are human approaches to the here and now of the human world. These approaches apply to observational sciences which are concerned with metaphysics, mathematics and logic; to applied sciences which are concerned with ethics and politics and to productive sciences such as economics and medicine.

The individual is required to engage in action and suffering to create a world out of his or her environment without surrendering to repressive patterns of thought or of values. Theories determine a formal structure which has pragmatic relevance. The attributing of transcendence to many-faceted theories is natural to the individual who does not experience the world as a given but as open to free application and production. True here is a quotation from the later works of the German poet Friedrich Hoelderlin: "Come into the open, friend."

Experience as a Guide to Knowledge

Science becomes practical as an opening of the life-space, either as systematic elucidation in the natural sciences or as structural elucidation in the humanities. In both cases it is neither a matter of mere reproduction of something given nor of abstract speculations. Rather, it is a matter of understanding what I have experienced, and experience is possible only when the body is involved. This concept of experience differs from the ideological dogma of having already experienced everything. Such a dogma becomes institutionalized, creating repressive-hierarchic structures of inhumane destructiveness. Experience guides knowledge only if it is able to lead to further experience. Experience is the essential instrument in self-understanding. Therefore, science is non-existent except as it throws light on experience.

Transference and Individuation

The individual's self-understanding results from analysis, which clarifies one's entanglement in oneself and the self-hindrances of the Oedipal drama. The powerful play of images initiates a process that frees the individual through an experience of the Self, of being oneself. Thus, analysis activates the Self's imaginative and creative powers. The healing of the Self and the healing Self mirror each other.

I and You

Analysis is a special case of a relationship which is directed toward wholeness; it is a reflected experience of the you. The I and the you are poles of a transcendent unit whose nature, according to Jung, can be comprehended only symbolically. In "The Psychology of the Transference" (CW16) Jung pointed out that such a transcendent unit does not mean identification of two individuals. Identification would be a symbiosis and therefore not transcendence. By withdrawing projection, an intrapsychic process occurs that lets us experience wholeness through the relatedness of one individual to another. Human relatedness is a condition that makes wholeness and transcendence possible. Thus, I and you, I and the Self, I and the world, the individual and God experience a transcendental freedom through which wholeness occurs as a practical utopia. In this process of self-understanding, everything has to do with everything. The necessity of this process includes the possibility of self-destruction. Theory, application and production reflect each other, in Jung's view, in such a way that we can see ourselves as instruments and witnesses of the work of cosmic love.

Translated from German by Sabine Osvatic

Dream Psychology
and Jungian Clinical Attitude

Federico De Luca Comandini
Rome, Italy
Associazione Italiana per lo Studio della Psicologia Analitica

A young man is lounging on a boat, basking in the warm Caribbean sun. It is a clear day and the sea is perfectly still. Suddenly a wave throws him off the boat and pushes him underwater, where he finds himself face to face with an octopus, staring at him across a desk. The octopus' expression is insistent and demanding, and seems to be saying: "Either you change, or I'll destroy you."

This is the dream that a man in his late twenties took to his first analytic session. His problems were intertwined with a drug addiction that he could not break, and with a rebellious attitude against his father, a businessman identified with the idea of success. The dreamer was trapped in a conflict of values.

These few details are all we know about the dreamer. Nevertheless, in view of its archetypal potential, the dream serves as an imaginal stimulus for what I have to say. The dreamer had sought out Zurich analyst Marie-Louise von Franz. She referred him to a colleague but gave me permission to mention this dream here and in another paper (1988).

The beginning of the dream seems to be a response to the need to relax and rediscover the natural rhythm of the psyche: within ourselves in feelings, and outside as harmony with the environment. To all appearances, the young dreamer is in an ideal situation, one that most of us have desired at one time or another. Warm tropical seas, the sun and snowy mountain peaks stand as mirages of ecstasy and escapes from the frustration and stress of city life. Yet the dream follows a stereotypic sort of representation; one can day-dream about this desire without having to use imagination, just as it can be bought in any travel agency or passively absorbed from a television commercial.

But we must realize that the stereotype of desire makes no distinction between managers and drop-outs, between upright citizens and rebels, or between the dreamer and his father. Collective consciousness sees pleasure as being only material and concrete. Missing is an active fantasy of Eros and a feeling for its value.

What happens in a situation like this? The young man is hurled out of his artificial paradise and finds himself underwater where an unnerving vision awaits him. His rejecting the dominant values of a culture exposes him to the risk of being overcome by the dark side of existence itself.

If one is completely absorbed, as is the case with drug dependency, the confused need for Eros gives way to the pleasure of obliterating oneself and the world. Thus the attitude of the rebel son prefigures the unconscious self-destruction of the well-adjusted father. This is a sinister metaphor for the state of Western people.

But now in the objective depths of the psyche an image breaks through. There are many stories of the presence of a mysterious octopus under water, but the image of this octopus seated at a desk is something new indeed. Polynesian myths associate the octopus with the creation of the world, and ancient Greek writers Plutarch and Aelian used it as a model of intelligence. The French writer Victor Hugo, drawing on the frightening aspects of medieval lore, attributed obscure metaphysical qualities to the octopus. In the light of all these imaginal precedents, the desk may have a legitimate place here. But none of this takes away from the astonishing, synthetic and essential quality of the image, supported as it is – thank goodness – by a generous dose of humor. None of us would want to underestimate the danger of the ultimatum that is delivered here, but the humorous element lightens the archetypal tension.

But we ask ourselves: What change is called for? Who is it that calls for the change? The question of the drug dependency comes to the fore. The dreamer can fool himself no longer: heroin is the octopus, which sucks him in with a force greater than anything the ego can imagine. The dreamer is forced to assume responsibility. Over and above the warning that is given, this unusual desk behind which the octopus is seated points to the need for the young man to take a hard look at his motives: the anesthetic use of pleasure and the necessity for him to respond with depth of meaning to this driven need of his. It is not enough simply to avoid whatever he is seeking through drugs. He must meet the need actively in a creative effort.

The desk is the place where the symbol is at work. Here the personal drama of the dreamer opens to the archetypal dimension. His self-destructive flight has brought him face to face with the Great Missing One: that element that is not to be found if the alternatives are simply duty versus pleasure, or work versus leisure. The Great Missing One is not pleasure as a concrete content nor is it affective gratification as reward, nor sexual release as a form of hygiene. The Great Missing One is the spirit of all these things. It is the Spirit of Eros as feeling for relationship; and as the criterion of an intelligence less split apart between giving and receiving, between the means and the end, and between reason and instinct.

The many arms of the octopus, arranged around a central eye, point to the link between the opposites within the vision of togetherness. Aristotle coined the expression *poluplokon noema*, the multi-modal intelligence of the octopus.

Our modern fear of being sucked in by the octopus is really our lack of psychological preparation in the face of the subtleties of Eros. Behind the monster stands an animated being capable of arousing potentialities close to its own nature, rich in polymorphic and polychromatic transformations. In ancient times, this archaic symbol served as a bridge between the human spirit and the totality of the Anima Mundi (soul of the world) – a bridge that is in the shadow of our modern conscious orientation. In the dream, the octopus sets foot on that bridge again, proposing once more –

in modern dress – the archetypal reappearance of the Spirit of Eros as the fundamental question of our time. This symbolic perspective is at the root of everything we have to say here.

In the language of the dream, let us imagine ourselves seated at that desk. Here the psychology of Jung, which is connected so intimately with the creative factor of Eros, occupies an important place. Beginning my paper with a dream acknowledges the dimension within which Jung carried out his work. By keeping the dream in the center, reason can educate itself to see its processes and conclusions as relative. At the same time reason is stimulated because the inexplicable opens new possibilities of understanding.

When the dream is no longer reduced to an object, Eros becomes an active part of the very act of understanding; it develops its own logos, its own way of reasoning. The novelty of such a psychological attitude is that it connects the search for meaning to the spiritual possibilities of Eros. The development of this openness in consciousness is a necessity of our age. Jung testified to this necessity, but we are far from understanding all the cultural implications contained in his work. The originality of our Jungian work is in the relationship with the dream; this is the humus where the connection of meaning and Eros can sink roots. In order to deepen our psychological identity, it is indispensable for us to orient our reflections around the dream again.

I am hesitant about re-proposing here a perspective that is basic. And yet work on the dream is the original arena for a relationship with the unconscious. We cannot avoid going back there to reformulate our point of view. Rational and technical models have shown themselves to be psychologically sterile. Hence, I return to the dream to show how the Jungian connection with it picks up the new contents that are emerging into the collective psyche: the space where an archetypal advent is taking shape, the gateway by which the function of Eros is permeating the spirit of our age.

In placing such great emphasis on the dream, I want it to be clear that I am against any sort of ideological simplification and that I have no intention of reducing the psychology of Jung exclusively to the archetypal perspective of Eros. I find that Jung's attitude toward the problem of truth is an effective vaccine against any such reduction. Even if I place my emphasis on the richness of dream work, I do not mean to neglect the creative complexity of Jung's work nor the various registers in which it can be understood.

Thus, by seeing the spiritual dimension of Eros as the backdrop, we emphasize also the mythical depth of Jungian psychology. This emphasis must not be confused with attempts to make a myth out of Jung himself. We want to examine here the psychological approach that unfolded as he went about his work and how it responds to a central archetypal necessity of our age.

Now to the question at hand: In what sense does Jungian dream analysis define a new psychic relationship? Jung was not the only one who paid attention to dreams. Following Freud, schools of depth psychology have variously considered dreams, but what interests us here is something deeper. The Jungian approach to the dream does not treat the dream as an instrument, a means to get somewhere else. Nor do we presume that behind the dream is a plot that must be explained. Jungian psychology recognizes the reality of the psyche in the dream. Thus, confronting the unconscious is not just a question of solving enigmas but rather one of staying close to the mysterious source of knowledge from which dreams naturally flow. Hence, rather than being a tool for therapy, dreams are the sense and meaning of it.

We can find evidence of this view in the testimony we have of Jung's analytic work more than in his more general essays and studies. Take, for example, the dream seminars held in Zurich at the end of 1920s (Jung, 1984). Let us examine the various details as we might do with an artist; it would be completely out of place to ask for an explanation of everything he or she did in terms of the general motif being applied. If we look at the dream work from the bottom up, we avoid getting stuck in the airy world of theories and we can ask simply: "What happens when one does this or that? What is it that we are making space for? What comes into our thinking mind?" These questions come from a perspective that is suited to the psyche.

A relationship develops around a well-defined center; the analysand and the analyst follow the thread of the dreams – from the beginning, when we are gathering background information and establishing the basis for the human relationship. As the new analysand tells his or her story, attention to the dreams creates a middle ground: between what the analysand confesses and what is proposed by the psyche, between the life story that is told and the dream. Stereotypes are depotentiated; for example, the passivity of the analysand and the power role of the analyst. A common substance takes shape as the basic element of psychological communication.

The orientation of the dreams helps us avoid getting bogged down in the complexes of the analysand and protects the authentic thrust from the unconscious toward development. A careful following of the priorities of the dreams takes us beyond the complex. The dream does not simply take a snapshot of the complex; it also indicates the pregnant aspects of it that must be taken into consideration. As Jung (1984) stressed, dreams have a guiding function and should be seen as attempts at a solution of a problem. The analytic relationship is entrusted principally to the dreams, for they lead the ego elements of the analytic couple toward flexibility, receptivity and reflective introversion. The analysand will learn to recognize the plurality of souls within, tempering with patience the feeling of urgency. The analyst will circumscribe his or her intervention in the life of the other, thanks to the thread of dreams.

What comes to mind immediately is the objection that each of us probably has heard many times: Does Jungian analysis pay attention only to dreams? What happens when there aren't any? There are many elements that make up the psychological process and that require time and accessibility if they are to be assimilated. Dreams give us the symbolic frame for the relationship. No matter how few dreams there may be, only rarely do they cease to be remembered altogether. Usually if the right importance is attributed to the dreams, they enter frequently into the process. In those rare cases where there is very little dream material, it is best to give value even to the smallest dream details.

I remember a man who, for the first two years of his analysis, managed to remember only one fragment of a dream: *an image of himself, holding a suitcase*. We kept that image alive and it became a frequent point of reference. Eventually, he remembered a dream: *He was at home, involved in a new activity – painting. On the wall there were various portraits which showed details of his life. Open on top of a wardrobe was the suitcase from the first dream fragment*. The introverted reflection which this man so desperately needed was now mature. The image had been able to contain the tension over a long period of time.

By staying with a single detail or the path of a series of dreams, the Jungian approach distinguishes itself by its faithfulness to the expressions of the dreams. It returns again and again to the scene presented, without setting off on a search for meaning independent of the dreams. Analysis seeks to achieve the consciousness that is within the language of the psyche. It trains us to assume the perspective of the unconscious. By observing a series of dreams as they move, by assonance and dissonance, from one theme to another, we can see the maturation of the complexes within the dynamic of the psyche. We can begin to discern a rhythm that oscillates between big and small motifs, between observations of a general nature and personal elements. Psychic reflection requires us to be in tune with this rhythm. From the dark beginning, the orientation of the Self comes to bear on the process. In keeping with this spirit the Jungian approach sees every dream situation as entirely new. The image of analysis that emerges is one of an encounter and a clash between realities that are different but support one another and which, rather than contradicting each other, are involved in a kind of heroic *agon*. On the one hand the dream, as Jung (1984) wrote, "walks in like an animal.... I may be sitting in the woods and the deer appears" (p. 21). On the other hand, there is the need for us to enter into a relationship with this event. As the image says, the sudden appearance of the deer touches us and gets the hypothesis of meaning moving, but it also remains a fugitive. In this elusive space of impressions that cannot be pinned down, we find our chance to dip into the message of the unconscious. We should not forget that, for Jung, this message is the principal aim of analytic treatment.

How can the experiencing of this message be made possible? What is the spiritual attitude that is open to receiving it? The deer confronts us with the irrationality of nature. If the intellect can sacrifice its desire to understand conceptually, the psyche is not violated but is brought face to face with the need to reason. Thus, in a disenchanted way, "from step to step ... from fact to fact ... the irrational sequence is to be understood as a causal sequence" (Jung, 1984, p.132). The convergence of these sequences, which we are accustomed to experiencing as opposites, is indeed paradoxical. But, as Jung (1984) reminds us, "When we think of the unconscious, we must think paradoxically" (p.672). It is just this paradox that moves along in the space between the "two ways of thinking" (CW5). The irrational sequence does not explain the causal but draws reflections from it; the causal recomposes everything into new images. The metaphor of relationship is not a conquest but rather a junction and meeting point.

In this view, Jungian psychology is different from other psychologies, for it treats the problem of meaning with Eros. And Eros guides the meaningful message of the unconscious. As spirit, it includes both logical connections and the irrational experience of meaning. It incorporates the reasoning process with all those sensations and intuitions by which the psyche comprehends. It unites our efforts to understand with the mysterious fact that we are understood, that from the center of the unconscious personality a sense of meaning comes to us.

Eros is then the mediator between the archetypal background and the personal dimension or, as in the ancient world, between the divine and the human; it is the messenger that is necessary for the orientation of the individual. The Jungian attitude toward dreams unblocks the spiritual potentialities of Eros and allows for its function to become truly psychological.

Thus, Eros is connected with relationship, with the complexity of a bond, with the subtleties of mutual influence. It seeks to elaborate the model of a broader kind of intelligence, rooted in the psyche and in the depths of instinct.

Our task is to continue to enlarge Jung's perspective, thus meeting the demands of our times. This perspective is essential for therapy and for human relationships. It is important for us to clarify for our culture the fact that Eros is the basis of intelligence, that it is not some dark object of desire but the very compass of our subjectivity: "The creator mother-father of every higher consciousness," as Jung said (MDR, p. 325). We experience Eros psychologically in dream analysis when it activates the symbolic message and gives a synthetic expression of intelligence to the ambivalence of the psyche.

Collective consciousness confuses Eros with the inclinations of the instincts. Philosophical tradition has relegated it to the place of an obscure dynamic of knowledge. The shadow of disorder has been projected onto Eros. At the beginning, creative chaos was its twin brother/sister, but Eros has become above all the image of a chaotic undercurrent of desire. It is seen as something to be contained, not the great container. Our civilization sees itself in contrast with Eros and does not know how to experience it as a value. Jung helped us to understand how, on the mythical plane, all this is the sign of a split in the Christian divinity which, by being identified with the *summum bonum*, sees the essential traits of the spirit of Eros as being related to the negative principle of evil.

But as long as disorder is projected onto Eros, consciousness will be obsessed with order. The computer has become the new Golden Calf. We have reached the point of inflation, with all the threatening overtones that term implies. The fundamental merit of Jung rests in the fact that he interpreted our need to turn around our way of perceiving Eros: he presented it as an element of order. This, it seems to me, is the great enantiodromia of Analytical Psychology. Jung understood that Eros is orientation for consciousness and he made this understandable. He also understood that in the face of the split which the collective psyche faces, the spiritual attitude of Eros is indispensable for a greater and more deeply felt sense of order. But we promised at the beginning not to get carried away, not to fly too high. "We must cultivate our garden," Voltaire's character Candide would say.

Let us get back to the analytic relationship. We must ask ourselves how this new orientation can be seen in the practical side of the psychological relationship. How does it change the style of our present attitude? Reflecting on Jung's style but also on what happens today to all of us, I find that the intelligence of Eros expresses itself essentially in depth of feeling. This explanation needs to be developed and examined more closely, but it is a good starting point. Jungian analysis helps the growth of feeling, a growth necessary for the collective psyche because of the way feeling has been twisted in the course of Western history. This twisting is something that concerns everyone, even those who have differentiated feeling. Psychological Eros is not monochord; it touches all the functions of consciousness, making itself felt according to each individual's personal equation. But in the totality of the personality, Eros gives depth and lucidity to feeling. We can see this relatedness more clearly by reflecting on the analytic setting and the transference.

The ordered structure of the analytic setting enables us to get into the subject at hand. From the Jungian point of view, the problem of setting is a false problem. Jung tended to downplay the various details and arrangements of his sessions, thanks to the trust he had in the relationship itself. The relationship is not just a personal factor but rather a psychological force which is central to the Jungian approach.

If the intelligence of Eros and the prudence of feeling are strong enough, there is no need to insist on rules. One need not be a giant to walk this path; it is enough to be an honest pioneer. What is true of any working relationship is true of psychotherapy. We need some agreement about collective necessities such as time and money. But beyond those the Jungian approach is flexible. We follow a general procedure as long as that proves useful, but we are open to individual adaptations. Jung altered the frequency of sessions, depending on the person and the life that person was living. There is no generalized technique just as there is no one theory. We recognize the centrality of the unconscious by basing analytic work on dream analysis.

There is much talk currently about the therapeutic contract, a prosaic term coined in a psychological school other than our own. I find that it takes its toll in terms of feeling. From the Jungian point of view, the psychological relationship is a unique fact that needs no other container than its own imaginal and human sphere. Keeping this sphere in tune with the rhythm of the psyche by means of dream analysis, we can meet its shifts and swings without being heavy-handed. A certain amount of flexibility stimulates the relationship to greater maturity and responsibility.

In contrast, when the relationship is bridled by rules and contracts, it remains infantile and dependent. For Jung, the uniqueness of the human encounter was the fundamental value, and no presumed technique could betray it. This value again is the perspective of Eros in the psychological relationship. If Eros is taken seriously, one moves away or draws closer as two movements of the same organic process. Personal conflict finds a bridge toward the archetypal matrix. We can experience passion or rage or disappointment without running away because there is a common base to stand on and not simply because some analytic cage opposes resistance. As the thread of the dreams unravels, it is preferable that there be fewer and fewer rules around it. The person who feels free nowhere else should at least have that freedom when the work at hand is the deepening of oneself. Therefore Jungian analysis is not defined by the setting. If we must use that term, the dreams are our setting.

Now let us turn our attention to the transference, the crux of the psychological relationship; we have an obligation to define clearly our attitude toward it. When Jung said that it was "the alpha and omega of the analytical method" (CW16 par. 358), he seemed to mean that the transference was everything. But its being everything takes it beyond all our efforts at understanding. The analytic method is contained by the transference and cannot, for even one moment, contain it. Rational approaches and outlines which try to describe it lose touch with the psychic meaning of the relationship, like trying to capture the sense of music by taking a snapshot of an orchestra. We have to resign ourselves to not understanding, at least not in logical terms. How then are we to keep our bearings?

Jung wisely chose to deal with the transference in an imaginal way, on two levels, viewing the analytic event as a parallel to the alchemical *coniunctio*. Thus, he revealed the sense of spiritual creation that is linked to Eros. The archetypal character of the psychological relationship becomes apparent. The alchemical parallel, which seemed so obscure when Jung introduced it, has begun to come clear. What many once considered abstruse holds great significance today on a wider cultural level.

Analysis conserves its secret which, in the relationship, gradually moves toward fullness and maturity. That secret is the creation of an individual sense of meaning, a new dimension for consciousness in that it has rhythms and modalities that are different from the various types of pressure that the collective exerts. Psychological work on dreams educates the perspective of the individual, bestowing ethical substance which encourages the person to formulate the unique meaning of his or her life.

The Jungian attitude, by carefully marking off this space and not rationalizing the transference, protects the new king from the onslaughts of the old one. Here the psychological culture of Eros unfolds, freeing the personal spirit. Flexibility, personal judgment and evaluation, the courage to contradict oneself, the unique and original bond between one person and another – all these take on meaning within the sphere of Eros. Jungian analysis makes it possible to overcome the many prejudices that can undermine our faith in the analytic relationship. Jung was very direct. Even in the face of the most awkward questions, he responded in a genuine way to the authentic personality of the other person. Similarly, if his interpretation did not meet with a feeling response on the part of the patient, he did not insist. He did not become rigid in the face of the embarrassment that comes from undifferentiated feeling. Such embarrassment can result in resentment-filled thoughts which often disguise the inadequacy of our erotic intelligence and our difficulty in feeling.

There is no need, in analysis, for all our responses to be perfect. On the contrary, it is only natural that the shadow should become evident in the relationship. At times our dreams invite us to recognize and declare the shadow openly; this openness bears positively on the relationship. Thus, the psyche can digest what stands in the way of trusting the relationship. In this way the Jungian approach lives the transference from the perspective of feeling.

But let there be no confusion; the result is not some sort of generic goodness or tolerance. A subjective brand of intelligence gives order to that which escapes rational logic. Jung recognized an historical current of ideas that runs along the shadowy margins of the West. The reason of the heart follows another kind of logic and is of one nature with Eros. We can appreciate in it qualities that are connected with the feminine: a sense of the measure of things, of detail, of the personal, of what is more or less opportune, of the lightness of gestures and so many other shades of expression which patriarchal civilization has yet to find within itself. The psychological approach comes into tune once again with the potentialities that exist at the very roots of our collective personality. We need only think of that Greek idea of *metis* – a model of intelligence involved in all of the subtleties of life, which was represented in the mythical perspective of Hermes, in the herotype of Ulysses and in the natural cleverness of that octopus we saw at the outset.

I conclude with some observations on the expression "clinical," a key word in the title of this paper. I have not mentioned it thus far, saving it for these final reflections on the meaning of our commitment to Analytical Psychology. Just what do we want to say when we speak of "clinical work" or "clinical experience"?

In using this term we refer to the medical tradition; psychotherapy is one of the healing arts. In addition, "clinical" seems to give a guarantee of concreteness and objectivity, and of immunity to ideological contamination. These would be sacrosanct aspirations, if only they were adequate for singling out the specific nature of the psychological approach. Unfortunately, the matter is far more complex than that. We have to admit, with Jung, that "In order to get closer to the sphere of the psyche, the ideas derived from the sphere of medicine are not enough" (CW16, par. 84). What is clinical is not exempt from ideology; virtually everything reflects the culture of its time.

Today behind all that is clinical lies the scientific method that believes only in repeatable and verifiable facts. But this attitude is unsuitable for the expression of psychic subjectivity and its uniqueness. The clinical case is something that is not communicable. When he was nearly 60, Jung remarked, "I have yet to come across a respectable specimen of neurosis of which one could give anything like an adequate description in a short lecture, to say nothing of all the therapeutic intricacies that are far from clear even to the shrewdest professional" (CW16, par. 84). He was not reflecting any personal shortcoming on his part. Psyche calls for its own approach and style of communication, which the clinical report does not capture. The root of the term "clinic" conjures up the image of lying in a state of infirmity. As a technique it is the art connected with infirmity. As an ill patient one entrusts oneself to the ability of the doctor.

In the background, however, there is another, less passive experience: the experience of incubation, of self-healing. Kerenyi (1959) wrote that going into the temple of Asklepios "was no visit to a doctor who simply administers medicine; it was an encounter with the naked immediate event of healing itself" (p. 34). The relationship with the unconscious, at least in the Jungian sense, dips down into these pre-technical depths. It reaches for the psychic basis of healing and reactivates the archetype of healing. This process is indispensable for psychological therapy and enlightening for medicine in general – a pressing necessity for our times when the psyche is so stressed that it does not allow itself to lie back passively. With its understanding of self-healing, the Jungian approach holds great possibilities for broadening our clinical sense and renewing the symbolic profundity of it. Jung never failed to mention his training as a doctor. As such he carried out his personal enantiodromia, living the psyche as object and as the active subject in the coming to consciousness. In this experience rests the novelty of the psychology of the soul. Dream analysis is the Jungian clinic that cares for the instinctual basis of intelligence, because instinct has suffered at the hands of the sweeping rationality of the Western world.

Dreams illuminate human consciousness. This illumination is

basic and essential to the well-being of the individual who has been reduced to a neurotic social cog. The image of the Self is manifest in our times. The younger generations are more and more sensitive to this manifestation; their anti-authoritarian, anti-ideological thrust holds out prospects for and new demands on analysis. There is hope but also urgent need for more direct, natural, personal human relationships. This is the deep psychological need for new orienting values. Rational and technical schemes have very little to offer here, for the personal dimension belongs to Eros and requires feeling in order to become conscious.

Jungian dream work finds that symbolic space needed for the incubation of new forms of relationship. The middle road that was the original sense of the encounter with Asklepios stands between consciousness and the unconscious. But this is also the special realm of Eros who, at Epidaurus, is portrayed in an unusual and unique pose. Rather than brandishing his bow and arrow, he is shown playing the lyre. The force of this middle road, this symbolic mediator between the personal and the archetypal puts down its Apollonian bow in analysis too, in favor of a subtler spiritual function. In this spirit, the archetype of the anthropos moves away from social projections and toward the personal and individual consciousness. The link that I have proposed here connecting dreams, the psychology of Eros and the growth of feeling seems to be the perspective from which to view the change that is taking place, such that the individual can profit from the meaning and value of the analytic relationship.

Translated from Italian by
Roberto Mercurio

REFERENCES

De Luca Comandini, F. (1988). The octopus: Metamorphoses of an imaginal animal. *Spring: A Journal of Archetype and Culture*, 91-107.

Jung, C.G. (1984). *The Seminars*, Vol. 1: *Dream Analysis*. London: Routledge & Kegan Paul.

Kerenyi, C. (1959). *Asklepios*. New York: Pantheon. Bollingen Series 34.

The Abandonment Depression: Developmental and Alchemical Perspectives

Nathan Schwartz-Salant
New York, New York, USA
New York Association
for Analytical Psychology

Two qualities of consciousness inform our work as Jungian analysts. One quality allows us to experience events within a space-time matrix. Through this mode we are able to perceive separable, discrete events such as historical traumas and psychic objects. Another quality of consciousness allows us to comprehend events within a field characterized by a symbolic sense of oneness. Through it the parts we perceive in the space-time mode become part of an imaginal world of mythical forms rather than separable events and historical sequences. One way that we can know this form of consciousness in psychotherapy is through apprehending an interactive field between analysand and analyst. We are both participant-observers interacting within this field, with its energies and structures.

These two qualities of consciousness are complementary; apprehending the analytic process through one limits our awareness through the other. Furthermore, each mode requires the other; if our imaginal perceptions do not link with an analysand's developmental-historical data and associated fantasies, imagination will tend to be fantastic rather than real. And if we focus primarily upon developmental issues that reflect individual suffering, integration of the affects and structures stemming from the early-object world becomes a person's valid lot in life, curtailing a sense of meaning.

Jung described the soul as "the living thing in man, that which lives of itself and causes life" (CW9-I, par. 56). There are, however, deeply alienated areas of the soul which appear to be lifeless. Integrating these split-off areas requires linking the two modes of consciousness, and with them personal and archetypal dimensions within the transference/countertransference. These dimensions cannot be separated but are related aspects of an indivisible process. To use Jung's metaphor, the sea is "the carrier of the individual wave" (CW16, par. 354).

The alienation of some areas of the soul is a result of abandonment, a catastrophic experience. The abandoned one suffers doubly: a consummate betrayal in the loss of a loved and needed person, and persecution by that same person. As a result, one's sense of reality is threatened; the good has become the bad, the nurturing persecutory. A chaotic state of panic becomes imminent because the entire fabric of one's perception of reality has come into question.

A frantic search for a good object takes over but the persecutory despair remains so intense that the search is doomed to failure, undone by the chaos and pain that defy the attempt at restitution. The individual's makeshift reality is threatened with each additional possibility of abandonment and a deep-seated depression dominates the inner world.

In general, the difficult act of engaging this depressed and persecuted quality of an analysand's inner life must include establishing a heart-centered, imaginal awareness within which one can experience the dread suffered by the soul. The analyst can make a contact but only with the awareness that his or her own soul suffers as the analysand suffers. First, however, the two must travel a tortuous path, lacking empathy or any real contact.

When we suffer abandonment from a loved and needed person, do we experience only pain and dread connected to early developmental issues? Or is another kind of inner process also at work, weaving a larger story? As Jung (CW14) noted, in the abandonment experience – known in alchemy as the *nigredo* – a deep melancholy affects the adept, but the inner world of the Self is being transformed through this dangerous state. Thus an inner process, a myth, is actualized under the impact of abandonment experiences.

For this transformation to occur, abandonment must be experienced consciously, as part of a purposeful archetypal process.

The archetype infuses our reality with its order, disorder, imaginal life, and pattern of behavior. But when we enter into its reality we encounter a different sense of space, time, and scale. For example, we experience the scale and power of the archetype when we know the *coniunctio* with its capacity to draw together, then separate, analysand and analyst. This experience, so important to Jung, is essentially religious and thus open to the unknowable rather than limited to the causality that comprises the shadow side of a developmental model.

The power of the emotions experienced in abandonment deflects an individual's capacity to relate to the archetypal level. But if a person is without an awareness of that level, the abandonment experience remains terrifying, begging for repression as a defense against its pain. The Eleusinian Mysteries dealt with the return of Persephone, an archetypal image of the abandoned soul. As part of the ceremony, there occurred a birth of a divine child, Brimos. This was announced with the cry, "Brimo has borne Brimos." Brimo, Kerenyi (1949) explains, means "the power to arouse terror [and] to rage" (p. 142). Out of the chaotic, rageful and terrifying experiences of abandonment, a new birth of the Self emerges. As part of his discussion of the *nigredo*, as shown in woodcut seven of the *Rosarium*, Jung also commented that "the birth of a 'divine child' or… the inner man" (CW16, par. 482) may be the underlying issue. As these myths indicate, something creative may emerge from abandonment, not the least of which is the capacity to dissolve old structures and allow new ones to form.

We cannot assume that our analysands will gain much from being told about mythical images such as those of Eleusis. Perhaps, however, analysts who suffer countertransference reactions that touch their own chaotic and persecutory levels of abandonment may be able to reflect on the larger meaning of these experiences and thus facilitate an attitude change for the analysand.

The Abandonment Depression and the Alchemical Nigredo

In Jung's investigations of alchemy he found that the *nigredo* "brought about a deformation and a psychic suffering which... [compares] to the plight of the unfortunate Job" (CW14, par. 494). If the alchemists are correct, investigating the depths of abandonment will bring about psychotic transference and countertransference. Thus, we experience the inherent rhythm of personal and archetypal levels when the Self does not function in a containing way. At such a time, we feel in danger of being overwhelmed and we are at least potentially psychotic. Symptoms of such behavior are: losing a symbolic capacity, being driven by persecutory anxieties, distorting reality, and being unable to differentiate inner from outer.

When I speak about psychotic levels or madness I emphasize that I find these levels in everyone. We as analysts can know the rhythm of personal and archetypal levels from a positive Self-connection. But knowing this linking through experiencing "the limit of our freedom," as we are driven there by our analysands, has a particular healing potential.

Alchemy maintains that the *nigredo* follows upon the *coniunctio*; a union state often precedes the dark and dangerous affects of the abandonment depression as we encounter it in analysis. If we do not know this, we may see such states of mind always as replays of infant experience. Sometimes, rather, they are part of a new creation. The union state may be perceived imaginally during the here-and-now of analytical work. But if it eludes our perception, we may discover it only retrospectively, perhaps through a series of dreams.

Union, the alchemical *coniunctio*, is not merely a connection of the analyst's and analysand's unconscious contents; also, energy is released through this experience. In negative, unconscious states of projective identification a release of energy occurs that tends toward compulsion and acting-out. A positive form of the *coniunctio* is a fusion state that can be used consciously without either person's ego coopting the released energies for power or defensive purposes.

Jung recorded alchemical texts that depict the *coniunctio* and its results. The alchemical imagery can be likened to X-rays that show us what lies far beneath personal-historical phenomena. At the beginning, Jung wrote, the *coniunctio* has undesirable results. He explored the nature of one of these negative images, the rabid dog, in a text that I have found particularly useful in the clinical material I shall discuss.

The infant hermaphrodite, who is infected from his very cradle by the bite of the rabid Corascene dog, whereby he is maddened and rages with perpetual hydrophobia; nay, though of all natural things water is the closest to him, yet he is terrified of it and flees from it. O fate! Yet in the grove of Diana there is a pair of doves, which assuage his raving madness. Then will the impatient, swarthy, rabid dog, that he may suffer no more of his hydrophobia and perish drowned in the waters, come to the surface half suffocated.... Keep him at a distance, and the darkness will disappear. When the moon is at the full, give him wings and he will fly away as an eagle, leaving Diana's birds dead behind him. (CW14, par. 182)

We see how the source of madness, the rabid dog, is viewed as dangerous but also as the source of a new spirit, the eagle that ascends from its transformation.

As Jung noted, the text is preceded by a remark that links the rabid dog to chaos, the *prima materia*, or to lead, which "contains a demon that drives the adept mad" (CW14, par. 183). In another text the enemy of the new birth is called the "thief" (CW14, par. 193). In clinical practice this dangerous quality has various roots, but one that connects with the case I shall deal with is the abandonment of the soul through the violation of incest. The alchemical symbolism of transforming the rabid dog or thief can reflect the arduous process of creating an analytic container for previously unbounded, incestuous energies. This process is especially difficult in cases of actual incest. In my experience, the transformation represented by a dog becoming an eagle can reflect the emergence of a creative, idealized transference in Kohut's (1971) sense. But more important, the eagle symbolism can reflect another possibility: after working through the madness associated with the soul's abandonment, the person may begin to experience a new-found integrity of spirit and, eventually, a passion for his or her own individuation process. When we struggle, often for years, with the unbounded, chaotic and distrustful states of mind to which imagery such as the rabid dog refers, such transformations are felt as miraculous, like a dog becoming an eagle.

Clinical Example

I turn to material from the fourth through the sixth years of my work with a 45-year-old woman analysand. During the first four years the theme of incest was hardly mentioned. It had gone unnoticed also in her previous therapies. One of her initial complaints was that her previous therapist told her that he found her spiritually but not sexually attractive. This was a grave injury to her, but there was also something strange in her affect when she spoke about it. She was in a state of mind-body splitting and became mentally blank. But what was most significant, in retrospect, was my willingness to sidestep these dissociated states of mind and focus on her statement, as an injunction to me not to reject her in the same way.

After four years, she began to recall memories of sexual abuse by an older brother when she was six years old, and much earlier by a nursemaid. As we focused on her brother-incest trauma, we explored the sadomasochistic nature of her inner life; it expressed itself in brutal self-attacks for what she took to be her role in the incest episode, and then even harsher ones that she had made it all up and was really crazy.

As this theme of incest became more central to our work, I found myself internally resisting the idea that it really happened to her. She then began a session with a question: "What do I do with my feelings when I feel no connection with you?" The affect-field that accompanied the posing of this question was charged with a hostile and accusatory challenge, leading to confusion in me. I thought she said: What has happened to our connection? Feeling challenged and angry, I was bewildered by the intensity of my reaction, but I mostly sidestepped it and focused on being irritated with her. I took this feeling, along with my tendency to dismiss her question as unimportant, as representing an induced reaction to her masochism. I challenged her by insisting there was a connection between us – on a sadomasochistic level – and I focused the session on exploring these dynamics. I thought a good deal had been accomplished, but a psychotic transference emerged.

In subsequent sessions the patient was blank, withdrawn and terrified. She took what I said in a very concrete way, believing that I hated her and had said so. For example, at one point in the previous session, while engaged in what I took to be her inner fantasy life, experienced through projective-identification, I had said: "You expect me to hate you and find you a disgusting whore." My language was her own, derived from the many previous sessions in which we had dealt with her self-attack stemming from memories of her brother's sexual abuse of her. I had come to believe that by now she knew that she was an incest victim. But this knowledge, I was soon to learn, had been assimilated, at best, by her normal-neurotic ego, and not at all by her more psychotic parts. With the interactive field enlivened, I believed that I was experiencing the analysand's sadomasochistic couple in which her inner sadist was blaming her for the incest and, in effect, accusing her of being a whore. I thought I was bringing this dynamic out and into consciousness by giving it voice.

The analysand, largely through my blunder, entered into her psychotic part, but with a certain degree of containment. She was filled with distrust and terror of me. Yet she also knew that she had to work things out with me; an alliance did exist. She had written up the session which began with her question about feelings and her connection to me, and her belief that I had said that I hated her. I was committed now to help her more normal ego qualities to recognize the distortions of her psychotic part. I was looking at her – not my or our – madness and trying to help her sort out reality. When we finally returned to her initial question, I recalled it, as I had heard it, and told her that I felt angered by her question which I experienced as an attack upon our work. I thus had looked for where we really did have a connection, and this, I could see, was a hostile act on my part. Only after this kind of exploration, in which I began to reflect upon the validity of her perceptions, did she find some relief. Now there was an analytic space in which she could work again on her incest issues and her psychotic qualities which had been manifesting as extreme splitting, withdrawal, reality distortion, and suicidal drives.

If we are to engage the potential available to us in fostering the integration of an analysand's psychotic part, rather than fortify his or her normal-neurotic ego, it is necessary to acknowledge the truth of the analysand's perceptions which stem from the psychotic sector, even if these perceptions seem partial and distorted. This can help the analysand to risk recognizing and expressing beliefs such as feeling hated by the analyst. This woman, I learned later, was terrified that such an assertion would lead to my destruction or to her being thrown out of analysis.

Acknowledging the truth of the analysand's perceptions may be quite hazardous. The danger is not, however, because such a procedure could be used by the analysand to further reify his or her distortions. The concern usually is based on the analyst's introjection of the analysand's fears of abandonment for having been confrontational.

There are, however, important grounds for not acknowledging such perceptions; to acknowledge them can undermine the analysand's capacity to be honest and, thus, it can seduce him or her into taking care of the analyst's feelings. This seduction is the shadow side of validating the accuracy of an analysand's perceptions, and it must be taken seriously and analyzed later. Nevertheless, unless we find a way to mirror the accuracy of the soul's vision, we shall not succeed in helping the analysand to integrate the depth of his or her being that is trapped in psychotic distortions.

In a subsequent session the analysand said: "I cannot trust anyone. I'm in a cold, withdrawn place and I am terrified of the power you have over me. If I tell you anything of what I thought last night you can annihilate me in an instant. I have never before felt the total power you have over me and it terrifies me. I just want to withdraw and totally leave everything – this process, life."

Her terror now centered upon what I had said when we went over the session, for I told her that she heard me say she was a disgusting whore. I explained that I didn't believe this but was playing out a fantasy with her, a process I thought she was aware of while it was going on. She listened intently, and I thought I was making progress in helping her to see her reality distortions. In the next session I learned that it wasn't the "whore part" that got to her but rather that I had said that she "heard me say" what I did, implying to her that I had not said it at all, and that she was psychotic. She felt that I had annihilated her perceptions and she was left not knowing what to believe or trust.

She was especially terrified by the possibility that I thought she was crazy. She felt that now I was just soothing her and lying to her. I explained again that I actually did say what she believed I said, but that she took it in the wrong way. It was becoming clear, even to me in my absurd attack on the psychotic elements between us, that I was having little effect. I then asked myself: where is she correct? She believed I said what I did because I really felt she was a disgusting whore, but was now denying this feeling. This belief could stem from her psychosis. Or it could be a result of a trickster-like force dominating our process, Mercurius in his demonic form, like the rabid dog. Or was her belief rooted in a perception of my own mad parts, with which I have had, when with this analysand, too little awareness?

It is clear that at times I distorted what she said, as when I did not accurately hear and process her question concerning what she should do with her feelings when she felt no connection to me. When I insisted that only a change of form in the connection had occurred, I denied her perceptions and what she experienced, namely a space in which she had absolutely no link with me, or with herself.

After another session, feeling the stress of my work with her, I recorded the following imaginal process:

I want to thrash her, drown her in a stormy sea, throw her body to and fro in the waves until she will stop this torture of me with her withdrawals and masochism, leaving me always the guilty party. More and more I feel as if I have committed incest with her. I feel as if I am her guilty brother who did it to her and then denied it. I feel the edges of losing the as-if. Did I do it or didn't I?"

I then recognized that unconsciously I may have felt this identification for some time, namely that I was her older brother, who had incestuously violated her. As a consequence of denying this level of psychotic countertransference I had been forcing interpretations while trying to feel empathic and related to her, rather than feeling the air of unreality and disconnection which actually pervaded our work.

After these attempts at sorting out our process together she asked the inevitable question: does this mean that I have been putting these reactions into you? How easy it would have been to say yes! Clearly, something like this had been going on but I also felt that, in becoming aware of the psychotic countertransference, I was opening up to a much larger realm that seemed to have a goal or purpose; a classical projective-identification approach would undermine that awareness. This domain included incest fantasies with my mother and sister, but the experience of a larger domain, an interactive field, and the sense that we were going through a process together – a process determined by this field – offered a sense of meaning.

The larger domain needed exploration, yet it soon began to feel too mental and non-substantial. Consequently, I turned back to a projective-identification view: parts I put into her and she into me. In turn this view felt too small, a killing of a realm of meaning. An emergence of the awareness of the oscillation between personal/historical and mythical/archetypal levels resulted. This awareness had a changing form along lines of the two modes of consciousness; the one oriented toward perceiving discrete parts within a space-time framework, the other toward a unity of process and imaginal forms. Thus, there was a subjective element, experienced as differing modes of consciousness, and an objective one as well, the interpenetrating personal and archetypal elements of the interactive field.

Our interaction could be understood, thus, as inclusive of a "third thing," a mythical realm that had been ordering and weaving together the psychotic parts of our psyches. To consider this we could look at the background of our psychotic episodes. They were preceded by an unconscious union state, usually indicated by dreams of a marriage or wedding. Then a devastating *nigredo* would set in. For example, a wedding dream preceded the session in which I had insisted that we had a connection. I recognized that all my difficult times with this analysand had been preceded by such dreams; I could document three.

The symbolism of the *coniunctio*, as Jung's research amply demonstrates, is varied and subtle. It is usually not so overt as the marriage and wedding imagery was in this case. It is easy to overlook dream images that can imply the existence of the *coniunctio*, such as fighting animals, a fire starting in the cellar, a burglar breaking in, or the dreamer's father dying. But such images can be taken easily as representing only the patient's intrapsychic existence, or as reflecting childhood material emerging through the transference. What is seen as developmental arrest is often a result of a *coniunctio* between two psyches.

In this case, as a consequence of experiences that were traumatic for both of us, we had found and contained our *nigredo*. In this blackness, the unconscious incestuous couple could be transformed. Could we, then, having gotten our bearings, play with the material that had so devoured us – without losing feeling?

The analysand and I, at times at her urging, often went back to the fateful session in which I sought to deal with our relationship in terms of a sadomasochistic quality. I was perplexed and at times felt persecuted by her insistence that we still had unfinished business, although by now I had learned to respect her reticence to go on as if we had cleared up what occurred in that session.

Then another *coniunctio* dream occurred. There had been no conscious feeling of union between us. There was some sense of calmness, which was unusual, but that was all. Whereas she previously rebelled at my saying that she "heard me say" what I had actually said, after the dream she was deeply upset at the content as well. She believed I really felt she was a disgusting whore. I felt anxious about her dropping more deeply into a psychotic state; suicidal drives mounted from her despair over the loss of her capacity to think and from her fear that she would never emerge from this state.

I respectfully recalled to her that I had believed that we were in tune together, that she understood that I was role-playing with her, and that I did not feel that she was disgusting. In fact, I felt the opposite – a deep kinship with her, a common effect of the *coniunctio*, as if she were an intimately known sister with whom I could say or feel whatever I chose. I only now learned that this belief was my own and not shared by her. She felt no such right for herself and, if anything, totally in my power. She could sense in herself, but only barely feel, a deep anger. Through these so-called kinship feelings our psychotic parts were secretly running the show, and a sadomasochistic field was being acted out, rather than enacted. So I had to ask myself: did I believe she was a disgusting whore? I had to recognize that in some place, I could say, "Yes," for to the extent that I felt I was her brother in incest, I also experienced her as seducing me.

The imagery of the whore is abundant in alchemy. In the *nigredo*, for example, the dark side of the moon wounds the sun. Gradually, I was able to recognize that such imagery was pertinent to my own psychotic sector, structured by such mythical forms as the Near-Eastern myth of Attis and Kybele. Attis is the son-lover of Kybele, the Great Mother. Driven mad by his mother's insane love for him, and by his inability to free himself from his passion for her, he is destroyed by a wild boar or, in many other versions, castrates himself under a pine tree.

I am sharing here my relationship to such material in which, as Jung says "a man is only a dream of the mother" (CW5, par. 392) because I have seen its presence in so many analysts. It is acknowledged by some and denied by others. Surely, this son-lover archetype was a dominant factor of Jung's psyche, as can be seen in his work with Sabina Spielrein (Carotenuto, 1980). I believe that this archetypal constellation, to one degree or another, exists as a dominant structure for any man today, a result of patriarchal domination of thousands of years and reinforced by personal incest issues. Men have been conditioned to be narcissistically injured by its presence.

When my normal ego-state was affected strongly by this archetypal pattern, I felt in danger of being overwhelmed by the analysand's needs and desires. In the near-total nature of this experience, engulfment and a loss of my autonomy felt very real. But through being able to relate imaginally to the presence of this archetypal sector and its associated ego-state, I could now begin to see my projection onto the analysand, even though I had not felt her to be seductive or dangerous. Then it was clear to me that, through the constellation of this archetypal pattern, I would see her as a whore, both hating her for the power she had over me and desiring to fuse with her to neutralize that power and regain a sense of safety.

Unless I owned consciously Attis-like levels in myself, my analysand would be left feeling delusional, her imaginal perceptions and her real vision denied. She would have no clear idea of what was occurring between us. Her vision would manifest through bodily pains and distress about that particular sadomasochistic session. It took courage for her to contain her confusion and discomfort, not to disengage from her perception and become her compliant and competent self. For me, awareness of this archetypal level and its overwhelming nature in me was the key to entering a heart-centered link with her which could perceive her process. Rather than reducing her concerns to paranoia, I had to recognize that I said what I said, not merely as an actor in her drama.

The qualities that often create the greatest difficulties in the analysis of the psychotic part of a person are precisely those that go back to ancient substrata of the mind, such as the son-lover mythologem. Here we confront shadow qualities that are not capable of being integrated into the ego sphere. Instead they must be seen, felt and experienced as devotees of a god or goddess would experience that deity's rite. The scale of such phenomena is far larger than that of the ego, but it can imaginally perceive and experience them.

Near the end of the two-year span I have been considering, the analysand's rage became mobilized by what she perceived as my lack of connection to myself. This issue surfaced after yet another dream of a wedding. We both wondered what would happen next. Two weeks later her rage came as never before and, with it, intense despair. She was filled with hatred of me for not letting her just die, for my faith in our process and for what she experienced as my torturing her with it. At this time her madness surfaced ever more forcefully. I feared that a delusional transference would emerge, for her madness did not have the form of a child-part lost in overwhelming anxieties and rage, but felt like a mass of formless fury aimed at me.

She then dreamed of *an insurance man named Hinckley*. She identified Hinckley with the deranged would-be assassin of President Reagan. Evidently her insurance against loss and abandonment was to come from being mad. The pain of the loss of connection with me was mounting to a new level of intensity. She felt she knew union – with me and with herself – at moments probably linked to her wedding dreams. But there was no continuity and embodied sense of linking. A soulless state tortured her and its lack of containment was, at times, very anxiety-provoking for me. Was there, as Jung's alchemical research suggests, an unconscious process also at work, a process in which the desired heart-connection was being sought and, perhaps, wrought?

Several months later there was another dream of a wedding and the resulting *nigredo* was the most devastating yet; she spoke now of feeling "totally dispensable." In spite of its intensity, however, and while suicidal thoughts and emotional isolation were still present, she was now far less schizoid. It was as if the young part of her that had hidden as a child, in hopes of not being found, was now integrated into the analytic process. This new spiral downward contained the previous material but included an important structural change as well. Feelings of withdrawal and unrelatedness still plagued her, but they were less intense in general as well as in our sessions.

In the next session she said that during the previous hour she was different. I told her that I also felt her to be different now, introverted and reflective rather than withdrawn. She said that she noticed the same changes. When she left my office she said good-bye. Previously she had said nothing, but had just left.

At the moment of her leaving I felt that she finally was separating from me and feeling her own interiority, rather than splitting off from her affects. But quickly this optimism gave way to another thought: what did she mean by saying good-bye? Would she now kill herself? In fact, this stage in our work ushered in the analysand's new-found capacity to wrestle consciously with whether she would live or die. Now, instead of a death-urge rushing over her and fought back only with splitting defenses of a manic nature, she could face death actively. The renegade that lurks in suicidal drives became more visible to her, and the threatening vulnerability of embracing life became a pressing issue that challenged her courage.

Recovery of the Heart

As the analysand gradually became more able to connect with her split-off soul, her withdrawal lessened, and a heart-centered imagination became possible. I was able to feel an aliveness in my heart and less drive to enforce control and connection through knowledge or interpretation. The process is difficult to describe because it exists within an imaginal reality in which one's attention flows through the heart and out toward another person. In the process imaginal sight emerges, a quality of consciousness that perceives the presence of the archetypal level. This sight can be experienced through the eyes, the body or the emotions, but it is a level of perception that gently penetrates in ways that a discursive process fails to achieve. To the abandoned soul, knowledge without heart feels like abandonment. The heart offers a way to connect without violating the soul.

The *nigredo* states that continued to emerge were difficult to manage, especially as they plunged the analysand ever more deeply into states of distrust. Yet these states always proved to be rooted in the process of creating a new analytic container; for example, for incest violations by other family members – abuses which, she feared, I did not really believe occurred. For the woman, dealing with her persecutory doubts was like the motif, in the alchemical text I referred to, of keeping the rabid dog at a distance.

My analysand suffered terribly when her heart-connection, and mine with her, was absent. The loss of heart was the main abandonment issue in our work, as it had always been in her life. Guntrip (1969) referred to the "lost heart of the self" (p. 87) in the schizoid personality; this metaphor well describes the schizoid quality in everyone. What was remarkable about the process of unions and ensuing *nigredo* states was that this process continually integrated the heart, while diminishing my analysand's schizoid withdrawal.

Jung quoted the alchemical maxim: "Take the foul deposit that remains in the cooking-vessel and preserve it, for it is the crown of the heart" (CW16, par. 496). I believe that we had implicitly followed this saying. The foul deposit of the pain and grief of our interactions, especially those which denied the absence of relationship and sought to force some connection, and those in which psychotic levels of transference and countertransference dominated, became the crown upon which a new heart-connection could grow.

REFERENCES

Carotenuto, A. (1980). Sabina Spielrein and C.G. Jung. *Spring*, 128-45.

Guntrip, H. (1969). *Schizoid Phenomena, Object Relations and the Self*. New York: International Universities Press.

Kerenyi, C. (1949). The myth of the divine child and the mysteries of Eleusis. In Jung, C.G. & Kerenyi, C. *Essays on a Science of Mythology*. New York: Harper and Row.

Kohut, H. (1971). *The Analysis of the Self: A Systematic Approach to the Treatment of Narcissistic Personality Disorders*. New York: International Universities Press.

Countertransference Dynamics in Analysis

The Hurt that Heals

James Astor
London, England
Society of Analytical Psychology

Jung's ideas about countertransference present us with a difficulty. On the one hand he seemed to imply that unsystematic, idiosyncratic behavior – the analyst's relying on his or her personality – is a desirable way of proceeding. On the other hand, he recommended that analysts be analyzed, indicating that the two people engaged in the process must bear the psychic pain and work through it. Thus he reduced the importance of the analyst's personality.

Fordham has examined this latter point of view in detail in a number of works (e.g., 1957, 1974, 1979, 1985). He has emphasized Jung's open systems view of analysis: two people together, mutually influencing one another. Fordham (1979) distinguished such "interaction" from countertransference, which he described as the appropriate term "when the interacting systems become obstructed" (p. 208). The beauty of this approach is that it preserves the individuality of the analysand and recognizes the potential therapeutic value of the influence on the analyst of the analysand's affects.

I am concerned here with ways of thinking about pain and analysands' difficulties in metabolizing the painful truth of their experiences. They discharge this mental pain partly in the form of sensations and emotions and partly in the recounting of action in and out of the sessions. This evacuation of discomfort can be accomplished, also, by the reverse: by being acquiescent in analysis, doing what is expected rather than thinking for oneself.

The Challenge to Collective Values

A problem arises in analysis of a woman when the intimacy of the analytic relationship challenges the collective values of the analysand, values suitable for adaptation and survival but not for individual development. This situation can arise when the animus, as part of the shadow, begins to be the focus of the work. Jung described the animus as consisting of "a priori assumptions based on unconsidered judgments" (CW10, par. 90). The animus often manifests itself in a preformed transference, the aggressive aspect of which can present itself in an erotic form. While analyzing this phenomenon I have had the experience of being invited by an analysand to move closer to her so as to be available for her pleasure. The invitation to action pushed away all my thoughts about the connections between the analysand's sexuality and her argumentative attitude to analysis. I am making a link between opinions, which Jung called "a priori assumptions that lay claim to absolute truth" (CW9-II, par. 29), and the presence in the analysand of unassimilated experiences with men. I inferred that there was an equivalence in her mind between an opinion and a man's penis. I am suggesting, following Jung, that the animus does not think; it has thoughts. In order for the animus to change, the transformative potential in "the mother" has to be found and the maternal transference analyzed.

Cognitive Processes in Emotional Development

Analysis requires of analysand and analyst alike that they become aware of their feelings and recognize them. Recognition is the meeting of a preconception – an archetypal expectation – with a realization. The formulation of a concept follows. Some analysands have learned the words but the concept (as described by Money-Kyrle, 1978) is absent. Thus the experiences to which the words refer are not available for use in emotional development. Should they become psychotherapists, these analysands are likely to try to fit the material to their limited experience. This procedure is a form of imitating the grown-ups. But in growing up we do not leave behind our childlike feelings; we incorporate them structurally, by reintegration or by splitting. In analysis this process of digestion is facilitated by containment within the analyst's mind of the analysand's feelings and thoughts; they are allowed to play on the conscious and unconscious processes stirred within the analyst.

This containment is similar to the way the mother, in thinking about the infant's feelings and her own, metabolizes them so that they can be given back with an increment of meaning. By so doing, the capacity for symbolic thought is fostered.

Fordham's Development of Jung

In London the model that has profoundly influenced analytic thought has been Fordham's work. It is congruent with Jung's attitude to the psyche but radically different in its understanding of maturation and development. I have written about this elsewhere (Astor, 1989a & 1989b). Central to the model is the idea of an individual Self. Its manifestation in adult individuation processes can be thought about in relation to the child in the adult, not as one of many archetypal images but as central to the analytic process. The procedure values the impact of memory in action, in the dreams and clinical material. Pain has to be suffered for growth to occur. Fordham (1985) wrote that, if the analyst identifies with an analysand's projections "and believes that he can sustain them all the time, he has been caught by a defensive illusion. He has lost his shadow" (p. 216).

Thinking as an Emotional Process

The work thus occurs in thinking about the feeling. Thinking here becomes an adjunct of attention, the conscious valuing (thinking) of an unconscious process (feeling). The link is between experience and thought. Not to think is to avoid the meaning and significance of the mental pain.

Jung's account of his own struggle with the unconscious is testimony to this point of view. By thinking, then, I am not referring to an intellectual activity that can be used defensively, but to a process of digestion resulting from paying attention to the meaning of mental pain. Thinking in this sense is an emotional process.

Intuition

Central to the dialectical procedure, when working in the area of primitive defenses against mental pain, is the analyst's reliance on intuition checked against the dreams and clinical material of the analysis. Intuition is described by Jung as "the matrix out of which thinking and feeling develop as rational functions" (CW6, par. 770). This description is congruent with the value Jung put on the irrational fact as an aid to the advancement of knowledge. Closely linked is my understanding of the connection Fordham (1985) made between Jung's concept of individuation and the development of depressive concern. Jung described individuation as "the process by which the individual beings are formed and differentiated. In particular it is the development of the psychological individual as being distinct from the general, collective psychology" (CW6, par. 757). Those analysands who cannot bear the pain of being introduced to themselves and who fight off understanding live in the collective undifferentiated parts of their personalities, expressed in opinions, attitudes and behavior dominated by socially-determined values.

Clinical Example

Miss K., in England for further education, enveloped her oriental appearance in the look of a 1960s flower child. She was in her twenties when she came to me for analysis. Underneath the "flower child" veneer, however, lurked an ideologue: one in whom the idealism of youth, which led her to espouse causes and feel passionate about injustice, had rigidified. On closer inspection, motives had more to do with an idea of herself than with a wish to change society. Her objectives were personal and goal-seeking: concerned with an end rather than a direction. In the consulting room she presented considerable difficulty.

At first I did not realize how important insignia were for her in denoting attitudes of mind. For example, men who wore jackets and ties were in a uniform that indicated extreme right wing opinions, an enemy of her ideology. Her outward demeanor concealed an inward sneer of contempt.

These attributes of her personality, hierarchical and

unexamined by her (part of the collective that had been internalized), were fiercely protected by paranoid ways of thinking beneath a touchiness that led to argumentativeness. She could not bear to have her fixed ideas investigated for the infantile transference aspects of them. The collective attitudes were a barrier to the experience of the analysis; they were the ally of the parts of her personality that evaded the discomfort.

This abortion of the analytic experience was equivalent to the literal abortions of her personal history. But it was never possible to sustain a consideration of the enviously destructive abortionist in her. She took my interest in the relevance of this experience to the transference as an authoritarian wish to cut her down to size. In terms of the dynamics of the analysis she was identified with a mother who, to the child in her, knows it all. Like the animus-ridden analysand I mentioned earlier, she avoided the pain of her experience by metaphorically climbing onto my lap and trying to see the world through "mummy's" eyes. The father's role was that of a dangerous and unsettling intruder into this psychotic world – the surgeon abortionist with his cutting knife of a mind. Internally the alliance between the abortionist and the ideologue sabotaged the work: the former not allowing the child to come into existence in the consulting room and the latter greeting the analytic process with slogans. Slogans are the antithesis of thought – vehicles for prejudice often dangerously near common sense. This woman's slogans, as expressions of an internal collective mentality, reflected the move from struggling within a framework of objective relations to a retreat to narcissism.

Transformative Potential

Jung referred to the transformative potential within the mother and the obstacles in the way of experiencing this in the conscious mind. They include moral difficulties and the power of the internal establishment that cannot allow change. But "the conscious mind often knows little or nothing about its own transformation, and does not want to know anything. The more autocratic it is and the more convinced of the eternal validity of its truths, the more it identifies with them.... It seems that all true things must change and that only that which changes remains true" (CW14, par. 503).

Combining Fordham's and Bion's (1965) ideas with Jung's, I understand that, in work with adult patients, the analysis of childhood – as memory in action in the present – is a prerequisite for change and development; collective values in the form of an internal establishment can obstruct this process. While analysis does not aspire to remove conflict, it can equip the analysand to resolve conflict. A central factor is the capacity to experience pain and metabolize it. It is important to bear the pain, to pay attention to its meaning and significance and not to be diverted into abandoning thinking.

REFERENCES

Astor, J. (1989a). "The breast as part of the whole: Theoretical considerations concerning whole and part objects. *Journal of Analytical Psychology*, *34*-2, 117-28.

Astor, J. (1989b). Michael Fordham, e L'analisi d'ell'infanzia. In *Psicologia Analitica Contemporanea, a cura di Carlo Trombetta*. Milano: Bompiani.

Bion, W. R. (1965). *Transformations*. London: Heinemann.

Fordham, M. (1957). *New Directions in Analytical Psychology*. London: Routledge Kegan Paul.

Fordham, M. (1974). Technique and countertransference. In M. Fordham et al. (Eds.), *Technique in Jungian Analysis*. Library of Analytical Psychology, Vol. 2. London: Heinemann.

Fordham, M. (1979). Analytical Psychology and countertransference. In L. Epstein and A. Feiner (Eds.), *Countertransference*. New York: Jason Aronson.

Fordham, M. (1985). *Explorations into the Self*. Library of Analytical Psychology, Vol. 7. London: Academic Press.

Money-Kyrle, R. (1978). *Collected Papers of Roger Money-Kyrle*. Perthshire, Scotland: Clunie.

Homosexual Countertransference

Robert Bosnak
Boston, Massachusetts, USA
New England Society
of Jungian Analysts

Homosexual countertransference between males is the focus of some short vignettes from my analytical practice. The first story, which took place in Switzerland in the mid-1970s – before AIDS – is about Marco, a 38-year-old military officer from a family of several generations of professional soldiers. When he came to me initially, referred by an older woman analyst, he was shocked to find me in my late twenties. In the first session he kept saying that I was too young to work with him. Since the referral was by a well-respected doctor, an acknowledged authority in the field, Marco came back for a second session. Authority was extremely important to Marco.

It soon became obvious that he was very attracted to me and that a deep-seated fear of his homosexual urges was at the core of his depression. He would hold himself back from these desires, until they became too strong. Then he would go to a distant city and indulge himself in several one night stands; these left him feeling extremely guilty. He would torture himself for months in a depressive self-punishment laden with feelings of utter worthlessness. After a while the urges became too strong once more and the cycle repeated itself.

His father had been a violent man and had beaten Marco viciously. It was always the inner voice of his father who chided him. We worked a great deal on the image of the little boy abused by his father. An event occurred that made it clear to me how important it was to differentiate carefully each sexual feeling that came up in me while working with him:

Marco sits opposite me. His face looks contorted. He is obviously suffering. After a while I ask him what is the matter. He doesn't answer. His face twists even more. "What is it?" I ask. "I want to take my penis out of my pants and show it to you," he replies, blushing crimson. I get a slight tinge of sexual excitement in my groin. But much less than at other times when I have had lewd masturbation fantasies while feeling the attraction between us. I sense down into my penis once more. The sexual desire is gone. All I can feel is embarrassment, about the sexual fantasies I have had about him. I chide myself viciously for enjoying them too much; such enjoyment is unprofessional. The image he is presenting me, of showing me his penis, is hardly sexualized and I am filled with feelings of self-flagellation. He can't stand it any more and changes the subject. "I dreamt that *my father was holding me at gunpoint. All I could feel was terrible shame. Then he shot me and I fell into a deep dark well. It looks like a sphincter.*"

We work on the extreme sense of shame. I believe that his desire to show me his penis was less a need to exhibit himself to me than a set-up for a torture by his father. My countertransference response supports this. I must keep an eye out for the transference of his humiliating father who gives him the sense of being an asshole.

A countertransference response of an entirely different nature comes up a week later. He dreams: "*There is a man closely monitoring my sex life. He finds me a disgusting homosexual. I shoot him.*" "What do you feel?" I ask. "The man is right. I have to admit that I do love men." He had always said that he would never admit to that. Seeing the look of embarrassment on his face again, I wait. "I see an image of a huge erect phallus," he says and looks extremely uncomfortable.

At that moment I begin to feel my breasts develop and I become soft and mother-like. I want to pet him and have oral incest with him. "I don't hate women. I just like men better," Marco tells me, twisting uncomfortably. I sense my nipples call out to him and I feel like a woman, wanting to seduce him. Marco begins to talk again. "I see a woman. I am undoing her bra. It excites me. I turn around. I see my mother in a see-through negligee." He is very embarrassed again, ready for self-punishment. This time, because of my feminine erotic countertransference response, I ask him about his sexual desires toward mother. He tells me how seductive she was, showing off her large breasts. It is striking to me that the incestuous mother emerges at the first moment he acknowledges his homosexual preference.

In the first scene I follow the direction of the punishing father. In the second scene, because of my countertransference response, I follow the incestuous mother. Countertransference led the way.

The third scene comes about three months later. "Do you love me?" he asks me. I feel instantly very distant from him and do not answer. "I want you to tell me that you love me," he repeats. The sense of distance grows and I feel very bad that it does. I didn't realize I felt this distant from him. In fact, there have been moments of intimate closeness in our relationship. But I can't feel any of it at this moment. Just the distance. I suddenly remember a memory he once told me about his father spanking him. The image becomes stronger, until it is all that matters.

"I am reminded of the memory of your father spanking you," I say, feeling that it is an awful response to his request for love. He is immediately inside the memory, as if he had forgotten all about his demand that I tell him I love him. "I see myself lying on your lap," he says. "You're spanking me and my pants are down. You stop spanking me and then you put your finger up my rectum." I feel a pressure on my sphincter myself, as if I have to defecate. Then it feels as if Marco enters me. At once we are very close.

"I've always wanted my father to do that to me," he says, without shame. "I've always wanted him inside me." The question about whether I love him seems answered. He never asked me again for the rest of our work. From then on the feeling between us is genuinely intimate. The distance between Marco and his father has been bridged.

In the following period of analysis Marco begins to develop an inner sense of authority. My strong countertransference response of distance and my allowing the spanking image to emerge constellated me strongly as the distant punishing father who could then penetrate Marco and give him his power.

Today, little more than a decade after my work with Marco, the looming of AIDS has made homosexual life radically different and changed analytic work with homosexual men. In many cases it has become a matter of life and death.

The next vignette is about Christopher (see Bosnak, 1989). He is 37 and so am I; it is 1985. AIDS has already hit wildly in many places, including New York, San Francisco, Houston and Los Angeles. Boston is still slightly off the track of the whirlwind. Christopher comes up from Houston to work with me in Boston. He wants to quit being gay, he says. The degree of intensity of that desire remains unclear to me. Three months after the beginning of our work, Christopher develops pneumocystis pneumonia, the dread opportune infection that kills many AIDS patients. I realize that we had never discussed AIDS even though Houston already abounds with it. There must have been a deep unconscious desire between the two of us not to address the issue. His passionate urge to leave the gay community and our joint silence about AIDS must belong to the same image: repressed dread.

Christopher's desire to stop being gay disappears entirely after the onset of his AIDS. We had fused together in a resistance toward feeling the ever-present dread of that disease. Everyone around us was hysterically afraid of AIDS as well. Thus, Christopher and I more or less fused with a collective background.

A fusion between us happens about half a year later, when I make an observation about a strange countertransference response. Since the first time I saw Christopher after he had come out of the hospital from his first attack of pneumocystis pneumonia, I had washed my hands directly following my sessions with him. It was a ritual to cleanse myself of AIDS. After about two months I dropped that ritual, though I wasn't aware that I had dropped it. I had become unconscious of my need to wash my hands. The change had been imperceptible. A couple of months after I stopped washing my hands he came in with tiny scabs on his hands. He had been biting his nails again. The scabs looked quite fresh.

During the next hour, when another patient dreams about blood, I realize that I haven't washed after shaking hands with Christopher. I was not quite sure that there had not even been some fresh blood on his hands. I am startled. Next week I begin to have fantasies about drinking his sperm and his blood. Highly eroticized fantasies. Then I realize: "My God, I want to get AIDS!" Thus I discover my unconscious passion to fuse with Christopher. To become one in AIDS. AIDS is the great daimon in his world. This unconscious urge to become brothers in AIDS is dangerous. It could make me want to be blood-brothers with him. Maybe accidentally to smear some of his blood on an "accidental" fresh wound of mine. At the same time I have this violent countertransference response, my passion for fusion, Christopher dreams:

> I am in a restaurant and dance with this man. At once I find him very attractive and not my type. We kiss on the floor and it is very deep and passionate. It takes me a moment to come to myself and realize where we are and that we can't do that there. But it is too late. People are already upset and a ruckus ensues. I try to avoid it, but he seems more of a brawler and doesn't particularly mind. He seems to need to amorize everyone: the women, me, other men. Something seems to have come clear about the difference in trying or wishing to be a woman, and letting her live and be manifest beautifully in a man.

When Christopher describes the brawler in the dream – the character starting all the ruckus and upheaval – the man looks very much like me. In me he sees the transformation of anima, from identification with woman to inner femininity. About the same time that I begin to feel my hitherto unconscious urge for fusion, Christopher is able to disentangle his femininity from a desire to be a woman. The importance of this new-found interior femininity is presented in a later dream in which *Christopher caringly holds on his lap his most beloved friend, who is dying of AIDS* – the posture of the Michelangelo sculpture of the Pieta holding her crucified son. When you feel cared for, dying is different from when you feel abandoned, the way Christopher had felt all his life. During the bout of pneumonia before the one that killed him, Christopher experienced his death twice. Once, feeling utterly abandoned by God and the world; once in utter bliss, feeling totally cared for and accepted.

Since working with Christopher I have been very involved with the problem of fusion. I had always felt that the words transference and countertransference stem from a root metaphor of a ball bouncing back and forth on a tennis court. I believe this to be a useful paradigm only on a surface level, where there are obviously two individual players. In this game, you transfer to me and I transfer back, as at the Wimbledon matches. On a deeper level, however, I find Jung's chapter "The Conjunction" (CW16) relevant. At the point of dissolution there are no longer two clearly individual players, but one mixture of images. The King and the Queen stop being two; they conjoin and become one.

I believe that in any analysis of some intensity such fusion takes place spontaneously. This is the raw *prima materia* that needs to be processed. In the examples I have given it becomes clear that my inner experiences in analysis are not exclusively mine. They only seem that way. In fact, my emotions can be treated as ore from which we can extract the atmospherics of the analyst/analysand relationship. Romantic atmospheres feel different from guilt and embarrassment. Incest with mother rouses me differently from incest with father. When we were in Marco's maternal incest, I felt seductive; when in the paternal incest I felt distant and punishing. In their raw form, these feelings were incomprehensible to me. My personal emotions had to be led back to their source – my own most private experiences of the seductive mother and the punishing father – since, at the melting point of our most intimate experiences, the personal and the archetypal are identical.

Working with AIDS patients makes fusion occur on a deeply unconscious level. I could only become aware of it by observing carefully my countertransference responses. In working with gay AIDS patients we have to differentiate the greatest possible range of our own homo-erotic emotion. The greater the range, the better the sound. Each consciously-experienced moment in analysis can be viewed from this perspective, as if it were personal material mixed by the forcers of fusion. Then each of our most personal experiences becomes a fluid mirror in which to reflect.

REFERENCE

Bosnak, R. (1989). Dreaming with an AIDS Patient. Boston: Shambhala.

Affect and Agape in Analysis

Johanna Brieger
Cambridge, England
Society of Analytical Psychology

"Love" plays a role in the search for individuation by persons in whom the psychically inexpressible affect becomes bodily suffering. Jung wrote:

> The way of the transcendent function is an individual destiny. But on no account should one imagine that this way is equivalent to the life of a psychic anchorite, to alienation from the world.... Fantasies are no substitute for living; they are fruits of the spirit which fall to him who pays his tribute to life. (CW7, par. 369)

Inner conflict is required for change to occur. When the body speaks, energy is lost from the psyche and the individuation process is hampered. The key to retrieval of affect is agape, as an attitude and as energy.

One definition of affect is "emotion or feeling of sufficient intensity to cause nervous agitation or other obvious psychomotor disturbances" (Samuels et al., 1986). One has command over feeling, whereas affect intrudes against one's will and can be repressed only with difficulty. An explosion of affect is an invasion of the individual and a temporary takeover of the ego.

In considering expression of affect via the "body way" or somatic channel, I have in mind a woman of 50. She was referred to me by a colleague who, knowing of my interest in psycho/soma, thought I might be able to help. This highly intelligent woman had been depressed and felt constrained, set in a fixed pattern from which there seemed no escape. She had suffered from severe migraines – like her mother – from an early age and, as a married woman of about 32, had had a seizure one night, in her sleep. She was told about it the next day but did not remember it. Her husband had given her an ultimatum: a child or no husband. She desperately did not want to lose her husband, but since childhood she had been determined not to bear children.

Her own childhood had been marred by "appalling parents": father hidden behind a newspaper and mother never there. A good grandmother rescued her for eight years. Then a brother was born who was also handed to grandmother; she introduced him to the little girl. She felt hatred flaring up, possessing her. She had lost her loved possession, her grandmother; she was alone. Shortly afterward, her grandmother had a stroke, was paralyzed and never recovered. The little girl also never recovered from the treble shock: a rival, a God who had struck the wrong person and, in her internal inferno, the little girl's belief that she had destroyed her grandmother.

The boy became the apple of the mother's eye; envy and jealousy joined the girl's hatred. The boy became violent and unmanageable, expressing through his behavior outwardly what she shut up inwardly: punishing, cutting, hammering and splitting thoughts in her head; rage, fury, guilt and shame in her heart. She was unbearably numbed, silenced for many years until a seizure betrayed her inner state.

All tests proved negative; she was labeled as suffering from idiopathic focal epilepsy and was sedated. At the time of our first meeting she had had no seizure for several years; since then she has learned to drive. Only a very occasional headache reminds her of her past severe migraines.

She was and is a "good" analysand, well-supplied with talents but also with rigid views and strong opinions. It became clear as we settled down to work that she was anxious for change but, understandably, terrified of losing control, lest the tightly jammed lid on the pot of unimaginable stuff would come off as the contents boil over. She would be "lost" like her brother, who had not been seen or heard of for many years. "Maybe," she volunteered, "the escaping fumes are making me ill." Yet she raised her son well, almost single-handed as the marriage soon broke down, so that she lost her husband after all. During one of her most difficult periods she told me she had stuffed all external cracks with newsprint and internal cracks with opinions.

It seemed clear that even partial recovery was possible only if she could modify her survival skills and redirect her energies to allow an altered balance in her cramped self, allowing a shift in the ego-Self axis. That this would be accompanied by stress perhaps mingled with relief, by fear of destructive behavior and hope of becoming a human being was clear to both of us.

Neither she nor I, however, had bargained for the extreme difficulties inherent in recovery. At first there was outer activity and no imagery. Later, and for some time, she had dream fragments but considered them futile; all my attempts to put them to use were to no avail. I was invaded time and again, session after session, by almost intolerable impulses and feelings. Words came to my lips unbidden and uttered themselves: cutting, hammering, splitting and scathing. But to me my most shaming responses were platitudes, fixed views and outdated attitudes, like hers. It was uncertain whether we would tear down brittle structures by opening up cracks stuffed – metaphorically speaking – with newspaper, resulting in collapse and total helplessness.

Parts of two dreams – one about a year ago, the other very recently, proved useful to us both. The first dream: *She was in a house, like hers but much more spacious and light, to which many things were being done. There were workmen about but they did not always seem to know what they were supposed to do and there was no organizer. Suddenly the room was full of people, some of whom she knew, saying to each other and to her that it was really no use. It would take far too long, would probably never be finished. There was not enough money, and what sort of a house did she really want?* All this reflected her mixed feelings – at that time mostly hostile – toward herself, me and our work. She realized that all those people were "sides of herself."

At my invitation she began to confront the people. A great deal of imaginative work went on, not excessively hampered by fixed ideas. The crippling grip on her grandmother and on me loosened. She began to mourn – she who had not been allowed to attend her grandmother's funeral because she was too young.

As she gained ground I began to wonder whether she possessed the inner resources to un-know – a process the medieval mystic, author of *The Cloud of Unknowing*, saw as essential for the spiritual journey. Would she, could she, indeed should she risk finding herself other than she wanted to be? My anxiety grew. I realized gradually that much of what was happening to her was happening also to me. Thus I had to question my willingness and capacity to un-know, although I had thought I had given up having a goal other than being there with my six senses – the five traditional and mind. I had to sacrifice all narcissistic gratification. Such sacrifice characterizes agape, the attitude that alone facilitates the individuation process.

The second dream is, I think, a clue to the role ritual plays in this awful – full of awe – process: the Agape Feast, the feast of sharing "in love." In the dream *the woman was in a group of unknown others, a conference involving the "Samaritans." The hotel was of stone, cavernous and dark. Other groups were around and Harry* (a friend and important person in real life) *was there too. At lunch time he appeared with a tray of beautifully arranged and ordered goodies and came over to offer her, gracefully, one piece. They both knew*, she emphasized, *that this was a ritual and, though she had a choice, the piece was preordained. She took a thin slice of carrot, disc-shaped, divided into sections. She was aware that Harry also knew the piece for her to choose. The task satisfactorily completed, he rejoined his friends and offered pieces to them.* (I was reminded of the Biblical statement, "Many are called but few are chosen.") As the dream continued, *she was practicing the ritual under instruction.*

She grew softer and more feminine and her voice more flexible. Instead of snatching greedily at everything I said, she seemed content with one item. I was aware of not feeling forced to go on offering her the dish. The resulting economy was enormous relief. I had noticed on many occasions my willingness to be emptied until the moment of resentment and consequent withholding – the negative aspect of the archetype. Had both of us discovered that we need not hate, that there is choice and will, a growing capacity for making decisions?

A short story about Bashu, the haiku master and his haiku, is an illustration of that inner attitude that we should strive to develop in our work, an attitude strange not only to us in the West but also to the disciples working under the master's instruction in the East.

The master was sitting in his riverside house on a spring day, bending his ears to the soft cooing of the pigeon in the quiet rain. This is the haiku:

Breaking the silence
of an ancient pond
A frog jumped into water
A deep resonance.

The disciples had been invited to contribute the fourth line. They, however, looked for something they could see; they saw the flowers of the yellow rose. Moving from the frog to the flowers, they completely lost the deep resonance vibrating in the heart of the master, echoing in the air of the garden. They offered other beautiful fourth lines but the mystery escaped them.

With the power of imaging the poet hears Hibiki (echo) coming from the depth of an ancient pond and makes it resound in poetry; a painter discerns Hibiki in the heart of mountains and rivers and recreates them in lines and on canvas; a theologian perceived Divine Hibiki from the abyss of creation and from the rough and tumble of human life in the world of suffering and hope – our world.

I was planning to end here, confessing to that goal for myself and I hope for us – neither slave nor master but servant of the Self. One week before this writing however, my analysand appeared for her session, quite transformed. She had dreamt a wonderful dream:

I was in my house, quite a large one and not the cottage I own, with a number of rooms light and comfortable. With me were several people familiar but not known. The bell rang and I opened the door. A friend stood there – not known. She brought me two plants and handed them to me: a Yucca plant and a Eucalyptus tree. By the front door were two small sheep (not lambs) frolicking. All around was beautiful country and health. The woman had disappeared and I went inside.

The dreamer explained: "This Yucca plant is a house plant with thorns instead of leaves. Every three to four years it bears on a stalk the most beautiful bell-like flowers." I, the listener, could smell and inhale the pungent scent of the crushed leaf of the Eucalyptus tree, freeing my breath as she went on to inform me that it has a tap root and where it grows is a water level which it taps to live. My breathing had become very constrained and now was getting rapidly free. The dreamer then added, "*There was another woman there facing me. She also was familiar but unknown.*"

Silence then reigned for what seemed a long time. We looked at each other comfortably. She said very quietly, almost with reverence, how wonderful it was to see the flowers emerge after three to four years of caring for thorns. She had, she mused, been coming for nearly three years. I continued to breathe more and more freely, savoring the pungent scent, freeing soul and spirit. The session ended; Chronos yielding to Chairos permitted us to experience the mystery.

REFERENCE

Samuels, A; Shorter, B., & Plaut, F. (1986). *A Critical Dictionary of Jungian Analysis*. London: Routledge & Kegan Paul.

Destructive and Creative Forces in Analysis

Destructive and Creative Forces in the Analyst

Margitta Giera-Krapp
Berlin, Germany
Schweizerische Gesellschaft für
Analytische Psychologie

When we think of destructivity it is usually that of the analysand. Here I am considering the destructivity of the analyst: not deliberate destructivity but unconscious destructive powers which, like creative powers, profoundly affect the analytic process on the archetypal level. The first of my two illustrative cases shows how destructive events in the analyst evoked or intensified destructive powers in the analysand. In the second case destructive powers of the analyst initiated a creative process in the analysand.

I present my first case with the consent of my late colleague. She gave her permission in order to contribute to a fundamental discussion on a subject that she had always considered very important.

Anna, a 31-year-old student, entered analysis because of depression and strong feelings of inferiority and inadequacy. Her suffering stemmed from her dwarfism and affected especially her female identity. When Anna was five years old her beloved father died of bone cancer. When she was nine, her mother married again. But the loving stepfather, who encouraged her a great deal, died four years later. Anna's childhood had already been marked by many hip surgeries, hence long separations from mother. For years the beautiful mother, of normal height, had not wanted to admit her daughter's dwarfism. Anna felt that, because of her handicap, she could never win the love of her idealized mother.

In the socially- and politically-involved analyst, Anna found a positive mother figure by whom she felt accepted. The positive mother-transference determined the course of the first year and a half of analysis. Anna had broken off her studies before undertaking analysis. She was advised by her analyst not to resume them because she was stressed by her physical limitations. The positive climate of the transference continued despite Anna's not finding her analyst's support for resuming her studies. Knowing that the analyst herself was engaged in studies, however, provoked strong feelings of envy in Anna.

The analyst attempted to mitigate the envy by saying that she did her studies because she experienced her profession as unsatisfying. In the evenings she felt empty; her energies and emotions were exhausted. She felt devoured by her analysands and envied them their privileged role in the analytical relationship. Anna wanted to be a good analysand – not demanding and devouring. Hence, she had to repress her angry feelings at the analyst's repeated complaints about the insatiability of her analysands.

Anna became depressed again. In addition to her fear of life and of the future, suicidal thoughts occurred which were interpreted by the analyst as a beginning of a process of detachment. Then, because of her own increasing depression, the analyst decided to give up her profession. In order to conclude Anna's analysis, she set a period of four months for the process of termination, convinced that Anna would not need further therapy afterward.

Although Anna felt let down, she wanted to remain the good analysand and contribute to a successful end of the therapy. In the analysis she avoided talking about her increasing feelings of meaninglessness and about her compulsive suicidal ideas which, however, were given expression in her paintings (Figures 1-3). In Anna's dreams the mother of death appeared in the form of child-murdering, witchlike grandmothers or of raging forces of nature which exterminate all life.

The analyst did not recognize the threat of death, which became visible in the dreams and paintings. Rather, she continued to interpret these images as expressions of a forced and therefore

Figure 1

Figure 2

Figure 3

dramatic process of detachment, which activated the negative mother complex – the bad mother who sends the child away. If she had gone more deeply into the topic of death, which Anna brought up, my colleague might have been confronted with her own suicidal tendencies and with the question whether these tendencies had evoked or, at least, intensified destructive powers in Anna. Only when Anna brought the following dream and connected it with continuing therapy did my colleague agree to a change of therapist. Anna dreamed:

With my two-year-old child I come to therapy but the house is empty. In the garden in a swimming pool I see a woman in black floating dead on the water, her arms stretched out, her head downward, her long black hair loose. I feel that this woman is my analyst. Terrified, I take my child into my arms and walk up a spiral staircase, feeling that from now on I have to take care of us all by myself.

The depth of the unconscious communication between analyst and analysand was evident in the period of Anna's analysis with me, during which my colleague committed suicide. Anna had been coming to me for nine months. During the previous two months positive mother aspects had recurred in her paintings and dreams. The transference climate was positively tinged, too. Anna could now mourn for her former analyst. More and more often she expressed her wish to speak with her once again, to make it easier to take leave of her and of their time together. I understood Anna's longing and supported her plan.

Figure 4

Figure 5

When they met, only a few days before my colleague died, she appeared rather serene and relaxed. At our next session Anna seemed depressed, but told me that their meeting had been a very positive experience for her. Consequently, she was shocked when, after the meeting, she painted two landscapes of death (Figures 4 & 5). They brought back her old longing for death and the feeling that everything was ultimately meaningless. Against this negative attitude to life she wanted consciously to depict a positive mother-child relationship. To her dismay the im-

Figure 6

age became a mother of death who threatens the child (Figure 6).

I offered the explanation that the destructive mother complex had been reactivated by the meeting, along with the loss of the good mother and Anna's fear of further losses. Anna agreed to this interpretation but during the next sessions she remained threatened by archaic, destructive ideas and fears. She finally said that she could not feel anymore and that she only longed for eternal peace and eternal sleep.

I saw Anna's longing for death, evoked by the meeting with her former analyst, as an expression of a still-existing symbiosis that enabled Anna to communicate with her on the deepest level and unconsciously to grasp her willingness to die. In order not to lose the good mother, she wanted to follow her to the sphere of death and live with her there.

Sensing her mortal danger I followed a sudden inspiration. I asked her to lie down at home on a big sheet of paper and to have her friend draw her body contours which she could then paint in colors and bring to analysis. As my request was urgent Anna followed it and painted the picture that gave her new courage to face life (Figure 7). That night she dreamed:

Figure 7

In a market place I see two circles of dancing people, blacks and whites separated. But then a black man seizes a naked white woman, and they dance a wild orgiastic dance. The two circles of dancers slowly close around the couple and form one big circle in black and white.

In the analytic relationship, too, the split into a good and a bad mother, which had existed up to this moment, slowly dissolved. The image of her former analyst had now light and dark aspects, as did Anna's image of me.

My second case example is that of Eva, a 32-year-old teacher, by now in analysis with me for 2-1/2 years, initially because of sexual disorders and relationship problems: she had difficulty in establishing contact with other people and she felt insecure among them. On the basis of an idealized transference the analysis began in an uncomplicated way. But Eva's powerful fears of separation and loss as well as defensiveness became obvious whenever I did not function perfectly. By the end of the first year of analysis the transference had become intensely erotic.

Eva suffered but did not talk. Instead, she showered me with quantities of anamnestic dreams, love letters, and poems. All my interventions and attempts at interpretation fell flat. Eva's strong infatuation and my feeling that I was manipulated made me assume that there was more than the symbolic constellation of the primal relationship in the transference, which had been uninfluenceable for weeks. I suggested that she paint her dreams or ideas. Obediently she brought along dozens of hastily painted pictures but could not say anything about the demonic faces that appeared here and there (Figure 8). She repeatedly dreamed that *she and her family broke into my apartment, occupied every room, rummaged about and kept a watch on every move I made*. Once again she could not realize that there was a parallel to the analysis, that she wanted to restrict and control me and make me lose my power. When I approached her about her resistance she replied, smiling indulgently, that I introduced this term only because it belonged to a classical analysis. She claimed also that she did not show resistance but I did, and I was reluctant and nasty.

Figure 8

I had been unusually touchy but now a veritable demon got into me. In cold fury I said that I was fed up with her gabbing and fuss, that I could not listen to her any longer and had to pull myself together in order not to throw her out. At the end of my outburst I said a bit more gently that I did not know how to go on;

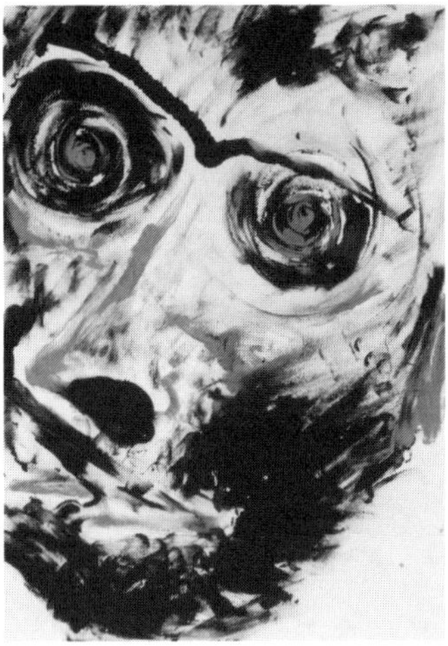

Figure 9

Figure 10

if she wanted to continue analysis, it would be up to her to find a solution. I only knew that I did not want to drop her. My later reflections on this aggressive countertransference reaction went back to Benedetti's (1984) thesis that the therapist can communicate with the inner demon of the patient only when responding to it on the same level.

Figure 11

When Eva came to the next session she was filled with fear. She reported a dream where *she had been pursued by a man armed with a stick and disguised with a black cloth*. She said she was not worried about herself but about me; she could see a big black figure standing behind me, his right hand on my left shoulder. This was death who threatened me. Eva felt threatened by this figure. I suggested that she capture it in a picture so that we could examine it together.

The drawings of this shadow-figure and a seven-page state-

Figure 12

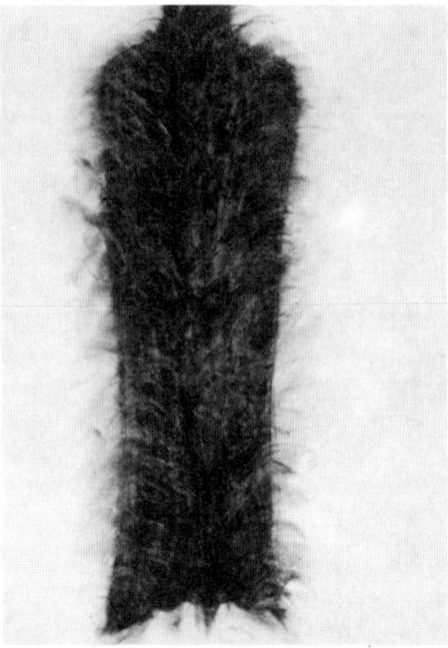

Figure 13

Figure 14

ment that the demon had dictated are impressive documents of the encounter of two unconscious archaic powers I call demons (Figures 9-15). From the threatening and then pleading speech of the demon, it became apparent that, although he was dangerous, the demon had acted only once in a destructive manner, and he might be able to protect Eva against a fragmentation because of his compulsive-rigid structures. I suggested that he cooperate in the analysis. Eva's demon decided to cooperate and opened the way to the deeper layers of her psyche. In the following two pictures (Figures 16 & 17) a boa holds a child in its jaws. In the dream the 1000-meter yellow-black poisonous snake pursues the dreamer. The snake symbolizes the mighty archaic power which threatened Eva on the deepest level but in the dream comforted a two-year-old child.

In her further dreams Eva learned about her deep injuries. She

Figure 15

saw herself as a two-year-old child alone in a hospital, crying out as doctors tormented her with injections. It was only now that she remembered that in fact she had been isolated for several weeks at that age because of a serious bowel infection. The personal mother had been threatening for Eva and still is. When the mother fell ill with breast cancer she asked her daughter to give up everything and to take care of her at home until her death. Accordingly Eva dreamed that *her mother, armed with a pistol, asked her to commit suicide and that she answered Eva's question of what she, the mother, wanted to represent with her illness was "a wolf, a wolf like the one in the fairy tale of the Little Red Ridinghood." And she added two words: symbiosis and death.*

Protected by my aggressive countertransference, which was now also directed toward the real mother, and with the consent of her demon who worked more and more creatively, Eva was able

Figure 16

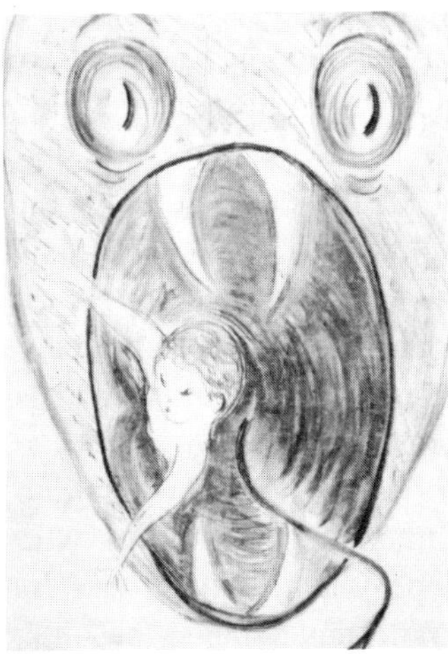

Figure 17

Figure 18

to dissociate herself from the threatening mother and from the auto-destructive tendencies evoked by her. Also, Eva could admit constructive aggressive impulses that contributed to a more appropriate mastering of reality and finding of identity. In one of the last imaginations the child freed herself from the snake's jaws and, with the protection of the demon who threatened the snake with his stick, crawled under my armchair while snake and demon disappeared into the desert in order to settle an old score with each other (Figure 18). In the imagination I had stood between Eva and the two opponents as a protecting black figure. Thus, in the countertransference I had taken, partly, the role of the protecting and structuring demon.

The question is: which was my own demon? Like Eva I must deal with power and powerlessness; an unconscious demoniac aspect of power may have been evoked inside me. It wanted to find out the secret kept by Eva's demon and did not accept the limits which were set for it. Here, this demon could contribute to the healing process and thus become creative out of destructiveness, but in another case it might cause a complete fragmentation of the fragile ego complex and be nothing but destructive.

We have to face the question again and again, to what extent the analyst's personality has an influence on the process and what conceptions and techniques are effective. The vitality and creativity of the analyst seem to be decisive. When we show openness and honesty regarding our own human limitations and vulnerability, our analysands will be able to experience us as authentic personalities who encourage individuation and give hope for individuality. I conclude with a quotation from Jung: "Who understands the images to some extent but who believes that it is enough to know is the victim of a dangerous error. Who does not consider his knowledge to be an ethical obligation becomes a slave to the power principle. Destructive effects can develop from it which do not only destroy others but also the knowing itself. The images of the unconscious impose a great responsibility on the individual" (MDR, p. 196).

Translated from German
by Sabine Osvatic

REFERENCE

Benedetti, G. (1984). Die Symbolik des schizophrenen Patienten und das Verstehen des Therapeuten. In: Hartwig & Menzen (Eds.). *Kunsttherapie*. Berlin: Verlag Ästhetik und Kommunikation.

"My Body Belongs to the Earth but My Spirit to Heaven": Psychotherapy in the Final Stage of Aids

Wolfgang Kleespies
Berlin, Germany
Deutsche Gesellschaft
für Analytische Psychologie

A 32-year-old man who suffered from AIDS turned to me in the final stage of his disease. My experience in this therapy has convinced me that there can be individuation even in a hopeless situation. Such a therapy does not prepare for life but it facilitates death.

Because of the very short life span that was left to him his analytic treatment was only six sessions. The setting was unusual, too. After the first out-patient consultation we continued therapy in the hospital; he had been admitted because of increasing febrile infections. I wore a sterile coat and cap; the patient had to be protected against the therapist.

During the sessions it soon became clear that it was not only the fear of death behind the symptoms; central unsolved matters emerged, frightened him and made it difficult for him to die.

Each session was characterized by a different experience. My initial "archaic fears of contact" with the patient wore off quickly. During our conversations, however, gradually an archetypal dynamic developed between us; it was characterized by fear, hope, resignation, and acceptance.

The Fear

A spontaneously reported dream became the starting point of the therapeutic process:

I was swimming in the ocean. It was very deep and I was very far out at sea. I could hardly make out the shore, which was very distant. I knew that I would not reach the shore because of the surf and the high waves. They dragged me out. Perhaps I should have tried to get to shore. But I felt fine in the sea. It was so tempting to swim, to drift and to let myself sink.

The man felt the tempting suction of the sea to which he only had to surrender – drifting, not doing anything, letting everything happen. But there was also a harassing fear arising in him. He said: "I won't die too soon, will I? I still have such a lot to do and to sort out." In my countertransference I felt a great deal of courage and the will to fight. Perhaps I would succeed in strengthening the man psychically. The therapy took place at his sick-bed; he was too weak to get up. Very quickly it became evident that two complexes especially kept the patient in movement, worry and anxiety: an unsolved aggression complex and a positive mother complex.

Life-space and Life-time

He wished to see the ocean one last time. Lying in his hospital room he was overwhelmed by this wish. Instead of its being realized, the walls of his room came a little closer each day. His way of experiencing space seemed to change: "The room shrinks every day," he said with a trace of humor. "One day it will have the size of a coffin and then they will carry me out of here in it." When saying this he got an unpleasant feeling of narrowness. He became painfully aware of his small scope of action. Only last week he still could leave his bed and walk around in the room.

He turned his attention to his childhood: father, mother and younger sister started to take clearer shape. Our sense of time changed; time seemed to expand and our talks seemed to last much longer. The subject of time and space continued in his next dream:

I flew backward, lying on my belly with my arms stretched out so that my feet were in front. I flew through a very big, boundless space. It was strange that I flew along a lot of closed doors. Behind these doors there were rooms: known rooms and totally unknown ones.

He immediately associated the closed doors with all that would now remain closed for him in life. Everything that he had planned to do and all the surprises for him would now remain behind closed doors which could never be opened. Next he occupied himself with the subject of spaces and their arrangement, something in which he had been interested since childhood. It had always been a matter of concern for him to create free spaces [German: "Freiraum" = "free space" and "freedom"]. He had painted gardens and horticultural scenes. This made him think of his father, a busy internist. The son had always felt deprived of his father's time and attention. In addition, the father appeared angry and despotic, restricting the free space (freedom) of his son.

Then the young man thought of the motif of flying, from his previous dream. He now associated it with lightness but also with remoteness from earthly life. He had the feeling that he was in a spiritual/intellectual sphere. He spontaneously connected this with a male/paternal sphere which, finally, he had now reached, at least in his dream. But in his dream he could not yet stay in this sphere. He rather felt drawn past and along these many doors, the known and the unknown.

To have his feet in front meant for him that they were directed toward the earth, the matter that was waiting for him and by which he felt drawn. This made him feel uneasy because he also connected matter with something maternal. I pointed out to him the linguistic similarity between "mater" and "materia". The transference had taken positive archetypal father-son form, characterized by acceptance and understanding and in clear contrast to his experience with his own father. This archetypal experience was of greatest importance for the young man's development. From this basis, which gave him security, he could now deal critically with the image of his mother. Up to this moment she had always appeared only as a good, sweet and noble woman who, silent and suffering, had endured the aggressive eruptions of her husband.

The man recognized basic patterns of his life surprisingly clearly. He was helped by the mature transcendent function that was at his disposal. His ego could turn actively to the spontaneously emerging symbols of his dreams and take them in. In this way, he gained self-knowledge.

In the elaboration of his dreams the analysand was occupied with this attraction to matter, which he now could feel so clearly. He thought of his own body, which consisted of matter, and said that he did not wish to be subject to an autopsy. To think that his body could be dismembered was unbearable for him. The body was his link to this world, in which he was still living. In the dream he already was in an unlimited, spiritual space which he spontaneously understood as paternal and male, but he was still endowed with a body whose feet pointed toward the earth to which he belonged. This session ended with the unsolved and torturing question: whether all of him would really enter into the earth?

The following night he had another dream:

I saw from above, that is, from a bird's eye view, how a coffin was slowly let down. My body was inside it. The coffin went deeper and deeper into the earth – without an end.

He was very much impressed by this dream. It was the first time that he had dreamed of his death. This brought us back to Mother Earth and to the fact that the body which belongs to matter also returns to it. He was a little relieved that he had seen everything from a bird's-eye view. There was something inside him which could observe the scene and which was separated from this terrible event. He said, "that was me – without a body." But the grave into which the coffin was let down was endless and without return.

The Labyrinth: Dissociation and Self-finding

During his last days the man thought time and again of a copper engraving that his mother had given him; it seemed to show a labyrinth. But this labyrinth, with its many fine lines and patterns, proved to be a spiral which led to a center. "This center was my mother," the man said "and my life is this spiral. I always circled around my mother." He said that this initial confusion, this labyrinth, corresponded to his life whose secret order he had not understood. Now his life disentangled to a meaningful structure in whose center stood this powerful mother figure. All his life he had adapted himself to his mother and had become as gentle – and inhibited in his aggression – as his mother. To become like his father – loud and aggressive – was something he could not do to his mother. This attitude was the source of his defense against his phallic aggressive side and consequently against his male identity. In spite of the previous idealization he now started to discover her shadow side. He worked intensively on her gentle and restricting ways, which had dominated him. For the first time I saw him angry.

In the following week a change occurred. I met his mother in the corridor. She complained about how her son had changed: he was so brusque and cold and wanted to be alone. I told the mother that she had to let him have his own way, that her son was in a critical phase. During the short life-span that was left to him he kept this new course of separation, which he had developed for the first time in his life. He seemed firmer and inwardly more relaxed. The complexes which had held him in a state of worry and conflict seemed to fade and the libido that had been bound up in them flowed to a calmer Self. In the following days his diffuse states of anxiety decreased. As we could state with satisfaction, he had acted in a combative and male manner for the first time in his life. In my countertransference I noticed that I felt more relaxed, too.

My Body Belongs to the Earth but My Spirit to Heaven

The last two archetypal dreams show a special dynamic: a separation of the spiritual/paternal principle from the maternal earthly sphere, that is, an unfolding of the opposites. The man had lived in a one-sided manner in the labyrinth of the mother archetype. This unfolding of the opposites had been prepared by the father archetype which he transferred onto me. Thus, he allied himself with the spiritual-paternal sphere and it was only from "this safe ground" that he could turn to his complexes.

In the first dream *the dreamer is in this upper spiritual space but the body is oriented toward the earth and subject to a pull toward the archetypal image of the Magna Mater*. The man's increasing dealing with the mother image reveals its pull on him. He starts to work on the underlying negative character of the mother archetype. Her pull increases through his progressing sickness so that the man comes under additional pressure. In this period of strongest elementary tension, of fight and inner reflection, he increasingly realizes the binding and devouring qualities that lie behind the positive mother imago. He starts to defend himself against them.

At this point let us recall the psychology of the Self. Our natural movement toward individuation is controlled by archetypes whose sequence is determined by the dynamic of the Self. For a lifetime the analysand had longed for a father to free him from his captivity in the negative maternal character. Psychologically this striving for a father makes sense; the young man's sexual orientation represents a motif of union with the Great Father, acted out on a concrete level in homosexuality. But the real struggle for liberation from the sphere of the Magna Mater was still ahead of him as something he wanted to achieve in his life. It might have remained unfulfilled forever. But during his last days at least part of it was fulfilled in impressive symbolic motifs which led the man out of his one-sided fixation on the mother.

The negative archetypal character of the Magna Mater becomes especially evident in the dream in which the goddess of earth opens her deep gullet and the coffin endlessly sinks into it. I have rarely come across a more impressive image for the devouring character of the Magna Mater. Relentlessly she demands her children back. But this second dream already contains the transformation. In the first dream the man is still completely subject to a pull toward the earth; he is located in the gravitation center of the Magna Mater and thus he is directed by her. In the second dream he remains in the upper spiritual sphere, he stays with the father who had always been the aim and object of his life. But he has to pay tribute to mother earth. In the end the body belongs to the earth, dies, becomes part of it, while the spirit turns to heaven and lives.

I saw the man one more time. He was shaken by phases of high fever; these were the "waves" which washed him farther and farther from the shore. I could not talk very much with him and noticed a distance between us which became larger and larger; he was gliding away while I remained behind. Deep sorrow seized me. The next day I learned that he had died in the night.

Translated from German
by Sabine Osvatic

Life against Death after a Neonatal Loss

Nadia Neri
Rome, Italy
Associazione Italiana per lo Studio della Psicologia Analitica

When I first met Marianne, my immediate impression was that of a helpless, fragile and "spooky" woman. She had pale features, was dressed all in black and appeared to be overwhelmed by an undefined, dull pain. It was palpable in her body, which seemed to be nothing but skin and bones. Marianne had introduced herself by phone stating that she wished analysis because of her pregnancy – she was in her fifth month – and the emotional problems thereof.

This child-like, inexpressive woman revealed from the first diagnostic session a boiling rage and a rigid rationality. Yet she desperately tried to suppress her emotions. And her belly signalled that we had to give priority to it, even if it was just a little swollen.

At the same time, Marianne was an educated woman with two doctoral degrees. She was politically active and had experienced a short period of militant feminism. She had entrusted herself to a woman obstetrician who favored home delivery. Marianne was convinced that she had made the right choice but at the same time was filled with such a growing fear and uneasiness that she felt it necessary to start an analysis during her pregnancy.

In the first of the three diagnostic consultations she told me the following dream: "*I am with friends. I am amazed about my clothing, as I wear light, floral trousers*. (Actually she wears black.) *Then I suddenly see a person's hand protruding from a concrete wall, moving around. I am deeply frightened.*" I imagine how frightening the scene must be for her. It is a hand asking for help, not knowing how to liberate herself from the concrete wall and it is just one free hand, perhaps not enough.

During our second consultation Marianne reported the following dream: "*I am in an elevator that is suddenly jammed. The doors open but I have a concrete wall in front of me. I wake up and I think that the child is not moving!*" As soon as she had finished telling her dream, a clear feeling struck me like a flash: this child will not succeed in being born. I sensed that this woman had a great vitality, but it was completely stunted.

Consequently, a great deal of patience and a readiness to wait was needed. Using the image in the dream: the concrete is impenetrable and not easy to crack. Nevertheless, I managed not to be infected by a frenzy of healing or by thoughts of being a saving mother to her. It was vital for me to take a constructive position, based on my experiences in infant observation during my analytic training.

I had done this observation in Rome, at the first Tavistock Biennial, with English Kleinian analysts such as Donald Meltzer and Martha Harris, Beta Copley and Gianna Henry Polacco. It was Esther Bick who, in 1948, introduced infant observation. Today such observation forms an integral part of the training of child analysts in many European countries. The English Jungians have had it for many years, the Italian Jungians for two years. Observing a newborn child provides an emotional training that makes us more sensitive to our countertransferences. It also teaches us to accept the fact that, with regard to our analysands, we live in uncertainty.

In the first months Marianne often returned to her childhood experiences and regressed to her infantile anxieties. I had to bear my own fears, anxieties and hopes and to accept the fact that there was nothing to do but await an uncertain outcome. Also, I must not confuse the emerging inner child of the analysand with the actual one about to be born.

The experience, in infant observation, of being powerless is fruitful; it helps to reduce our sense of omnipotence as persons as well as therapists. In my view, of equal importance with personal analysis in training is observing the development of a newborn child and its relationship with its mother. Such observation – over a period of two years – evokes deep and often regressive sentiments and memories in the observer.

In addition, observing the newborn child lets us become more "conscious of the infantile aspects of the transference and of the psychosomatic nature of the experience; it also renders us more sensitive toward the difficulties of our countertransference" (Wittemberg, 1986, p. 3). "Both mother and analyst can... feel uncertain and confused because of a particular position of the baby, and the mother's reaction can go so far as to be turned into action. The analyst would then have a rather reflective function and... always avoids action. The fact that the observation techniques [developed] by Bick do not allow action turns out to be very useful in developing the ability of not intervening directly" (Maffei, 1984, pp. 147-48).

My training experiences supported my decision to take Marianne into analysis. From the beginning I knew that I had to accept the uncertain outcome of the delivery and to take care not to intervene in matters that were dictated by reality; for example, go to the doctor or have an echography done. Furthermore, I wanted not to provoke my analysand's anxiety that she would give birth to a child who was not healthy. My attitude must be that of seconding nature. As one knows, nature generates death as well as life. Nature is not subject to human wishes; it has its own terms that are to be respected. Pregnancy is an example.

The day before one session Marianne telephoned and told me with a totally emotionless voice that she had given birth at home. The baby had shown extreme pains while being born and was taken to a hospital, where it died after three days. She let me know that she would keep our appointment the following day.

The month that followed the birth and death was a very hard time for her and also for me; I recalled the sensation I had during our second session, when she told me her dream. I had to come to terms with my feelings of guilt and inadequacy and confront this actual death. The death of a newborn child is unbearable in a double sense: witnessing the child's signs of desperation and fear and, even more, accepting its death.

In analyses we always confront the fear of death, often in the inner form of destructivity and anxiety. Sometimes we confront the actual death of a person important to the analysand. We then help the bereaved to work through the period of sorrow and the terrorizing reality of death, which is part of every human being's experience. The process is much more difficult and painful if one confronts the death of a newborn child. It triggers what may be the origin of mortal fear, connected with the moment of birth.

In psychoanalytic theory the question of death has always been thorny. Freud, conscious of his own fear of death, first theorized on such fear as an anxiety neurosis before he postulated, in 1920, the concept of a death drive in "Beyond the Pleasure Principle" (SE18). But we have known for some time that it was a woman, Sabina Spielrein (1986), who first mentioned – in 1912 – this drive as determining the psychic life alongside the pleasure principle. Another woman, Melanie Klein – who was sorely tried in her personal life by the death of a sister at the age of four, followed by a brother and a son – also wrote extensively about the anguish of death. She supported vigorously the idea of the death drive and its derivation from the experiences a newborn child has with this drive. Indeed, she dedicated herself to a profound understanding of grief and to the paranoiac, manic and obsessive-compulsive defenses that are used to limit such suffering.

It was not accidental that a woman first realized the existence of a death drive. Women have a direct and immediate contact with nature and are therefore capable of comprehending its most secret and mysterious aspects. Von Franz made numerous observations on this theme, including this one: "The secret of nature seems to consist of killing with perfidious cruelty and on the other side of giving life to the most beautiful things" (1983, p. 176).

For Jung as well, death was not a specific drive linked to fears and desires but rather something natural, connecting the individual to the species and confronting the person with the inscrutability of nature. Jung also perceived death in regard to religious and philosophical thinking of the Orient and to the concept of rebirth. These are surely useful and valid positions for the mind of the analyst, yet not always immediately helpful in the analytic setting.

In any case, grief work has to start at the personal level. Deep inside I felt guilt, having in a sense sacrificed the child, while concentrating on the non-synchronous rhythms of the analysand. On the other hand, I felt that Marianne experienced her own body as damaged and as a contagious carrier of misfortunes and death, making a pregnancy unbearable. She risked being overwhelmed by grief in the face of such a clear failure of her femininity. She did not need explicit answers, but rather the right kind of attitude. In similar situations it has seemed fruitful for the analyst to be capable of tolerating and imagining the analysand's suffering. In so doing, the analyst "helps the patient tolerate his/her own anxiety and leads him/her to identify with an object that is strong enough and able to think," emphasizes Wittemberg (1986, p. 8).

This interior attitude is a silence that contains the analysand. And if we consider the narcissistic wound of the mother of a handicapped newborn child – studied by Mannoni (1964) – the death of Marianne's child seemed such an irreparable event that a psychological digestion after just five months of analysis is simply impossible. My countertransferential attitude strengthened Marianne's feelings of hope, confirming the possibility of a new inner journey.

One month after the death of the newborn, she told me the following dream: "*I am with one of my friends. It is night. I have to go down a winding road to the base of a palace. At my left there is sand, the kind that is used to make concrete. Within the palace, there is a newborn baby, suffering from shortness of breath. With others we try to cure it. Then I see my aunt on a terrace above the palace.*" While listening to the dream, I was touched by two elements, the crumbling concrete and the return to a primary situation shown by the sand and, of course, by the presence of the newborn; both seemed to free the vital force that had been bottled up.

An aunt is observing from high above. This unmarried woman, the father's sister, had lived with the family. Preferring to go out to work, the mother had delegated Marianne's upbringing to the aunt. This situation of having a "double mother" generated an emptiness and a deep anger. And because she lacked the primary contact with her mother, Marianne started to develop a fear of the feminine and a hatred toward her own body. This went so far that her body became the object of furious attacks in her imagination. She neglected her appearance, dressing as a man. She thought she could do without her mother and get all her strength from the world of her father. Therefore, it pained her to realize that the relationship to her father was also doomed by the thought of death. The beginning of a relationship with her unborn baby – risking a life of isolation and loneliness because the baby probably would have needed extensive care – gave rise to hope in this fight against pain.

The analysis is still going on. After two years Marianne gave birth to a daughter; now she is a much sweeter and stronger woman, more vital and feminine. We have touched the subject of death on only one occasion, but it will surely arise again in another form, when we approach the end of the analysis.

I conclude with a quote from the Portuguese writer Pessoa. The poem expresses the difficulty of life, which we analysts encounter every day.

Second guard: "What is eternal and beautiful is only the dream....
But why are we still talking?..."
First guard: "I do not know.... Why does one die?"
Second guard: "Perhaps because we do not dream enough."

First guard: "It could be.... Would it not be worth locking oneself up in the dream and forgetting about life, so that death forgets about us?"

Translated from Italian by
Helena Nyberg

REFERENCES

Maffei, G. (1984). Perché l'osservazione del bambino? In *La psicoterapia infantile junghiana*. Rome: Il Pensiero Scientifico editore.

Mannoni, M. (1964). *Il bambino ritardato e la madre*. Torino: Boringhieri.

Spielrein, S. (1986). La distruzione come causa della nascita. In *Comprensione della schizofrenia*. Napoli: Liguori.

von Franz, M.-L. (1983). *Il Femminile nella fiaba*. Torino: Boringhieri.

Wittemberg, I. (1986). Infant observation e angosce infantili in pazienti adulti. Seminario fiorentino del 5. april.

Analytical Psychology and Women
(Workshop)

The Feeling of Creativity and Fantasies About the Child

Martine Gallard
Paris, France
Société Française
de Psychologie Analytique

In my practice I see many women who have managed, without too much difficulty, to become "adults" and to establish their lives. Such a woman has either succeeded in setting up a family life (with or without a professional life) or else she has put all her energy and creativity into a career. She comes into analysis because she has the feeling that nothing is working out right any more, everything is falling apart around her, everything has lost its meaning. The analytic process brings to light her affective relationships and parental imagoes and allows her – and me – to understand the reasons for her dissatisfaction and sense of failure.

I am especially interested in being attuned to what I call "the subjective feeling of creativity," which may or may not be connected to the development of femininity. At such moments of doubt the woman says to me: "Despite all the things I've created, my feminine being is not recognizable as belonging to me. Giving birth has not made me into a woman. Living with a man has not given meaning to my life. Creating a business has no interest for me because I no longer know who I am nor what it is to be a woman."

As an analyst, the questions I hear are: "Is it possible to develop the Self without first having realized one's femininity? Is there a way of realizing the Self that is unique to women?" Clinical observation will give us a partial answer to this question.

In order to accept fully one's femininity, one must first become detached from the maternal role. This process is often expressed by an act of abortion – in reality, in dreams, or in fantasies; the abortion is lived as a symbolic event. It shows both the possibility of having a child and of refusing the child. This symbolic act can open the way toward one's individual and spiritual creativity which is rooted in the Self, and in so doing permit transcendence of woman's biological destiny.

A young woman with a borderline structure dreams that, *while with her mother and aunt, she is going to have an abortion. Her mother and aunt find it impossible to believe that she could be pregnant. In the dream she has no choice; she must have an abortion.* The dreamer's associations bring out the painful circumstances of her own birth. Her parents, very young at the time, had plans to buy a car. They never accepted having to buy a baby carriage. Since the beginning of her life this young woman has been weighed down by the feeling that she has no right to live. When, during her analysis, she has this dream, I understand it as a way of coming to terms with this early trauma: an attempt to put to death the suffering child inside her, in order to symbolize a new beginning. We can only hope that an archetypal process will help to create in this woman a new attitude toward life.

A woman of 50 also dreams that *she is going to have an abortion.* Actually, she has no sex life and she has never expressed the desire to have a child. But this dream comes during a period of extreme resistance in her analysis, when she is angry with her analyst for the suffering caused by realizations of the necessity of making real changes in her life. The dream helps the analysand to express her negative transference. She then experiences a surge of new energy which enables her to take charge of her desire for transformation. It is by saying "no" first that one can then say "yes."

Another woman, in her late thirties, decided that above all else she wanted to have a baby. After many failed sexual relationships, she met a man by whom she quickly became pregnant. Because the man was not ready to make a firm commitment, he decided that the woman should abort. She agreed, although against her wishes. On the way to the hospital the man changed his mind and said that he wanted her to have the baby.

This experience was fruitful for both of them: for the woman because she was forced to give up her desire for a child, a desire that did not take into consideration her partner's wishes; and for the man, because it forced him to give up his wish to keep her all to himself and to acknowledge her desire and its consequences.

A few weeks later she had a miscarriage, which proved to have beneficial consequences. It led to a necessary process of mourning the loss of the potential child, and it helped her to understand that the desire for a child represented the wish for a phallus. She recognized also the difficulties between herself and the man: both partners needed more time in the creation of a relationship, given their two very different personalities. These events in her life helped her to become aware of a symbolic castration; this awareness had not been possible before. Feelings of omnipotence had always controlled her life; now it became possible for her to accept feelings of emptiness and the idea of not being all-knowing.

These women have in common an extraverted animus during the first part of their lives. Women's struggle for liberation during recent decades has resulted in a collective development of the animus, of the so-called masculine qualities. Now acknowledged as being as intelligent and capable as men, women have overcome society's resistance and have proved themselves worthy of the best positions, even in the military establishment. But questions concerning their affective development and their femininity remain unanswered: What does it mean to be a woman? How does one become a woman?

Having based their life choices on exterior criteria of success, they reach a point where this success is no longer enough to hold their lives together. Thus they are forced to stop the constant forward movement – toward the exterior – in order to look into their interior, affective lives. I have found that the question of the inner child, which comes up in all treatments of women, plays an important role in working through various aspects of early affective life:

The identification with the mother.

The problem of the difference of the sexes results in anger or depression due to the discovery of the absence of the penis.

The wish to have a child with her own father, which – assuming that the wish is later abandoned – can represent a positive resolution of the castration complex. No woman can avoid following this path of libidinal development, discovered by Freud, which I think corresponds to an archetypal structure.

But now I propose that we consider how a woman – either by having an actual child, or by dealing with the possibility of having a child – is able to work through childhood problems and, in so doing, to begin to realize her femininity and creativity. We have already seen how many women mechanically go through the biological act of childbirth without experiencing the corresponding creative process.

Abortion – actual or fantasized – enables the woman to give up her masculine identification and phallic desires. Such perception, of a visceral nature, brings the woman to realize that her sex is not an absence or a lack and helps her to take more active control over her life and destiny.

I have in mind a young woman whose relationships with men have always been violent and aggressive. Her sex life with her husband is marked by ambivalence. In order to feel pleasure in the sex act, first she must go through feelings of disgust. During her first pregnancy she suffered from intense anxiety and feelings of unreality. After a few years in analysis she began to want a second child. In contrast with the first pregnancy, the second was a fulfilling experience.

Because of the restoration of her maternal function, she became physically more relaxed and began to enjoy sex. During moments of intense sexual pleasure she felt her vagina and uterus become integrated into her body. Thus, making love with her husband at times took on cosmic proportions, with far greater meaning than her individual existence. This woman, who had been very uncomfortable with her bodily functions – suspicious and easily disgusted with anything related to the body – learned to let herself go and deeply enjoy physical pleasure. At the same time she discovered that she was a whole, separate entity in the universe.

These new sensations of pleasure were not without anxiety, as she saw that she would have to modify and soften certain aspects of her behavior and ways of thinking. She came to understand that the discovery of pleasure – and of her femininity – was possible only because she had allowed herself to give up the need to control.

Although she was a talented professional painter, her work suffered because of this need for strict control. During the course of her analysis I observed a parallel between the creation of the actual child and the evolution of her artistic work, which became a more authentic personal statement. Previously she had not been able to risk a regressive movement, although such a movement would have allowed her to find a new source of primal images which she could have used in her creations. Through such an archetypal dynamic she found the Self.

The woman was very much bound to the objective, outer aspects of life; she had difficulty coming into contact with her subjectivity. Living through the physical process of pregnancy afforded her more confidence in giving herself over to the process of creation, much as she had let her child grow in her.

To return to my initial question: how does one become a woman? I think that a woman cannot attain her Self in its totality until she has given up her masculine identification and wish for a penis. I have attempted to show that desire for a child and abortion fantasies, which permit the symbolization of loss, play a role in the transformation process.

The extraversion of the animus places women on the path of doing and interferes with their ability to hear this internal voice which can lead them to their being. This path is not easy. It is reserved to the fortunate who have the courage to suffer and to confront their solitude, and who have a certain creative genius to initiate new paths of development for the future.

Women are by nature sensitive and drawn to symbolic processes – perhaps because of their familiarity with hidden and secret things. Thus they seek individuation in their lives. Consequently, they find themselves living in a world different from that of the men they meet. However, we can help each woman at a given moment in her life, when confronted with difficulties, to make use of what her psychic gifts provide and what society offers, and to find a compromise and the possibility of investing herself in what interests her.

On a Road to Nowhere

Françoise Caillet
Antony, France
Société Française de Psychologie Analytique

Four women analysands of mine had in common the situation that the mother archetype had not been awakened; it had no dynamics, it had not been embodied. As Jung said, the archetype in itself is an empty form.

The relationship of these women to their mothers had been disturbed at an early age or, more precisely, had never reached a level where the emotions could be lived. Although the daughters were well cared for physically, the mothers could not allow their maternal feelings to come alive – because of depression or pathological grieving, or because the attachment to their own mothers still precluded any emotional connection.

Each of the four analysands has, even today, an intense relationship with her father. This relationship has monopolized her consciousness and her affective life. Each says: "He has been a marvelous father."

The Frustrating Mother

It becomes apparent very soon that each analysand rarely alludes to her mother and that the few memories of her are frustrating. She hardly exists. When she does, it is as a mother who is not "good-enough." The archetypal mechanism is stuck and becomes repetitive in these little girls. Yet it is the mother who is "good-enough" who stimulates the development of tools which enable us to deal with life's vicissitudes and obligations.

These analysands have had to protect themselves against their identification with the mother, which is made dangerous by the destructiveness of her depression. But we know that the baby's identification with mother, which is one way in which the ego develops, can take place only if the mother identifies with the baby. In these cases, the mother – for various reasons – has not been able to see herself reflected in the mirror which her baby girl presents her. As a result, the basic pattern of identification does not exist and the child remains stuck in a repetitive and hopeless quest for this original object. An initial mother-child pre-Oedipal container, in which the baby can grow, is simply not there. The unconscious of such a daughter tries to deny the pain this situation produces. This defense mechanism prevents the little girl from using the other women she meets as substitute models of identification.

The Father as Carrier of the Feminine

The only remaining model of identification available to the little girl is her father's anima, which he has already projected onto her instead of onto his wife. As a result, the daughter is prevented from creating an inner image of her future adult sexuality. She stays permanently at the pregenital stage. If the father allows his daughter the right to a non-incestuous genitality, he loses the object of his anima projection. (The girl's right to a non-incestuous genitality should have been confirmed or even provoked by the mother, but she has not been emotionally available.) The father is put in a perverse position. He enjoys the father/mother role and tries to assume both functions. Although he originally assumed this ambiguous role in order to protect his daughter from her deficient mother, the mother's deficiency and the father's trespassing do not make for the growth of an ego which would allow the child to withstand the inner tensions.

Time

The femininity into which the father initiates the daughter is sterile, whereas the femininity that the maternal feminine introduces is fruitful. It gives access to time – to cyclic time – as it relates not only to that which repeats itself but also to the basic drives. It is only by being related to both cyclic time and basic drives that one can have access to historical time.

The analysands I am describing all look much younger than they actually are; their personal histories have not left any marks on their faces. They seem to stand outside time. Even so they belong to it via their successful studies and their academic degrees. Nevertheless, their professional lives remain unsatisfactory because they are not really involved.

Adolescence

For these "motherless" women, the breaking point usually coincides with adolescence; childhood had been a protection. Ordinarily, adolescence allows the girl once again to be close to her mother in their shared, potentially homosexual femaleness, reviving their early fusional relationship. When this type of regression takes place, it provides the energy needed for the separation. Through this structuring dynamism the daughter emerges ready to face life and her first sexual awakenings.

In the cases I am citing, however, separation from the mother does not act as a stimulus but creates an abyss, a desperate solitude. One of these women has attempted suicide, one is living a totally marginal life, the other two have lost themselves in a pseudo family life. These women have no inner space, no inner psychic territory where erotic or aggressive investments can be experienced fully. They are unable to hold on to any positive images of themselves. They are constantly searching for the primordial object – the "good mother" – in an endless and exhausting repetition. The result is a feeling of emptiness which these analysands often mention.

Non-differentiation

In fact, these analysands are not Oedipal. They have not been introduced into the mother-child circle. They have been pushed instead into the father-child circle. The psychologically missing mother has let the father take all the space. The masculine and feminine poles of the archetype cannot be differentiated when the father does not accept being a man and only a man. Such acceptance would give him his rightful place in the couple and allow his wife to occupy hers. The child, and later the teen-ager, is introduced into a dual relationship instead of an Oedipal triangle which would have given her the opportunity to develop in a psychologically diversified way. The ego remains infantile, the narcissistic compensations cannot develop and the ego becomes rigid so as not to upset the precarious equilibrium.

Because, psychologically, they have not had two separate parents, the masculine pole of these women has not been differentiated. For their personalities to be well-structured, their father's masculinity – which is an aerial masculinity – should have been counter-balanced by their mother's masculinity, which is earthy and carried by her animus. The combination would give the daughter the means to adapt to new situations, to initiate new relationships, to face the unknown.

The Role of the Analyst

In cases such as these – where the mothers were absent, where a firm basis is missing – what is the place that, as a woman analyst, I should occupy? These seem to be cases where the gender of the analyst is important even though the transference is not a maternal one to begin with. On a conscious level, the analyst is not even seen. Then, little by little, the transference takes place at a level where there is confusion: the analyst is experienced by the analysand as similar to herself, and the analytic setting is charged with negative potentialities. There occurs a repetition of the frustrating situation, previously experienced with the mother, where nothing good could happen and yet where hope brings the woman regularly to her sessions. Then the analyst becomes someone for the analysand to attack and make sure she is still alive and still welcoming. The transference occurs in the space where something is missing. In these cases, it is the place the "good mother" should have occupied. During the sessions, the analysand constantly wonders: Is the analyst going to stand up under my attacks? Is she going to take an interest in me even though my own mother has not done so?

At the same time, the analyst must be very discreet. The analysand has always identified herself with the other's (the father's) desires instead of her own desires, which could never be perceived by her ego. I must be careful not to dream her future and my interventions must be gentle and nondramatizing.

In the second phase of the work the mother archetype has been constellated; the analysand is able to imagine the ideal mother and to confront her with the real mother. The archetypal process takes over. The transference is then less ambivalent. The dreams which precede this moment are dreams where women of the same age as the analysand begin to appear, positive similar women and complementary shadow figures.

Then, and only then, come the dreams in which the real mother appears. From then on the analysand, without being destroyed, can experience rivalry toward her mother and toward other women without being destroyed. She can imagine, she can feel, she can live the pleasure of being a woman.

Refusing To Be A Woman

Monique Salzmann
Paris, France
Société Française de Psychologie Analytique

The women who consult us are searching primarily for their identity, whatever they overtly ask for. They come to us to find out what it is to be a woman.

Until relatively recently, society decreed what was womanly and what was not. And, no matter how much this definition differed from one cultural group to another, or from one period to the next, there was only one way to be a woman at any given time and in any given society.

Consequently, women did not have to worry about what was womanly. The universe was divided clearly into what was masculine and what was feminine. This dichotomy was reflected in every field of human activity. Daily tasks, social, religious and family roles, behavior, even character traits were assigned according to sex, down to the most minute details. Initiation rites separated the young girl from the world of the mother and did away with the sexual ambivalence of childhood. The most concrete form of initiation rite was the ablation of the clitoris. More generally, these rites permitted a girl to enter the world of women, where she was taught the language, the sexuality, the gestures. From the beginning of her life she knew that her world was different from the world of men.

The fact that such customs have existed, in one form or another, in every society, indicates that they are archetypal. That is, they belong to those primordial patterns which, like instincts, organize the human aspects of life.

The problems we encounter today come from the fact that the collectivity no longer offers the means by which to make these separations and differentiations. Initiation rites, even those that have evolved in our societies, have grown obsolete. Sexual differentiation no longer takes place on a collective level. Most activities, even typically virile ones such as driving a truck, can be entrusted now to either sex.

That which was really important in the traditional division of roles according to sex, was not so much the fact that men tilled the fields and women prepared the dance ornaments; in another group it could have been the other way around. What was important was that the masculine was differentiated clearly from the feminine, one being defined by opposition to the other.

The individual psyche develops, distinct from the collective, but the archetypal structure does not change. The same separations and differentiations which, previously, were assigned by the group now must take place in the individual psyche, in order to activate the dynamics that push a young girl to become a woman.

It is hard today for the individual to find her bearings. Society no longer provides structures that are suitable for furthering the life urge. The only way is that of the individual; all of us are obliged to become aware of the archetypal processes within our psyches.

The old dichotomy between masculine and feminine is still at work, however, in the social, religious and family world. In our culture the encounter with patriarchal values is one of the major difficulties that face contemporary woman in her attempt to become a complete feminine human being.

This difficulty seems to be the common denominator of two types of avoidance of the feminine: the woman who has not found her place as a woman cannot deal with the world of men and, consequently, she may deny the difference between the sexes.

In one instance a woman avoids a genuine encounter with the man, whose "otherness" she denies. Instead, she repeats with him the uroboric symbiosis of the primal relationship in which each partner plays alternately the role of the mother or of the child.

The instance that I am considering here is the opposite; she denies the woman and takes the place of the man. She is the daughter who refuses to be like her mother. Through fear of men, or because she refuses to occupy what she considers to be a position of humiliation and impotence reserved to women in our society or – more generally – in compensation for a feeling of inferiority, she refuses the form of femininity that our society has to offer. Such a woman is likely to lack any relationship with her father because he was too violent, larger than life, or absent.

The adult female who refuses to be a woman identifies with the masculine pole of the archetype. For her the function of this pole, as animus, is to render possible the relationship of the feminine ego to the unconscious. In such a situation it seems not proper to speak of a negative animus.

One can understand the feeling of omnipotence in such an analysand. It results from the experience she has of the androgynous totality that characterizes the archetype in its original, pre-differentiated state. This archetype seems to be the origin of her formidable energy. But we know that this totality has to be sacrificed for us to be human, endowed with a masculine *or* feminine identity.

One can imagine how intolerable will be the sacrifice of a position that places these women above others, above everyday life which they consider banal and contemptible, above their own instincts, feelings and sensations. In these lives, driven by a superhuman will, psychotic episodes are quite common. To defend herself against such episodes a woman may develop a rigid personality. The real losers in this kind of situation are the young girl and the animus.

The rejection of her mother by such a woman – or the feeling of being rejected – has not allowed the separation from the mother to take place. But it has also excluded the woman from the world of the mother and prevented any sort of triangulation; both experiences are necessary to enter into the world of the feminine.

By trying to force her way into the non-maternal feminine by means of the heroic masculine short-cut, she expresses an immense attraction to the woman she perceives but cannot attain.

This attraction manifests itself in an idealization of the woman she would like to be or, possibly, by homosexual behavior which aims at being reunited to both the lost mother and the abandoned girl. Her refusal of her humanity has been so violent that it is moving to see her slowly become more gentle, cry without violence, abandon her megalomania, dream that her parents are tender with her, take pleasure in daily routine and, very slowly, begin to re-evaluate herself.

But for any of these developments to be possible, the woman must come down from her position of power, experience the humiliation she feared and perhaps even come to the bottom of the pit. Thus, castration is imposed from the outside. Finally, she must let go of the desired penis and accept the sacrifice without which there is no access to the animus. There comes a time when the analyst also must accept a loss of power, in one form or another.

It is only then that in these women's dreams there appear normally-sexed men toward whom they experience both desire and tenderness. (Until then, any relationships to men were of a masculine homosexual character.) Now they become less demanding and dream analysis is no longer immediately re-appropriated by the ego for its own purposes.

I insist on this particular type of process because I do not see the problem as a negative animus. On the contrary, I rather think that there is no animus at all. It has been squeezed out of the picture, deprived of its otherness by the ego's usurpation of masculinity. This is a pseudo-masculinity, not related to the woman's inner being, but imprisoned in the unconscious. The identification with the masculine, however, may be the woman's attempt to possess a father to whom there was no other way of access.

This manner of approach to the feminine, this aborted attempt at obtaining the ingredients of the *coniunctio*, is becoming more and more frequent. What is its deeper meaning? We do not know yet the type of woman that is in preparation and with what type of partner she will be able to relate. Is she going to recreate the symbiotic couple? And if, alternatively, a woman should become more of an autonomous being, will her lot be solitude? As we know, the archetype does not provide the contents, but attracts and organizes them. Therefore, there is an infinite variety of ways to be a woman now that there is no longer a single model available. All that we analysts can do, probably, is to keep out of the way of our analysands' living aspects of the feminine that have been outside the collective field of consciousness. Then, perhaps, they can enter that world and, perhaps, transform it.

Child Analysis: Transference/Countertransference

Adolescents with Bulimia

Brian Feldman
San Francisco, California, USA
Northern California Society
of Jungian Analysts

The inner world of the adolescent bulimic woman is filled with anxiety, dread and terror. She comes to analysis in a state of confusion, despair and hopelessness, having tried to stop the repetitive bouts of binging and vomiting but unable to reduce their frequency or length. During the evaluation interviews she often talks of being unable to cope with depression, internal chaos and feelings of self-hatred, some of which are in response to the bulimia itself.

The level of psychic pain has become so intense that bulimic episodes have become the only form of emotional relief. They take on the quality of magical rituals whose purpose is to calm, soothe, and reinstate some semblance of psychic balance following periods of disintegrated mental states. The bulimic episode can occur in a dissociated mindless state where there is little capacity for reflection or integration. The bulimia takes on an addictive behavioral pattern in which food is used not for nutrition but rather to change and negate distressing states of mind.

My thesis is that bulimia represents a disorder of the Self in which the deintegrative/reintegrative processes are damaged, and that the bulimia can be conceptualized as a desperate attempt to forestall psychological breakdown. Fordham's (1985) concept of deintegrative processes has been important in helping me to understand the clinical material of bulimic women.

Fordham conceptualized the infant as having a primary Self from which psychic structure evolves through the process of deintegration and reintegration. One of the first deintegrative/reintegrative processes occurs during the first feeding. As the infant experiences the breast and the maternal care associated with it as reliable, and an empathically attuned relationship develops between mother and baby, the baby begins to introject an image of a good breast that comforts, soothes, calms and provides important nutrients. When the breast is absent, for tolerable lengths of time, the infant begins to form images of it as a response to desire and need, and symbol formation slowly begins to evolve.

When there is not a good enough fit between mother and infant, Fordham postulates that defense systems can arise spontaneously out of the primal Self. These defenses are designed to preserve a sense of individual safety and intactness, but they also create an impermeable barrier between the infant's Self and the environment at a time when the infant is beginning to develop a symbolic function. When the defenses of the Self are operative, they interfere with the processes of deintegration/reintegration and thwart the unfolding of archetypal and symbolic experience.

In the analytic treatment of young bulimic women I have found that their symbolic function has been either poorly developed or severely damaged. There has been a basic and early failure of the deintegrative/reintegrative processes of the Self. The bulimic behavior and the atypical use of food as an addictive substance are used as defenses of the Self against further impingements, hence against introjection and assimilation of psychological experience. The parallel between the bulimic symptoms and the underlying psychological processes is striking. Psychologically thoughts, affects and images cannot be assimilated and meaning cannot be attributed to them. Physically, food can neither be utilized for nutrition nor held within the body to be digested.

The bulimic behavior creates a feeling of isolation that is impenetrable. During the beginning phases of analysis these women have great difficulty using the analytic space and the analytic relationship. They have a hard time both holding onto and digesting what transpires in the analysis. They are unable to create meaning out of their internal experiences, and they seem unable to rely on their own internal resources for self-care and self-soothing.

As analysis progresses, few memories are reported of good feeds or good early empathic interactions with mother. Instead, the young women remember experiences of feeling mistreated, misunderstood or even neglected. They have encapsulated themselves in their bulimia as a response to the dysfunctional infant/mother relationship. Fears and suspicions stemming from the original mother/infant interaction predominate in the transference relationship; these women are often exquisitely sensitive to failures of empathy or potential misinterpretations of their psychological experience. They are fearful of becoming dependent on the analyst and want to give the impression that they can care for themselves, yet all the while feeling a great need for support and care.

In analysis, as the early developmental roots of the conflict become clearer, the meaning and function of the bulimia begins to unfold, to stabilize a fragile sense of self. Through binging and purging there is present the fantasy of ejecting the bad parts of the self: getting rid of bad thoughts and feelings, especially rage, anger and self-destructive fantasies. These feelings and fantasies are often related to murderous impulses which have been initially directed toward the mother but, in her absence as a containing and detoxifying agent, they are redirected against the self. Binging and purging helps to get rid of anger and rage and helps to create the illusion that things inside are manageable.

The analytic approach that I have evolved with these women entails creating a safe enough space for them to begin to explore their own internal conflicts. I have found that it is important not to attribute meaning to their experiences prematurely but rather to create an environment that helps them to find and generate meanings of their own, with the help and support of the analyst. They tend to become suspicious and withdrawn if they feel that the analyst has some magical understanding of them; they easily feel that their autonomy can be taken away. This type of relationship with the mother has helped to create the bulimic symptoms. Thus, we work to evolve a collaborative relationship that respects their sense of individuality and integrity.

We also give attention to the early infantile and childhood

origins of the disorder, but this is helpful only if the actual emotions are experienced within the analytic relationship. As the bodily and preverbal aspect of the problem is profound, it is important for the analyst's unconscious to be present and involved as fully as possible. It can act as a tool to understand the developmental origins of the disorder.

Some of these women have been able to enter successfully into deep analytic work, three to five times weekly. I have found some striking similarities among them in both the personal origins and the archetypal patterns that emerge during the course of analysis. At the personal level the women describe feeling inadequately responded to in childhood by self-absorbed, absent or immature mothers. In the transference, deep feelings of wanting to be held and cared for emerge along with fears of merging and loss of a sense of self. These feelings represent the unresolved, infantile root of the disorder. At the archetypal level the image of the all-giving and nurturant breast-feeding Great Mother, Neumann's (1963) Good Mother, alternates with the image of the devouring and negating Terrible Mother. The young woman yearns for the archetypal image of the bliss-giving mother, with whom she can feel fused. It is this archetypal image which the personal mother has not been able either to incarnate or mediate during the girl's infancy. It remains in the mind of the adolescent as a frustrating object of desire.

The archetypal image of the castrating, devouring, withholding, and abandoning witch-mother predominates. This image has been consolidated around the experience of the personal mother. In the transference the desire to restore a feeling of lost union with the good aspects of the breast-feeding mother/analyst alternates with a fear of being caught in the clutches of a devouring, frustrating and negating mother/analyst. It is important for the analyst to be sensitive to countertransference responses in order to make sense out of the analytic material at both the archetypal and personal levels. The adolescent often has difficulty with verbalization of internal experiences.

This difficulty with verbal expression is related to the failure in the development of the symbolic function. Because of this failure the expression of fantasies and affects remains stuck in bodily processes. Offering a safe and containing analytic environment is essential for the unfolding of the personal and archetypal unconscious. The analyst needs to be able to contain and help the adolescent to integrate the affect that threatens to be overwhelming.

Diana began her five-times-weekly analysis when she was 19 years old. It took a good deal of intense and careful analytic work for her to begin to experience security in the transference relationship. As she felt safer, early infantile emotions and memories emerged. She felt anxious about weekend breaks when she feared becoming self-destructive and suicidal. She thought that I would neither think about her nor hold her securely in my mind during the separations, and she felt panic. She felt terrorized by her emerging needs, and began to realize how unsatisfied they were. The only way she felt she could cope with her emptiness and emotional hunger was through binging and purging. I discussed with Diana how her emotional response to me was linked to her early infantile experience with her mother, and how her yearnings were related to the depth of the unfulfilled infantile needs for emotional holding and care. She began to make some sense out of her experience when these links were made.

As her needs for support and nurture emerged, her rage and anger increased toward her mother and toward me. She described a relentless search for a lost breast which, if found, could restore a feeling of wholeness, but what she found was only a substitute, food, which could not satisfy her deeper emotional needs. Recurring dreams and waking images of falling down dark holes and being inside empty caves pointed to her terror of disconnection from a supportive maternal milieu. Inner blankness alternated with intense psychic pain. She wished to be reunited with a mother who would take care of her, but the mother was nowhere to be found. Her binging became a frantic attempt to find a connection to the archetypal breast-feeding mother, but she was left with feelings of longing, emotional hunger and depression.

During the third year of her analysis, a childhood memory emerged. She recalled a good experience with her mother when she was encouraged to paint, draw and engage in playful, creative activities. She began to paint. Her work consisted either of self-portraits or abstract paintings with large quantities of paint layered on the canvas. With her self-portraits she seemed to attempt to create a sensation of having a psychic skin (Bick, 1968), which could contain and hold together her often tortured and fragmented experiences.

She was able to build on these experiences. As they provided her with a symbolic means of expressing, containing and digesting her internal experience, some healthy disintegration could occur and a nascent experience of self began to emerge. The development of this symbolic capacity appeared related to her capacity to work through, in the transference, her intense rage, disappointment, and sense of betrayal as well as her murderous impulses toward a mother who was unable to help her detoxify and assimilate her early emotional experiences. A defense of the self dating from the infantile period had been set in operation at adolescence as she became encapsulated by the bulimia. The self-defense had thwarted the possibility for healthy deintegration/reintegration processes to occur. As the self-defense was dismantled in the analysis some possibility for reparative symbolic functioning eventually could emerge.

In the treatment of the bulimic adolescent I find it necessary to go back to the early infantile origins of the symptoms. It is through this deep analytic experience that the early damage to the deintegrative/reintegrative processes and the symbolic function can be repaired, the defenses of the self dismantled, and the individuation processes of adolescence can be allowed to unfold.

REFERENCES

Bick, E. (1968). The experience of the skin in early object relations. *International Journal of Psycho-analysis*, *49*-4, 484-86.

Fordham, M. (1985). *Explorations into the Self*. Library of Analytical Psychology, Vol. 7. London: Academic Press.

Neumann, E. (1963). *The Great Mother: An Analysis of the Archetype*. Princeton, NJ: Princeton University Press.

Adolescence: Archetypal Second Chance

Denise Lyard
Paris, France
Société Française
de Psychologie Analytique

René is 14 years old when he first phones "for an analysis." He has not yet reached puberty. He has been failing in school for the past three years and is faced with especially demanding parental superegos; they demand heroic deeds, academically and socially. René himself feels unadapted to and persecuted by his peer group.

The transference develops quickly and gives rise to numerous dreams that are primarily René's response to what he imagines makes a good analysand. However, the dreams of sessions seven to nine reveal the plan of the psyche, which is of a completely different tone. First dream:

> I am with my mother in Grandma's car. We are on our way to my grandparents' (on my father's side) house where we are going to meet Daddy and my grandmother (mother's side). My father has found an old bike in the attic, but it is too big for me; I could fall. At a corner, at the edge of a cave, is a boy about my age. His father is pretty mean. The boy has killed my mother. A chase follows. The boy leaves with his father.

This dream brings the grandmothers of both sides together; the dynamics lead to the world of the fathers. René's father offers him an old bicycle, an antiquated means of getting around. It is as unadapted to the son's needs as are the father's demands of social success. At the climax of the dream the meeting with the shadow, carrier of the plan of the Self, takes place. The son of a mean father is standing at the edge of the cave/uterus. The father is mean in that he separates the boy from the world of mothers. It is not the René of today, but the son of this father who kills the attachment to the mother and goes off in the direction of the masculine world.

René's comment on the dream, "My mother pushed me to destroy her by sending me for therapy," shows that he is aware of the task before him, although he is as yet unable to accomplish it. The comment also implies that René's mother has some foreknowledge of her son's future development and that part of her consents to this development. Second dream:

> In the jungle. Four men and one woman have to kill the last monkey of a very cruel race. The monkey has to make babies and the others chase him. The monkey kidnaps the prettiest woman in the camp. The men search the jungle, but they get there too late. The monkey has already made two or three children. The men have failed. I see all of this.

This second dream places the confrontation on another level, that of the instincts, which must be rendered human. René emphasizes that the woman is the tool the monkey uses to replenish his race. However, René does not like the monkey; he feels that the monkey is too close to human and carries something of himself that he disapproves of because of his own fears. I suggest that here the woman and the feminine serve as a bridge between the animal and the human and that the birth of these babies is very important. The woman serves to humanize wild and primitive nature which speaks of violence and sexuality.

René is moved by the fragility of the babies and thinks that "the monkey has been doubly successful; he has made a further evolutionary step and he is no longer being pursued." René is willing to accept the idea that the monkey represents something instinctual which René himself represses – violence, but definitely not sexuality. This is the first but not the last time that René experiences me as a dangerous woman. Third dream:

> With my grandfather on my father's side. I asked him something. He was not sure that he could explain it to me. At the end he did. He was pretty satisfied with himself.

As the carrier of the law in the family, the grandfather also gets the projection of the father archetype. Thus, he acts as an indispensable support for René in the ensuing confrontation. The fourth dream confirms this:

> Three men and one woman are around a table in a luxurious house. They have fallen asleep, lying on the table. They had quarreled about the maid. The maid calls to tell us to pay close attention to what she says; otherwise we may not be able to come back. A man of about my father's age is listening. He is the only one who really understands. Robots attack him but we help him to get rid of them so that he can continue listening.

The maid (French: maid = "the good woman"), in all of her ambiguity, holds the key to this luxurious habitation where René's adult totality (three men and one woman) lies sleeping. This maid is the servant and at the same time the good mother/analyst. Only a father figure can assure the connection with her and understand what René calls his "automatic attacks." (I call these "attacks" his negative complexes: his negative father complex and his mother's virulent animus.) Therefore, I insist on joining in the fight and giving up the spectator position.

With these proposals of the psyche in mind, I foresee several ways of proceeding with the work. The main point is to help the establishing of an ego capable of standing up to the conflict inherent in adolescence: between the demands of the Self, which are pushing for the adolescent's development, and the often contradictory demands of the parental superegos. The demands of the body-Self, represented by the monkey, trigger the process. They call for the acceptance of the sexual body and its drives. The way leads from the collective thrust of the instincts toward their integration in personal experience. As for the demands of the parental superegos, they are conveyed by the parental imagos which the adolescent must experience in their positive and negative aspect, in order to differentiate himself from them. René's unconscious is especially vigorous and demanding; it could lead him to an agonizing re-assessment of his parents' values.

It is equally important for René to attain his masculinity in a transference relationship in which differentiation will be more essential than identification. Thus, I foresee how important the support of my animus will be for René in its quality of precursor of the paternal logos. My animus will have to avoid both stumbling blocks: the doubt of the mother and the rigidity of the paternal grandfather. But woman and the feminine will also have to be met in a different way than was possible thus far, with René's mother and with his father's feminine side. I am drawn in from the start, therefore, in my totality. I shall have to pay attention to maintaining difference and distance, although *coniunctio* is of the essence. The French analyst Elie Humbert (1987) described the countertransference as a long, drawn-out death.

The accounts of the weekly events gradually become the proof of the development of a growth in awareness in daily life. One type of dream takes up day-to-day situations and shows René's mechanisms of defense. Such dreams lead to a dismantling of the persona as well as to a confrontation with the shadow. Thanks to these dreams René becomes aware of the evolution of his attitude and his feelings toward his parents.

A different type of dream plots the psychic organizers at work. Their progress prompts me to speak of the "second chance" of adolescence. The psychic dynamics first of all accentuate the body; this forces René to abandon his state of identity with his mother. This prologue ends with the search for his origins, as the son of a couple and no longer merely as the son of a parthenogenetic mother.

The next stage prepares the confrontation with the maternal dragon via the restoration of a positive father image. It includes a dream *of the king, the father and the dragon*. The constellation of a masculine Self capable of dealing with the dragon's, as well as the old father's, attacks is supported on the one hand by the paternal uncle, as a positive figure in René's life, and on the other by the analyst's animus, as the dream well shows. This sequence marks the beginning of a more trusting relationship between father and son.

Although René in day-to-day life takes on a healthy autonomy and now has the height of a man, his dreams point to situations in which he is still fascinated with childhood and the maternal world. In session 72, René has an image of himself imprisoned in a subterranean grotto. For my part, I fantasize here a uterus contracting at the beginning of a birth. I offer René this prospective interpretation.

A month later a spaceship from Mars carries René off toward the unknown – sexuality, I suggest. But René cannot accept this interpretation. The following month, furious, he reports a dream: *"I was making love to my mother. It is an initiation, something I have to get done with.*" This is also the turning point of the analysis: the deepest point of regression, but also the moment of rebirth. René's attitude toward his mother is no longer passive; he sees himself in the relationship as a man. He can also show aggressivity toward me.

The last year of the analysis deals with the re-evaluation of masculine values, with René's finding access to his real father and to men in general and with a critical evaluation of his parents' superegos. This confrontation leads to the progressive establishment of a negative maternal imago which leads the way toward the process of separation and differentiation.

In session 91, René is 17-1/2 years old. He dreams that *his mother interrupts the session and that he cannot get her to leave*. He recognizes the intrusive and suffocating aspects of his mother and relies on the analyst to free him. The functioning of her animus serves to separate, but also plays the role of a guide: "You kind of know where I am going, like a football trainer who says, 'You'll get there'." The development of the transference during the hour shows another way of relating to the analyst: love and aggressivity are both there. For my part, I feel René developing into a subject that can face his two mothers.

The feminine figures are evolving: "It is the image which the feminine in me has of the masculine which is changing. She is coming to accept my virility and no longer fears the world of men." From now on the woman, rather than the mother, becomes the partner in the transference; she welcomes his virility.

The acceptance of sexuality ends with a confrontation with homosexuality. This confrontation finds its place between two images of the Self. The first is something round which envelops and asphyxiates the stars: a negative primary Self. The second is an organizing crystal, like a surveyor's pole. To possess it would be destructive, but fascinating, comments René.

These four years of work began with the challenge of the body; it triggered the archetypal process. The work terminated with the attainment of genital sexuality. René drew from an ancestral experience to which we gave meaning. It confronted him with parental imagos in an initiation process which was constellated by the transference. The task of managing this experience and keeping it up to date remains. Here is the dream of the end of analysis:

> I am at the seaside with my mother, but I don't see her. We are swimming along the coast. Here the sea is the ocean, a hidden masculine force, Poseidon. I see several boats with huge sails like wings. I think that they can fly. Then I see that they are fishing nets. I am swimming the crawl, badly at first. But then I understand that it's like crawling. My mother is there more like an advisor. At the end she is hardly there any more.

The mother who served as a link with the unconscious disappears. But the search for the anima is about to begin. René is 18 years old.

Translated from French
by Joanne Wieland-Burston

REFERENCE

Humbert, E. (1987). *C.G. Jung: The Fundamentals of Theory and Practice.* Wilmette, IL: Chiron.

Images of the Archetypal Mother in Early-Disturbed Children

Verena Rossetti-Gsell
Rancate, Tessin, Switzerland
Schweizerische Gesellschaft
für Analytische Psychologie

My current research is intended to contribute to a better understanding of severe cases of psychopathology. The diagnosis of the 20 or so children I am considering here ranges from autism to borderline, from early infant anorexia to severe types of narcissistic and developmental problems. Some of the case histories reveal pre-natal and perinatal organic difficulties.

By their behavior and symbolic play these children have communicated their unconscious images; I observe a spontaneous and autonomous transferential process, which is guided by archetypal content. As therapist I am invited to take part in this process, to understand and interpret it.

The first transferential images are maternal in character. This is not surprising, for the archetypal mother is both the cradle of childhood and the foundation of all material existence. In the transference of the Great Mother and her images I can distinguish three phases or levels. Using evolutionary terms, I call them mother/world, mother/belly, and mother/breast or symbiotic mother. Each has a positive and a negative or destructive aspect.

I have concluded, also, that these children's experiences are dominated by the negative mother archetype. Thus the therapy will produce, initially, the compensatory positive mother image. However, the constellation of a negative mother archetype in the transference is equally indispensable for any positive therapeutic development. Often we can see signs of the negative mother even in the initial phase of therapy. But in most cases it takes time and requires a well-established positive transference, along with a more consolidated ego, before it is possible for the child to confront these destructive images. Consequently, I speak of phases as well as levels.

I shall present my examples according to their evolutionary order. I am aware that each archetypal image, as it emerges from the unconscious, takes a personal shape and may have various interpretations. But my focus is on the archetypal contents.

It is important to consider what precedes the maternal and its images. We know that behind the image of the Great Mother there is the image of wholeness, the archetype of the Self: from an evolutionary point of view, the primary Self.

During my work with three autistic children I observed that they transferred to the therapy room the image of the undifferentiated totality that revolves on its own axis. They sought the perfect image at the level of sensations and of proprioception, looking for spherical or revolving objects – balls, balloons, marbles, discs, wheels, screwdrivers – or created rotating motion in their bodies. Such an image seems to compensate the terrifying and paralyzing archetypal image of the black hole that annuls everything and makes the universe disappear. For example, an autistic boy of five years lives in terror. He is waiting for the light to disappear during a thunderstorm and for the world to be lost in blackness, or for him to dissolve into nothingness with the flush of the toilet.

I come immediately to the images of the Great Mother of the World, the magnificent goddess, the goddess of matter – of the vegetable and the animal life. She can appear in each of these manifestations.

With the autistic boy I mentioned earlier, I must often play "going through the seasons," when the leaves burst out in the spring and fall in the autumn. Another five-year-old boy, after four months of therapy, suddenly calls me "Signora Mappamondo," which means "Mrs. World" or "Mrs. Worldmap." A little girl's drawing with a female figure carrying little bags of seeds toward a border of soil expresses the same transferential reality, as does the game of a seven-year-old boy, in which I must continually provide him with soil, so that he can sow, plant, and have the herd put out to graze. In other games material goods keep falling from the sky or animals come out of the desert, one after another, to obtain the desired water.

I also witnessed a direct identification with the great magnificent goddess. A boy created a princess with a canopied bed; she wore ever more beautiful clothes. For months he was occupied with the sewing of ever more beautiful robes. Dressed with a skirt of innumerable frills, he moved around his own axis, while insisting that I admire him. In my countertransference, I was fascinated by the beauty of his dance, which helped me to overcome my prejudice against his transsexual fantasy.

The image of the negative mother is terrible, however. Instead of "Mrs. Worldmap," "the lady with the hair" appears, a deadly Gorgon who paralyzes the little boy. He suffers from terrifying phobias when he looks at dolls with hair or at leaves being moved by the wind. The mother/nature is presently the mother of chaos, of natural catastrophes, of coldness, of frost, of the volcano and the burning fire, of earthquakes and the flood which destroys the world of plants and animals – the world of life. The situation is characterized by hopelessness: "nobody is coming; everybody is dead." These are the answers of the children. The therapist must take part in this despair and still survive.

The child with the autistic past keeps creating a marvelous mountain. He instructed: I must be a boy who innocently admires it and who later must witness its destruction. Every time I must cry out, louder and louder, in grief, desperation and rage. I must express the same feelings, in later sessions, when the boy becomes the creator of the earthquake and the universal chaos, throwing around all the play material.

I am not far from being overwhelmed. A nine-year-old, severely destructive borderline boy, during the second year of his therapy, starts to transfer directly the image of the deadly archetype to my person. Especially at a moment of separation, his capacities of symbolization are flooded with his unconscious. I become the mortifying destroyer for him. Many times he destroys the games that, with meticulous attention, he has created. Later, he throws up into the air anything he can. My attempts at interpretation are without effect. More than once, I am left with my countertransference desperation: everything is useless, I shall never be the therapist capable of helping him. Later, during psychotic crises, he physically attacks me with all his power. He screams that I am a thief; I have stolen everything: his house, his therapy, everything. I am left with nothing but my physical strength that is greater than his and my tears of desperation in the chaos that is left after he has gone.

Fortunately the majority of children are capable of expressing their negative transference in the imaginary. Another boy, who also attacked me physically at the end of the third year of his therapy, assigns to me the role of the terrible spouse, envious and malicious ever since the times of the ancestors. She has come to steal all the pictures he has painted and to destroy the town with the help of the devil. In his desperate struggle, the arms of his friend Jesus have no effect at all. Only as the master of the volcano does he succeed in destroying the monstrous spouse, in killing her after three resurrections, and in consuming millions of watts and volts.

We come now to the images of the mother/belly. It is the maternal container that protects, gives warmth and security and reminds us of the uterus that is often evoked in the transference of these children. They create caves, houses, tents, niches, or swimming pools. The container must be tightly closed, dark, equipped with cushions or soft carpets. Sometimes the children also take food in there, or music, and often the game consists in sleeping there all alone. The house of the boy we already know for his marvelous dance is called "Uiticasa," a neologism which could signify "house of life." He creates a self-catering system there for his "nectar," which is reminiscent of the umbilical cord.

The corresponding negative image of the archetype is one of inadequacy or destruction of the contents. The swimming pool, for example, has a hole through which the contents run out, or the water gets green and poisoned. The house breaks down, sinks or burns. It is destroyed many times by natural catastrophes or is attacked by bombs. The little boy who called me "Mrs. World" often empties the little dollhouse and carries it into the cave. It is "badly done," and he never wants to see it again.

In this phase the child's ego is capable of activating its resources of restoration. The floor and the walls can be reconstructed, the dividing walls repainted and the roof repaired. But the destructive archetype continues to manifest itself. It must still be borne and defied.

The third phase, the mother of the breast and symbiosis, appears in the image of a baby and its nourishing mother. It can show us the transference of the symbiotic union. Sometimes the need for the therapeutic symbiosis and motherly care is projected onto animals that belong to me. A seven-year-old girl with anorexia drinks out of the feeding bottle in the second session and takes care of her baby in the little house. Afterward, she prepares herself large quantities of pudding. The consumption of pudding and mashed potatoes (using ingredients in my office) is considerable. At first, it often is I who must prepare the food. The relationship during this phase is characterized by the child's omnipotence. Later, many children succeed in preparing their own food: bread, cookies, or even whole meals.

Even in this phase the negative mother image is terrible. Again the little boy, the son of Mrs. World, gives us an impressive example. At first, he directly transfers the symbiotic mother to my person. Cowered down in the corner of the stove – "vicini, vicini" (very, very close) – I have to feed him with white yogurt. All of a sudden he pinches me hard. It is the first time that he plays this intimate game, and I am unprepared. He really hurts me; I cannot help bursting into tears. Moreover, in each session, he wants to know what I have eaten. When I tell him, he pinches me. I perceive the primitive envy; when I eat, I take food from him. But later, when he dramatizes the situation in the dollhouse, the image also reveals the condition of the baby's victim. The mother dies while feeding the little child. The abandoned child cries and cries but the mother does not wake up. Other children demonstrated this deadly abandonment by the symbiotic mother: the baby drowns or ends up in the children's cemetery.

Finally, the devouring or poisoning aspect of the negative mother/breast also is transferred in the protected room. It becomes visible in the form of a wolf with his mouth wide open, a shark with 50 teeth, a devouring crocodile or a poisonous snake. The borderline boy wishes to be threatened by puppets with ferocious mouths and to photograph them. During the sixth session a little boy of three, who has been unable to masticate ever since his weaning, puts the same puppet over his hand. I must imitate him with the tiger. He gives the order "Let's eat!" and we walk around my office, devouring everything. The child has identified with the devouring mouth.

Many times I also observe the projection of the devouring image onto a vacuum cleaner. Once again, it is the little boy of "Mrs. World" who is afraid of being swallowed up. At first I have to switch on the monstrous vacuum cleaner at a distance while he is taking refuge on top of some cubes, far above the floor. Later he exorcises it by calling it "tesorina" (my little safe – in the feminine). Then he washes it and builds a house for it in order to use it, ultimately against other enemies.

This example shows us that the possibilities of the infantile ego are increasing during this phase. With the aid of the therapist the boy can dare a confrontation, using his magic and cunning, and later make a heroic struggle.

Translated from French
by Sabine Buken

Clinical Workshops

Abaissement du Niveau Mental in Analytic Treatment

Niel Micklem
Zurich, Switzerland
Association of Graduate Analytical Psychologists
of the C.G. Jung Institute Zurich

Jung made frequent references in his writing to *abaissement du niveau mental* (lowering of consciousness), each time with a respectful recognition of Pierre Janet, the originator of the term. Jung used abaissement in describing psychopathology, especially psychosis and neurosis. We still hear the term today as pathology, with undesirable associations implying a state of some mental inferiority. I want to illuminate another aspect of abaissement that belongs more to psycho*therapy* than to psycho*pathology*, drawing attention to abaissement as a feature of the transference and to its place in the movements of healing. The term bears so immediately on therapy that we may well wonder how it comes to be overlooked.

Today we take progress and achievement for granted as a way, if not the only way, of life. Inevitably, the dominance of this attitude plays its part in the work of analytic psychotherapy, deceiving us into assuming that analysis means increasing and broadening consciousness. This assumption is not valid, though increased consciousness may follow as an outcome of treatment. If this statement sounds like hair-splitting it is nevertheless an important differentiation, for the deception of progress is no trivial matter. To mistake the results for the work itself puts "the cart before the horse," and the psyche goes out of psychotherapy. To respect psyche we must be prepared to risk diminution.

Jung (CW3) said that, by abaissement, Janet meant a form of depression: a lowering of consciousness together with a reduction of attention. This abaissement, said Janet, is a constant characteristic of neurosis. It is not, as we often understand it, a cause, but one of what he called the regular stigmata of neurosis. Janet's observation sounds foreign, though it should cause no surprise if we recall that we see the same abaissement in other morbidities – in all severe organic illnesses and especially in those associated with fever. But the question arises: How is abaissement relevant to the treatment of the morbidities?

Turning to history, we find abaissement in all ancient medical practices. The magic rituals of tribal medicine healed its patients in a state of trance. We note also that, in the ancient Greek practices in the name of Asklepios at Epidaurus, depression was necessary for the healing dream to appear. Similarly, all exorcism for mental derangement has required a state of trance for its effects, with abaissement as a common central feature. In the late 18th century Franz Anton Mesmer's use of animal magnetism became a bridge between medieval treatments and modern scientific psychotherapy. His method produced an hypnotic state of trance, the so-called magnetic crisis. This scientific approach marked the beginning of active research into the ways of psychotherapy. We see in retrospect that the crisis of Mesmer's treatment as well as the states of exorcism and the earlier magic practices were in themselves examples of the abaissement of somnambulism.

The magnet proved superfluous with the discovery that similar trancelike consciousness could be induced without it. Neurypnosis then became the field of investigation and this, halfway through the last century, became the hypnosis we recognize today. Hypnosis was then, and to some extent still is, surrounded by an aura of magic unacceptable to orthodox medicine, though Jean-Martin Charcot gave some acceptable medical status to this new form of sorcery when he discovered close affinity between hypnosis and hysteria. At much the same time Ambroise Liebeault and Hippolyte Bernheim drew attention to the phenomenon of suggestion, to suggestibility in hysteria and to the role of suggestion in hypnosis. Abaissement continued its role as a feature common to these therapies.

Today we are familiar with the particular form of psychotherapy we call analysis, and though relatively new, it differs little in essence from the other practices. All the more surprising is that the attitude frequently adopted in analysis is inadvertently against its own best interests: its orientation toward heightening and increasing consciousness. Explanations, interpretations, teachings and even exercises in fantasia address the intellect more than the imagination and these well-intentioned endeavors to heighten and increase consciousness overlook the message of thousands of years.

The evidence of abaissement in the history of therapeutics is convincing. This is no series of chance events, but the imprint of no less an archetype than that of individuation. But can individuation be reconciled with the depression of abaissement? Individuation, as understood by Jung, may be observed from many different viewpoints. From the viewpoint of illness and treatment it is the way we live our morbidities, whether as an isolated ailment or the sum of all life's morbidities. Individuation is also the story of healing. If we seek the features of this pattern we have many examples in Jung's works. The best known quoted by him are the Night-Sea Journey and the *Rosarium Philosophorum*, the alchemical series of pictures he chose to demonstrate the individuation process in terms of the transference. In these and other images we do not see the familiar striving for progress and attempts to improve ourselves. The psyche presents a contrasting picture: not an ascent to bigger and better things for the individual, but a process of decline – an alchemical "emersion in the waters" on the way to death (CW16). Individuation, like healing, is an encounter with death to which we are all bound by the gods of abaissement in various underworld guises.

In pointing his finger at the abaissement of neurosis Janet opened the door directly onto the magic world of hypnosis, suggestion and much that is held in ill repute by analytic therapy. Furthermore, at a time of mounting disapproval Janet risked saying that hypnosis counts for something after all. Indeed it does, if not always as it is practiced. But, we may ask, if abaissement as hypnotic consciousness is the heart of psychotherapy, why does hypnosis not work? More accurately, why are the practices of hypnotists not therapeutically more satisfactory than they may seem at first – as Janet, Freud, Jung and many others recognized long ago? The likely answer is that hypnotists do not themselves partake in the abaissement. They may suggest, but they are not available for the transference. Jung (CW14) was addressing this theme indirectly when he said he gave up hypnosis early in his career because, in his opinion, suggestion by the physician's personality was so much more important than any abreacted contents.

In spite of its ill repute we cannot dismiss hypnosis lightly, for it reaches back to the original use of the term transference when physical symptoms were magically displaced by the magnet, and hypnosis was recognizable as the rapport. When hypnosis reached the height of its fame 100 years ago it was for many people virtually synonymous with suggestion. Or we might say that rapport and transference were indistinguishable. But Janet did not subscribe to this view. He saw hypnosis as consciousness with a predominance of imaginative faculties and a reduction of intellectual initiative. Suggestion, on the other hand, was not hypnosis but a natural condition which nevertheless might be enhanced in hypnotic consciousness.

Janet went further and attempted to define the difficult concept of suggestion by contrasting it with persuasion. Indirectly, this distinction says much about the place of transference. Persuasion, Janet said, is guiding. But suggestion is inciting. We may hear this as a comment on Jung's reference to the therapeutic influence of personality and the limitations of hypnosis. Jung was saying, in effect, that the suggestion of hypnotism may bring an unreflected change in behavior, but in analytic psychotherapy the transference moves suggestion into another place where paradoxically it is persuasion – a place where impulse and reflection mediate a response within the personality. By way of example we may see this in the treatment of the cigarette habit. The attitude of the hypnotist is a suggestion to stop smoking. That of the analyst is equivocal; to stop smoking, but also to go on smoking, to inquire and reflect. In this way analysis brings a change in attitude rather than in behavior; from Janet's contrast we sense how paradox is a moving feature.

Janet observed that abaissement is already present in the patient's neurosis, but he made no comment on the challenge it poses for the therapist. That challenge is daunting for, as Jung pointed out, "Abaissement... reduces one's self confidence and spirit of enterprise" (CW9-I, par. 214). Not every therapist can find sufficient trust in the psyche to risk that sacrifice. But the question is, how does this apply to our practices? Should all good analysts fall asleep regularly in the analytic hours? The question may not be as facetious or ridiculous as it sounds. The late John Layard used to tell of falling asleep, dreaming and, on waking, recounting the dream to his analysand. It is certainly an abaissement and one way of being imaginative in therapy.

So let us reflect well on this theme: on hypnos and hypnosis; on sleep, induced or otherwise; on the ready access to the dream and spontaneous play of images as imagination in the setting of transference. Abaissement is indispensable. We may say that must be obvious to any psychologist. And perhaps it is, but it is disregarded in practice nonetheless. We have only to note how people readily confuse imagination and its paradox with the whims of fancy more akin to the heights of an intellectual consciousness than to the depression of abaissement.

By way of example let us take a dream that tells of following a trail until progress is halted by a locked door. What now? From those preoccupied with progress and achievement we may expect a recommendation to fantasize about what happens on the other side of the door. This sort of fantasy knows no obstacle. Another view is that the obstacle of the locked door is an experience with much to say if we stay with it. Jung himself was able to stay there and meet such situations with an abaissement that enabled him, though awake, to "dream" it further. He called that practice "active imagination." Many of his followers still fail to distinguish this from the more familiar exercise of simple fantasy. For such fantasy is "in." It belongs to the heights of a culture preoccupied with "trips." To save analysts and their analysands alike from mistaking their rich and ready fantasy for the movements of imagination we must recognize abaissement.

However much we may achieve by outright sleep, I suggest that an ideal therapeutic consciousness borders on paradox. Consciousness is defined in terms of levels – not in a hierarchy of values, but simply as many different levels. In respect of abaissement in psychotherapy we may see this as two levels manifest at the same time. If this sounds foreign, it is largely because of the way ego and its exclusiveness are taken for granted. We learn, for example, that the pairs of psychic functions, sensation and intuition or thinking and feeling, are mutually exclusive. But we overlook the fact that this is no absolute truth; it is rather a limitation of ego consciousness that we assume to be absolute. Thus we miss the other dimension that makes it paradoxical. Someone dreams: "I was hiding behind dustbins in fear of Mr. Smith at the end of the road. But then I saw it was not Mr. Smith." Or similarly in a dream: "I saw my sister in the crowd, but it was not my sister." We are familiar with this dream language. It is paradox, and paradox is commonplace in the psyche. In abaissement we find the other consciousness and the dimension to contain that paradox.

Images of God in the Transference

Rudolf Müller
Stuttgart, Germany
Deutsche Gesellschaft für
Analytische Psychologie

Freud saw a connection between the father image and the image of God but regarded the image of God as nothing but an overpowering, interiorized father image. His works on religious criticism dealt with the dissolving of infantile fixations and taking the greatest possible responsibility for oneself. Jung, too, was concerned with confronting, differentiating and making conscious these ultimate ideas, principles, and images because they tend to determine our thinking and behavior. At first, he called these "affective centers" and "primal images," later "dominants of the collective unconscious" and, since 1918, archetypes.

Jung's View of Images of God

Jung spoke of "guiding principles" (CW8, par. 632) that determine our ethical behavior and moral decisions, on which depend the weal and woe of our existence. These dominants result in a positive or negative concept of God. Psychologically, this concept of God includes every idea of the first and the last, the highest and the lowest. The archetype of the Self, as the center of the psyche, is endowed with the strongest energy charge. As symbol of psychic wholeness the Self is a transpersonal dimension that cannot be delimited. In being superior to consciousness, the Self is experienced as "completely other." This archetype reflects an image of God and thus unifies consciousness, which is limited, with the infinite and unfathomable unconscious. Symbols of the Self cannot be distinguished from symbols of God.

For Jung, God is a secret experienced as numinous and as an extraordinary psychic event that cannot be connected with any cause within human experience and, at the same time, a mythologem with an archetypal base. As visible forms of the instincts, mythologems underlie the psyche's structure; they have a certain autonomy. Thus, God is a biological, instinctual and archetypal "arrangement" of individual, contemporary and historical contents. In spite of its numinosity this concept must be exposed to intellectual and moral criticism. In his work "Answer to Job" (CW11) Jung dealt specifically with the image of God. This work shows clearly Jung's struggle for autonomy and for the dissolving of infantile fixation.

Archetypal Transference

An archetypal transference was one of the experiences that occasioned Jung's developing his theory of the collective unconscious. In his work "The Relation between the Ego and the Unconscious" (CW7) he described an analysand who had shown particular difficulties in detaching from Jung, until the image of an archetypal transference appeared in one of her dreams: *the figure of her father with superhuman qualities, while "the wind swept over the wheat-fields"* (par. 211). Only after working through the problems that this image made evident and after dealing with the non-personal point of reference, which had been unconscious, could the analysand detach from the transference and overcome the stagnation.

Religious Attitude and Neurosis

According to Jung, many neuroses are expressions of disturbed religious function; the psyche's religious demands are no longer apparent "because of a childish passion for rational enlightenment" (CW16, par. 99). The psychoneurosis is "a suffering of a soul which has not discovered its meaning" (CW11, par.

497). A search for meaning is at the same time a search for the numinous, for the transcendent.

Thus, neurosis is rooted in the attitude toward the ultimate. Jung described religion as a psychic healing system and the religious attitude as important for psychic balance. He was the first to realize that depth psychology must accept the religious question as a central factor. Without it, an analysis remains incomplete; this is especially true for the second half of life. Indeed, for Jung the access to the numinous is the real therapy.

Dealing with Archetypal Transference

In order to dissolve personal fixations and one-sidedness in psychotherapy it is necessary to make the unconscious conflicts conscious. A neurotic attitude toward the parental images, for example, can be healed only through analysis, working through and integration of the opposites.

Similarly, to overcome a harmful God-image, analysis and integration of the opposites is needed. The individual and archetypal projections must be worked through and taken back. Only then does it become possible to dissolve infantile-incestuous attachments and to develop an adult attitude. It is the nature of the individuation process "that we are conscious of the image of God which is constellated in our unconscious as well as of its effects on our way of behaving and experiencing and that we are able to distinguish from it our humanness with all its faults, limits, and incapabilities" (Dieckmann, 1980, p. 14).

Becoming conscious and differentiating the collective unconscious comprise the contribution Analytical Psychology makes to the integration of humanity. For a mature humanity it is no longer possible to project the divine as only male or only female, as only good or only evil. A split image of God has disastrous consequences. Such a splitting causes and legitimates misdevelopments and repression in politics and ecology. For the world's redemption – through unification of the opposites in the deity – the human being is indispensable. As Jung wrote: "I am concerned with the fate of the individual human being ... on whom a world depends, and in whom ... even God seeks his goal" (CW10, par. 588). Neumann (1971) wrote that the task of the future is a conscious orientation toward the unconscious and a responsible dealing of human consciousness with the powers of the collective unconscious.

Dialogic Therapy

In this process of change we as Jungian therapists are asked to change our psychotherapy which has been patriarchally determined. Jung understood the relation to the Self as one which is also a relation to the other person; he saw the numen entering human relationships. This understanding is especially true for the therapeutic relationship. Therefore therapy can be understood as a dialogic process which includes the therapist as someone who responds. "No longer is he the superior wise man, judge and counsellor; he is a fellow participant who finds himself involved in the dialectical process just as deeply as the so-called patient" (CW16, par. 8). This encounter of two personalities "is like mixing two different chemical substances; if there is any combination at all, both are transformed. In any effective psychological treatment, the doctor is bound to influence the patient; but this influence can only take place if the patient has a reciprocal influence on the doctor. You can exert no influence if you are not susceptible to influence" (CW16, par. 163).

Transformation of the Parental Image and of the Image of God

A series of pictures made by a 34-year-old, married, severely depressed female analysand demonstrates that, behind each personal transference, archetypal and transpersonal contents can be recognized and must be worked through in the therapeutic process. I have reported on this case elsewhere (Müller, 1985). The close connection between the unconscious parental images and a harmful image of God becomes evident here.

In the first picture (Figure 1) the father is mistreating the analysand. He kicks her in the abdomen so that she defecates. Her internalized experiences with the father form an image of God which – as subsequent pictures show – left her no room for her own development.

Figure 1

In the second picture (Figure 2) the analysand painted her head equipped with a big figure of Buddha, several devils, and a host of medicines. (For many years she could ease her troubles only with the help of medicine.) The "puffed-up Buddha" shows the underlying inflated image of God.

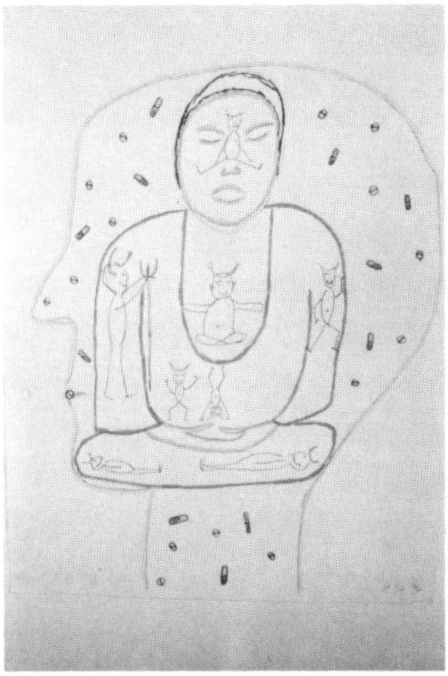

Figure 2

Then (Figure 3) God is shown with scorching eyes, which exterminate the people. At God's left and right side are the redeemed. Influenced by her husband, the analysand had become a member of a strict religious sect. This affiliation intensified the polarization of the "condemned" and the "redeemed." (The motif of God's eye also can be found in some of her other pictures: Figures 2 & 13.)

Figure 3

In a picture (Figure 4) of a sculpture, the "hunger child" shows how emotionally neglected the analysand felt. Painting herself

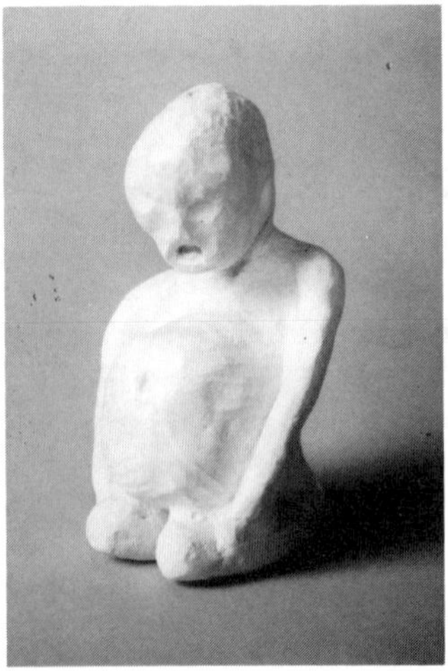

Figure 4

"in the clutches of an expert" (Figure 5) reveals her negative father complex, which was stirred whenever she encountered authorities. In an image (Figure 6) of the analysand kneeling in front of a telephone receiver, an oversized hand prevents her from speaking. Her inner hunger corresponded to excessive need for and expectations of the therapist, leading to a feeling of privation and rejection.

In the next picture (Figure 7) the analysand stumbles over the oversized, black left leg of the therapist, who sits on a throne like a divine figure, with a rainbow above him. Our work included countertransference aspects and open dealing with the limits and shadow aspects of the therapist. His aggressions and rejection led to a deepening of the therapeutic relationship and to a gradual correction of the image of God.

Figure 5

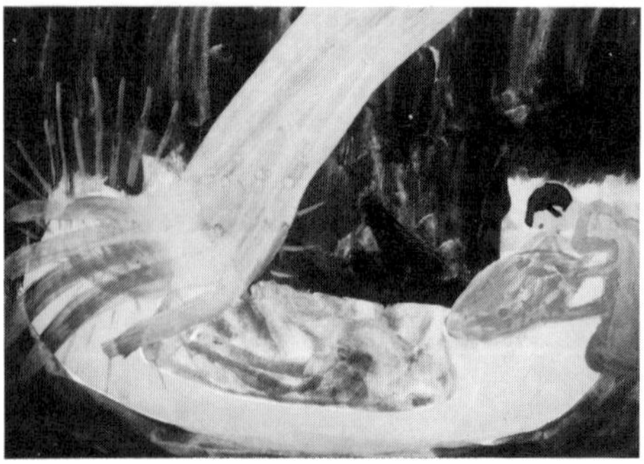

Figure 6

The eighth picture (Figure 8) was made just prior to an attempt to commit suicide. It shows the black quaternity in the form of a cross, represented by fists that knock the patient down.

In a picture (Figure 9) showing the patient's "way of the cross" she stands, in front of a wall, run through by a cross. Behind the wall there is water or sky and a setting or rising sun. In the upper left a gray, dead tree can be seen. The number of bricks in the upper part of the wall corresponds to the analysand's age. The hand, the cross, and the perspective toward the left side correspond to decisive times in her life: separation from her father, marriage, the birth of her son.

Figure 7

Figure 8

In the tenth picture (Figure 10) the analysand painted herself walking into a forest in great pain and deep sorrow. She is bleeding out of her vagina. The first picture in which she painted herself as a woman, it coincided with the return of a regular menstrual period. The working through of her anger and her helplessness as well as dealing with her mother problem in a process of deep sorrow enabled the woman to reconcile herself gradually to her

Figure 9

Figure 10

Figure 11

fate and to develop a new feeling for life.

In this context she made the sculpture (Figure 11) which shows a woman on a cross. The analysand wrote a quotation of Vergil on the crossbeam: "Sunt lacrimae rerum." A free translation is: "These are the tears of reality." In this picture the reconciliation with her own cross and fate becomes visible, leading to a fundamental transformation in the therapeutic process and a lasting stabilization. The woman on the cross is also a shattering collective symbol of the role and helplessness of the female in our society.

In this period she also painted (Figure 12) a falling person, caught by hands. The growing trust in the therapeutic relationship as well as

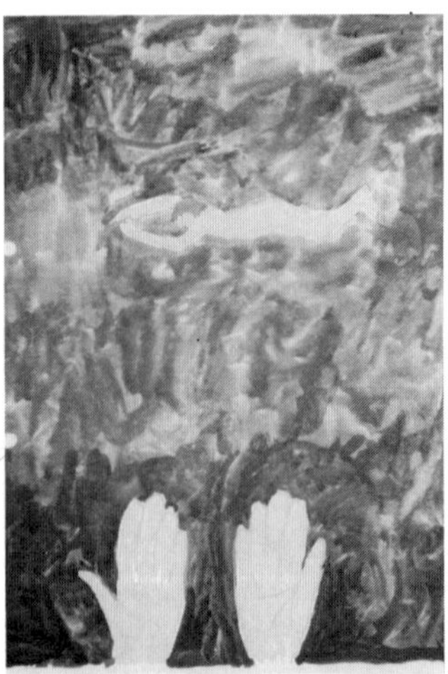

Figure 12

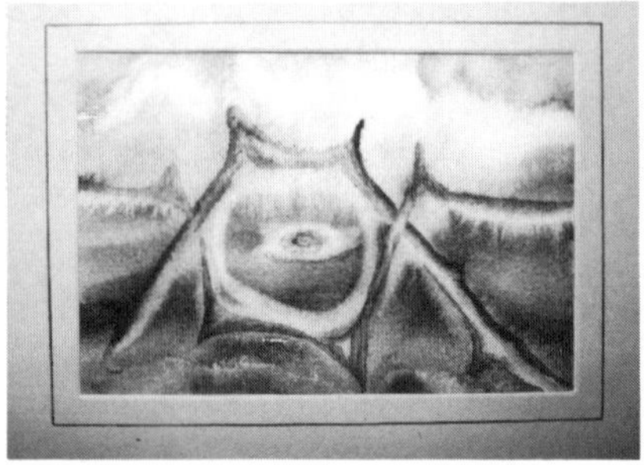

Figure 13

in her own capabilities becomes visible.

The last picture (Figure 13) of the series shows a crown of thorns with the eye of God in the middle. The patient called it "Good Friday." It is a water color in soft blue, purple, brown, and green shades. Compared to her other pictures it conveys reconciliation and calmness. The pictures in this series show the transformation of the image of God, the change of a disastrous ideal and thus a correction of the inner attitude. Working through these problems has given the woman a new relation to her life. I thank the analysand who permitted me to show her pictures.

Translated from German
by Sabine Osvatic

REFERENCES

Dieckmann, H. (1980). Das Problem der Übertragung und Gegenübertragung in der Analytischen Psychologie C.G. Jungs. In H. Dieckmann (Ed.), *Übertragung und Gegenübertragung*. Hildesheim: Gerstenberg.

Müller, R. (1985). Heil und Unheil von Leitbildern – Gottesbild im Wandel. *Zeitschrift für Analytische Psychologie*, *16*-2, 132-56.

Neumann, E. (1971) *Ursprungsgeschichte des Bewußtseins*. Olten: Walter.

Dependency, Trust, Perversity and Addiction in the Analytic Relationship

Barry D. Proner
London, England
Society of Analytical Psychology

> Interpretation in terms of the parents is ... simply a *façon de parler*. In reality the whole drama takes place in the individual's own psyche, where the "parents" are not the parents at all but only their imagos: they are representations which have arisen from the conjunction of parental peculiarities with the individual disposition of the child.
>
> C. G. Jung

The relation between the inborn potential for true creativity within the individual's mental life and the phenomenon that Jung called "psychic mass destruction" is at the center of the analysis of the infantile transference/countertransference. It is well known that in the mental events that unfold, twist and turn from minute to minute and day to day in the analytic relationship we can study the interactions among parts of the self implicit in Jung's comment quoted above. Written in 1912 (CW5, par. 505), it is startlingly fresh today. Some forms of relation to the therapist enable psychic growth and development to proceed relatively steadily, if not altogether unopposed. Conversely, there are extremes of fear, suspicion and mistrust of the analyst/parent and of the psychoanalytic or truth-seeking parts of the personality (see Bion, 1959). These extremes arise out of potentially overwhelming anxieties which have to do with being lost through being controlled or devoured – wholly or partially – in the process of making a relation to the object. Such anxieties may result in the formation of a psychological system in which a "do it yourself" shadow part takes a leading role.

This "bad member of the internal family" may dominate the emerging Self in its struggle to establish loving and trusting relations to its internal and external objects. Ledermann (1979) has written about do-it-yourself trends as a feature of narcissistic personality structure. She referred to grandiosity and the replacement of oral dependence with anal control, a control that leads to perversity in the transference. These are not "do-it-yourself mother" analysands, but "do-it-yourself without mother." The "do it yourself" part essentially aims to present the dependence of the child parts of the personality upon the parent parts. The importance of acknowledging dependence upon the creativity of one's internal parents was described by Money-Kyrle (1978). He maintained that to deny their importance was to assume a parthenogenic ability which he called "a megalomanic delusion." He wrote, "All you can do, and surely this is enough, is to allow your internal parents to come together and they will beget and conceive the child" (p. 442).

The part of the personality I am considering stands at one end of the spectrum of perversity and dependence which, for these purposes, I consider to be in opposition. The mentality of perversity has – as its ultimate affect – despair, which is to be distinguished from hopelessness. In this state dependency upon good parents is replaced by a passive, addictive relation to a tyrant. As will be seen, this model closely relates to Jung's theory of complexes. The part that dominates this state of mind is a "do-it-yourself" part by virtue of its distortion of the normal deintegrative and reintegrative process. I refer to Fordham's (1969) model for the infant's means of making a relation to the object – an instinctual capacity in which the baby makes some form of contact with the object and has some experience of it which furthers knowledge of it. The infant then "reintegrates" – through sleep, perhaps. The process suggests that, by means of projection and introjection, archetypal potentialities unfold, with vast importance to the further development of object relations. Internal object representations become established, populating an inner world with "objects" that have individual characteristics and specific relationships. These representations are crucial to further relations to the outside world, and vice versa. This is the collective unconscious life of infancy and is present, one way or another, throughout life.

True dependence in the deepest sense has great importance in analytic psychotherapy. Part of the infantile structure of the Self acknowledges appreciatively the relative strength and goodness of the analyst/parent in its creative and nurturing functions. This part results in the establishment inside oneself of creatively combining parents upon whom one can depend for psychic nourishment. Such acknowledgment is a profoundly humbling development, equivalent to "a certain experience of God" that Jung described in "Answer to Job" (CW11). He referred to God as "a totality of inner opposites." Job's torment brings him to terms with God's imperfection. This experience includes the development of the ability to bear the proximity of one's love and hate for more realistic, less idealized parents.

Lambert (1960) used "parent figures" and "God" interchangeably. He reprinted Jung's letter to *The Listener*, written after his interview on the "Face to Face" program earlier that year. In the interview Jung seems to have shown his implicit relation to his internal parents when he said "I do not need to believe [in God]; I know."

Jung wrote extensively of the *coniunctio*, a symbol derived from alchemy expressing the archetype of the union of opposites. He viewed it as a symbol of relatedness between two people and it is at the center of the psychology of the transference (CW16). We can think of it for these purposes as the equivalent of the primal scene. Meltzer (1973) described the relationship between dependency on the mother and the primal scene: "The coital relation of internal objects has an overwhelming relation to dependence of infantile parts of the self on the internal mother which is the foundation of all stable and healthy psychic structure" (p. 68).

On the analytic stage there is a process of integrating into psychic life a good linkage or bond between the opposite parts which represent the parents. This process can lead to symbolic activities such as dream-life, fantasy, constructive thought. It can lead also to the qualities of gratitude, generosity, patience, self-sacrifice and improved relations with authorities and with siblings – symbolic and actual – to name but a few possibilities. Jung

(CW16) depicted the image of a child, symbolizing the emergent Self, which may develop through the interplay of analyst and analysand. Hubback (1983) wrote of the importance of the *coniunctio* in depression and in its amelioration. Bion (1984) wrote about the disturbance of emotion and of the impulse of curiosity, upon which all learning depends, as part of what he called "the attacks on linking."

The difficulties in analyzing these shadow parts are well known. As Jung wrote, "When [the shadow] appears as an archetype, one encounters the same difficulties as with the anima and animus.... It is a rare and shattering experience... to gaze into the face of absolute evil" (CW9-II, par. 19). The very nature of the conflict in this area expressly interferes with the analysand's making use of what the analyst says. Nevertheless, as Fordham (1974) remarked, such analysands continue to come to analysis.

Glasser (1979) drew attention to the wish to experience a "fusion" or "merging" with the object against which the analysand defends through a flight from the object. In my experience, extensive use of "intrusive" or pathological projective identification makes claustrophobic anxieties very common. That is, analysands who in fantasy put parts of themselves into the analyst or the "analyst/breast" to control the object and to rid themselves of unwanted parts, come to fear loss of themselves through being devoured, controlled, or taken over. They can experience these anxieties at a conscious or unconscious level. For instance, I have noticed a common observation by these analysands that they "can leave analysis at any time without the slightest twinge," or else they state plainly that they fear feeling trapped or brainwashed by the analyst. Thus, sadistic attacks on the object may be motivated by a wish to be certain of what the object is feeling. I have encountered many situations, in which this motivation is the dynamic. By putting, in fantasy, one's most hostile and destructive parts into the object, one knows what the object is feeling and can defend oneself accordingly.

In talking about establishing the trustworthy analyst/parent within the inner world, or the failure to do so, I am referring to a combination of interdependent qualities, which usually first appears in analysis as a combined "part-object." This precursor of a creative relationship between two whole parts in the inner world combines hard and soft, nipple and breast, or separation and togetherness, and challenges the person's tolerance of frustration and jealousy. This is the part-object prototype of Oedipal development. In the analytic relation forces are continually at play to separate these opposites as well as to permit their integration. The analyst often identifies with the anxiety and unwittingly cooperates with the cleavage. The result in the transference/countertransference may be excessive hardness, withholding or sadism. The analysand may be attempting to make an incestuous union with the analyst to the exclusion of the analyst's partner, whether in a whole or a part-object form.

In a part-object experience, the part of the analyst with which the analysand may seek to link can take, in unconscious fantasy, one or the other of alternative forms. The fantasy is infantile or archetypal. The forms are the hard or the soft, the sadistic or the masochistic, the erect phallic penis devoid of nurturing or inseminating functions, or the soft breast which has been separated from the modulating and controlling effect of the nipple. Indeed, there may be acted out a fantasy sexual relationship between the analyst and the analysand. A failure to make a recognizable link with the analyst/parent may indicate that the analysand wishes to exclude the combined object with the intention of projecting into the analyst/parent couple the experience of being the outsider. Once again the fundamental motive in these operations – out of despair – is to destroy relatedness and linkage, notably between the two members of the primal scene.

In this context the anxiety is of a paranoid nature and splitting is a characteristic defense. The object is a bad object, a terrible mother; often no good object is available in one's mental life. Thus the experience of overwhelming persecution gives way to despair and the door is opened to attack upon the combined object. The purpose is to take over the object by substituting, for its system of values, one's own. The relation with the object may be sexualized and the sexual zones and their functions thrown into confusion, a process made possible by the polymorphic nature of early infantile sexuality. In the system I am describing, the "bad part of the Self" leads polymorphism into perversity. The analytic material contains much evidence that – at a deep level – functions are interchanged for perverse purposes. Examples are the penis and the feces, the mouth and the bottom, the breast and the bottom, and the vagina and the bottom. Furthermore, the relation to the object is perhaps both eroticized and highly charged with aggression. Consequently, the formation of a harsh and excitable superego, consisting of retaliatory bits of the attacked object, appears to be inevitable.

Thus, strong feelings of guilt and badness arise which have to be denied through further attacks, and a vicious circle of attack and persecution takes the place of trust, dependence, and psychological nourishment. One defense against such a dreadful sequence is the establishment of relationships in which the constant presence of the object is sought, for external comfort and not for interaction and nourishment. In this case it is usually the surface qualities of the object that are important to the analysand.

REFERENCES

Bion, W. R. (1984). Attacks on linking. In *Second Thoughts*. London: Maresfield.

Fordham, M. (1969). *Children as Individuals*. London: Hoddard Stoughton.

Fordham, M. (1974). Defences of the Self. *Journal of Analytical Psychology*, *19*-2, 192-99.

Glasser, M. (1979). Some aspects of the role of aggression in the perversions. In I. Rosen (Ed.), *Sexual Deviation*. Oxford: Oxford University Press.

Hubback, J. (1983). Depressed patients and the coniunctio. *Journal of Analytical Psychology*, *28*-4, 313-27.

Lambert, K. (1960). Can theologians and analytical psychologists cooperate? *Journal of Analytical Psychology*, *5* -2, 129-46.

Ledermann, R. (1979). The infantile roots of narcissistic personality disorder. *Journal of Analytical Psychology*, *24*-2, 107-125.

Meltzer, D. (1973). *Sexual States of Mind*. Perthshire, Scotland: Clunie Press.

Money-Kyrle, R. (1978). The aim of psycho-analysis. In *The Collected Papers of Money-Kyrle*. Perthshire, Scotland: Clunie.

Suicide and the Shadow

Lawrence K. Brown
Lyme, New Hampshire, USA
Society of Analytical Psychology

A focus of the long and difficult analysis of "Mr. A" was whether he could bear to come alive or his frequently enacted suicidal wishes would prevail. Issues included the importance of regression, the use of reconstruction and difficulties in the use of interpretation. The maintenance of the analytic attitude was the cornerstone of the work; the alchemical model helped the work to be contained. Jung's emphasis on the positive value of the symptom informed my attitude.

The issues of method and management presented by this work led me to explore Jung's seemingly negative attitude to regression and to working with infantile material. I found that he was not objecting to work with such material but to a simplistic, reductive approach to it. His criticism has proved valid and is now shared by most Psychoanalysts as well as Analytical Psychologists.

Mr. A presented for analysis with a crippling depression that reflected his very difficult past. His secret and compelling sexual fantasies were an aspect of this depression but were also his lifeline in that they provided a place for a "true self" (Winnicott, 1965).

Immediately after Mr. A's birth his mother developed an abscess on her breast. In the hospital he screamed so violently that he developed a hernia. His mother brought him up, largely on her own. He came to feel that he was the cause of all her troubles. She told him that, if he had been a daughter, all would be well. He expressed his yearning for closeness with his mother, from about the age of 11, in written fantasies about intimacy between two women. He continues to have a compulsive interest in these fantasies.

Mr. A left school when he was 19 and spent a year at home, not working and in a demoralized state; he made the first of several suicide attempts. At the end of that year he moved to London and obtained work with a large public body. He lived alone and felt extremely isolated. He was receiving medication for his depression, and his mother would travel to London for some of his outpatient appointments. When he was 25 he made three suicide attempts a couple of months apart, combining pills and alcohol with slashing his wrists. He nearly died on the third attempt and was admitted to hospital, for six months' psychiatric care.

In the early years of our work Mr. A had a positive, uncritical attitude to analysis. He identified strongly with me and imitated my reflective attitude in his dealings with others. During interruptions he experienced intense loneliness. He bridged these periods by writing to me, sometimes daily.

In the past he had done quite well at work and received promotions at appropriate times. However, he despised himself for "performing" well for his bosses, fearing that his performance had to do with underlying homosexual wishes. By the time he came into analysis, he had become remote and hostile on the job. A vicious circle developed as he was bypassed by younger, less able men. He withdrew into feelings of contempt and superiority, becoming less and less willing to cooperate with his "inferiors."

This period of analysis was punctuated by "breakdowns" when he would spend large amounts of money on pornography. In his early teens, his mother had discovered his stories; they provoked one of her attacks of possessive rage. The decision whether to let me know about the sexual wishes and stories became crucial. He feared that I, too, would go into a rage.

A pattern developed of his bringing in a paragraph he had written. He would become quite dissociated and his speech would deteriorate. Eventually he would read it aloud but claim vehemently that he had not written it. The fantasies now found the two women in impassioned sexual contact lasting many hours or even days. I felt that he had wishes for fusion with me, but it was a long time before he could feel such wishes. Sometimes the dissociation was complete: he would claim that he had not read the fantasy, he had not written it, he was not in the fantasy, the phallus was not connected to a man.

At some subsequent sessions, he would feel extreme guilt about having read the fantasy. More often, he would go into a rage, assume contorted positions with his hands and face and laugh madly, shouting that the only solution for the rat was poison. He sometimes enacted mock self-poisoning scenes with tremendous affect and murderous shouts. At other times the rage would take the form of prolonged silences when he would proclaim calmly that nothing was wrong.

I was shaken profoundly by an event that became a focal point for the analysis. In one session he had been particularly attacking toward me. I was irritated and said so. The following session he reached into his pocket and, concealing a light bulb in his hand, smashed it against the wall, proclaiming "Nobody crosses me!" My involuntary "Oh, my God" showed him that he had achieved his aim. (He reported later that he had gone to hospital for stitches and to have the glass removed.) My response is an extreme example of a frequent countertransference feeling of fear – a fear that was his but that, for many years, he could not acknowledge.

During his "good phases" he would put all of his aggression away and talk of his hopes for the future. He started going out with a woman he had met following his time in hospital. He was pleased that they could enjoy a good sexual relationship. He feared that I would try to break up the relationship out of jealousy, as his mother had done during his adolescence. The situation appeared to be a mixture of an attempt to become more related and of an escape from fears of homosexuality in the transference.

The relationship in the ensuing marriage was very difficult. What had "worked" on a dating, mainly weekend basis was quite different now. He began to feel controlled by his wife and her demands, mainly unspoken. He felt he had to watch television with her all the time or just "be there," and he became increasingly frustrated and demoralized. It was a repetition of life with mother and mirrored the debilitated state he experienced at work.

He became negative about the analysis, blaming me for the difficulties he was in. He declared that his marriage was killing him and he wanted to end it. To do so would mean giving up the house into which he had put so much, but he claimed that the loss was worth it to regain a sense of himself. He complained that he was so swamped in the marriage that he had lost touch with the feelings about himself which he had experienced previously in the analysis. He reported that he was increasingly withdrawn and uncooperative at work. Keeping me in a constant state of alarm seemed to be the only way he could feel a contact with me. He had been taking Valium for many years and felt that taking it was the only way he was managing.

The fantasies surfaced again. He alternated between bringing them in and keeping them out. He would declare that I had forbidden them and would get into frightening rages. The "slasher" emerged as someone who knew how to deal with such matters. Castration was the only answer and he produced a pocket knife more than once. These times alternated with periods when he read me his fantasies. In me, fears of sudden attack changed into more continuous states of alarm, despair, excitement – and a willingness to persist. Although he had no conscious emotions about days between sessions, he observed that his behavior deteriorated on those days. He would be likely to destroy something at home, to get into blind rages and sit up all night, or to walk the streets "patrolling." We made various arrangements for telephone contact; the most useful of these was his phoning at an agreed time midweek and on weekends.

Dreams were infrequent but important. During this period he had a dream which was a precursor of an ability to relate differently to me – a precursor that was to lie dormant for a further difficult two-year period. He dreamed that *there was a large room with a painter sitting in the middle, painting pictures in vivid colors. Mr. A was a shadowy figure on a bed with a woman at the side of the room.*

He rejected my suggestion that the man in the center of the room personified an aspect of himself. After all, he said, that man was a painter and all Mr. A produced was filth. His decisions not to bring his fantasies to the sessions were followed by periods of rage, but he discovered the connection only slowly.

He made repeated demands that I intervene in his marriage to help him break it up, and that I arrange with his doctor for him to receive a period of time off work. I did neither, in the interest of keeping the analytic framework intact. More than once he decided to terminate and wrote formal notes to that effect. He described his plans to go to a doctor, after termination, for an operation to be castrated. As the time of the planned termination approached, he became fearful of the ending of analysis and asked to continue. A more positive phase followed for a brief period.

It was difficult for me to make interpretations during this phase; Mr. A was not capable of reflecting on what was going on. I experienced in my body the powerful affects that were split off in him, before Mr. A could experience them.

But something was going on, for a dramatic change took place. It again related to a dream, from some months before: *Mr. A was sitting in a waiting room with a group of homosexual men who were waiting to see an eye doctor.* At the time of the dream he found it frightening. Following the change, however, he gave it a new interpretation.

The change happened in relation to his fantasy material. He had brought it and rejected it, as before, but now he began to reflect on it. I was amazed and richly rewarded to hear him say, "I can see that the intensity of the feelings in the fantasies has to do with how much I want to be loved by you." I had never used these words and was staggered by the admission itself and by the quality of reflective activity that lay behind it.

Following this admission, he was more willing to consider the meaning of the fantasies and to experience the feelings as his. Indeed, experiences of intense bodily feelings and the ability to think about the meaning of the fantasies developed at the same time. He became able to relate each fantasy figure to the transference. He thought the "eye" was "I" and that the dream meant he was not ready to analyze his "I."

This ability to reflect corresponded to a transition in the content of the fantasies. As before, they began with two women, but now one was older and more experienced, introducing the younger one to the art of love-making. He understood the older woman variously – as dimly remembered figures from other rooms in the houses they lived in during his childhood, and as me. The change was that the fantasies consistently had an "I" figure who entered at just the right moment, when love-making was at its peak but when satisfaction was incomplete. This male figure, to whom he referred as himself ("I"), had intercourse with both women and provided satisfaction to them.

Sessions when he was able to discuss the fantasy and to relate it to his feelings about me were followed frequently by feelings of greater completeness. He gradually became more aware of the meaning to him of interruptions in analysis. Intense rages occurred, but less frequently.

He felt more "involved" at work. Deciding that, to foster job security, he would try to master something special for his department, he took on a major computer project. He also bought a small home computer and, on his own time, installed a system at his wife's workplace.

In the fantasies there were no longer two women, but instead one woman and himself, and there was a much greater feeling of mutuality in the love-making. Generally, the descriptions began with an overwhelming wish on the part of the woman to feed him, followed by an intense overwhelming of her by him.

It was "essential" that each session begin with a fantasy. There was a difference in his attitude to dreams from that to fantasies. Fantasies arose from a state between consciousness and unconsciousness; he wrote them but did not direct them consciously. He brought dreams more frequently, but they were less under his control; their sometimes disturbing content made him wary of them.

His bodily presence changed. While he frequently made a powerful impact on me with his feelings, he had lain on the couch nearly motionless and quite stiff, making almost no impression on the cushion. This posture changed into a more relaxed one, and he came to make direct eye contact with me when he left the room.

In another dream *he was on an island and was establishing communication with the mainland. There were four kilostream cables linking the two. The task was to establish telephone lines. Only two would be possible and there was difficulty over placing the call boxes to receive them; one box would need to be in a pub.*

The large amount of information via the kilostreams seems to represent the force of the feelings that were packed into our four sessions per week, but the need was for more personal communication. Placing the call box in a pub represented a difficulty because of his extreme emphasis on privacy, which got in the way of his attending any social function. However, I took the pub to represent other aspects of him that needed personal communication between us.

The analysis no longer felt under such threat. Rages still occurred but he had more understanding of why they happened. He perceived his feelings to be like a mill race. If they were allowed into the mill they created enormous power, but if the gates were down preventing the water from getting through, there was a dangerous build-up, leading to potential disaster.

Conclusion

Coming from a very deprived background, Mr. A had retreated into a world of fantasy to make up for the lack of a containing maternal relationship. Through the two women in his fantasies he imagined the relationship he would have had with his mother had he been the wished-for daughter. His castration fears were heightened by the hernia operation at the age of three when he thought his penis was going to be cut off. The alternating seductiveness and rejecting behavior on the part of his mother, combined with his father's frequent absences, encouraged utterly ruthless solutions to his fantasized wishes. His suicide attempts were an acting-out of his feeling of being cut off and rejected. His ambivalence over the fantasies reflected his uncertainty whether they were something exciting but dirty which were to be enjoyed from behind and then extruded in shock or something that could be experienced in a way that could lead to a more loving relationship.

Issues for me centered around maintaining the analytic attitude. Because Mr. A had limited capacity for symbolic thought, for a considerable time the analyst's body had to function as the alchemical vessel. Interpretation was of little use until later stages of the analytic work. As it became apparent that I could receive the impact of his powerful affects, work with them and gradually hand them back to him, the capacity for symbolic thought developed and increased interpretive thinking could take place between us. Allowance for regression was essential in permitting a working through of Mr. A's childhood experience in which so much vitality had been locked away. His screaming in his earliest days was mirrored in the breakdowns in the analysis and his wishes to cut off from it – wishes that he had acted out in his earlier suicide attempts. Yet these powerful shadow aspects contained his creativity and the possibility for life itself.

REFERENCES

Fordham, M., (1974). Defences of the Self. *Journal of Analytical Psychology*, *19*-2, 192-99.

Winnicott, D. W. (1965). *The Maturational Process and the Facilitating Environment*. London: Hogarth.

Negative Countertransference: A School for Individuation

Thomas Patrick Lavin
Wilmette, Illinois, USA
Chicago Society of Jungian Analysts

I am honored to contribute this paper to the Congress in Paris, the home-city of Elie Humbert and Jacques Lacan. Both men of genius have mirrored for us the importance of the language and speech we use in the art and science of depth psychology, and have clarified the epistomological aspects of Jungian and Freudian approaches. Through their work, depth psychologists of both schools have come to a deeper dimension of our mutual and central focus: the dialogue with the Other.

The language and images to which we associate an experience give us a cognitive and emotional context through which we can understand and support or reject that experience. Our speech and images reflect our attitudes toward these experiences and their place in our development as analysts. When we look at a certain glass, we can perceive it as half-empty or half-full. When we look at our own negative countertransferences toward our analysands, do we see them as embarrassing faults or a call for continuing personal individuation? Negative countertransference, its language and images, is the subject of this paper.

In 1913 Freud wrote to Ludwig Binswanger: "One must always recognize one's countertransference and then rise above it; only then is one free" (Binswanger, 1957, p. 112). This statement is typical of the negative view of many early theorists of depth psychology regarding countertransference: an inappropriate response on the part of the analyst. Freud imaged countertransference as a heavy, leaden, and imprisoning substance resembling the *prima materia* that sinks to the bottom of the alchemical vessel. In many respects, Freud's image accurately portrays those countertransference phenomena that are unconscious to the analyst. Such an unconscious countertransference experience can indeed imprison and make heavy one's creative spirit. Yet, every time I have tried to rise above a negative countertransference in order to free myself from those negative feelings – instead of delving into them as Jung has suggested – that analysis has ended disastrously.

In my 20 years of therapeutic work, one particular flight from a negative countertransference remains a source of embarrassment even today. The analysand was a middle-aged mental health professional with whom I had struggled for a year and a half. Our major source of conflict, from my viewpoint, lay in her tendency toward grandiosity in dreamwork and active imagination. This grandiosity elicited in me negative feelings which I rarely had the courage to make explicit. I repressed these emotions in order to cultivate in myself as a professional the "same evenly-suspended attention… in the face of all that one hears" (Freud, SE12, pp. 111-12), which Freud advocated as the optimal therapeutic stance. Notice that Freud's word, "suspended," depicts the analyst's attention as something that hangs down from above.

In what became our final session, the analysand presented her dream and her interpretation of it. I responded by saying that I could not understand how anyone could honestly deduce such a meaning from that dream. She coyly replied: "Perhaps you need to go back into analysis, so that you can learn to interpret my dreams better." I arose instantly, compulsively, and explosively from my chair, telling her to leave my office and that our therapy had concluded. Eighteen months of repressing my countertransference feelings had exploded into a negative action.

The analysand's grandiosity about her unconscious contents rubbed against my inflation from having received an analyst's diploma. Through this mutually painful action, I became aware of the difference between being and becoming an analyst.

The diploma on the wall of my consulting room says I am an

analyst. Yet I know that I must spend the rest of my life becoming an analyst. Without this terrible event, now 15 years in the past, I might still hurt those who are wounded, with my inflated analyst's persona. (The analysand later completed a successful analytical journey with a colleague who handled negative transference and countertransference feelings more capably than I.)

The action I have described has proved to be a source of self-reflective analysis regarding the mutual meanings of negative countertransference. In suspending my attention and flying like Icarus above my negative countertransference feelings, I also succeeded in leaving behind an essential ingredient to the *cura animarum* (cure of souls). "The crucial thing," Jung wrote, "is no longer the medical diploma, but the human quality" (CW16, par. 174). Note that Jung referred to our work as *cura animarum* (plural) rather than *cura animae* (singular). More than one soul is cured in the dialogue we name and image as therapy.

Reviewing the literature, we find that the best and brightest of each school of depth psychology have given words to the multi-complexed and multi-imaged experience of countertransference. Klein (1952) imagined four persons in the consultation room: the analyst, the analysand, the good mother, and the bad mother. Guggenbühl-Craig (1971) underlined the "power in the helping professions" with bold strokes. Roustang (1980) named the unconscious dimensions of transference and countertransference: the game of the other. The Berlin Research Group (Dieckmann, 1976) on transference and countertransference postulated four levels of images: the projective, the objective, the antithetical, and the archetypal. By these four we see more clearly the hand of the Other in our transference and countertransference experiences. Fordham (1957) elucidated the archetypal dimension in the transference and countertransference dialogue with the terms participations, identifications and syntonic processes. Jacoby (1984) used Martin Buber's I-Thou to express the deeper realities of the dialogue of analysis.

In our negative countertransference experiences, we deal with a highly emotional source of energy that comes from what Jung called the archetype of the Self. We must name and image this energy in many ways in order to integrate it constructively into our work and our lives. The more names and images we have for our countertransferences, the better we will be able to heal instead of wound. We Jungians might do well to reflect on our countertransference experiences by listening to the words and seeing the images of the savants of other schools – such as Mahler (1968), Racher (1968), Winnicott (1971), and Searles (1979) – in order to heighten our awareness of our unnamed and unseen emotional and cognitive complexes.

Owning my classical Jungian preferences and biases, however, the best theoretical and practical framework I have found about countertransference is contained in a 22-page monograph, "Problems of Modern Psychotherapy" (CW16) that Jung wrote in 1929. This framebreaking document presented his understanding of the parallel processes occurring in the clinical experience of transference and countertransference. He observed four stages in the psychotherapeutic process: confession, elucidation, education and transformation.

On one level of understanding, we may apply these four stages to the developmental history of depth psychology. Breuer's cathartic or cleansing method marked the first stage of Psychoanalysis. In its second stage, Freud's genius introduced elucidation or interpretation of the unconscious shadow material into psychoanalytic practice. Adler recognized that social education – the third stage – must follow insight into personal and collective shadows. In its final stage of development, analysis reflects upon itself and sees itself mirrored by the Other as an instrument of personal and collective transformation.

On the second level of understanding, we observe that in every successful analytic dialogue, the analysand moves and is moved through the same four stages of personal development in which successive transference and countertransference feelings play a crucial role. Painful secrets are confessed, shadows come to light and are elucidated and interpreted, the analysand is drawn out (e-ducare) or educated into other meaningful modes of interpersonal relationships. Finally, the analysand comes to the cognitive and affective realization that the Other has given life a new form, widening and deepening the boundaries of being.

A third level of examination applies these four stages to the process of becoming an analyst, a never-ending process. Jung courageously admitted that those who are continually becoming analysts journey with their teachers or analysands through the same stages of development. The four images and words that apply to the science and art of analysis and to the journey of the analysand are astoundingly and humblingly relevant to the individuation process of the analyst. To quote Jung directly, the confession is "nothing less than that the doctor is as much 'in the analysis' as the patient" (CW16, par. 166). I continue to be in the process of becoming an analyst because I need to be "in analysis" for the rest of my life. I am called from a very deep place to attempt the very same uncomfortable work upon my own darkness which I hope and expect my analysands to perform. If I face my negative countertransference feelings, I realize that I need my analysands to draw out of darkness those complexes that I have avoided and defended myself against for years. My analysands act as my educators. It is ironic and humbling that they pay me so that I can become a *mensch* (genuine human being).

Jung warns us that the final stage, the stage of transformation, demands that "the doctor must change himself if he is to become capable of changing his patient" (CW16, par. 170). He exhorts us to respond wholeheartedly to our profession's greatest and most difficult ethical imperative: become the woman or man through whom you wish to influence others.

Without an introspective attitude toward negative countertransference feelings, analytic work becomes unethical and these feelings degenerate into negative countertransference actions. Moreover, by failing to recognize such feelings, the analyst is deprived of another opportunity to be drawn out of pseudo-professional narcissism into a deeper, richer dialogue with life.

I conclude with a dream reported by a middle-aged mental health professional with whom I had worked for three years:

I come into Dr. Lavin's office for a session. He is seated behind a desk. This office is a larger and more rectangular area than his normal office, with an adjoining large area for a busi-

ness office. I am struggling for words, trying to speak about a process, a discovery of images from my inner work. I am dissatisfied because what I am saying doesn't express me well. I then realize that I am at a long distance from Dr. Lavin and that there is no door between the area I am in and the business office.

For some reason, probably frustration with myself because I am unable to verbalize and frustration with Dr. Lavin because of his distance, I leave the room. Later, I return and Tom is on a couch to the right of the entrance. He is eating grapes and is very cheerful. We begin a conversation in which I have no trouble finding the right words. I can not express how grateful I am that, after all these years, the Other is pointing to the possibility that a balance might yet be found between the Apollonian Dr. Lavin who cannot leave his distancing desk and the Tom who can enjoy the Dionysian delight of a dialogue on the analytic couch.

In this paper, I have followed Jung's guidelines by making a confession about a negative countertransference action, giving that action an interpretation, referring to colleagues from several schools of depth psychology and especially to Jung himself for education, and reporting a dream that may point to the possibility of transformation. May we grow into a greater consciousness that, at the center of our many complexes and *trans-fere*, there bubbles up the energy and hope of *trans-formare*. For Jung's complex psychology is, at its core, a psychology of and a call to transformation.

REFERENCES

Binswanger, L. (1957). *Sigmund Freud: Reminiscence of a Friendship*. New York: Grune.

Dieckmann, H. (1976). Transference and countertransference: Results of a Berlin research group. *Journal of Analytical Psychology*, *21*-1, 25-36.

Fordham, M. (1957). *New Developments in Analytical Psychology.* London: Routledge & Kegan Paul.

Guggenbühl-Craig, A. (1971). *Power in the Helping Professions.* New York: Spring Publications.

Jacoby, M. (1984). *The Analytic Encounter.* Toronto: Inner City Books.

Klein, M. (1952). The Origins of transference. *International Journal of Psycho-analysis, 33*: 433-438.

Mahler, M. (1968). *On Human Symbiosis and the Vicissitudes of Individuation.* New York: International Universities Press.

Racher, H. (1968). *Transference and Countertransference.* London: Hogarth.

Roustang, F. (1980). *Psychoanalysis Never Lets Go.* Baltimore: Johns Hopkins.

Searles, H. (1979). *Counter-transference and Related Subjects.* New York: International Universities Press.

Winnicott, D.W. (1971). *Playing and Reality.* London: Tavistock.

The Analyst as Intermediary

Maria Luisa Spinoglio
Milan, Italy
Centro Italiano
Di Psicologia Analitica

> Who, if I cried, would hear me among the angelic orders? And even if one of them suddenly pressed me against his heart, I should fade in the strength of his stronger existence. For Beauty's nothing but beginning of Terror we're still just able to bear, and why we adore it so is because it serenely disdains to destroy us. Each single angel is terrible.
>
> Rainer Maria Rilke

These dizzying verses begin the first of the *Duino Elegies*, the most mysterious and fascinating of Rilke's works. The lines serve as our entry into the complicated problem of archetypal relationships.

The angel to which Rilke referred may be the primordial image. This image is representative of that pre-existent and impersonal form which is the true archetype, in itself unrepresentable. The yearning for the Angel – the tension, the presentiment of catastrophe were this distance to disappear – these all make the poet's condition universal, and we feel that humankind – perceived by French philosopher Blaise Pascal as suspended between the infinitely small and the infinitely huge – must continually invoke the Angel and must not fear its intimacy. A human's psychic health depends on this tension, like that of a tightrope-walker. "He who is near me is near the fire," says Jesus (in the non-canonical Gospel of Thomas), "and he who is far from me is far from the Kingdom."

The poet finds one of his intermediaries in Beauty. Perhaps for a few this path is travelable even if not free from danger. Or perhaps Beauty is the changing veil of maya, the only condition for loving and accepting life. If so, Aphrodite's multi-colored girdle propels all toward love and makes "beautiful" a life otherwise unacceptable.

Mythology is rich in warnings about the danger of wanting to see the gods too closely or of competing directly with them. Zeus presents himself to his non-divine lovers in maskings and transformations (e.g., bull, golden rain, swan) to protect them from an impact like a bolt of lightning. The sight – voluntary or involuntary – of a god is the cause of disasters and even death. An example is Actaeon, a hunter of mythology who, having seen Artemis bathing, was changed into a stag and devoured by his own hounds.

Competition with divinity – inflation of the ego with respect to the gifts of the Self – is also destructive to the individual. Arachne, who wanted to vie with Athena, was reduced to the subhuman form of a spider. Marsias, in his rivalry with Apollo, was conquered and flayed alive. The relationship between humans and gods demands the greatest respect and prudence. One cannot have excessive confidence in it. One's abandonment to God must be regulated by the rites that God establishes.

In Rudolf Otto's (1936) work we see how, within the numinous, fascination and *tremendum* are closely linked; every religious sentiment is an attempt to enter into a relationship with the archetype without letting oneself be overwhelmed by it. Mediations are necessary. Angels have ever moved back and forth as messengers between God and human; Hermes, as psychopomp, is the mediator. Esoteric doctrines quite naturally draw their inspiration from him. Wherever someone seeks to go beyond the limits of human consciousness centered on the ego, Hermes or one of his equivalents appears.

Humanity needs its specific intermediaries before God. Priests, shamans, prophets and kings – persons especially prepared and protected in their relationship with the numinous – have assumed this function. Without such mediating functions, humans have exposed themselves to tragic consequences.

Kohut (1969) singled out the "traumatically rigid devaluation of both Christian and traditional tribal values" as the determining element that spurred the narcissistic regression of the German people in the Nazi years toward the "grandiose self and toward archaic forms of rage" (p. 85). Without a basis of dangerous exposure to the eruption of the archetype, a narcissistic wound does not justify the explosion of a psychosis – even at the collective level. An analysand of mine noted that the desire to eliminate God from the conscience of the Russian people led, as a direct consequence, to the personality cult and Stalin's setting himself up in God's place.

From the chaos of the collective unconscious in which the newborn is immersed, the first figure who brings order and mediates the organization and the humanizing of the conscience is the mother, or one standing for her. Here again we find Rilke re-evoking the humanizing power of the maternal figure, this time in the third elegy:

> Did he ever begin himself, though?
> Mother, you made him small, it was you that began him;
> he was new to you, you arched over those new eyes
> the friendly world, averting the one that was strange.
> Where, oh where, are the years when you simply displaced
> for him, with your slender figure, the surging abyss?
> You hid so much from him then; made the nightly-suspected
> room harmless, and out of your heart full of refuge
> mingled more human space with that of his nights.

Such an undertaking is not once and for all. Rather, we are involved in it essentially our whole lives, just as the victory over the dragon is never definitive and the autonomy of the complexes gathers force anew in crisis situations, in transit toward new phases of life.

Knowing of the existence of the archetypal background can be of great help when the analyst is beset with projections from the analysand. The analyst is not merely a substitute for parental figures, as in the Freudian model, but functions through a complicated process wherein the imagos stand behind the parents. Further, the more the parents seem distant, innocuous and inactive, the more the imagos become powerful and dangerously active.

Witches, often, do not develop from mothers who are really bad but are activated when mothers are absent and thus, for the child, dead. In many tales the wicked stepmother is substituted for the good mother who has died; so too in the psychic space left vacant by the maternal function, the child is swallowed up and destroyed.

Awareness that the only therapeutic function possible is that of mediation can protect the analyst from ego inflation, for the true healer remains the Self of the analysand. To help is to loosen the dependencies that develop in a contact as close as the analytic one.

The great difficulty in the therapy of psychoses lies precisely in acquiring the right distance, one that permits true relationship. Indeed, the starting point may be a symbiosis – a virtual fusion of the two beings. Alternatively, there may be an excess of separation, a psychic void in which one of the two cannot exist because the point of reference that allows for the structuring of the ego is lacking. An apt image is a bird that cannot fly in either too dense a medium or in a vacuum.

In the therapy of anorexics, I have noticed particular difficulty in that psychic space which permits the birth of autonomy. Used to symbiotic relationships, anorexics defend themselves against maternal intrusiveness through the desperate, concretistic attempt not to have anything more enter their bodies.

Francesca was an anorexic who began analysis at 16. For several months she remained behind a screen of formal neutrality. The relationship between us was empty of real content. Her fear and diffidence paralyzed all attempts at communication. In the story of Hansel and Gretel, Hansel gives the witch the chicken bone to trick her, so that he will not be eaten. Similarly, Francesca became ever thinner in her attempt not to take up space. Thus, she tried to escape identification with her mother. The analytic work slowly reinforced her right to have secrets and a shadow. In the analytic relationship, in which she was respected, she found the right to intimacy and to the "corporeality" she had rejected previously. Her dreams revealed her wish to be nourished by the mother. This wish put Francesca in the paradoxical situation of wanting to be born again without giving up the maternal symbiosis. Analysis gave back to Francesca a genuine concreteness which permitted her to accede to that second birth which guarantees completeness.

Carla came to analysis at 25, suffering from schizophrenic disturbances coupled with the deep anguish of depersonalization and fears of persecution. She was continually exposed to the destructive aspect of the mother archetype, as before the petrifying glance of Medusa. Her mother, a seriously narcissistic personality, had on the one hand filled her daughter's psychic space with herself and, on the other, had exposed her to the danger of abandonment and therefore to the void. The mother used the threat of withdrawing love if Carla did not always remain the good daughter who would mirror the motherly perfection. Carla remained a perpetual child, as in the story of Snow White wherein the paralyzing envy of the mother is activated by the birth of the daughter.

For a long period I had to restrain attacks on me that arose out of Carla's identification with the destructive maternal archetype. Gradually our work made room for a more human and less archaic relationship. Fortunately there was always, along with Carla's psychotic fantasizing, a plane of easier personal connection that permitted, even in the most difficult moments, the continuation of analysis and the repeated re-emergence from a stormy situation.

The dream of another analysand summarizes perhaps better than any formal discussion the significance of the analyst's role as intermediary with respect to the archetypal plane. The analysand was a lesbian in her thirties, identified with a weak father who had absorbed her mother's anxieties. The young woman was perennially looking for a female figure by whom to be loved and treated with tenderness and understanding. Despite her appearance as a mannish woman quite sure of herself, she suffered great anxiety and insecurity which – during vacations and trips – approached phobia in their intensity. The dream occurred shortly before a trip to Jerusalem, a journey desired intensely but conflictually because of a series of experiences. Here is the dream:

My analyst invites me to her home. I ask if I can also bring my friend and she consents. We enter without anyone opening the door before us, as if the door were already open. It's a period house with glass-paned doors which open onto a long corridor. I begin taking lots of gift packages from a suitcase. From one doorway I see a large room with a table set. A middle-aged woman greets us with a smile and explains that the analyst has left for Denmark where she will touch the center of the Earth. I am sad because I greatly wanted her to meet my friend but, at the same time, I also feel a sense of joy. We go off, leaving the packages behind.

In working on the dream, the analysand referred to her imminent trip and to Jerusalem as the center of the world. She marveled that in the dream the analyst is going to Denmark and that the center of the Earth is located there, but immediately afterward she understands because the Denmark mentioned in the dream is the image of a wild and solitary land, near the sea. She had seen this land in a beautiful film, "Babette's Feast." In it a woman offers an extraordinary and costly banquet. She has prepared it with great skill for the community that has welcomed her and for her benefactors, two sisters whose lives are dominated by the memory of their father. The banquet permits, symbolically, the renewal of the sense of a complete life.

The dream alludes to the possibility of putting oneself in contact with the center and, therefore, with the Self, through the process of analysis. The desire for a more direct and personal relationship hid the therapeutic meaning, leaving to the analyst the task of keeping the true goal in sight. The goal was not one of a good personal relationship, but rather activating the therapeutic factor that operated in the center of the analysand's psyche.

Translated from Italian by Walter A. Blue

REFERENCES

Kohut, H. (1969). *Potere, coraggio e narcisismo*. Rome: Astrolabio.

Otto, R. (1936). *Il sacro*. Milano: Feltrinelli.

Psychodynamics in Training

Birth Trauma and Training

Jo Ann Culbert-Koehn
Santa Monica, California, USA
Society of Jungian Analysts
of Southern California

Birth trauma is a particular life experience that can be reconstellated during the analyst-training process – at times of passage from one stage to another and, especially, in the final interview. Jung's only reference to birth trauma is found in *Psychology and Religion* (CW11), where he wrote about *The Tibetan Book of the Dead*. This book describes an initiation process to restore to the soul the divinity lost at birth. Jung chided Freudian analysts for not looking far enough, contenting themselves with conjectures about intrauterine existence and birth trauma – not searching back far enough, to the collective unconscious. He called birth trauma a "famous obvious truism" (CW11, par. 842).

Many Jungians take this attitude; birth trauma is such a truism that we don't need to talk about it much and certainly we don't need to feel it. Obviously, one can get stuck in the womb or in investigating womb trauma and lose a good deal of living. On the other hand, one can miss something that is causing the analysand pain in mind and body by minimizing or intellectualizing birth trauma. I became aware of this lack as a result of my own experience in training: with a control case, my personal process, studying such theorists as D.W. Winnicott, and in my final meeting with the Certifying Board.

Control Case

In retrospect, there were clear references to birth trauma in a control case I had. My case report included a lengthy description of the analysand's complications during her pregnancy:

The patient was deeply depressed from the time she suspected she was pregnant until the birth. I never saw her smile. She was often mute. Her interest in her physical appearance deteriorated markedly. There was not a moment of joy. Shortly after the pregnancy was confirmed she dreamed: "*I went to the bathroom and saw that I was bleeding. I went to the doctor. Two female obstetricians and my therapist were all there talking. There was some kind of infection.*"

As the pregnancy culminated I found and wrote about a link between the analysand's birth and the difficult pregnancy:

> I believe Frances was afraid that the baby would not be healthy because of her own sense of badness and deficiency. She suffered this terror from the time she found herself pregnant until she saw her healthy child. I think it was this terror as well as memories of negative feelings about her own birth that accounted for the unrelieved depression throughout the pregnancy.

In the last months of the pregnancy physical complications increased and the woman was hospitalized. Again, from the case report, is a description of the birth:

> The last time I visited the hospital I said, "Frances, if you tell the baby the world is as negative as you think it is right now, it's never going to want to come out." She looked startled and said, "That's what my husband said yesterday." This exchange took place Friday afternoon. I left, wondering how I could have sounded so harsh. Friday evening the labor started and early Saturday morning Mitchell was born. It was a difficult labor and he was born by Caesarian section. His umbilical cord had been wrapped around his neck. Frances was groggy when I talked to her on Saturday. Her throat was sore from the tube in it, but there was an excitement in her voice. The baby was beautiful. I cried on and off for three days. I had been aware of the depth of her fear, but not of my own.

Personal Process

It would take additional years of analysis and supervision before I realized that I also had a powerful identification with the baby undergoing a difficult birth. In retrospect my final interview for certification was filled with painful birth trauma/separation anxiety which I defended against with what looked to the committee like narcissistic rage. There had been no mention of birth trauma as such in my analysis, in my control work, or in the certification interview. No one asked the question, "What does this powerful countertransference have to do with your own birth?" In the certification interview we talked about my rage, but we did not get to the fear or terror beneath it. We did not discuss the fear that in making the transition from trainee status to analyst the door was open for the possibility of death as well as rebirth. The archetypal aspect of this transition was clear but not the personal birth trauma component. I continued to feel the effects of the certification interview for many months. In a dream I had after certification *my recently certified husband, two recently certified colleagues – one male and one female – and I had all been in a mudbath*. The mudbath seemed to me a very primitive way of removing impurities. Although I had been through an archetypal initiation, more fine-tuned work on infantile shadow would be needed. In the same dream *a woman analyst trained at Tavistock was walking around the perimeter*. Several months later I sought her out as a supervisor. In the course of the supervision she read my control case. I still had a feeling of something important being unanalyzed either in the transference or countertransference. The year following the control work and certification had been marked by increased somatization in the analysand and in me. My supervisor, after reading the case, suggested that the somatic aspect might be approached best by reading a chapter of Winnicott on psyche-soma. When I did, my strongest associations were to my own experiences of giving birth. In both labors I experienced terror and pain shortly before the birth. My fear of pushing the baby out was severe. I attributed this fear to my generalized problem with separation but was never able to pin it down. After reading the Winnicott material (1975) I began to pay more attention to the details of my experience of separation, especially analytic breaks. During one very anxious period I tried to draw a picture of a baby being born and myself cutting the umbilical cord, as the moment of traumatic separation. This had actually been a fantasy around the birth of my first child. I became very frustrated as I drew. I ripped up a number of drawings as my hand moved spontaneously toward the baby's head, not her belly. The cord wanted to attach itself around the baby's head. With a shock of recognition it occurred to me that I had been born with the cord around my neck. I had been a baby that barely made it out – like the baby in my control case. I realized how much the anxiety related to my birth was reflected in my life. Birth trauma could be seen in the process of my control case and my countertransference reaction. It manifested in my own experiences of giving birth, in the process of the final interview itself, and in all my major experiences of separation.

Theorists

Winnicott (1975) wrote of two times of birth trauma: the actual birth and the first days of extra-uterine experience. Tustin (1981) made a similar distinction between physical birth and psychological birth, calling mismanaged or premature psychological birth a psychological catastrophe. Melanie Klein (1984) also made a connection between physical birth and the first days of life. She wrote, "External circumstances play a vital part in the initial relationship to the breast. If birth has been difficult and if it results in complications such as lack of oxygen, a disturbance in adaptation to the outside world occurs and the relationship to the breast starts at a great disadvantage" (p. 179). In Jungian terms (Neumann, 1976) a difficult physical birth leads to a difficult relationship to the mother and hence to the Self unless compensated by an unusually sheltering and sensitive mother or by later strong transference experiences in analysis. The infant catalogues or memorizes the birth process as it occurs, according to Winnicott (1975). When there has been a physical trauma the premature use of the mind, in response to the trauma, becomes an encumbrance to the relation between psyche and soma. It is also an encumbrance to analysis. It is very difficult for the birth-traumatized analysand/trainee to get into a position of not-knowing, just being, letting the analyst carry the continuity. Winnicott went on to discuss psychological birth. He said that any disturbance of continuity or containment, such as the mother's being unable to pay sufficient attention to the infant's needs after birth, is experienced by the infant as an invasion or impingement. A premature use of the mind becomes a false self. One sees this in trainees who cannot "be in training." They are forever seeking a perfect environment. Winnicott wrote: Clinically one may see such a person (therapist) develop who is a marvelously good mother to others for a limited period of time (a therapy hour). In fact, a person who has developed along these lines may have almost magical healing properties because of an extreme capacity to make active adaptation to primitive needs. The falsity of this pattern for expression of the personality however becomes evident in practice. Breakdown threatens or occurs because what the individual is ... needing is to find someone else who will make real this "good environment concept." (1975, p. 247)

To summarize Winnicott in Jungian terms, birth trauma leads to a fracture of the ego-Self axis. The ego separates prematurely, inflates and acts as if it were not dependent on the Self.

Training

For many trainees, if the final interview goes deeply it is experienced archetypally as a rebirth or initiation experience. For certain trainees, however, it may arouse intense anxiety on a personal level. Trainees will be affected most if: 1) the personal birth experience has been traumatic and involves a near-death experience; 2) the trauma is unconscious; 3) analysis proceeded with little attention to traumas of infancy; 4) frequency of the trainee's analysis is such that early trauma is not constellated in the transference and the training institute has carried the projection of mother or womb in a way that is split off from the analytic process. The birth-traumatized trainee's experience of the interview will include feelings of extreme vulnerability, fears of being thrown out in the cold, or fears of being kept in and suffocated. Such a trainee may feel attacked or killed off, raw or skinless. He or she may become emotionally paralyzed, be unable to communicate emotions verbally, feel dead, or become aggressive and attacking.

Conclusion

I have shared this material out of my feeling that its discovery, although anxiety-producing and painful, enriches a connection to the core of one's being. The need to be in contact with what is primary – for each of us – links us together as Jungians. The material that I have presented here may be difficult to locate in oneself, but after a personal experience it becomes quite easy to see in one's analysands. I am bringing this matter to light, not out a sense of anger at the analysts with whom I worked; they helped me to bring to consciousness other important aspects of my personality. I want to say simply that this basic area of psyche brings with it deep anxiety. If it is not analyzed there will remain a feeling of not having gotten to the core, of a deep body-mind split and a strong propensity to somatization. My hope is that more understanding of the birth trauma dynamic will facilitate work with analysands and trainees and that they will be freed to enjoy more of life. The French author Antoine de St. Exupéry has written, "To live is to be slowly born."

REFERENCES

Klein, M. (1984). *Envy and Gratitude and Other Works*. New York: The Free Press.

Neumann, E. (1976). *The Child*. New York: Harper & Row.

Tustin, F. (1981). *Autistic States in Children*. London: Routledge & Kegan Paul.

Winnicott, D.W. (1975). *Through Pediatrics to Psycho-Analysis*. New York: Basic Books.

Countertransference in the Selection Interview

Mario Jacoby
Zurich, Switzerland
Schweizerische Gesellschaft
für Analytische Psychologie

After many years of experience in training future analysts, I have come to the conviction that the selection of trainees is crucial. Insofar as the practice of analysis is more an art than a science, it basically cannot be taught or learned; it calls for a natural, inborn talent. Usually people with such a talent as well as the corresponding motivation can make the best use of their training, can integrate it into their personality, refine and differentiate it, and apply it creatively. Training may provide psychological knowledge, some methods and skills and, I hope, develop sensitivity and psychic differentiation needed to grasp what analysis is.

Even in the light of modern psychotherapy research the old Chinese saying remains valid: "If the wrong man uses the right means, then the right means have the wrong effect" (Tschang Scheng Schu). Training, ideally, should provide the "right means" to the "right" man or woman. But how do the right applicants reveal themselves and how are we to recognize them?

For many years, in the Jungian tradition, the applicant's personal analyst recommended the applicant for training. But this practice had disadvantages for the "objectivity" of the selection as well as for the analysis of the applicant / candidate.

Even with the formation of selection committees, committee members have felt a certain reluctance to give final judgments concerning the applicants and their potential for becoming Jungian analysts; at least this is so in Zurich. In a good Jungian spirit, one wanted to "give a chance" whenever possible, because one never knows what the Self has in store for a person. Leaving it to the Self and to the potential of a Jungian analysis seemed to be the best and most modest attitude toward this intricate problem. Perhaps there was an overestimation of what an analysis can do to overcome decisive shortcomings.

It became evident that most of the candidates whose suitability had been doubted greatly in the beginning were never able to dispel those doubts. At the end of their training it seemed inhuman to stop their graduation. Once they were graduate analysts, the doubts still remained justified and we regretted ever having accepted them into the training program. But sometimes the committees found courage at the last minute and refused to grant the diploma – the certification of the Jungian analyst – never, though, without guilt feelings.

But who are we – who am I – to say who would be a good-enough and trustworthy analyst and who not? We cannot avoid the issue of selection altogether because so much of the analytic process depends upon the analyst's personality. We cannot leave the choice to train open to anyone who fulfills the formal academic criteria. Our training institutes carry a responsibility toward future analysands who may trustingly choose an analyst because he or she has been trained at a Jungian institute and is a member of the IAAP.

But how can we arrive at an objective enough evaluation? What images do we have of a Jungian analyst, what criteria? I am sure we could agree to certain personality features such as emotional reliability; openness toward the symbolic realm; a certain intelligence of the heart and a capacity to question oneself; empathy along with the ability to set firm, yet flexible boundaries. Qualities that indicate unsuitability include: paranoid tendencies, moral deficiencies, borderline conditions, psychotic states, unmanageable vulnerability, pseudo-health, and rigid defenses toward the unconscious.

But some of these tendencies may be present in each of us and sometimes even can be of use in the analytic encounter. There are neurotic trends that may help our effectiveness – the image of the wounded healer applies – but others hinder it. A major consideration is: what does the personality of the applicant radiate and constellate in others? A candidate who is a charismatic personality may become a very effective analyst, yet be dangerous. Which tendency prevails depends on ethical awareness and differentiation, as well as talent for analytic work. A useful guide for arriving at a broader evaluation may be the fantasy question: would I recommend this person to my dearest friend?

But in selection procedures the power issue is always involved. How can we deal with this issue and its various subtle and often quite unconscious ramifications? How do we come to terms with our ambivalence and guilt feelings? These are important questions which have to be asked and yet cannot yield generalized answers.

In Zurich we have adopted a workable procedure. Three members of a committee of seven each see a particular applicant for two separate individual interviews. The three discuss their evaluations in a meeting of the full committee, which reaches a decision. Thus, four members have not seen nor been personally involved with the applicant but listen to the reports of the three members who have done so. The advantage of this arrangement is considerable: the three interviewers sometimes have difficulty in reaching a conclusion – very often due to countertransference issues. The more "neutral" committee members often sense those countertransference issues and can offer some clarification.

On rare occasions I have felt that a power complex has invaded the group spirit of the committee of seven. In general, however, the committee's composition keeps the power issues of the individual members in check. It is important to see applicants twice at an interval of a few days. Both interviewer and applicant can digest the first session's impressions, which can be checked during the second meeting. There is also the possibility of discussion between the interviewer and the applicant of the impact the first interview has had on both. Such discussions can reveal a great deal.

It is definitely an advantage to evaluate an applicant in two separate steps. At the first step one attempts to grasp the applicant's personality as well as possible. At the second step reflections follow on the suitability of someone with this particular personality make-up for a career as an analyst. These two steps cannot be clearly separated, of course, but the effort must be made. Not making it brings the danger that we measure every insight about an applicant against a personally-preferred image of a Jungian analyst, an image each of us carries half-consciously. We must remember the wide variety of personalities among Jungian analysts and that the "right" person is right only with certain analysands.

Some analysts are "right" for a wider spectrum of people than others but each has limitations. I remember for example, a young man who was in analysis with a renowned senior woman analyst, saying: "My analyst is such a wonderful, cultured and refined lady; how can I, in her presence, reveal my rather crude sexual fantasies?" The question arises here: should such an analyst be aware enough of the particular atmosphere in her space and be able to sense those resistances which are likely to arise because of her particular personality-emanation?

But again, who are we to judge? It is obvious that countertransference plays a decisive role in many ways. Most important, the interviewer must beware of unconscious projections – illusory countertransference – which can distort perception of an applicant and falsify any evaluation. But the "syntonic" side of the countertransference experience also comes into play. Although the interviewer is not involved in a deep analysis with the applicant, an emotionally-charged situation exists between them. Thus, contents belonging to the applicant's inner life may be parts of the interviewer's experience. Yet it is difficult at times to distinguish between perception and projection, that is, between syntonic and illusory countertransference. I will give some examples from my own experience as an interviewer.

Applicants, when coming to interviews, are more or less tense and apprehensive. They usually are cooperative, trying their best to make a good impression in order to be accepted. As they don't know me and my criteria of evaluation they tend to replace me by a figure of their own fantasy. Sometimes I can feel what kind of figure I am expected to embody – usually a more or less accepting or rejecting authority-figure. Often that expectation creates a disorientation, together with embarrassment and insecurity. The question arises in me whether I should leave applicants in such a stress-situation where their complexes and defenses show up much more clearly, or whether I should try to calm them down, perhaps by expressing empathy for their understandable feeling of stress? If I do the latter, I must ask myself, am I doing this because I cannot tolerate the stress?

Trying to reduce their stress produces a variety of effects in different applicants, from complete denial that they feel any tension to crying fits for having finally been met by an understanding parent. Sometimes the result seems to be genuine relief, but I may sense some hostility hovering around our psychic space. I may address this, but if a candidate denies having any such feelings I am faced with the question: Is he or she unconscious of it or simply afraid to admit hostility for fear of being rejected? Or is it just my own hostility, which I unconsciously harbor against the candidate? These questions require soul-searching. In some instances, applicants admitting their hostility are cooperative enough to trace with me its source, which usually lies in the resentment of having to undergo such an ordeal as selection interviews or in the narcissistic injury of being brought into question at all. Sometimes there is aggression against having to surrender to judgment by a power- figure meddling in one's private affairs. These are understandable reactions and do not in themselves contra-indicate acceptance into training. The decision depends on the applicant's manner of dealing with an authority complex.

In general I try – at least in the second interview – to focus some attention on what is happening in the psychic space between the applicant and me. I prefer an applicant to express some awareness of this space. Failure to do so shows either a conscious or unconscious resistance or a lack of feeling for those crucial analytic tools of transference / countertransference.

Another example: There are applicants who seem to know instinctively how to make me feel good and to engage me in an interesting dialogue. But a sense of mistrust, of being manipulated, may come up in me. It is difficult to discern whether this suspicion belongs only to my own mistrustful side or whether I am becoming aware of something taking place in the applicant.

Some people have this intuitive gift of tuning in to the wave-length of their dialogue-partner and can use it in a manipulative way to their own advantage. Is the trickster working in such people? If my suspicion leads me to some evidence concerning their conscious or unconscious manipulation, I may experience a negative reaction. But does this necessarily prove the applicant's unsuitability? This "tuning-in" may represent a great analytic gift, provided the candidate can develop in analysis a sense of moral responsibility and of integrity in knowing his or her own psychic boundaries. Control over the inner trickster needs to be learned. But to what extent this is possible may be difficult to anticipate.

As a last example I offer the case of an applicant, a middle-aged woman, toward whom I felt an intense dislike from the start of the interview. She seemed clearly motivated, had excellent recommendations and very good reasons for wanting to train, but I suffered more and more from the unusual intensity of my dislike. I felt as though a watch-dog were barking incessantly inside me, trying to chase this person away. Our likes and dislikes have to be taken seriously, yet they are by themselves never a sound enough basis on which to form an evaluation. In her case it took a good while until I could find enough evidence to explain my dislike. That came when I asked her how she felt about her analysis. Her response was an outburst of enormous hatred against her analyst, a hatred stemming from a delusional transference. From that moment on her delusional rage became more and more apparent in the interview. At the beginning, it had been well concealed, but my "inner watch-dog" picked it up. This woman was too ill to be accepted for training.

These are just a few examples to show the value of counter-transference in the selection procedure. Yet the illusory counter-transference and the interviewer's personal bias also interfere. We are thus left with more questions than answers.

One thing is certain: The interviewer can form an evaluation based on subjective experience, but only under the condition of the corrective element of the other two interviewers and of the committee as a whole.

Shame in Training

John Talley
Santa Fe, New Mexico, USA
Inter-Regional Society
of Jungian Analysts

Those of us who were drawn to becoming Jungian analysts saw in the profession a way to understand ourselves better and to help others. It also offered a second chance to be the kind of person we would like to be, in a more ideal family than the original one. In Kohut's (1977) words we chose an "idealized self object" which carries for us a vision toward which we can aspire in personal analysis and training.

The choice of an ideal suggests something fundamental, probably a necessity for everyone. Hultberg (1987) has suggested, following Kohut, that "between basic ambition and basic idealization ... is an intermediate stage of basic talents and skills" (p. 171). Thus, realization and achievement take place to the degree that one comes to terms with the tensions between actual self and ideal self.

The shadow of the inevitable and necessary idealization is shame. In the training situation both candidate and analyst are vulnerable to the shame of falling short of the ideal. Training includes understanding and accepting impossibility as well as possibility, limitation as well as expansion, disillusion as well as hope, fate as well as free will. We are well acquainted with the realities of power, anger, fear, depression and the capricious vicissitudes of eros even as we also know joy, curiosity and surprise. All are the warp and woof of training as they are of the human condition.

However problematic and disillusioning these realities are, at least we know their signatures. As the old familiars they are ever ready to bring us down to earth where we must grapple with the truth about ourselves and with the pain of distinguishing the hopes and ideals of training from its realities.

Shame

With shame it is a different story. Ubiquitous and rarely acknowledged, shame is the emotion – perhaps above all others – that calls attention to the failures of our ideals, hopes, and endeavors. Shame is exquisitely sensitive to any hint of recognition and will feign a mask of indifference. If cornered or threatened with exposure it can seethe with arrogant contempt.

Solitary and alienated, shame does not know its own value. It experiences as valueless its own secret liking for honesty, openness and simplicity. These qualities are scorned by a rejecting world preoccupied with other matters. As a hidden and denied part of ourselves, perhaps our true selves, shame has much to teach us. Not the least of these teachings are humility and acceptance of our own creatureliness.

Theoretical Considerations

Because it is such a devastating emotional experience in and of itself – so shameful if you will – shame has begun only recently to be explored by the various schools of depth psychology. Hultberg (1987) and Sidoli (1987), at our 1986 Congress in Berlin, presented papers on the subject. Stewart (1987) singled it out for clarification in his research into the archetypal system of the Self. Analytical Psychology can assume that, as an archetypal affect, shame/contempt is part of the Self at birth and has a typical developmental role to play in species survival and in individuation. For the archetypal affect of shame/contempt Stewart sees rejection as its stimulus and alienation as its image. As this affect becomes differentiated by reflection, the feeling and a social-cultural attitude evolve.

Kohut, according to A. Morrison (1983), seemed to place shame at the very foundation of development of the bipolar self. Kohut insisted that there are two parallel developmental tracks, while Morrison, a later explicator of Kohut's self psychology, saw the mirrored self as prior to the idealized self.

Morrison stated that a more or less successful experience of mirroring is a prerequisite to experiencing shame; to experience the rejection and alienation of shame one must have known the acceptance and inclusion of adequate mirroring. One might say that the self sees its own "image-as-it-wants-to-be" (Morrison, 1983) in the idealized self object. Repeated experiences of the congruence of self and self-image reflected by another (self object) provide the psyche with its sense of solidity, reliability and security. Incongruence results in the opposite. The specific reaction to this incongruence is shame.

John Beebe (1987, 1989) has suggested that what Jung (MDR) referred to as the "creatura" in his "Seven Sermons to the Dead" is the "small s" self, as later described by Kohut. The "capital S" Self, as Jung used it, in that context is "The Pleroma." Using words Jung might have used, the creatura (self) seeks confirmation in the reflecting Pleroma (Self).

The specifics by which the individual comes to experience self and Self as distinct aspects of one's own psyche is the essence of the individuation process. Fordham (1985) described this process developmentally as occurring through deintegration/reintegration. It is quite possible that the capacity to experience shame is a major stimulus to the individuation process.

An Analytic Session with a Candidate

Dr. X is a highly skilled practicing psychotherapist and an analyst-candidate. He had a disturbed childhood with a psychotic mother and ineffectual father. During a session the analyst was twirling his glasses as the candidate was talking. Suddenly the candidate said, "You do that a lot. Is that so you won't have to look at me?" Unthinking, the analyst said, "Sure. When I don't have them on everything is like an impressionist painting." Silence. The candidate's face became flushed and his eyes tearful. "You mean you haven't seen me for all these four years?" Then followed a tirade of contempt for the analyst's lack of ability as a therapist, insensitivity and betrayal. He left the office early, for the first time in his therapy.

The analyst was confused and defensive at first about this seemingly innocent remark, then recognized how wounding he had been and experienced the shame of failure. Later that day the candidate left a helpless message on the analyst's answering machine. Now knowing his own shame and that of the candidate the analyst returned the call and expressed his genuinely felt regret for having been so insensitive. Later, in discussing the matter together the candidate said, "If you had not called me I don't think I could have ever faced you again." As is often the case when analyst failures are acknowledged, this encounter with shame led to an opening and deepening of the analytic work.

A Supervisory Session

A control stage candidate is discussing with his supervisor the thesis he must write as part of the final examination. The supervisor, interested, suggests another possible way of approaching one aspect of the material. The candidate becomes quiet and after a silence says, "That's what always happens. All of a sudden I got a terrible headache." The supervisor, realizing his suggestion was somehow disturbing said, "Did what I say sound like criticism?" The candidate, in the saddest voice, said, "I just suddenly felt stupid and hopeless."

An Admissions Interview

An applicant to training is being interviewed by an Admissions Committee. An analyst, known for aggressive questioning, asks the applicant who her personal analyst is. The applicant says the name. The analyst then says, "When are you going to get a real analysis?" The applicant freezes and is barely able to answer later questions from other committee members, who attempt to redeem the shame situation.

The Return of the Suppressed

An analyst allows a training analysis to end and the trainee becomes an analyst. Each partner in the analysis knows that each had been avoiding crucial issues in their relationship: any hint of negativity. Each had maintained a good face and had colluded in terminating the analysis. Each felt anger and each felt betrayed. Subsequently their professional relationship was characterized by distrust, anger, and resentment. The analyst felt shame. The former trainee felt contempt.

Shame in Training

Any training situation is a potentially perfect medium for the cultivation, proliferation, and massive denial of shame. The trainee idealizes the training analyst, the body of knowledge professed by the training analyst and the training institute. These idealizations represent a trainee's searching self reaching toward models with which to identify, learn from, and grow. At the same time the trainee is vaguely and sometimes acutely aware of the incongruence between the actual and the ideal; this incongruence is the catalyst for a shame experience. The trainee aspires to perform in approximation to the ideal. Failure to achieve the level desired and expected leads to shame. However, a trainee who has learned well how to defend against feeling shame will not acknowledge failure but will express contempt for the failure of others: trainees, analyst, faculty, institution.

The resolution and transmutation of the tyranny of unrecognized shame in training must be borne by the three primary providers of the training experience: the personal analyst(s), the institute (seminar leaders, committee members, examiners), and the supervising analyst. At the same time, training requires conscious attention to provide optimal learning anxiety, the inevitability of an often painful "learning regression in service of the professional ego" (Alonso & Rutan, 1988). Let me repeat: shame is secret. That which one is ashamed of is secret. Unlike guilt, shame is not easily confessed. Unlike guilt, which implies an action, shame is an inaction, a passivity, a failure. One can confess a guilty action and be forgiven for that action. But confession and forgiveness are not part of shame's signature. Shame, as an experience of the Self and by the Self will be relieved only by acceptance of the Self by the Self. A crucial role of the analyst must be one of understanding and acceptance of the reality of the experience of shame. This role requires no less than the analyst's acknowledgment of his or her own shame experiences: the pain of alienation, rejection, and helplessness. This is not the heroic reaching for the stars of perfection. It is the true acceptance of the possibilities for relationship in the ordinary world.

Stewart (1987) wrote that shame is one of the seven archetypal emotions; it has a basic role in self-preservation and individuation, and in the development of the capacity for feeling and relatedness. Isolating and humiliating as shame is, it becomes the very emotion which, when accepted and understood, leads outward to pleasure, community, self-esteem and capacity for empathy.

Training analysts, training programs and institutes must become aware of the inevitability of the shame dynamic. This dynamic is implicit in the discrepancy between our human limitations and our tendency to idealization of the value systems underlying Analytical Psychology. All of us want good, challenging training. To the degree that we can become conscious of our failures and accepting of our shame reactions, as with all shadow consciousness, we will be less dangerous and possibly more helpful to ourselves and to our colleagues.

Finally, the dream of a trainee about to take his final certifying examination:

I am in an army induction center, standing naked in a long line of naked men. Behind me is a Nobel laureate in deep thought. In front of me is a famous man known for his brilliance. He is with a prestigious university and is author of many well-known books. He is talking to me brilliantly. My heart sinks. I feel inept and stupid, and know I will not pass the exam.

The dream abruptly changes scene. *I am sitting on a wooden kitchen chair on a surfboard riding the waves toward the beach of the city where my exam is to be held. I suddenly realize I am not alone. Standing behind me on the surfboard with his hands on my shoulders is Robert Frost. He is diffidently, quietly "talking me in" : "A little to the right ... eeassy ... now a little to the left. Good ... You're doing fine." It is a brilliant sunny day, the sea is rolling and blue and I am excited, happy and feel strong and able. We are approaching the beach for a safe landing when I awaken.*

Needless to say, the candidate passed his exam. In his dream a supporting Self figure changed a shame situation (the induction center) into one of excitement, play, joy and achievement.

REFERENCES

Alonso, A. & Rutan, J. (1988). Shame and guilt in psychotherapy supervision. *Psychotherapy*, *25*-4, 576-81.

Beebe, J. (1987, March). "The ante has gone up: The conscience of the post-modern artist." Paper presented at a conference of the C.G. Jung Institute of Chicago, "Civilization in Transition: Jung's Contribution to Contemporary Culture."

Beebe, J. (1989). Personal Communication.

Fordham, M. (1985). *Explorations into the Self*. Library of Analytical Psychology. London: Academic Press.

Hultberg, P. (1987). Shame: An overshadowed emotion. In M. Mattoon (Ed.), *The Archetype of Shadow in a Split World*. Zurich: Daimon.

Kohut, H. (1977). *The Restoration of the Self*. New York: International Universities Press.

Morrison, A. (1983). Shame, ideal self and narcissism. *Journal of Contemporary Psychoanalysis*, *19*-2, 295-318.

Sidoli, M. (1987). The shadow between parents and children. In M. Mattoon (Ed.), *The Archetype of Shadow in a Split World*. Zurich: Daimon.

Stewart, L. (1987). Affect and archetype in analysis. In N. Schwartz-Salant & M. Stein (Eds.), *Archetypal Processes in Psychotherapy*. Wilmette, IL: Chiron.

Analytical Psychology and Art (Workshop)

Yesterday's Myths to Today's Creation: Genesis of a Work

Christian Gaillard
Paris, France
Société Française
de Psychologie Analytique

The "work" in my title is that of the German painter Anselm Kiefer. He was born in 1945, immediately after the Second World War. His work won its place in the art of his country during the 1970s and, since the 1989 retrospective in Chicago, Philadelphia and New York, has provoked lively controversy and even impassioned polemics both in Europe and in the United States.

Kiefer's painting turns away from the style of art favored by the two preceding decades, art that was deliberately conceptual and minimal, characterized by the aesthetics and international ideologies of the avant-garde and thus by the taste for breaking with traditional forms. He stages the most disturbing, and perhaps dangerously regressive, return to the primeval essence of the most ancient German myths – whose devastating effect in recent history is all too familiar. Kiefer's solitary and singular art jars and fascinates us just when political and aesthetic debate, especially in Germany, is focusing on the virtues and pitfalls of memory and simultaneously on liberation and revolution.

The therapist is also concerned with the primeval, which is rooted in the body and in history and nevertheless is so strange to the individual that it could be termed collective. How can the therapist confront such a work, make room for it and intervene in the all-too-violent controversy that it arouses?

First of all, by forcing oneself to remain silent. The analyst and the artist are both grappling with an uncertain, hesitant becoming, one which bears and finds its own judgment within itself. This is the apprenticeship of waiting.

Vast, somber canvases without escape, where the pastose heaviness of the paint bears the whole weight of the German soil – devastated by the war, devoid of human presence, still smoking and smoldering; a dumb, opaque, badly sutured scar.

How can one dream of avant-garde here? How and what should we think of the perspectives of art when it is so close to reality that it represents itself – as the recumbent statue represents death – so massively that we must limit its importance? And the corpse here takes on the dimensions of a region, of a country. Even the words written on the canvas by the artist – the names of places, the scene of disaster – double the crude memory of such oppressive painting. Kiefer's early works are massively encysted in the landscape of contemporary art and inscribe the project of painting with the impossibility of any future. Nevertheless, Germany was not born of this cosmic cataclysm, which occurs without leaving room for a living soul.

Kiefer painted far from the towns where the future of art supposedly is decided, far from Dusseldorf and Cologne. Parallel to the vast landscape canvases, he painted the inside of his studio on the same scale. This empty room is an abandoned village school. He calls it *Innenraum* (Interior).

Will this space be as inanimate as the landscapes? Yes, is the first impression. But with a closer look it becomes clear that the emptiness of these interiors is appealing. The painter inscribes on his canvases the names of the heroes of ancient Germanic mythology with its disturbing dynastic sagas. On one of the canvases depicting his studio the artist has written the name Amfortas – the aged king, wounded and impotent. Another is called Notung, the name of the legendary sword at the center of the painting. Sigmund was not able to use the sword but his son Siegfried, his son of incest, would make it into a new weapon. On another canvas, where the flames of some obscure ritual are burning in the room, we can read the names of composer Richard Wagner and other

Spiritual Heroes of Germany, the title of the composition. Still others are dedicated to Arminius, the Germanic hero who once defied the legions of Rome.

Siegfried, the son of the fallen father, returned to a mythic genealogy and a heroic ideal to surmount the obstacle of a harrowing immediate past. Do the paintings evoke nostalgia? Provocation, perhaps, at the sight of this young German of today reappropriating the most notorious Nazi edifices in his painting, though still under the heading of *Innenraum*. What archaic dream is haunting this painter who has so patently broken away from the avant-garde? A cry of scandal is raised.

But the critics were not seeing properly. Kiefer's art is deliberately regressive, but in order to see properly. And to demonstrate that those archaic dreams are hollow. These canvases do not reanimate anything; they remain soulless. The appeal to mythic ancestors is a vacuous appeal. The great spirits – late forebears of the Germanic soul – do not reply to the appeal, even to the ritual invocation of their names: philosophers Hegel, Feuerbach, Marx, Schopenhauer, Heidegger, Nietzsche. Their bodiless heads – wraith-like, grey or diaphanous – float in procession. The mystery has been drained; there is nothing more to be expected of it. These collective values ring hollow.

And now? Kiefer's work is still only on the threshold of itself. His work to date has known how to outwit these seductions from various sides by bringing them into the light. The work did so, focusing on the aching wound of the earth and of the country: wounded fathers, powerless or guilt ridden, obsessed, whose sons are trying, frantically, to raise them again. But the dream of his work has not yet been put to the test.

The dream image of Kiefer's work frequently takes a shape which is as elementary as unexpected: that of the Palette. Nearly round, more a contour than a tangible object, its essence almost conceptual and nevertheless fitted to the hand of the painter. A balanced shape despite, or perhaps because of, its eccentricity. The line of its contour, like the shape of an observing eye, has been watching over the landscapes of Germany since 1974.

The Self is at work; Kiefer might be astonished that I mention it here. Sometimes we think we have attained the goal. We would like to believe it but it is only potential. Kiefer with his Palette would like to believe in unity by transfiguration. An artist's dream. An alchemist's dream, when the alchemist is taking refuge in his oratory; he wants to forget time and the labors awaiting him in the laboratory.

But the raw materials remain ponderous: all this abused land, all this war without a face. Only against a background of disaster and destruction does Kiefer's Palette seek its most fitting countenance.

Unity and the quest for balance add up to destruction.

Thus painting and art itself are questioned. The verb *malen* (to paint) is written around one of these Palette canvases. But what is painting, after all? Is art, which aspires to the sublime, innocent? The art of the great Germanic spirits who have lost their power of seduction today, though Nazism made such use of it: did it not transpire to be destructive? And not only their art. Kiefer calls another of these canvases of ravaged earth, encircled by the same palette, *Nero malt* (Nero paints). How can we still believe in art, knowing what we do of the art of yesterday?

At the commencement of his work, the cataclysm seemed cosmic, anonymous, out of all proportion. It was approached slowly, gradually; it had to be examined more closely. Then names began to surge from the depths of time. Great names that seemed to imply some form of support. The rediscovery of a few values above all suspicion. And now a suspicion is born of history. Some kind of guilt has insinuated itself into the landscape, implicating us.

But the Palette does not want to have anything to do with guilt; it wants to play the angel. Kiefer paints it with wings, slightly ridiculous but almost touching. In fact, it is struggling. A black-winged Palette plummets to earth, the same ravaged German earth. And this canvas is called *Icarus-märkischer Sand* (Icarus – Sand of the Marches). It is another story of blood ties and heritage but the heroic ideal is falling from the heights, despite Siegfried. Jung also had to grapple with the promises of this lofty figure. And he had to decide to sacrifice it. He did this in a dream of necessary murder which left an aftertaste of shame and remorse.

The Palette is threatened. Thus *Palette am Seil* (Palette on a Rope), 1977. Kiefer chose this title because the Palette is hooked on a rope, tightrope walking and fragile, in an aerial excursion. The painter reveals it as close to falling, with tongues of flame lapping at the rope supporting it. We can feel the fall, expect it, hear it. This is nothing less than we expect of painting, even if it teaches us to abandon our illusions.

The Palette is suffering, as if it were a wounded bird. Kiefer introduces the use of lead. A lead Palette is pinned to a tree on the canvas; ribbons of real lead hang down from it. Thus, it is submitted to gravity. This is the *Baum mit Palette* (Tree with Palette), 1978, 2.75 x 1.91 meters, for me one of Kiefer's most attractive works. But this beauty does not take flight. It has returned to earth, as much sculpture as painting. It starts to invent its own history: without future, but in the here and now of its future.

The Palette is broken. Cast on the ground now, shattered by the implosion of its own tensions rather than from the onslaught of the tanks beleaguering it. Kiefer calls this 1980 canvas *Bilderstreit* (Conflict of Pictures) which reverts to the great debate, the iconoclasm controversy which raged in the Byzantium of the eighth and ninth centuries, opposing the zealots of imagery against those who wanted to rid humans and gods of their images.

But there is nothing esoteric or abstruse here. Kiefer, quite formally, is taking stock of a fragmentation. His very quest has subjected the Palette to such extremes that it imploded. He uses the term Bilderstreit, rather than "Zerstückelung" (cutting up), which Jung would have chosen. Kiefer emphasizes that, for the contemporary artist – who could not forget the debates of yesteryear projected into theology – that it is the very shape of the images, which appears all the more brutal because it is by no means clear what will follow. For the time being, Kiefer's art idles there, without a way out, from one canvas to the next. These canvases emphasize their meaning by the sensorial play of the most crude materials and elements – here sand and fire – which the artist strives to articulate, like a language.

Between avant-garde and regression, with all the resources and risks of contemporary art, this work seeks and, gropingly, finds its path. The Self is indeed at work. But not as it was expected. The path is also a transition from the Self, at first imaginary, to the work. Kiefer undertakes it. That is his work.

The work attacks him as a painter in his presentation of himself. A Palette beats its wings above a grave, on a small canvas this time. Here he is, and here we are, on a human scale. A tomb, a supine corpse of a man. They are on a human scale even in their bulk, quite different from that of the early canvases. For only humans know how to experience mourning, the mourning of others, of their ideas, and their ideals of themselves. Kiefer calls this canvas *Resumptio*. The word does not exist; it is *Assumptio* turned inside out, its contrary.

At this juncture we must look at the works in which Kiefer makes use of angels. He has broken away from Germanic mythology with Icarus and with Denis (Dionysos) by transforming this specialist of the heavenly hosts into Dionysos the Areopagite. The artist plays with everything, perhaps he does not know that he is working on inhumanity and destruction within humankind. But in darkness, to be able to see more clearly, he devotes himself to painting ladders. We think of Jacob's ladder. When Kiefer depicts cherubim and seraphim there are stones attached, suspended from lead wires, which he represents in *Die Ordnung der Engel* (The Ordering of the Angels), 1982-83. One can feel its whole weight. A smile is permitted.

With this sleight of hand and others, this work reveals its seriousness. For us, it is a question of discovering feeling by sensation, to understand how the painter/sculptor managed to do it, with his hands and his techniques. Kiefer is no longer depicting the ravaged earth as from a distance. He starts to work his canvases by fire, which explains their texture from then on, and the depth of his blacks. The initial chaos is succeeded by the *nigredo* of loss and mourning, from the avowed inanity of the collective values to the collapse of a heroic ideal ego which is obscured by a suspicion of some sin.

The vast images have fallen. *Gefallene Bilder* (Fallen Images) is a 1986 canvas, 1.02 by 1.41 meters. Working with lead on the basis of a photograph, the artist constructs a perspective in greys and blacks – empty frames, one inside the other. The work affects us with the air of a compulsive ritual.

Here art is generated from torment. With logical consistency the meaning of Kiefer's work becomes literal. The artist never ceases to explore his relation to recent history and that of the traditions important to him. He introduces and works real sand into his portrayals of German landscapes, sandy and war-scarred. He really burns them and reverts to this practice with such insistence that his work forms a palimpsest with every layer opening on the preceding one and at the same time covering it over, as memory does. But in realizing this he also discovers that this operation applies salt directly to the wound. It leaves indications that it could be right and even beautiful. He signed his name, as he did with *Ausbrennen des Landkreises Buchen* (Scorching of the Buchen District), from as early as 1974.

Let us consider more closely this work and its function within Kiefer's work. It is a book (60 x 42 x 8 cm.) – very black of course, and open; the pages are canvases with the fold at the center. This form is a response to the Palette. Like the Palette, it is a container. But the Palette was aerial or at least it wanted to be, whereas the book has been placed there. It does not promise transformation.

The projection into the imagination is always menacing. But Kiefer works these books physically, by fire or with sand on the canvas or by adopting and transforming old photographic plates and by his use of lead. The books stand on the side of the earth and the body. It is the "Resumptio" of the Palette, the artistic creation of a shadow self.

And then it rains. It rains as one cries. Always materially, of course: water falls as rain, in tears, on the canvas. Kiefer, who has composed his work in the heaviest pastose, remembers water colors. Just as, after the earth and the air, he resorted to fire, here he discovers the gifts of water. This elementary cosmology is the motive force of his creation.

His water colors have always followed the black manner of his

Palette landscapes. which reveal themselves as more human; faces and human bodies appeared, wounded but alive and as if refreshed by the water and the color. He painted the face and body of his wife Julia. Hers was the first, and long the only, name which was not mythological among his titles. And his own face and body, also wraith-like, but reworked from actual photographs.

Whereas the heroes of the great Germanic sagas were nominally or emblematically taking all the room on these large, somber and soon sacrificial canvases, female figures appeared as if between two waters, more sleeping than recumbent – Brunhilde in particular. A sort of light, coming from afar, fragile and hardly credible, uncertain whether this is more an initiation or a trace of life. Wagner's Brunhilde could be Shakespeare's Ophelia.

Then Kiefer discovers Paul Celan. At the beginning of the 1980s, he reads *Todesfuge* (The Fugue of Death), which this excellent poet wrote in 1945 in a concentration camp. He committed suicide in 1970 at 49. This poem has a poignant music which resurges from one verse to the next, haunted by the most brutal, murderous violence. The poem finds its breath, its soul, in this invocation, this incantation which punctuates it: "Dein goldenes Haar, Margarete – dein aschenes Haar, Sulamite" (Your golden hair, Margarete; your ashen hair, Sulamite). This blond Margarete is certainly German. In Goethe's *Faust* we saw her seduced but, sentenced for crime, she also experienced the straw of a prison. And the Sulamite, with ashen hair, emerges from the Book of the Jews. In Germany she experienced the most terrible of fates, a concentration camp.

Room is made for the feminine, an anima which is not just half-glimpsed but which has become embodied, really burned, so close to us. And it is not only a question of loss and castration, of mourning and sacrifice, but also of culpability. As is the case of every one of our psychoanalyses, life is generated, but at a high price. Paul Celan restored their presence, both this Margarete and this Sulamite, linking the one to the other inexorably. Shadow is not only the hidden face of innocence; the ideal can be the harbinger of death.

Kiefer takes Celan literally, word for word. The poem was already charged heavily by the weight of the words and of the feeling formed by the events. Under the title "Dein goldenes Haar, Margarete" the painter composes on his canvases, always against the background of the German soil – real sheaves of straw and corn, golden light on this earth, but physically fragile and threatened, as from the interior, by tongues of flame which are lapping at the sheaves and will destroy them.

After this, Kiefer created *Johannisnacht* (Mid-summer night). It is still night. But midsummer night, the summer solstice. Here again the implications of his celebration, both pagan and Christian, are familiar. It is the date that Hitler chose, in his mythological hubris, for the invasion of Russia. All this is the heritage of history. In fact, Kiefer produces a masterpiece here. His great sheaves of corn are alive, even in their fragility, the fragility of art. They have found a role which links together life and destruction, the rhythms of time. In the material dynamism of this creation, at this moment, the essentially cosmic is rejoined by the essentially human, via history.

The work continues.

Translated from French
by Jacqueline Gartmann

The most important catalogs about Kiefer's work are published by the Städttische Kunsthalle, Düsseldorf; Stedelijk Museum, Amsterdam; Philadelphia Museum of Art; Thames and Hudson, London.

Picasso's Belle Époque and Blue Period

Rafael López-Pedraza
Caracas, Venezuela
IAAP Individual Member

Modern psychology has tended not to appreciate the contributions that art can make to psychology. In psychology's assumption that it knows what is going on in the psyche of the artist, we see too much projection of the psychological theories and cultural background of the psychologist, too much interpretation. An attitude of learning from a person's expression through art is fundamental. For me, the arts cannot be excluded from psychotherapy, especially if we consider the "talking cure" in relation to the history of the culture which sustains the reading of the image.

Pablo Picasso's Blue Period (1901-1904) presents an unexpected picture of the Belle Époque, which is associated with optimism and gaiety, by showing its shadow side. The themes, the expressions of the figures, and the monochromatic blues all point to depression. Picasso himself said that the blues were his sadness and depression. He was a living example of creation and depression acting in unison; his consciousness was rooted in the depressive level of his psyche and nature.

My view of Picasso's pathology and depression – specifically his depression at the time of the Blue Period – needs an image to support it. This is a complicated image with four levels. The first is primordiality, which includes a primitive instinctiveness. To see Picasso in terms of such an image allows me to look at him as a man for whom life was basically full of fear but who, at the same time, lived it as a mythic-poetic event. This primordiality was the force behind the continual psychic transformation of Picasso's life (1881-1973) into a flow and finding of poetic images. My conception is of a consciousness close to the sources of life, death, and psychic creativity.

Just above this primordiality we can differentiate the second, archetypal, level of his psyche, and connect Picasso's depression with the imprint of two archetypes ruling his personality: Hermes and Dionysos. Picasso had exceptionally good health, which I attribute to his loyalty to those archetypes. He never had psychiatric treatment or a serious illness. One of my interests is to look at his psychopathology, but from the angle of a psychically healthy rather than a sick person. At the time of the Blue Period, a specific depression is present, quite different from the depression revealed during other periods of his life.

Elsewhere (1989), I have discussed the classical image of Hermes' appointment as guide of the soul into the realm of Hades, finding in it a suitable metaphor for approaching the depressive level of the psyche. The image of Hermes guiding the soul into the realm of the dead provides a commerce between psyche, the realm of the dead and depression; it provides an inner connection to death and an appreciation of how death feeds our psyches.

The third level is in the geographical and racial complexities of an old Andalusian soul. Such a soul is steeped in the traditional irrationality of embrujos (enchantment) and duendes (daimons), and in a strong and highly developed popular art in which tragedy, death and depression are always present. I refer to bullfighting and flamenco, two Dionysian art forms that were in Picasso's soul and that nourished his emotions and his imagination throughout his life. His old Andalusian soul has a great deal to do with his art's irrationality, which is of great value.

The Blue Period was the expression of complexes centered in the archetypal realm of Dionysos: suffering, pain, misery, illness, blindness, madness, shame, pity, fear and death, all dominated by the many blues. The images in these paintings are tragic images, expressing a tragic sense of life.

We are deeply indebted to Picasso for the expression of such tragic images in this century when the tragic sense of life has disappeared from art. We are living in a civilization based on systematic repression of the tragic emotions. As psychotherapists we are unable to live our conflicts with a sense of tragedy, let alone see those of our analysands that way. We are too accustomed to referring to our conflicts with the terminology of psychopathology. Likewise, our use of the word "empathy," which has to do with pity (a tragic emotion), seems more concerned with the technicalities of an approach than the tragic reflection of life's suffering. Our emotions are terribly repressed. Dionysos cannot function, and only the emotional Dionysos could induce the tragic reflection of empathy in psychotherapy. In focusing on Picasso's Blue Period my aim is to connect to its tragic aspect.

In my image of Picasso's psychology, there is a fourth level: his personal history. The limitation of life in Malaga forced his family to emigrate to La Coruna when he was ten years old, and five years later to Barcelona. Picasso's puberty and adolescence were marked by the psychology of exile and its uprootedness.

Once settled in Barcelona, Picasso adopted the Catalonian culture and language as his own. The atmosphere in Barcelona was full of tension and interest; the intellectual avant-garde and anarchism exacerbated the individualism of his Spanish background and stimulated his creativity. During that time Spain was marked by decline and shame after the Spanish-American War. Then there was the tension of Picasso's trips to Paris, with the avalanche of new images descending on a young man. And, something nearer and more overwhelming, which hit him with a terrible impact: the suicide in February 1901 of his friend Carlos Casagemas. In it tragedy knocked on Picasso's door and triggered the Blue Period.

I see the Blue Period as the catharsis of a massive depression compounded by historical complexities. Through depression Picasso plunged into the painting of human suffering at its extreme. Catharsis means, here, the purge of emotions Picasso was living at that time. In the process, which cured the excess of depression, Picasso learned about human suffering and started to sharpen his sensibilities to the tragedy of the human condition. Moreover, in his depiction of tragic suffering, he alone compensated for the bourgeois optimism of the Belle Époque. He showed the underside of the epoch; the Blue Period with its depression and tragic emotion heralded the finishing stroke to the Belle Époque.

In March 1904 Picasso painted La Celestina (Figure 1) – a masterpiece – in Barcelona, while he was submerged in the life and depression of the Blue Period. By then he probably had a certain intellectual knowledge of her, as well as the living experience of Celestinesque love: the procuration of sexual fantasies and encounters.

Five centuries ago, the first edition of Fernando Rojas' novel, today called *La Celestina*, was published. But La Celestina is classic. Euripides in the *Hippolytus* depicted her in the guise of Phaedra's nurse, who triggers the whole action of the tragedy. In her love for Hippolytus, Phaedra is caught in the psychological conflict between her aristocratic history, family pathology – her moralistic complexes – and sexual possession by Aphrodite. Her emotional conflict results in her suicide, pushed by the intervention of her nurse.

A psychological sketch of La Celestina will allow us to see the importance of this archetypal figure. If La Celestina stands for the procuration of sexual fantasies and the arranging of sexual encounters, then she is closer to us than we care to accept. She provides us with some of the most perennial and profuse of our imagery – sexual images. In a novel by Fernando de Rojas' La Celestina says, "I give form to your desires." Thus, her psychological function is essential to our psychic balance and health.

Picasso rediscovered and brought to the fore this archetypal figure. In our times La Celestina, unnoticed or disguised, has created the most extraordinary turmoil around sexuality, ranging from theorists trying with their psychological systems to catch their own and their patients' sexual fantasies to the most naive and superficial externalizations of sexuality. All this turmoil goes hand in hand with the technological age, where we can even detect La Celestina disguised as a computerized machine doing her work of procuring sexual encounters. Through his powerful portrayal of her, Picasso shows us that sexuality is not child's play, but it has to do with tragedy and death.

La Celestina as an inner figure has been prevalent in modern

Figure 1

psychotherapy, but a psychotherapy that has been blind to her archetypal validity. The blindness is complicated by the confusion of sexual theories. Picasso portrays La Celestina with a cloudy left eye. Her personality, though austere and enigmatic, transmits a self-awareness of her art – the art of the procuress. What I find so astounding, even more than this masterpiece painted in 1904, is what happened on a day at the Prado Museum in March 1898, six years earlier, when Picasso was only 17 years old. Out of 80 "Caprichos" (caprices) of Goya, Picasso's psyche chose to copy La Celestina.

What impelled Picasso to choose her? The choice was an

unprecedented *anagnoresis*: the soul's immediate recognition of what archetypally pertains to it. Here we are in the mysterious realm of psychic and archetypal analogies. We have some clues: Picasso's copy of Goya's Celestina (Figure 2) of 1898 and the enigmatic mystery of the tragic Celestina of the Blue Period. We have also a rough idea of what La Celestina stands for archetypally in Western culture. Although we know of her attraction for Picasso, any speculation about what happened on that day in

Figure 2

March 1898 would seem unnecessary and ridiculous, because Picasso's copying Goya's Celestina – a psychic, archetypal drama enacted at the Prado Museum – as well as painting the impressive portrait of La Celestina in 1904 tells us more than any intellectual speculation.

In addition to making an initial psychological approach to La Celestina, my intention here is to provide a classical background to the tragic emotions felt by Picasso over the suicide of his friend and to its influence on the Blue Period. Actually, after painting La Celestina in 1904, he began to move slowly out of his depression and the Blue Period. In Rojas' book La Celestina introduces herself as a healer and all the other characters recognize her as such.

Of all his friends at that time Casagemas had a special attraction for Picasso, who responded intuitively to the strange morbidness emanating from Casagemas; it was caught in Picasso's portrait (Figure 3) of him. I consider that, archetypally, Casagemas was ruled by virginity (Figure 4: Casagemas nude).

Figure 3

Picasso has left profuse and detailed drawings of the sexual life he and his friends engaged in, in the brothels of Barcelona. In 19th century art two frequent motifs were the Femme Fatale and the Brothel. One can imagine that going to the brothel was half a social meeting at a men's club and half a visit to a temple in which to enact the repressed carnal desire. The brothel was the

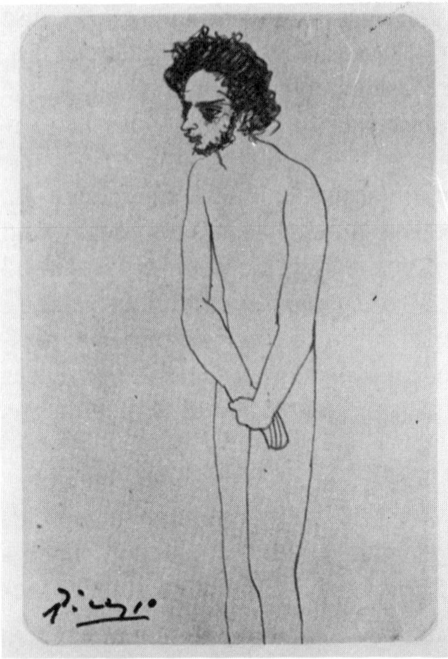

Figure 4

place of sexual initiation at that time. It is possible to conceive of the brothel as an inner theater of Picasso.

In this life of the brothels, Casagemas was notorious. He was always with a group of friends – painters, poets and writers – but in his relations with the prostitutes he suffered from impotence.

In February 1901 Picasso was in Madrid. Meanwhile, in the Cafe de Clichy in Paris, Casagemas shot himself with great histrionics, killing himself and nearly killing Germaine, the woman he was in love with. According to Germaine, their sex life was very poor. As a virginal personality, he was driven to suicide by the Celestinesque conception that all his problems could be resolved by sex.

Sexuality is an instinct, with two archetypal forms of life, two divinities of extraordinary force, conflicting upon it: Aphrodite, goddess of carnality, and Artemis, goddess of virginity. Between these two poles stretches the huge spectrum of each one's uniqueness, suffering the tension, conflict and pathology these poles engender. Sexuality, seen from within the historical Judeo-Christian tradition, is dominated by virginity. In the case of Casagemas, however, his virginity was seen from the view of sexuality, resulting in tragedy.

Undoubtedly, Picasso carried the conflict that was so ingrained in tradition, culture and history. Yet his own sexual nature needed initiation. It is impossible not to connect the many appearances of the theme of La Celestina and the brothel to his initiation into sexuality, to his recollections of the epoch, and even to Casagemas' suicide. But this event alone does not tell the whole story, for Picasso's interest in La Celestina predated the suicide. This tragedy radiated ever-widening repercussions throughout Picasso's life; its memory-images stimulated his psyche into endlessly varied creations of art.

When he was in his nineties, Picasso produced the last 156 of his etchings. I am including four of these. The first time I saw the first of these (Figure 5), what came to my mind was a young puritanical evolutionist Victorian scientist. In spite of the fantasy of resolving scientifically all the problems he might have to face, he was completely impotent when faced with this group of strange women. His hands are behind his back – a sign of impotence. The image conveys the archetypal distinction in an extreme polarization of virginal sexuality. In these etchings Picasso was inspired by his memory of the myth concerning Edgar Degas: that Degas

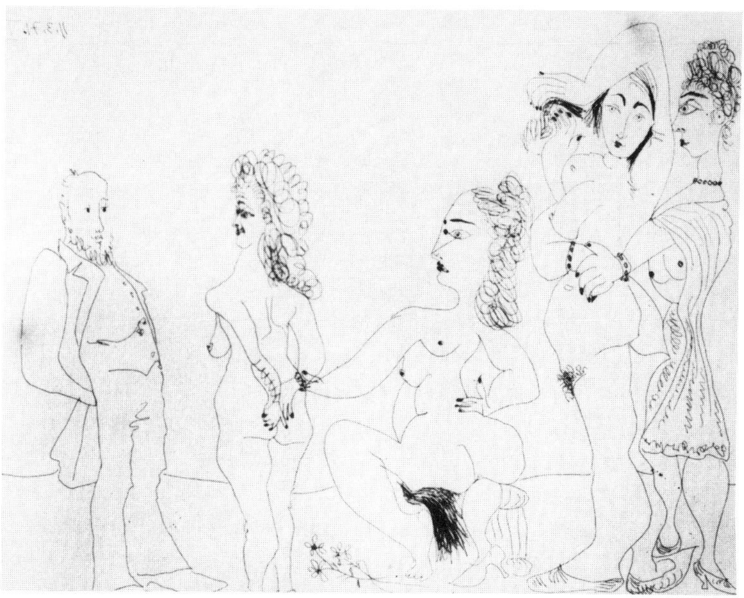

Figure 5

had no sexual contact in his entire life. In spite of his chastity, he painted beautiful nudes and also brothels, leaving us a legacy of this side of life during the Belle Époque.

The second of the etchings (Figure 6) is an image that stresses the importance of the brothel in the psychology of the Belle Époque; we see the Madame at the center of the scene. Symbolism of interest is the butterfly Picasso has placed on her head.

In the third etching (Figure 7), one of an imaginative brothel,

Figure 6

Picasso introduces La Celestina. Based on pictorial evidence we can say that the image of La Celestina had accompanied Picasso for at least 74 years, making her entrances and exits in his inner theater. Only God knows how many unrecorded times she must have appeared on that stage in order for Picasso to produce his vast iconography of her. For Jungian psychologists there is a lesson about the relationship of a man's soul to the images most congenial to it. We cannot associate this Celestina with the picaresque touch given to her by Euripides in the *Hippolytus*, or

Figure 7

with the vitality of Rojas' conception. This Celestina is bitter, as if she were expressing an aspect of Picasso's soul-memory which had left in him a deep remorse, a bitter wound.

With the same freedom of imagination that makes for art, the etching of Edgar Degas in the brothel comprises recollections of Picasso's history. This work gives me the basis to imagine that, in his extreme old age, the suicide of his friend Casagemas was still moving his creative psyche. I find it impossible to believe that there was not the memory of Casagemas somewhere in the background of these etchings: Casagemas, who, unlike Degas, did not stay loyal to the virginal archetype; he was trapped and overwhelmed by the archetypal conflict between the virginal Artemis and the carnal Aphrodite.

I close this paper on Picasso with an aquatint (Figure 8) depicting, presumably, one of the girls in the brothel in the embrace of a Dionysian-horned Eros. What one sees here is a bit different from what one has been watching previously. Picasso is introducing a mythological little god – the most joyful and, at the

Figure 8

same time, dangerous of all the gods. However, he is also telling us that the many, many images he transformed into great art throughout his long life are an Eros and Psyche business. Furthermore, he is pointing out the main affinity between art and psychotherapy. No matter what our theories or speculations, religion or race, at the core of the many disguises covered by human madness, Eros and Psyche are there. And this is what the observer Degas, in this etching of Picasso, is observing.

REFERENCE

López-Pedraza, R. (1989). *Hermes and His Children* (New expanded version). Zurich: Daimon.

"The Sculptor's Studio": Picasso's Images of Transference and Transformation

James Wyly
Chicago, Illinois, USA
Chicago Society of Jungian Analysts

A truism among Jungians is that great works of art are images of psychological process, which has archetypal roots. Thus, art can evoke parallel psychological awarenesses and religious resonances in people far separated in space and time. Among great works of art, however, there are certain exalted examples that do even more than this. When we bring analytic abilities to them we discover that the works contain consistent languages – far more complex than the artist can have intended – which communicate statements of utmost importance about the human condition. We recognize such works as special, even undecoded.

As examples of this kind of work I need only cite Chartres Cathedral, Bach's *B-Minor Mass*, The *Four Quartets* of T.S. Eliot, Goethe's *Faust*, and the Taj Mahal. They overpower us initially on a kind of sensing-intuitive plane. Then, when we bring to them the analysis of thinking and the response of feeling, we discover in them an inner consistency of intent which seems inexhaustible in its richness of meaning.

A cycle of etchings within Picasso's *Vollard Suite*, known as "The Sculptor's Studio" (1985) seems to be such a work. (Permission could not be obtained to reproduce the etchings here.) It can be "read" in the language that Jung provided for discussing the transference. I doubt that Picasso knew or cared about the psychology of the transference. But we do know that he cared deeply about the creative process and devoted much of his work to exploring its manifestations.

When we speak of the transference, as Jung (CW16) did, we imply that an analysand's encounter with the psyche, projected on the analyst, can lead to a kind of creative union with previously alien psychic material. This union gives birth to a new psychological attitude that transcends the original opposition between ego and unconscious. In this way, the creative process produces a new psychological attitude. If one gives it form, one has completed a creative act, produced a work of art. Thus, transferential and creative processes are basically identical.

Picasso's lifelong preoccupation with the creative process led him to the awareness that art work involves the projection and objectification of inner material. He frequently portrayed the creative encounter in works that depict the artist, the model, and the work. To examine a series of Picassos devoted to this subject is to see how Picasso met his own psyche, and how this encounter affected him. Moreover, since he often used the impersonal language of classical representational art, his works can have much more general meaning as visual descriptions of some of the transformations that take place in any creative encounter. This includes the transference.

"The Sculptor's Studio" provides an especially cohesive and complete statement of this material. It is a set of 46 of the 100 etchings known as the *Vollard Suite*. Picasso assembled the 100 for his dealer, Ambroise Vollard, between 1930 and 1937. Picasso obviously conceived "The Sculptor's Studio" as a set, for his dates on the plates show them to have been made in two intense bursts of work in 1933 and 1934. During this time he sometimes finished as many as four plates in a day.

All 46 plates show relationships among the bearded sculptor, the young female model, and the sculpture. Hardly ever does the sculpture resemble the model. Instead, she serves as a kind of screen upon which the sculptor appears to project images from within. He captures them in clay or stone, as art. In this process sculptor, model, and sculpture are all transformed.

I see no basic difference between this situation and the analytic transference, where we have the analysand-as-sculptor, projecting inner experiences upon the analyst-as-model. The analysis moves when the analysand recognizes the projections as his or her own, as new perceptions independent of the analyst in whom they were first perceived. Then, as psychic works of art, these newly owned parts of the personality can go on to enrich the life of the analysand, who strives toward the awareness of "When I look at you I don't see you, I see this, which is part of me, which I didn't know about before."

But when we peruse the plates, we find more. In their sequence lies a story that Picasso could hardly have intended consciously. Images familiar to us from Jung's writings, however, depict phenomena such as regression, splitting off, transformation, separation, and synthesis. Their sequence tells a story of the relativization of ego, accomplished through repeated projections. The story is one of analysis – of transference – which can be traced by observing, without interpretation, what is happening in the successive etchings. Let us turn to the plates and watch the story unfold. (Plates are given here the usual numbers by which they are known in the *Vollard Suite* as a whole, where "The Sculptor's Studio" begins with Plate 37).

Plate 37. Here we meet the basic characters of the series. We must take note of a few of Picasso's conventions if we are to follow the players through their metamorphoses. The sculptor is almost always male. He generally has a beard. He gives his attention not to his model – who is always female – but to his work, which is recognizable as sculpture because it stands on a plinth. What he seems to require of his model is close physical contact; they are never far apart, and often touch. Thus, close contact with the contrasexual permits one to see inner images and to transform them into visible external things – specific works of art.

The first work of art resembles the model not at all, for it is male. It looks like a slightly older, more muscular version of the youngish sculptor himself. It holds a stick, as though ready to defend itself, if the sculptor's contemplative gaze should threaten its integrity. It is easy enough to relate this scene to one that occurs early in many analyses: the analysand encounters a threatening shadow figure, a carrier of unassimilated authority.

Plate 38 implies integration, for the sculptor has gained a few years; his face is that of the sculpture of Plate 37. He is working intensely on an abstract head which we know to be female – it is a form Picasso used often in the 1930s – although it does not resemble the model at all. Evidently whatever he gained from the phallic shadow of Plate 37 has enabled him to see a new, puzzling image, which is to occupy his attention for this and the following 11 plates. He is freed of his narcissistic need to contemplate an image that resembles himself and so is able to begin working on a mysterious opposite. We could call this a first appearance of anima-imagery, clearly independent of the model.

Plate 39. The sculpture seems to take on an autonomous power, for the vine has grown around its hair and rays emanate from it.

Plate 40 results. The head gains a body. Sculptor and model pause to look at this rough-looking but clearly feminine apparition. The sculptor must be mystified, for he calls in his friends.

Plate 41. They look as puzzled as he. This division of the sculptor into three – a beardless youth, a young man, and one perhaps in his late thirties – suggests a dissociative process in response to the incomprehensible form that the contrasexual tends to take in the first half of life. Meanwhile the sculpture has become more fluid and mobile, but less understandable, while the model withdraws behind a curtain – a parallel to the analyst's withdrawing when the mysterious manifests itself, leaving the psychic material to reveal itself in its own time.

Plate 42. Behind the curtain the model succumbs to temptations familiar to analysts confronted with the unknown. She requires the armor of additional persona, for she has gotten dressed. Also, a new female figure rises from the body of the model and draws the curtain aside, permitting light to illuminate the sculpture. It has regressed; it is again a head on a column. This image can be understood as the model's tendency to project her own material onto the sculpture. The analytic parallel is the tendency of the analyst to project something from her or his psyche onto the imagery produced by the analysand. Such a projection is prone to happen when the analyst does not understand the material and the analysand is dissociating or regressing.

Plate 43. We find confirmation of this projection in the next plate, for here the model has painted a picture – of a long-haired, prepubertal boy. She has infantilized the sculptor, equating the primitive anima-representation with an early stage of masculine development.

Plate 44. We see what this countertransference does. It freezes the sculpture; we see it as a primitive feminine head on a column here and through Plate 49. It tends to dissociate the sculptor/analysand from *phallos*, for he is confronting a little shrimp in a glass.

Plate 45. He is younger than he was when he could see the whole figure (Plates 40 & 41), while his perplexity and the model's appear to deepen.

Plate 46. As he regresses further he loses sight of the model altogether, and takes a knife to the sculpted head. The way he holds it is disquieting, more like opening the jugular vein than smoothing a carving. Here he can be hardly more than 15 years old. At this age, the struggle for independence from mother-figures will make threatening any contact with the contrasexual and its imagery. The complete denial of the presence of the model confirms this. In analysis, it suggests something important about regression: the encouragement of regressive transference can lead to the analysand's perception of the analyst as threatening enough to cause a rupture in the relationship. This perception seems of special importance in work with borderline disorders.

Plate 47. An enantiodromia occurs. The lush curves and elaborate drawing of the previous plates are replaced by spare, awkward lines. The sculptor is older than ever before and the model is surrealistic and primitive, while the sculpture has lost all signs of life, as though the entire process is reduced to lifeless formulae. Yet something is being prepared; to explain it requires the next three plates.

Plates 48, 49, 50. A climax is reached; the sculpted head has been transformed into a beautiful female figure. Its form in Plates 48 and 49 suggests violent movement – perhaps vibration – as rays of light stream from it, before the sculptor's astonished gaze.

This is an intrapsychic transformation, for the model is not even present until it is complete. When we see her again, her mask has been lifted. For the first time she looks at the sculptor rather than at his work. The sculptor has resumed his original age, but he looks healthier. His hair and beard have lost the unkempt appearance of the early plates and will remain full and curly through the rest of the series. Finally, we notice in Plate 48 a huge sculpture of the sculptor's head; it will play an important part in the coming developments.

An anima-representation has been realized. With Plate 50, the sculptor has achieved a clear vision of a psychic constellation, an inner opposite of what he had consciously believed himself to be. This vision has arisen through projecting the developing psychic material onto the model, and then noticing the projected material's effects on both of them. Now the projection is lifted, for the mask is raised. The model's face turns out to have been an illusion. And now she can see the sculptor more clearly, for her view is not limited by the structure of the mask.

In addition, the sculpted male head of Plate 48 can mean only that the sculptor has gained an awareness of himself. Instead of being identified with his persona, he has some knowledge of how it looks in the world. He can perceive himself as independent of it. The positive side of dissociation is disidentification with persona. The differentiation of the sculpted head and the mask mark a major transformation.

Now we can return to Plate 47 with even greater awareness of the importance its technical style has in conveying its meaning. The lines are rough, approximate and limp; the only visible energy lies in the directness of the sculptor's gaze and the musculature of his right arm. In contrast to the other plates, its effect is desolate and empty. There is a near-total withdrawal of libido from the images here, as though there were a realm beyond them, to which the regression has led. When libido withdraws to this secret depth of the psyche, a kind of depression is apparent. But changes are prepared, and the return of libido accomplishes a seeming miracle of transformation.

Plate 51. The miracle is confirmed. The anima figure remains and is capable of something like autonomous action; she seems to be drying herself in preparation for taking part in her new environment, the world of the sculptor's awareness.

Plate 52. Yet the first thing she does is to disappear. This is the only plate in the series lacking a female figure. It recalls Plate 42, where a female divinity reveals something about the meaning of the anima-representation to the model. In Plate 52 a male divinity involves himself with the sculptor and a totally new sculpted figure, that of a beautiful young man. We shall meet the young man again in Plate 70.

The divinity of Plate 52 recalls Dionysos, in the characteristic long hair braided with vines. (Picasso was well-read in classical mythology). His appearance has been anticipated by the grape or ivy leaves frequently seen in the sculptor's hair in earlier plates. When we recall that Dionysos was regarded as effeminate-appearing, and that he and his retinue were closely associated with the between-the-sexes realm of transvestitism, homosexuality, and ecstatic casting aside of convention, the message of this plate becomes clearer. The manifestation of anima in the sculptor's psyche is not to stop with the appearance of a demure young woman emerging from her bath. Rather, the sculptor must confront a new set of issues about his identity and the way the feminine integrates herself into his masculine way of being. Development is required of a quality of masculinity that we see here for the first time, of a still rather unstable-looking beardless youth. (Plate 70 permits us to identify him as the solar hero; the short sword he holds suggests Theseus' battles with the Minotaur. Yet he has a cup in his left hand: the connection to the feminine.)

Plate 53. Neither the sculptor nor the model looks happy as each contemplates the work – now a female torso – and the journey into the unknown that integration of the contrasexual poses for any sculptor or analysand.

Plate 54 begins the journey as sculptor and model confront some of Dionysos' retinue. It is as though the encounter with the god of Plate 52 has opened a new realm for the sculptures; they begin to carry masculine imagery, here in the form of acrobats.

Plates 55 through 58 continue this imagery: an equestrian, revelers with a bull, animal violence, and a merger of animal and human in a centaur who kisses a woman.

Plate 59. This outburst of the instinctual and magical masculine appears to be too much for the sculptor; we find him asking his model to pose for the first time in the series, while he shapes a realistic torso that reproduces her gesture. Clearly, he is trying to regain ego control over his creativity.

Plate 60. It doesn't work. The resultant sculpture is a puzzling abstraction; the reappearance of vines around it and the sculptor's hair tells us that the forces of nature are still working uncontrollable transformations. The sculptor does not look overjoyed to realize this.

Plate 61. The sculptor's anxiety is well-founded, for the transformative process he has unleashed takes an unforeseen turn. We see only the male head, being contemplated by a female. We are driven to see this as an egoless state, for the plate is inhabited by only a rigid persona-representation and an anima figure.

Plates 62, 63, and 64. The egoless state was momentary, for here the original triad is restored and the Dionysian revel continues. But the sculptor has had an experience which the next plates tell us he can neither integrate nor forget.

Plate 65 shows him contemplating the male head again. We see that this persona, not ego, must be the enduring quality of his original identity. His aspect has changed as a result of the egoless experience; in the last four plates he has appeared as older, more mature, and more kingly. He seems to have gained important knowledge about his own nature, and it gives him stature in the world.

Plate 66 finds him, thus, contemplating the revel from a remarkably merged identity that combines all three original figures: the anima-sculpture's head, the model's body, and the sculptor's gesture of gentle physical touch.

Plate 67. Again we are taken to a state in which the male ego is absent. This apparently is a deeper state, however, for we see only three female figures, seated in timeless meditation. The distinction between model and sculpture is no longer discernible.

Plate 68 and 69 continue this merged feminine image in a

single female figure, first with the sculptor and then with only a mirror-image, propped on the male persona-representation.

Plate 70. In this context of episodes of total loss of ego-identity and total merger of model and sculpture the sculptor goes to work on the figure of the solar hero. He carries a blade, to separate – presumably a new attempt to regain ego control over this process of merger and loss of familiar identities.

Plate 71. The blade works, for the feminine is again divided, but in a peculiar and not very satisfactory way. She is split crosswise; her heavily clothed head and shoulders confront her naked torso and legs, in a reversal of conventional modesty. The sculptor is again reduced to the carved head.

Plate 72. Another attempt divides her into a rather mature woman and a hermaphrodite. Attempts to restore the old identities are doomed to failure and they initiate ever farther-reaching transformations, the general thrust of which is to develop the chthonic and feminine aspects of the material at the expense of ego and persona.

Plates 73 through 77. The feminine's resources range from the sublime (Picasso's drawing conveys the texture of flesh in an uncanny way) to the ridiculously surrealistic and beyond, even to an apparent ability to transcend time by dressing the cast as 17th-century Europeans.

Plates 78, 79, and 80. Three more pairs of exotically beautiful women reinforce the statement of the creativity that can be tapped when ego-structures and limits are let go; in none of them does any representation of the sculptor appear. Then, as though to remind us how this works, we have the two final plates.

Plate 81. The sculptor, now definitely past middle age, gazes out at us with a knowing look while his creations continue their endless dance.

Plate 82, the last in the series, shows us the final state. Now there are five female figures, some clearly seen, some partially visible, and one almost totally in shadow. All are of great complexity and originality. But all that remains of the sculptor is his bust, now ensconsed on a handsomely carved plinth.

This bust, which we first saw in Plate 48, is of great significance. It is placed high in the center, where it stares out at us commandingly. Of all the figures and sculptures it is the most constant, for it has always been rendered as the head of a strong, middle-aged, kingly man with full, curly beard and hair. In contrast, the sculptor's representations evolve in relation to the bust: he begins younger and more disheveled than it is, taking on its facial characteristics only in Plate 50, when the model is unmasked and the lush, full-figured sculpture appears for the first time. He then goes on to age beyond it in stages that alternate with his total disappearance. What are we to make of this?

It can hardly be coincidental that Picasso was 51 years old when he made "The Sculptor's Studio" – approximately the age of the sculpted head. The relationship between the sculptor and the head contains the key to the psychological evolution Picasso is representing, seen from ego's point of view. Up to Plate 50 we see a kind of growing into a present, physical reality equivalent to Picasso's. Then total identification with it evokes growth beyond it. Thus, objective reality, once accepted, becomes merely a constant reference point, a kind of fixed persona-image. Within it, awareness learns to maintain a relationship to the increasingly compelling and bizarre phenomena the psyche produces without danger of being permanently overwhelmed by them. One recalls Jung's concern, voiced the year before Picasso made the "Sculptor's Studio," that Picasso was vulnerable to a psychosis (CW15).

The psychic evolution represented in "The Sculptor's Studio" reveals the process by which such a break was avoided. Instead of fortifying itself against an onslaught from the unconscious and thus making itself rigid and brittle, we see ego accepting the phenomena from an increasingly relativized position. Thus it arrives at a new and unexpected stance in regard to its environment.

Picasso laid the series aside for about eight months between Plates 76 and 77. The relationship between the head and the feminine is the same in Plate 76 as in Plate 82. The last six plates are a kind of coda, to show the infinitely varied potential for creative development that is inherent in the sculpture of Plate 76.

We can step back from contemplation of the individual plates and see a series of transformations in the images which make some very provocative points about the creative process – that is, transference. For Picasso, the encounter between ego and anima results in a steady lessening of the importance of ego, until it disappears altogether. Ego is replaced by a fixed, sculpted persona-image, which is clearly a reference-point. But it also is clearly incapable of taking any action except, possibly, as an observer of the intense drama that surrounds it.

Meanwhile anima – which began as a sculpture – assumes a varied, active role, to become indistinguishable from the model. Thus, the former division between subjective and objective worlds breaks down. Each becomes as important as the other, and their mutual interaction takes place without barriers of any kind. The question of what is "real" and what is "imaginal" becomes irrelevant.

Descriptions of such states are familiar to us in the literature of various religious traditions. Also, Jung's attitude toward active imagination, dreaming, and the psychological processes he observed in himself and his analysands leads in this direction. Whether a given analysis or a given individual's process arrives at the sculptor's final state, and whether it should, remain as open questions. But it seems clear that if we begin with the assumption that the transference and the creative process have something in common, "The Sculptor's Studio" makes a bolder, farther-reaching statement about their potential than has yet appeared in our psychological literature. When seen from a psychological point of view, "The Sculptor's Studio" becomes a *Rosarium Philosophorum* of the 20th century.

REFERENCE

Picasso, (1985). *Picasso's Vollard Suite.* (N. Guterman, Trans.). Introduction by Hans Bollinger. New York: Thames and Hudson.

Analysis and Culture
(Workshop)

The Magician and the Analyst: The Archetype of the Magus in Ritual and Analytic Process

Robert L. Moore
Chicago, Illinois, USA
Chicago Society of Jungian Analysts

The primordial image of the magus has had its careful scholars; among them is E. M. Butler (1948), a professor of German language and literature at Cambridge University, whose book is one of the most important studies currently available on the topic. From a historical and phenomenological perspective he outlined the essential features of the magus as characterized in myth and legend. He found the origins of the magi in ancient ritual practice.

Butler listed 10 characteristics of the magus imago found in the most highly developed forms of the legend: (1) supernatural or mysterious origin of the hero; (2) portents at birth, vouching for the supernatural nature of the hero; (3) perils menacing his infancy, from evil-wishers or the powers of evil; (4) some kind of initiation; (5) distant wandering; (6) a magical contest; (7) a trial or persecution; (8) a last scene frequently set in the present; (9) a violent or mysterious death; (10) a resurrection and/or ascension.

Butler's greatest contribution to our understanding of the archetype of the magus lies in his recognition of two points: (1) that the image of the magus is the primary imago behind the varieties of cultural expressions of the ritual healer and the archetypal image behind such figures as the shaman, wizard, and medicine man; and (2) that the magus is always associated with initiatory process and the extraordinary space associated with healing rituals. While he did not emphasize or elaborate this second point, he understood the internal relatedness between magus, initiation, and transformative space. The most serious limitation of Butler's presentation is his tendency to conflate the images of hero, king, and magus.

Butler has not been the only theorist to recognize the relationship of the king imago to healing process. More recently Perry (1966) has noted the importance of the archetype of the sacral king in the context of healing and presented the mythological expressions of the archetype of the king. Perry (1976) also detailed the role of the archetype in both the phenomenology and healing of psychotic process.

Although the archetype of the king is related to those of initiation and the magus, they are by no means the same archetypal structure and serve very different dynamic functions in the psyche. My ongoing research into the dynamic interrelations among the four archetypes of king, warrior, magus, and lover as they manifest themselves in psychological functioning – especially in male psychology – suggests that the king archetype has important functions in the personality's capacity for centeredness, order, and creativity.

While the king archetype is of central importance in the symbology of transformation, it is basically an archetype of extraversion; it relates primarily to the founding of a centered and non-chaotic world related more to Turner's (1969) concept of structure and ceremony than to my concerns of liminality and ritual. When this imagery occurs during "liminal states" – transformative experiences – it is to offer the transforming ego a paradigm for centeredness, order, and a blessing authority which is empowering of the initiand's creativity.

The king archetype is not an image of the steward of the transformative process itself. That role is served by the archetype of the magus. Based on my research into this archetype I offer ten conclusions as to its role in psychological functioning and psychosocial process:

1. The archetype of the magus is an image of a master of esoteric knowledge whose task is to act, through ritual magic, upon the cosmos; to control his fate and help others control theirs.

2. The archetype of the magus is the fundamental psychological structure that provides the matrix of such images as the wise

old man, the guru, the shaman, the prophet and the priest. Jung (CW9-I) discussed this archetype chiefly under the designation "wise old man." (In its feminine expressions it manifests, for example, as the wise old woman, the witch, the sorceress, the priestess and the prophetess.)

3. In every case the magus is an image of the potentiation for psychological awareness and inner work. Again Jung (CW9-I) clearly attributed this quality to the archetype.

There is a clear and archetypal tie here between introversion and the space needed for transformation and initiation. Introverts probably are more influenced by the constellation of this archetype than extraverts. The cultivation of an introverted life is the cultivation of an "inner garden," one of the most important images of sacred space (see Lau, 1981). Jesus' times of introversion were in a desert and in a garden on a mountain.

When the magus archetype is constellated, the psyche is calling for the location of and entry into Turner's (1969) "space-time pod," where awareness can be increased through exposure to "esoteric" knowledge heretofore ego-alien. This inner work is the basic ingredient of initiatory process.

4. The esoteric knowledge of which the magus is master has two fundamental and inseparable components: a knowledge of the structures and dynamics of power, creativity, and optimal order; and the ritual means to contact, channel, and disconnect from these powers at will and without incurring unintended harm to oneself or others.

5. The issue of proper ritual containment and insulation, then, is of central importance to the functioning of the magus. Metaphoric parallels in contemporary technological imagery are the master electrician and the atomic technician. Both must have extensive technical knowledge of the properties and flow patterns of "hidden" forces. These forces are dangerous to the uninitiated but they can be useful if channeled properly in carefully contained and insulated vessels. The mystification of the magus serves, like professional or guild credentials, to enhance his power and prerogatives. To the insider (Adept), however, the forces, dynamics, and flow patterns have less of a "mystical" or

theological reference – removed from everyday life – and are related more to the practical concerns of human life.

Hierophany for the magus tends to be manifest more as *kratophany* – the manifestation of the force or power. In our contemporary setting, a magus would be concerned, in a metaphorical sense, with circuitry, circuit-breakers, meltdowns, contamination, even unwanted flooding. In one analysand's dream, for example, the archetype was manifested as *a hydroelectric plant supervisor in hard hat and coveralls who turned the proper valves to drain excess floodwaters that were threatening a dam.* One could scarcely find a better metaphor for the practical functioning of the magus.

6. Implicit in the archetype, then, is the psychological function of creating a space appropriate for the dangerous transformation of structures and energies through controlled contact with extraordinary forces or powers. This function is expressed in occultism in the ritual creation of the magic circle or pentagram: careful utilization of the space, then dissolution of the space when the contact with the extramundane power or force is no longer desired.

We can hardly overemphasize the care with which practicing ritual magicians approach the consecration of sacred space, the selection of entities to call upon for manifestation (invocation), and the benediction or banishment of these entities prior to the ritual termination or dissolution of the space. Failures in stewardship of the space have negative consequences. At the very least, the transformative power of the process is truncated. Worse, partial transformations can occur that are monstrous in their effects and dangerous to the person of the practitioner. Occult Adepts, therefore, always seek to be masters of "psychic self-defense" in the knowledge that not to do so would endanger themselves as well as those who have come for assistance.

7. In Turner's (1969) language, at the archetypal level is a primordial representation of the necessary ingredients for liminal states: constellation of the archetype of initiation and knowledgeable stewardship and utilization of the transformative space by a magus.

8. Constellation of the archetype of initiation always issues in the quest for both a magus and a transformative "space/time pod," though the individual is often not aware of what is sought.

9. If a magus is located who has a "good enough" knowledge of the transformative process and a moral capacity for stewardship, a truly liminal space may be constituted, utilized appropriately, and exited.

10. If such a magus is unavailable, or lacks either adequate technical knowledge or capacity for stewardship, the Quester is likely to be limited to liminoid space – pseudo-transformative experience.

Whenever the archetype of initiation is constellated, the heterogeneity of space is experienced as a phenomenological reality. Whenever either liminal or liminoid space is experienced, then, the archetype of initiation has been constellated and potentially renewing archetypal energies are close at hand. Thus, whether a space is liminal or liminoid turns – not on the archetype of initiation – but on the constellation and appropriate utilization of the archetype of the magus.

A ritual elder may be present in liminoid space. For example, a contemporary clergyperson presiding at a typical worship service stewards a space which is for many a liminoid experience. Such an experience of the liminoid is often what some Jungians call "persona-restoring" experiences. Deep structural transformations are usually neither intended nor manifest in these forms of extraordinary space.

Alternatively, a magus may be present and intend the constitution of a truly liminal transformative space but be unable to bring such space into being. The inability may be that of the would-be initiand to submit, to trust the leadership of the ritual elder – and consequently to cross the threshold into transformative space – or there may be a lack of sufficient competence in the tasks of ritual leadership on the part of the would-be magus.

This possible lack raises the question of the presence or absence of "ritual genius" in the person of the magus or analyst. This concept is one used by scholars to refer to the power of a leader to manifest numinosity through the "dry bones" of ritual forms and formulas. Not exactly the same as charisma, ritual genius is tied more closely to technical virtuosity than to personal qualities.

Turner's interest in theater is relevant here; some of the best examples of ritual genius in contemporary culture can be seen when talented actors and directors make dramatic performances "come to life" on stage. The relevance of such theater to analytic practice merits more attention. Here I emphasize that a failure in the attempt to constitute transformative space may reflect a lack not in the postulant, but in the ritual skills of the magus/analyst.

A third possibility is that the magus or analyst may assist an individual over the first threshold into the phase of dissolution of old structures and still be unable or unwilling to assist the person in the pilgrimage through liminality to the second threshold and back into autonomy and structure. Such a situation occurs in the classic story of the "sorcerer's apprentice," who could begin magical process but did not have the skills to control or to stop it. A more extreme case is that of the "black magician," who uses knowledge of ritual and personality not to heal, but to manipulate others according to his own designs.

Once across the first threshold of submission to the magus and the magic circle of power, the postulant is dependent upon the magus' integrity and capacity for stewardship. In analysis this manifests when the power shadow in the countertransference overrides any therapeutic and/or other transpersonal aims; then the analysand is in a vulnerable position for exploitation by the analyst. In folklore this psychosocial reality in ritual process is often imaged as enchantment by a wicked sorcerer or sorceress; the result is often a zombie-like loss of soul on the part of the individual who has been "bewitched." As in the other examples noted above, the space thus constituted is not normative liminality. Again, it is at best liminoid, that is, pseudo-liminality. While it may manifest the actions and symbolic structures characteristic of liminality, countertransference difficulties on the part of the analyst render the space impotent for transformative purposes.

In summary, liminality is present when the archetype of initiation is constellated and the analyst is sufficiently competent and motivated to guide the individual in the pilgrimage across the first threshold into sacred space, to the empowering and renewing center, through related regenerative enactments, and across the second threshold back into autonomy and structure. This is the archetypal norm. In actual practice, any given ritual process is more or less healing or transformative according to the personal characteristics, gifts, and motivation of both the initiand and the ritual elder. Thus, the dynamics are the same whether the ritual processes under observation are those involved in premodern ritual or contemporary analytic practice.

REFERENCES

Butler, E. M. (1948). *The Myth of the Magus*. Cambridge, England: Cambridge University Press.

Lau, S. (1981). Garden as a Symbol of Sacred Space. Ph.D. Dissertation, University of Pittsburgh.

Perry, J. (1966). *Lord of the Four Quarters: Myths of the Royal Father*. New York: Braziller.

Perry, J. (1976). *Roots of Renewal in Myth and Madness: The Meaning of Psychotic Episodes*. San Francisco: Jossey-Bass.

Turner, V. (1969). *The Ritual Process: Structure and Anti- Structure*. Chicago: Aldine. This essay is adapted from the author's forthcoming book, *The Magician and the Analyst: Ritual, Sacred Space, and Psychotherapy* (Center for the Scientific Study of Religion).

Anger, Despair, Fear and Love in the Analytical Relationship

Manisha Roy
Boston, Massachusetts, USA
New England Society
of Jungian Analysts

My concerns in this paper are threefold. First is that of relationships between the analyst and the analysand, both in I-It and I-Thou aspects, as Jacoby (1984) calls them. Second is the analyst's emotions – frustration, anger, fear and love – and how vital they are in opening doors to the archetypal world, which contains and heals both partners. Finally is the importance of the cultural archetypes of both analyst and analysand in this process.

A woman of 39, who began analysis with me three years ago, was born of Jewish and Polish parents. She was brought up in a lower middle-class ghetto of New York. Her father, a mechanic and a crude, unlettered man, left his wife when the daughter was seven. The mother, an art teacher, is an attractive and egotistic woman who has had a series of lovers. She wanted the daughter, who has considerable artistic talents, to be an artist. From her childhood, the only time the analysand remembered her mother attending to her needs was when the girl developed diarrhea.

The woman came to see me because I was close to her geographically and she heard that I was flexible with my fee. Otherwise she wouldn't have considered me, she said. She needed help with her anger against men who were forever "stalking to abuse" her. She felt like killing every man in sight. She also declared that, although she lived in a sexual relationship with a woman for several years, she was not a lesbian. Right now she lived alone in a noisy, dirty, cheap neighborhood because that was all she could afford. She had a bachelor's degree in fine arts but earned her living by house-cleaning.

The woman looked like a hippy from the 1970s, clean but unadorned, somewhat overweight with a pretty but angry face. I disliked her defensive stance immediately, yet reduced the fee more than I wanted to. I told her that I would "give a try." She assured me that she was not making up her mind about me either. She disappeared for several weeks, then made another appointment, saying that she decided to work with me because of a dream.

In the dream *she came to see me and sat on my chair. I was pregnant, curled up on a sofa and had a white lace veil over my head. We had begun the session when she realized that I was not well. She asked if I wanted to wait. I said "yes." Later she came back to the session; I found her on the floor crying about her rotten life. I apologized for being late and we resumed.*

Actually she did sit on my chair each time. This dream left me with a sense of uneasiness about the reversal of our roles. We both associated the dream image of me with the pregnant virgin, although the full implication of the dream was not apparent to me at the time.

For several months she complained about everything and everyone: the glare of the sun in the room even when the shades were drawn, the chair was uncomfortable, the hour was too short and finally one day my perfume was horrible. First I was embarrassed, then angry. I told her that I did not like her constant manipulation to get me angry although this time she did succeed. She became a sulking child immediately, complaining that now I was going to throw her out. I realized that I was not being the "good enough mother," neither "mirroring" nor having "empathic resonance" (Kohut, 1977).

Such scenes occurred for over a year. She succeeded in getting me angry sometimes, but termination was never a possibility in my mind and I told her so. However, my increasing discomfort with her neediness and manipulations sometimes pushed me into animus reactions in the form of arguments against her outrageous accusations. Her only goal in life seemed to be to provoke me and everyone else to be disgusted with her. My natural inclination to emphasize a pleasant or a positive image in a dream or her artistic talent was always subverted by ridicule and mistrust.

Nevertheless, I kept encouraging her to paint some of her dream images, and she often did. One such painting moved me deeply. It was of a wailing figure of a woman in the middle of a wood; her wails penetrated the sky and the earth. The analysand gave the painting to me.

She brought many dreams and told me that she was not sure how much she remembered and how much she made up. Many of them had confusing and unnatural images; some had animals which were sexually seduced and abused by the dream ego and some were full of masturbation, feces, filth and dirt. I could not relate to many of them even symbolically and many produced instant repulsion in me. I realized how desperately she was trying to draw me into her regressive world. After all, it was diarrhea that captured her mother's attention.

She also wrote pages of her sexual history. These were long tales of manipulation, humiliation, drugs, petty crime and literal seduction of animals. All along she created situations where she was the initiator and the victim at the same time, to perpetuate the disgust and anger against the world and against herself – the only excitement she knew. As I interpreted this to her I let her know that I found it hard to enter this world of hers. She seemed disappointed yet relieved.

Meanwhile, she found a job as an assistant to the occupational therapist in a hospital, working with mentally retarded patients. We spent many sessions on her difficulty with her colleagues, the patients and the hospital environment. I supported her self-image as a normal person who could do a job. Gradually she seemed to be able to withdraw some of her negative projections and kept the job. But this achievement was never enough for her to believe in herself. Even a very moving dream image seemed to do nothing for her. I would be totally frustrated and lose interest in her dreams.

All my readings on narcissistic and borderline personality disorders helped little. I failed to be the mother the way she wanted me to be, although I was there for her the way I could be. Nor could I be the negative mother she kept projecting. I had a distinct feeling of being suspended in the middle; that feeling, I believe, created my despair. Now she began to have dreams with me in them, mostly in uncompromising and sad images.

Two and a half years after the beginning of our work, she had a dream that left me with a frustrated anger for several days. In the dream *I was an older woman of 70, sitting on a high chair, like a religious figure. She was opposite me, lying on a bed. I was telling her about my mother's death. I was the analysand, she the analyst. Suddenly I disappeared in a puff of smoke; in my place materialized the figure of the Buddha and, at one side, a smaller human being*. She awoke hearing the "clatter" of my voice.

This dream, despite the emergence of the archetypal figure of the Buddha in place of my incinerated body, left me very upset. I decided to let my anger envelop me. By the end of the week I had a brief image of a dream. *My analysand and I were sitting side by side instead of opposite each other*. A few days later she dreamed of *a book entitled "The Burning Bush."* She had no associations. When I mentioned the Old Testament story I could not be sure she even heard me. I asked her to paint the burning bush. Meanwhile, reading anything I could find on countertransference, I stumbled onto a book by the psychoanalyst Harold F. Searles. Opening the chapter entitled "The Patient as Therapist," it dawned on me that my struggle to remain the therapist to my analysand might be the key problem.

I remembered the first dream my analysand brought, in which I was unwell and pregnant. In many of her later dreams she was the analyst, I the analysand. In my desperate need to help her, I failed to see how she was trying to help me to become a good mother to her. For the first time I began to relax.

The next week she brought several paintings of the burning bush. In one the fire came out of the earth and encircled a woman's abdomen. I was reminded of the story of Sita, wife of Rama in the Indian epic Ramayana. Sita, daughter of Earth, was tested with fire by the people of the kingdom who needed proof of her incorruptible virtue. Out of shame and sorrow she prayed to Mother Earth to save her from humiliation. Mother Earth answered Sita's prayer by opening herself to give shelter to her daughter. I told the story to my analysand, who listened eagerly. I wondered, could she begin to trust the archetypal mother for her psychic home and shelter?

The archetype of the feminine that had been constellated since the beginning of this analysis appeared in three images: the pregnant virgin who is in pain, the wailing woman of the woods and the mistrusted queen who is tested by fire. All of them emerged in my analysand's dreams and paintings. The only time I could feel a connection to them was when I relinquished my power and responsibility as an analyst/therapist to her. Perhaps the analysand needed to see the sad mother shedding tears for her daughter, who manipulates her own individuation. The same mother also must be there to offer home and shelter when the daughter is put to test by fire. Many times during our sessions I identified with all these images.

Much later, I realized how her narcissistic rage triggered my anger. I could not transcend that anger to hold hers. She did everything to destroy that process as well. The pregnant virgin's pain in her initial dream expressed my inability to impregnate her, to help her.

Another person, a young man of 29, has been in analysis for nine months. He came because of his problems with women. In his own words, he felt sucked into women when he fell in love. They acted like sponges to him. He also had great difficulty relaxing and felt extremely agitated most of the time. He was born of an Irish father, who was a renowned poet; and a Portuguese mother, a well-known sculptor. The young man came to America to study photography, in which he already had made a name in his country. He held a scholarship and worked several nights in a pizzeria to earn extra to pay for analysis.

I saw him as a talented, intelligent and imaginative young man with a great deal of agitated energy. He carried a camera always and, even in the session, sometimes shot pictures through the window. Other times he appeared quite lost and agonized in his soul. He reminded me of El Greco's painting *The Christ* – thin and emaciated. I liked him from the beginning, but had a hard time getting him to concentrate in the hour. He seemed to be quite inflated most of the time. The only time I could engage him in the session was when we talked about art, films or literature. Rilke was his favorite poet and he also read some Jung.

When he was seven his father left his mother and had many women including two other marriages. My analysand spent parts of his childhood with his father's mother, a devout and strict Catholic. He spent most of his teens with his mother, who loved him but offered him no discipline. She was a frail, artistic and confused woman. She seemed unable to manage anything; leaking bathtubs and windows in her house needed repair. He fought against her and wished that she would become more independent. He admired her talents but felt sorry for her.

As a child, he saw his father only occasionally but spent more time with him later. The analysand admired his father's poetry, which the young man edited and illustrated. However, he disapproved of his father's bohemian life-style. When the father died a few years ago, the young man was very upset over the undignified death in a state hospital, where the father had been left unattended. As the young man spoke he tried hard to suppress his tears; they provoked great sadness in me and I could not help shedding mine. This touched him deeply. He relaxed suddenly and said, "you can weep so easily. It's wonderful!" In his presence, I often felt teary – a spontaneous reaction I could not quite control.

He claimed that he could not remember dreams. However, he reported a vision:

> In a cave he saw a cave-painting – an outline of a bull. A real bull was asleep on the floor of the cave. He began to complete the painting and later fell asleep near the bull's hairy body to keep warm. Next morning he awoke to see a bird pecking away at the pigment of the painting on the wall. This disturbed the bull. He awoke and stretched and became very restless.

I tried to interpret by telling him that his own restless energy was pecking away at the painting, and perhaps he needed to continue painting the bull. But he had a hard time listening to me.

A week later he came extremely agitated and declared that he had to stop analysis. He recognized a voice inside him whom he called "the teacher" and who told him that I was no good for him and analysis could not help him. His agitation was so strong that I decided to help him to an active imagination with "the teacher" right then. It took a while before he could calm down and close his eyes. After several minutes of silence, he reported that he saw his mother standing near his bed. He asked her why she was so incompetent, never getting the bathtub fixed.

I asked him, "Are these things that important? Do you hate your mother because of this?" He answered, "No, I don't hate *you*. Actually I love you very much. I feel like protecting you. But I cannot. You have to learn to protect yourself."

I had a strong surge of emotion. I became the mother he could not depend on and wished to protect. This identification on my part touched a deep vulnerable spot in me and opened an old wound. When he opened his eyes I merely said, "So, you see your mother when you try to talk to the 'teacher'." He seemed calm and pensive, and said, "But you are very different from my mother. You are independent and strong, although you do look a bit like her." Thus he protected me by his conscious judgment and put me back in the role of the analyst.

This session left me with a feeling of love and gratitude for him. I felt good about the way things had gone. The next week, however, he told me that he must stop analysis. He felt afraid of being pulled into a darkness like a dark womb. He assured me that this decision had nothing to do with me. I was shocked but understood why he felt that he must stop. I told him that I respected his decision and he had my blessings for whatever he decided to do. We said good-byes.

That evening for several hours I was in great pain – pain from this unexpected separation. Had I scared him off by my strong feelings? Were my feelings inappropriate and devouring for him? I felt terribly guilty and sad. That night I had a dream in which *he and I were swimming together very gently in calm rivers of a European city like Venice. We went under a bridge together. Before we emerged I awoke.*

This dream made me feel better but I could not let go my sorrow from losing him. Or was it the pain of losing my brief projection which was not allowed to live its full course? I lost a son/lover before either of us had a chance to face the dangerous challenge. Also, this sudden separation opened another set of old wounds of separations and losses including termination in my own analysis several years earlier. I decided to meditate and invoke the Hindu goddess Durga to help me and to protect him no matter where he was. As I concentrated on the image of the goddess, to my surprise the image of Krishna, the god of love, appeared with his flute.

Krishna's love for an older woman, his aunt by marriage, is the famous allegory of romantic love in Indian mythology. This love story has produced exquisite lyrics, music and paintings. It is the love between the deity and his worshipper and the ultimate romantic love of all times and places. It is also the love of incest which is not fulfilled concretely – the prototype of the analytic love which must live and transform in emotions and imagination only.

Without the image of Krishna I could not have felt this old truth so deeply again. For now, my analysand's fear of love must stay side by side with my love for him. His fear had to do with the fear of the death of the son in the maternal love – a death I must allow, in order for us to achieve further consciousness, whether we work together or not. "Too bad," I told myself, "I could not get a chance to do this with him."

About three weeks later he telephoned, asking if I would consider seeing him again. He told me how, at the last moment, he decided not to leave the country and how much he missed me and now he knew that he had to surrender to the analyst. I corrected, saying: "to analysis, to the darkness – the unknown journey." He brought me a clay sculpture of a frail but determined young man facing a charging bull. He said that he would like to make a figure of the dancing Shiva, the god of destruction and death. I pointed out that the bull was Shiva's animal.

I admired his courage to face the dangerous maternal energy in the symbolic form of a sculpture – his mother's professional medium. Together we made connections to the gods of love and creation as well as the god of death and destruction – Krishna and Shiva. I realized how important my awareness of the emotions was for both of us, to be connected to the archetypal depths and to begin the process of individuation.

Both these cases – one where I was unable to love and in the other where love was not repressed – could be interpreted variously. I could talk about the kinds of countertransference reactions – syntonic, concordant or complementary. While differentiating the countertransference reactions in the analyst is important, I chose to discuss my own emotional experience – the human aspect of the analyst without which the I-Thou relationship remains impossible. This recognition also allows me to acknowledge how much my analysands helped me and healed me in the process.

I am grateful to Drs. Adolf Guggenbühl-Craig and Robert M. Stein for their comments on this paper during its preparation.

REFERENCES

Jacoby, M. (1984). *The Analytic Encounter: Transference and Human Relationship*. Toronto: Inner City Books.

Kohut, H. (1977). *The Restoration of the Self*. New York: International Universities Press.

Searles, H. (1979). *Countertransference and Related Subjects: Selected Papers*. Madison, CT: International Universities Press.

The Analyst-Analysand Relationship: A Cross-Cultural Perspective

Luigi Zoja
Milan, Italy
Centro Italiano di Psicologia Analitica

Neither psychotherapy nor its deeper version, analysis, is mainly a technique. To look upon them as such would be to view the processes and therapies of the psyche in the medical model. This model is substantially fixed; the physical processes of a modern European are not different from those of an Aztec or an ancient Egyptian. In contrast, the psychic processes of these latter two groups, fused as they are into collective hierarchies outside of which the individual does not exist and is destined to go mad, differ greatly from our own.

Freud, with his psycho-biological model, took his cue from this positivistic psyche-soma analogy. One of the reasons for Jung's break from Freud rested in the intuition that, while the body and its organs change very little over the course of the millennia, the psyche is constantly being criss-crossed and re-formed by the history and culture surrounding it. Consequently, analysis is not simply a collection of techniques nor is it a fixed intervention upon some unchanging organism which, like the amputation of a limb or the administration of a drug, always would be done more or less in the same way.

Analysis, as a subculture of the West, was not invented but discovered as an already-existing potentiality within that same culture. "Talking cure" was the name given to the therapeutic relationship between Josef Breuer and Anna O; the therapist did not invent new techniques but rather gave full value to the possibilities contained in a conversation.

Even its principal "technical" aspects, the dynamics of the transference and the countertransference, were not constructed but rather recognized, almost out of desperation; they channeled already existing affective dynamics that were the offspring of the culture in which the work was underway. We need only think of the extent to which hysteria, that privileged object of analytical prehistory, was linked to the era and to social class. Such hysteria was exemplified in the intensity of the transference of Anna O, the transference that made Breuer flee.

In order to improve our understanding of psychic structures and processes, analytic schools often study the cultural phenomena of peoples whom Eurocentrism has expelled from the dynamics of history and relegated to the stagnancy of folklore. This very Eurocentrism is perhaps an obstacle to our attempts to relativize the more common objects of study; we tend to prefer technical analyses of the transference and countertransference rather than to attempt a cultural one. My purpose here is to point out the usefulness of such a cultural analysis and to put forward a hypothesis that may help us along this road.

Freudian psychotherapy encountered the transference unexpectedly and, at the beginning, considered it to be a form of pathology. The medical model designated the transference as a neurosis ("transference neurosis") and saw it as an important and delicate factor in healing.

Jung's model looks upon the transference not as a sickness but rather as a reflection of a deeper pathology. This model also distinguishes the personal dynamic from collective psychology and the cultural setting. For Jung, the transference directs the flow of libido. This flow does not disappear as the transference is resolved but is reintegrated into the analysand's process of individuation. The transference is seen, therefore, as a signal-light of a "vertical" personal dynamic which has failed to find an expression.

And yet, if we want to remain faithful to the Jungian idea of linking the personal dynamics of the psyche with collective ones, we must ask ourselves if the frequent occurrence of transference in analytic treatment may not be also a signal-light of a disturbance in the "horizontal" flow of energy. Such a flow links individuals with one another in a social context, and therefore is a form of compensation for collective one-sidedness. A person who is generally considered "healthy" rarely enjoys a very developed state of individuality but invests considerable libido in the establishment of pseudo-ties with others, for example, in clubs and sects.

Even more surprising is the ever-growing amount of libido that is invested in the things that we use, an investment not in the subject but once again in external objects. Such an investment points to a widespread difficulty in setting up simple and satisfying relationships. This difficulty predisposes the analysand, at the beginning of analysis, to an intense and passionate transference.

The deepest, even if the slowest, of the revolutions that have touched the West has been individualism. Unlike primitives or the populations of Asia, for whom the individual has meaning only as a function of the whole, European thinking has conferred upon the individual's personal well-being an ever-growing and central importance. This movement was announced at least 26 centuries ago in passages of Greek lyrical poetry. It was prefigured again in the kinship relationship that existed between humans and the monotheistic God, even though this relationship was modified by the idea of the fear of God.

This revolution exploded in the Renaissance and then received its theological and political credentials from Protestantism and the French Revolution, respectively. It reached its apex with Psychoanalysis, which opposes all the obstacles along the path of the development of the individual, automatically choosing the values of the individual over those of the family or the community at large.

Like all radical transformations, this revolution has lasted not years but millennia and has worked its way down to the roots of the Euro-American West. It is rapidly reaching the rest of the world as Western life styles spread to other countries. As is often the case with movements which affect every aspect of life, this revolution becomes evident in the compensatory elements that seek to correct it and that stand out against the background of the movement itself.

Studies of the sentiment of love, especially in its passionate form, stress the fact that this sentiment is typical of Western civilization and has grown over the centuries. This progressive development of sentiment is an unconscious reaction against the continuing growth of rationalism and individualism. The sentiment of love inspires creativity, ambivalence and fear. The passionate forms of the transference have both a personal and an archetypal aspect. Thus, these forms are to be classified as examples of that typically Western phenomenon of passionate love. The very term "passion" takes us back to the idea of pathology (in Greek *pathos* means suffering); our culture looks upon anti-individualistic sentiments as an illness.

In contrast, Socialist ideologies generally reflect a kind of feeling that reacts against excesses of individualism, thus appearing as the heretical version of the idea of Christian love. Those ideologies (and the feelings they stem from), in social-democratic and more decidedly Marxist forms, are now said to be in a crisis and even anti-historical. The same thing is being repeated regarding the sentiment of passionate love. This repetition may be unavoidable since openness to solidarity and fusion come to life as elements that correct the individualistic revolution but are not able to stop its triumphant, thousand-year march.

A more recent phenomenon is the "individuative revolution," the reinvestment of libido in the subject in the form of individuation. It, unlike the individualistic revolution, has reached only a limited number of cultured and sensitive people. Jungian analysts should take note of this fact.

Openly compensatory to the individuative revolution is the investment of libido in external objects by the majority of people. This phenomenon is obvious in the increasing indispensability of objects and the growing number of clubs, collective holidays and social get-togethers which have been contrived rather than felt.

Thus, the high incidence of strong transference in the analytic process is a compensatory and immature expression of an individuative potentiality in people who have a predisposition to this type of development. But for others it can be seen also as a strong form of corrective compensation, as the fabric of social relationships becomes more and more arid.

This point of view seems to be in keeping with another teaching of Jung's: before turning to an interpretation of what is disguised, before giving way to suspicions, before adopting the "nothing but" attitude, take a psychic phenomenon for what it is. The passionate transference is a strong affective link with another person. The most pathological cases, where it is hard to distinguish between the difficulties involved in resolving the transference and a refusal to get better, express the analysand's fear of independence and the overpowering force of the mother-child symbiosis. But the more general and less pathological transference seems to reflect a refusal to return to a lonely and ethically tricky form of well-being. Thus, we see an unconscious effort to regenerate feelings of solidarity, fusion, dedication, and of mutual obligation. These feelings, until a short time ago, made up the fabric of society even in our own culture.

Passionate falling in love, whether it be in the context of analysis or outside it, can come into being individually as an unconscious means of reaching other ends. But the fact remains that love is a valid goal in and of itself on the collective cultural plane, once we realize how wanting our culture is in terms of passion.

In a certain sense all deep one-to-one relationships are a recent invention. They are extreme forms of resistance to extreme forms of individualism and represent a bridge which is still open between the feeling of community that has been lost and individual autonomy which is feared as loneliness. We have only recently gone beyond marriages arranged by the community to marriages based on love. Only recently has the practice of having many children begun to wane and the parent, with the help of various cultural forms and models, has space for a one-to-one relationship with the child.

Within this framework, I hypothesize that the transference, from the collective point of view, shows a need for fusion, for community and for passion for another person. The transference therefore stands in harsh opposition to the illusion that every good is to be constructed upon the foundation of individualism.

Translated from Italian by
Roberto Mercurio

Analytical Psychology and Inter-Cultural Experience

Introduction

Donald F. Sandner
San Francisco, California, USA
Society of Jungian Analysts of
Northern California

Manisha Roy
Boston, Massachusetts, USA
New England Society
of Jungian Analysts

This workshop brings together analysts who have had significant experiences with cultures quite different from their own, to share such experiences with their colleagues. Although culture is a pervasive influence in every aspect of our lives, it often eludes notice. Like a fish surrounded by water, one tends not to be aware of one's culture until one separates from it and views it from outside. Then one realizes, sometimes with a sense of shock, how different other cultures are. Customs and traditions as well as pathways of spiritual and instinctual expression are molded by culture. Without an external standpoint in another culture from which to reflect and compare, one's viewpoint becomes narrow and parochial.

In addition to influencing its own people, each culture has a specific development that contributes to the sum of world culture. Each has certain values without which the whole cannot be comprehended, a key that unlocks all the others. Therefore, we need every culture's experience, and we would do well to cherish each one, no matter how undeveloped it appears to our culture-bound perception. The serious student finds in every culture a secret revelation that enters into the observer's personal life and widens the therapeutic perspective toward greater flexibility, life-enhancing tolerance and a deeper wisdom.

Anthropological Fieldwork in My Personal Life and Analytic Work

Manisha Roy
Boston, Massachusetts, USA
New England Society
of Jungian Analysts

When I was a little girl in a border town of eastern India, near Tibet and Burma, we children often saw tribal people from the adjoining foothills of the Himalayan range. They appeared very strange in our highly industrialized oil town. Our mothers told us that, if we did not drink our milk or take our cod-liver oil, those people would take us in their bark bags which hung from their shoulders. They were supposed to be headhunters. Somehow my fascination with those people overcame my fear. In addition, I observed that they took out harmless things from their bags such as raisins, honey, exotic bird feathers and animal skins, not children's heads. They bartered for tobacco, sugar and tea. This childhood experience, I believe, was the beginning of my anthropological interest. One of the hill tribes also became my first field of study when, years later, I embarked on research.

I believe that one is a born anthropologist, as one is a natural analyst and therapist. Otherwise both these professions are hard on one's constitution. My interest in observing people and their behavior began early because I was a stranger in language and culture to the place where I was born and brought up: a border town of the subcontinent. Thus, I had to deal with an outsider's position from the beginning of my life.

As a student of cultural anthropology I was gripped by one compelling question: the relationship between individual and culture. Coming from an old and traditional society I experienced the security of a culture grounded in the live myths and rituals of gods and demons as well as the occasional suffocating restriction of rigid customs. When I went to America to study I observed that the freedom of a young society confused individuals considerably as to their identities. Not until years later, after analysis and analytic training, did I begin to make sense of what really constitutes one's identity. I needed to face my own personal and professional crisis and delve into my psyche via my own cultural archetypes before it was possible even to begin to see what the question meant for me. It was my anthropological research that initiated this process for me.

The crisis happened during my first fieldwork. For a student of anthropology the first fieldwork, in its nervous excitement and anticipation, can be compared only to a long-awaited love encounter. Fresh from the classroom, fortified with all the theories and techniques, I soon discovered that theoretical and technical knowledge help little in understanding the people I set out to study. After the initial romance it was an emotional disaster.

The natural beauty of the Khasi Hills of Assam captivated me from the moment I arrived. At last, I told myself, I would find out if those strangers with long bark bags really stole children who were naughty. Of course, my topic of research was very different. I had to analyze the factors of political unrest between the Khasis and the Nepalese, who migrated to the Khasi land and were encroaching into its beautiful hills. My work was coming along fine until the second week when, to my great shock, I developed amnesia. I could not remember anything I was observing and trying to record. After initial panic I noticed that I could remember things that were not important for my research. I decided to record whatever I could remember. I recorded information on human relationships, their emotions and the commonsense strategies people used in order to live with one another. I became obsessed with finding out how people felt about who they were, within the context of their society and culture. This material later offered vignettes for my fiction-writing, if not for my dissertation.

When I was there in the 1960s, the Khasis were one of the few matrilineal tribes left in the world. I came directly from an American campus where the Women's Liberation Movement was well underway. I noticed how the Khasi women worked from dawn to dusk. Their work included cultivating the fields while the men sat in the tea shops drinking tea or rice wine, talking politics and women. Being trained to be objective, I suppressed my shock at such injustice. However, when I learned to use their language a bit, I discovered that the women were very proud of doing what they were doing. Indeed, they pitied the men, who did not own any property and therefore – in the women's eyes – had no motivation to work.

This was the beginning of my interest in the topic of gender, culture and psychology, and the relativity not only of the culture but also psychological experience within the contexts of individual cultures. This interest came easily because I was trained heavily in the school of cultural relativism à la Margaret Mead. My subsequent fieldworks in urban India and in southern California reinforced this theoretical conviction. In addition, my life experience in many cultures supported this. Yet, somewhere deep down, I also knew that relativity of any kind is valuable only if it is transcended by a unity on another level. It took almost another decade – when I came to analysis – before I had a chance to discover how that unity is possible.

My crisis in the field was due also to academic methodology. I was trained to be "objective" while studying another culture. I soon realized that objectivity is an artificial and untenable position. If I allowed my intuition, feelings and instinct to serve my creative ideas, I could not be objective. Moreover, I could not be satisfied with my professional work if I was not part of it, both objectively and subjectively. I have seen many casualties in academic research because of one-sided objectivity. For me this crisis led to analysis.

Paradoxically, analysis took me back to the cultural relativism via the cultural archetypes, but only to make me aware that there is another level – a deeper and more compelling one – where at last my intuitive hypothesis of psychic unity could be tested. I began to experience the healing power of the archetypes, but only through culturally specific symbols. At last my initial question of the connection between individual and culture became irrelevant. The question transcended itself.

Thus, the effect of anthropological work on my analytic profession is a cyclical process; each feeds back to the other continually. It happens on many levels: simple and conscious to complex and unconscious. For example, I learned in my fieldwork the value of the objective reality such as the everyday world of things, language, customs, and common sense ideas. This reality is vital, for my analysand and for me, in facing the unconscious, the world of the archetype. The needed rootedness comes from a well-developed persona offered by one's culture and tradition, no matter how objectionable that persona can be. The battle between the soul's needs and the persona's demands, I have found, is a natural one, a necessary tension which can lead one to look inward. In addition, facing the archetypal world is possible and safe only within the framework of the rituals that are culturally prescribed and practiced. My personal belief in religious symbols and rituals seems to help my analysands in a mysterious way.

Cultural relativism in archetypal experience is a necessary middle ground between the individual and the transcendental. It offers a protection for facing the gods and the demons.

My Experience of Anthropological Research Work

Vera Bührmann
Gansbaai, C.P., South Africa
Society of Analytical Psychology

Anthropological research, affording intimate contact with a culture foreign to my own, has been enlightening and growth-producing, not unlike analysis. Physical and instinctual aspects of my psyche, which are often relatively neglected, have become more real. At a community health meeting a black doctor said, "The white people do not understand that when part of a black man is ill, the whole of him is ill, physically, mentally and spiritually." These black people's approach to healing is much more holistic than the Western model. In the West we are now searching desperately for such an approach.

I experienced this healing – whole-making – process during my research, which included participation in rituals of the Xhosa people of South Africa, as well as their song and dance performances. A sense of mystery, well-being and zest for life became associated with a sense of community with the other participants and with supra-personal powers.

Much of the treatment by the Xhosa healers is of a symbolic nature. Thus, I became aware of the transformative power of the living symbol in people who believe in a mythical world and who have no urge to take the symbol apart; they leave it intact and let it do its work.

The rituals have to be performed correctly in every detail. The ineffectiveness of a ceremony is ascribed, often, to the neglect of ritual detail. Just as with Navaho sand painting, the ritual must be perfect and the chanting faultless.

Visits to the Xhosa healers, their families, trainees and the community became a psychic necessity for me, to such an extent that they said, "You are *thwasa*, you suffer from the Xhosa illness, you should come for treatment and training."

When I became depressed before visits to them, they entered my dream life to such a degree that I discovered how much I really was of Africa. Jung had comparable dreams while he was in North and Central Africa. In the Sudan, he dreamt about a Negro who wanted to make his hair kinky, that is, Negro hair. I never dreamt about becoming an African, perhaps because I was of Africa, but I dreamt about my black companions and about participating in their ceremonies.

Their interpretation of dreams is very different from ours. To them, dreams are fragments of reality. Dreamers' responses are concrete, causing much misunderstanding between employers and employees. An employee who has a dream – whether at the work-place or the living quarters – that could be interpreted as witchcraft or evil, will disappear without explanation.

The Xhosa attitude to dreams is open and accepting. Dreams come from the ancestors: "Our ancestors never deceive their children." The dreams are guides to understanding their life and world; meaningful life is not possible without dreams. Excessive dreaming, complicated and confusing dreams or nightmares cause much anxiety and are often the reasons that they visit healers for enlightenment. An old man told me that he had no need to visit healers; he had his own way of communicating with the ancestors. If he did not dream or had confusing dreams he would take his black stick, go to the gate of the cattlepen and ask the ancestors to send him clear dreams. (The cattle pen is the most important place for the ancestors to congregate). If there was no change in his dreamlife he would repeat the performance but be more emphatic. If there was still no change he would go for a third night but then he would have a real confrontation with them and demand that they grant his request, pointing out that he was a reverent and obedient child of theirs and therefore was entitled to their help. He claimed that this procedure was always effective.

The healers vary considerably in their ability to create an

atmosphere. This variation makes for differences between gripping, numinous ceremonies and lifeless, boring ones. In good ceremonies the participants engage fully in the rituals; in the others, they engage only in a half-hearted way.

In the good ceremonies, certain archetypes are stimulated and seem to grip everyone present, including me. Unconscious fusion seems to develop. When I told senior healers afterward about my experiences during these sessions and the images that were evoked, they confirmed most of my impressions.

My anthropological work has influenced my analytical understanding of the psyches of my Western clients, and my knowledge of Analytical Psychology has given me an understanding of the psyche, rituals and ceremonies of the black people, especially those who are still steeped in their culture. This work leaves one in no doubt about the universality and power of the objective psyche – the collective unconscious.

In addition, my experience has demonstrated the transformative power of the symbol. I frequently use my knowledge of the thinking and world view of the black people, especially their holistic views on health and illness, in my teaching of psychotherapy. These people have an easy relationship to the ancestors; these personified complexes of the personal and collective unconscious serve as illustrative material. Looking at their union of psyche and soma can assist us with our efforts to heal the split within our Western approach to health.

The Other Side of the World

Mary Jo Spencer
San Francisco, California, USA
Society of Jungian Analysts
of Northern California

When I was four years old I heard of a strange country on the other side of the world, called China. I also heard that anyone who went straight through the middle of the earth would come out on the other side to a place where everything was upside down. The earth was above and the sky was below; people's feet were above and their heads hung down into the sky. The houses, the chairs, the beds, the tables and dishes were all upside down. I tried hard to imagine this, and I could not control my fear that the people might just fall off into space. I knew I would, if I ever got to the other side of the earth, but I was also consumed with curiosity about this upside-down land and its people.

By the time I was ten and fascinated with geography I knew that the upside down land was nonsense. The earth was round and possessed something called gravity. The image was rather more like a giant pincushion where heads were always up and feet were planted firmly on the ground.

Now, in my seventies, I know that I was right at four and wrong at ten. China is the other side and it is opposite in many ways to my mode of life, my attitudes, my concepts and my beliefs. Even if I have not fallen off the earth into empty space in my journeys to China these last several years, I have fallen into another space of being, so different from my own that I can only observe and wonder with the same puzzled fascination that I remember in my early self and see in my great-grandchildren.

The upside-downness is there. But now, in good Jungian fashion, I call it the opposite or complementary. For example, I address a letter to a Chinese friend: Mr. Kun Yuan Gu, 115 YuYi Road, CITS Suzchou Branch, Suzchou, China. If he has not learned American customs, he addresses a letter to me: U.S.A., California, San Francisco, 262 Moncada Way, Spencer, Mary Jo Mrs. As in the marvelous Sung landscape paintings the human being is clearly there but located within a much larger perspective.

I eat soup at the beginning of my meal. He eats soup at the end of his, or at a banquet he may eat it in the middle of the meal and at the end. When I talk of directions I say north, south, east and west. The directions are named so that they intersect the center of a space; often I feel the center of the space is exactly where I stand. He, on the other hand, says east, south, west and north, traveling around the rim of the space he discusses. What are the implications to his psyche of this ordering of directions which encloses space rather than pin-pointing it?

Where does his psychic perception stand in the circle? At the rim? Above the circle? I favor the latter, but I do not know.

I have learned about time as a linear progression or a cyclical progression which nevertheless moves from below to above, or above to below, or from left to right or right to left. His image of time seems more like a long parabola that exists in many dimensions and folds back on itself. For example, in Chinese grammar there are no tenses; the past, present and future that are so necessary to us are indicated by completed or uncompleted actions.

The Chinese language has developed in a geographical vacuum, apart from outside influence. To Americans, whose language is a hodgepodge of Anglo-Saxon, Norman French, Latin and Greek, who cannot read what their direct ancestors wrote as recently as 700 years ago, the unbroken flow of language through the millennia can elicit wonder and fascination.

The source of Gu's language is largely visual, still holding ancient pictographs within its characters. Mandarin sounds are dictated by a system of five tones; there are nine in Cantonese.

The tones are rather like the sounds of the ancient bronze bells from 2000 years ago.

All languages originated in ideographs, which used highly simplified pictures to represent ideas. The sea-trading Phoenicians created a phonetic alphabet, however, which was used eventually by all the nations bordering on the Mediterranean; it is the ancestor of our 26 letter symbols, which can be combined in various ways to make thousands of words.

But in China primitive picture writing was refined into an intricate, highly sophisticated system of ideograms. A European child learns an alphabet and how to make words from it. A Chinese child must learn a different ideograph or character for every word.

Perhaps the matter of names can suggest something of the subtleties and complexities between Western culture and China's. My friend Gu, who is Kun-yuan when addressed Chinese style, has the title Xian Sheng – Mr. – as he would have in European cultures, but he has many others as well. To his parents and servants his name is also "second son." To his younger brother he is "ge ge," older brother; to his older brother he is "di di," younger brother.

He calls his younger brother "di di" and his older brother "ge ge." He calls his younger sister "mei mei" and his older sister "jie jie," no matter what their personal names are. His father's younger brother – Gu's uncle – Gu will call "shie shie;" his father's older brother will have still another name and so on.

Thus, a child in a large family has many names, descriptive of his or her relative place in the family. The names affirm a constant interplay of relationships. Through the names the person is knit into the fabric of the family. This fact alone tells us how the structure of the Chinese family and, by extrapolation, how the fabric of Chinese culture differs from our own in defining the relationship of the individual to the group. If the Chinese attitude toward individuals seems stifling to us, we must remember the variety and range of possible relationships, at the same time that each relationship may be defined rigidly by the rights and duties that accrue to that relationship.

By tradition, a person can take other names as an adult, sometimes related to formal social structure. For example, an emperor or nobleman takes a name connected with the position.

Calligraphers, painters and poets also give themselves new names from time to time, much to the despair of students of their work. Fortunately, they keep old names and continue to acknowledge the past identity. Often the names are very evocative and moving, seeming to reveal a vista within a personality.

During the 17th century, at the very end of the Ming Dynasty and the beginning of the Ch'ing, there was a school of painting called the Eccentric School. The most famous members of this group were educated and influential men who refused to serve at the court of the alien Manchu ruler of the Ch'ing dynasty and led the lives of eccentric recluses, wandering around the countryside or dwelling in Buddhist or Taoist monasteries.

The greatest master among these painters was a man named Tao-chi who was descended from one of the Ming emperors and took Buddhist vows in 1644. He wandered most of his life in the mountains. He absorbed sensory impressions of nature and tried to understand through them "the hidden forces of heaven and earth." His painting name was Shi Tao, which means "Stone Billow," a paradoxical image of permanence but with it the properties of a powerful billowing force.

In Chinese painting there is a tradition of rendering a single work from multiple perspectives. Many paintings were hand scrolls meant to be unrolled a foot or two at a time and followed as if one were walking through the scenery. But multiple perspective is used as well in large wall hangings. Thus, multiple perspective seems a rather natural process, perhaps another manifestation in the Chinese psychic structure of a comfortable psychological connection to the constantly shifting image of oneself in relation to the situation of the moment.

There is also the example of SuShi, a wise and able administrator of the Northern Sun dynasty, a man of outspoken integrity who was twice exiled to minor official posts. During one of these exiles, to the city of Hangzhou in 1080, he built there a famous dike that is still in use. It prevented the equinoxial tides of the

Qiam-tang river from flooding the town. SuShi was not only a first-class poet and prose writer but a distinguished painter and calligrapher as well. In addition he was, like most major Sung poets, a philosopher interested in Confucianism, Buddhism and Taoism.

About him Watson (1966) said, "The Confucian side of his thinking is less apparent in his poetry than in his political papers and his life as a whole – his strong family devotion, the fact that he chose a career in politics, the fearlessness with which he spoke out against abuses in government, the numerous public works for the local inhabitants that he undertook at his various provincial posts. In his poetry it is rather the Buddhist and Taoist aspects of his thinking that find expression. His mother was a devout Buddhist.... The influence of Taoism is most clearly seen in his sensitivity to the natural world" (p. 10).

SuShi is known to most of us as Su Tung-p'o, his literary name: the Layman of the Eastern Slope, after the plot of land he farmed in exile. He was a genius, but he was also a product of that culture in which one person could have many names. They were all meaningful expressions of his individuality and his place in his family and in society.

Why, since I am not Chinese and could not possibly live in China, at least as it has been since 1945, has this intense interest blossomed for me? A part of me stands aside in amazement, watching, as I struggle each day with learning to read and write Chinese characters and to speak the Chinese language, butting my head against grammatical structures which seem even stranger than to have my feet on the ceiling and my head dangling toward the floor.

I finish each study time tired, knowing that I am too old to learn very much in the few years left to me. But I can scarcely wait for tomorrow, to begin again, and I look forward to a whole day free for study, as I would to a secret tryst. Physical energy seems to have very little to do with my drive. What is this unexpected intensity of feeling? At times it seems almost laughable, but I want to make a reasonable case for it.

The French mathematician Henri Poincaré (1854-1912) used

the metaphor of a net for any hypothetical structure, providing a structured and ordered container for masses of indiscriminate ideas, thoughts and beliefs. The carefully-built net catches much, and often things of immense value, but allows other things too fine for its structure to slip back into the non-structure, into unconsciousness.

My belief is that each culture provides such a net for those who are born into it. The net is composed of generations, even millennia, of a given culture experiencing and re-experiencing itself, as new lives come to be enfolded into its being, gradually building itself a stronger, finer and more structured net. The net, with its contents, finally becomes a civilization, perhaps eventually even a high civilization.

The human psyche, in order to survive, has always had to make choices. We are finite and cannot use or respond to the multitude of sensory, psychic and neurological input we receive; we must be adaptively selective. It is our inherited culture that helps us to choose – unconsciously. We are necessarily unaware of what falls through the holes in the net. Thus an ego is formed with which we begin a dialogue between our being and our cultural structure.

Looking back to my childhood I can say that my interest in China was always there, although there was little in my early life in Colorado that had anything to do with China. A book of Chinese fairy tales, a porcelain Chinese garden stool used as a table for a fern, a doll from Panama dressed in Chinese clothes, an occasional newspaper story discussed by my parents and grandparents. A horrifying story of a group of missionaries being thrown over a cliff by a Chinese war lord and his gang; one victim was a young mother with a tiny infant in her arms.

Perhaps I recognized my interest first when I went east to college and saw the Dragon Scroll at the Boston Museum of Fine Arts and when at the Freer Gallery in Washington I saw my first Sung painting. The clouds in the Dragon Scroll and the misty emptiness at the core of the painting spoke to me as nothing painterly ever had before. It was less a shock than a simultaneous feeling of loss and discovery. Something I had missed, without knowing I missed it, was met and validated by those images. From then on I gravitated toward things Chinese, but I still did not recognize, until relatively recently, the depth of my interest nor its inherent value for me.

Evidently a latent aspect of my psyche has been activated and opens itself to my evolving ego. How or why this happened I am not certain. I know now that China is inside of me, though I never could quite realize it until I encountered that other China that is outside – actually being in China. I have no illusions that I understand the Chinese, or that in my visits I have seen "the real China now." Rather, now there are experiences and images that had fallen through the net for me in learning to be the child of my family and the person I am in my culture and my time in history.

An example of what I have recovered access to is the fascination I feel toward Chinese characters (ideograms); I even have Chinese characters in my dreams. I felt this was a little odd and over-involved until I came across a relevant statement: "As pictures of ideas, Chinese characters reveal the human mind at work. They travel directly from eye to brain, bypassing pathways of speech. Westerners,... whose deepest responses are to pictures, will find themselves drawn to written Chinese. Its appeal to the artistic eye is unequalled by the Western alphabet" (Chang & Chang, 1978, p. 14).

The effect of my interest in China on my practice is equally far-reaching. I watch more closely for what has fallen through the analysand's net, what is latent. What wants to grow, to be in the light? What, in short, is that person's China?

In three areas of life Chinese culture has made a major addition to my attitudes: humanity's place in nature, each person's place among other humans and, most important, the effect of formulating thought and feeling through images rather than through concepts.

REFERENCES

Chang, R. & Chang, M. (1978). *Speaking of Chinese*. New York: W.W. Norton.

Watson, B., Trans. (1966). *Selections from a Sung Dynasty Poet: Su Tung- p'o*. New York: Columbia University Press.

Friendship with the Hopi

Katherine Sanford
San Diego, California, USA
Society of Jungian Analysts of San Diego

I am grateful for this opportunity to acknowledge the inner as well as the outer enrichment I have gained from my years of friendship with the Hopi people.

The Hopis are Pueblo Indians whose ancient villages are located high on the mesas in northern Arizona. Oraibi, one of the major settlements, is the oldest continuously inhabited town in North America, dating from 1125 A.D. or earlier. One gets the feeling that these people and their villages have been here since the dawn of creation. To a remarkable degree, moreover, these people still retain their sense of a meaningful place in the universe.

James Kirsch, an early pioneer of depth psychology in Los Angeles, remarked that – as he understood it – the Hopi culture approximates that of ancient Egypt. My experience of the Hopi people is compatible with that view.

Traditionally the Hopis are farmers. In that arid land their religious ceremonies express a recognition of and a reverence for the awesome forces of nature on which their physical and spiritual lives depend. The Hopis identify these supernatural forces as Cloud People, or as rain beings, who appear in the form of their kachina dancers. In the kachina ceremonies the dancers become identified with the transpersonal deities they portray.

From my long-standing participation in Jungian psychology I was aware of the archetypal forces in the unconscious that play on our lives. It was my interest in these transpersonal dynamics within the psyche that first drew me to the Hopis, to see one of their major ceremonies, the Snake Dance.

Circumstances in my childhood environment had left the realm of the archetypal feminine sorely impoverished. The conflict resulting from such self-alienation brought me to therapy early in my adult life. Painting proved a valuable extension of my analytic work; here the deep disturbance resulting from this split-off spirit of nature found symbolic expression and integration. I had done much of this inner work before I was exposed to the Hopi ceremonies in which these dynamic forces play a central role.

On my first trip to Oraibi I had the good fortune to meet and establish a unique, personal connection with Henry Polingyawma, an important man among his people. Over the last 28 years this relationship to Henry and his family has endured and deepened, bridging the gulf of cultural differences with an unusually strong bond of mutual trust and acceptance. This personal connection has added depth and richness to my experience of the Hopis and their rituals.

The Hopi religious structure rests on a living connection to the primeval images of nature, both light and dark. These images are dramatically personified in the kachina figures, who are central to the religious ceremonies. Each year in February the Bean Dance announces the arrival of the kachinas to be with the people. The kachina ceremonies continue until July when the Home Dance signals the kachinas' return to the distant peaks of their sacred mountain. It is unforgettable to attend the kachina dances and, at daybreak, to see the masked, ceremonially-attired figures. As personified spirits, Cloud People, they emerge from the underground kiva or appear over the edge of the mesa to perform their ritual interaction with the Hopi people. The dancers' identification with the kachina spirits they personify energizes archetypal forces so that dancers and audience alike become part of the process. Participating in such an event can be truly awe-inspiring.

While my work in depth psychology gave me considerable appreciation for archetypes, the kachina dances added immeasurably by portraying these concepts in living, breathing form before my eyes, as if inner and outer realities had merged or been turned inside out. The wisdom of Mother Nature, so split off in the white people's culture, finds a celebrated acceptance in the Hopi rituals. For the Hopis the chthonic spirits are honored and dramatically represented by the various kachina dancers.

I recall a particular kachina who appeared in one of the more elaborate Bean Dances. As the ceremony progressed one dancer moved away from the rest, furtively, around the sides and backs of the dwellings. I watched this lone, masked, black-garbed figure creep up a ladder to the rooftop where a man sat absorbed in watching the drama in the plaza below. Sneaking up behind this man, the kachina threw him to the ground to enact a simulated rape. The people watching treated this as a great joke, laughing heartily at the man's discomfort.

Later, while I watched the dance with Henry and some Hopi women, this same kachina crept up on Henry and grabbed at his genitals. Henry was truly terrified and the women moved quickly to place their bodies in front of him to shield him from the kachina's sexual assault. Later, Henry's wife Mae explained that this particular kachina was called Popo Pu Mana, or the sexy woman who is out to get any man who is not paying attention. She added that it is the task of the human woman who is related to the man to protect him from being sexually violated by this dangerous female kachina.

The young boys who were with us then said something in Hopi which caused great laughter. Mae hesitantly translated that these young, uninitiated boys had mistaken me in my dark coat for the Popo Pu Mana and described what their reactions had been. The irony of this did not escape me, for I could recall times in my life when I had played such a role. There was obvious relief among the women that I could accept an association with the Popo Pu Mana, for the Hopi women have not yet disowned that dark sexual power that is an innate part of their being, even though in their religious ceremonies sexuality as a spiritual force is downplayed in deference to the white people who attend. My obvious enjoyment at the confusion of identities opened the way for a far greater acceptance of me by the Hopi women. It was as if I had passed a small initiation test.

I found very impressive the Hopis' instinctual awareness of the implicit danger of "a man's not paying attention" to the castrating, dark aspect of the feminine. Fortunately, the work I had done toward the integration of my own psychic depths allowed me a degree of objectivity in relating to the primitive energy expressed in this and other Hopi rituals. The Hopi world still exists within an undifferentiated state of uroboric wholeness. In order to relate to that reality I had to be able to translate the mythic drama of the Hopi into the more conscious framework of my own psychology. The Hopi accept naively and simply humankind's need to identify and serve the gods whose powers impinge on human lives. This acceptance reflects my more differentiated experience of the collective unconscious as an objective reality that, in my own way, I must recognize and honor.

Finding a personal welcome in a culture immersed in the spirit of the Great Mother energized the wellsprings of my own creative depths which, in turn, helped heal my split between the masculine and feminine archetypes within. To the degree that these deep psychic wounds find healing in the individuation process, a legitimate base of age-old wisdom becomes available from which one can draw in both personal and professional interactions. My relationship with the Hopi people has enhanced my sense of responsibility and awe for the nature deities that are both accepted and honored in the kachina rituals.

Conclusion

Donald F. Sandner
San Francisco, California, USA
Society of Jungian Analysts
of Northern California

My work with the Navaho of the southwestern United States has allowed me to see the archetypal spectrum from another cultural viewpoint. In Navaho mythology the archetypes are set forth clearly, just as Jung described them theoretically: the Great Mother, the Sun Father, the Trickster (coyote), divine animals, the ubiquitous snake, the story of creation through four wombs in the earth, the hero's journey, the initiatory process of death and rebirth. From this completely independent source – in no conceivable way connected to Jung – the whole stellar archetypal background is confirmed and, indeed, linked closely to the practical business of living.

Here also the entire mythology of shamanism has been envisioned by an ancient lineage of seers, and made visible in the form of exactly reproducible sandpaintings. These sand paintings – intuitive psychograms of a highly abstract order – fascinated me initially, and still do. Seeing them is like looking through a telescope to see a distant galaxy whirling in space. The more I work with the paintings, the more they awaken the deeper layers of my psyche. They depict a dynamism of the soul, which it has become my life's work to unravel.

The Navaho's world is wholly alive and vibrant; in it the cultural path of individuation is allied with the great events of nature. The clouds, the winds, the mountains, the thunder are markers on the soul's journey; the goal of the path is total absorption in the plenitude of the natural world.

In my analytic practice this absorption has carried over into a deeper appreciation of the healing power of the natural psyche as it is invoked in ritual. In our culture we focus intensely on technical means to deal with regression and transference problems. The Navaho system of healing pays no attention to personal psychology but invokes at once the archetypal process of death and rebirth or, stated another way, immediate submergence of the ego into a power greater than itself. The two systems come together where, as Jung has shown in the *Psychology of the Transference* (CW16), such a power is also at the heart of the transference/countertransference.

But I found a more personal meaning in my relationship with the Navaho through the medicine man, Natani Tso. He worked with me closely and cooperatively and he was a great teacher, even through the awkwardness of back-and-forth translation. In some way his relationship with me in the discussions of Navaho chants and prayers resulted in my taking the Father out of the sky and bringing him down to the earth, or my finding him there. It was only after Natani Tso's death in 1978 that I realized how much his being was a part of my learning – not only about Navaho mythology, but how to grow older with dignity and vitality. When I think of how I would like to grow old, and how I would like to die, it is his image that smiles shrewdly and beckons the way.

As this workshop has shown, knowing a foreign culture is an endless process of amplification of one's inner life, and a continuing contribution to its eventual completion in the natural Self that gave it birth.

Jung and Anti-Semitism (Workshop)

Opening Remarks

Jerome Bernstein
Washington, District of Columbia, USA
C.G. Jung Analysts Association
of the Greater Washington, D.C.
Metropolitan Area

When my book (Bernstein, 1989) was published, it was reviewed in the Los Angeles *Times*. The opening lines of that review were:

> Jung was – to put the best face on it – confused by the politics of his day. In Nazism he glimpsed an ecstatic Wotan; he babbled about the creative Aryan unconscious and the inferior Jewish psyche. (July 2, 1989)

The reviewer, Russell Jacoby, went on to ridicule various parts of my book. His antipathy for Jung, Jung's shadow, and also the brilliance of Jung's thought – which Jacoby could not grasp – caused him to use my book for Jung-bashing. I felt smeared with Jung's shadow. The value of my book as a new model for looking at superpower conflict and the collective unconscious, as it manifests at the macro level of international relations, was denigrated as well. So much for those who say that the issue of Jung's anti-Semitism is history and has no relevancy in the context of the contemporary *Zeitgeist*.

I am not presenting here my views about Jung and his alleged anti-Semitism; other contributors explore that question. Rather, I will tell you how this workshop came to be and describe what I see as a spiritual and intellectual awakening that has germinated and is unfolding within our Jungian community.

In the Congress program the workshop was entitled "Jung and Nazism." I changed it to "Jung and Anti-Semitism" because, after reviewing the literature – including the proceedings of the New York conference on "Lingering Shadows" – I found no credible evidence to support allegations that Jung was a Nazi sympathizer, whereas there was substantial evidence of an anti-Semitic attitude in Jung. I define "anti-Semitism" as "a personal prejudicial attitude or behavior toward Jews as individuals or as a group."

For me this story begins with my personal analysis in the early 1970s. When I first heard the assertion that Jung was anti-Semitic, I was dismayed. I asked my analyst about it. With great authority he said that there was no truth to the charge, that it was slanderous. At most, Jung – in the genesis of his theories of archetypes and the collective unconscious – had become psychically infected, momentarily fascinated with the archetype. My analyst's being Jewish, and having had dealings with Jung himself, put the issue to rest – I thought.

The next chapter for me was at the 1983 Congress in Jerusalem. A memorable spontaneous meeting took place one evening to discuss "the emotional impact of a meeting in the City of Jerusalem." About a third of those present were Jews, about a third Germans and about a third others. The meeting soon turned into a highly emotional connection between Germans and Jews. We talked about fear, about guilt, about victims, about grief and about loss. There were many tears. I remember my shock at hearing one analyst refer to Jung as anti-Semitic – two or three times, matter-of-factly. Most disturbing of all, for me, was that no one challenged his assertions. One analyst even mentioned "pro-Nazi leanings" and again no one challenged such a shocking statement. Those words lingered with me a long while. I did not know what to think about these allegations. My projections onto Jung were assaulted, if not cracked.

The group wanted the rest of the Congress to know that an important event had occurred that evening. I was designated, along with a German woman, to report to the group at the next morning's plenary session. To my dismay the request to make such a report was met with angry opposition by a segment of the Israeli delegation. I was subjected personally to assaults on my character as a Jew. I had become a traitor to my own people, it was said. I was astonished – although I did understand – at the controversy in which I found myself. I was hurt profoundly by the attack on my personal integrity. My hurt was deepened because, as a child, I had been stoned because of my Jewishness. This time, in Jerusalem, the "stones" were thrown by Jews, whose statements took on some of the ugliness of anti-Semitism. In the end, a five-minute report was given at the next day's plenary session, but not without vociferous objections by some participants and a confrontational vote on the floor whether to bring the matter before the Congress.

I was shaken by that experience. Only in the last year and a half have I realized that part of what I encountered in Jerusalem was Jung's – and our, yours and mine – unresolved shadow problem. I did not attend the Berlin Congress, but I noted with some dismay from the Congress Proceedings that there was little said about the specific issue of Jung's alleged anti-Semitism and pro-Nazi leanings; not a single paper dealt with it at a Congress whose theme was "the archetypal shadow in a split world." (I have since learned from Gustav Dreifuss of Israel and Ana Springer of Germany that there was an informal workshop on the topic at the Berlin Congress.) Thus, I suggested that there be a workshop on Jung and anti-Semitism at this Congress.

Independent of my proposal for this workshop Stephen Martin, a Philadelphia analyst, and Aryeh Maidenbaum, Executive Director of the C. G. Jung Foundation of New York, organized for March 1989 a three-evening program entitled "Lingering Shadows: Jungians, Freudians, and Anti-Semitism." (Maidenbaum's paper in this chapter reports on that meeting.)

This workshop was planned to address the important historical question of Jung's behavior between 1933 and his death, but not only that. To limit our focus to historical events will be to argue only at the level of Jung's attackers, one of whom, a respected psychiatrist, went as far as to compare Jung with Joseph Mengele. (Mengele was a Nazi physician who designed and implemented some of the most sadistic and grisly "experiments" conceivable on concentration camp victims.)

The participants in this workshop have been wounded by this shadow problem and by a man we all respect in some way. Some of us displace our hurt through anger toward Jung; some of us blindly defend Jung, to avoid our hurt and anger. Some of us prefer to discuss Jung's alleged anti-Semitism without taking a deeper look at our own prejudices, and some of us would prefer not to deal with the matter at all.

I propose a question. It is one thing to address Jung's shadow in the 1930s in the context of a world radically different and much less aware than our own. But what can we, as Analytical Psychologists, say of ourselves with our claim to greater consciousness and sensitivity to shadow issues, that it has taken until 1989 to take our dirty laundry out of the hamper and to examine it in depth?

This is a workshop. The intent is for all of us to process our thoughts, feelings, emotions and blindnesses. We have been and remain wounded by this issue and the only way to heal is to look into the darkness that hurts, and to explore together what light we can find and extricate from that darkness.

[The workshop was attended by 150 people the first day, 250 the second. These numbers did not permit the kind of workshop process I had envisioned.]

REFERENCE

Bernstein, J. (1989). *Power and Politics: The Psychology of Soviet-American Partnership*. Boston: Shambhala.

Report from New York

Aryeh Maidenbaum
New York, New York, USA
New York Association
for Analytical Psychology

In March 1989 the C.G. Jung Foundation of New York, of which I am Executive Director, held a conference entitled "Lingering Shadows: Jungians, Freudians, and Anti-Semitism." In arranging it, Stephen Martin – a Philadelphia Jungian analyst – and I attempted to approach the problem, which is undeniably subjective, as objectively as possible. It was important to us all at the Foundation that the conference be conducted on a serious, scholarly level and be perceived by Jungians and non-Jungians alike as neither a whitewash of Jung nor a witch-hunt that would polarize our Jungian community. I believe we were successful in these objectives and can look back with pride at the consistently high level of presentations. Along with historians, psychoanalysts, and other scholars, several Jungian analysts participated: E.C. Whitmont, Andrew Samuels, Hans Dieckmann, Ann Ulanov, Thomas Kirsch, Philip Zabriskie and Foundation President Jeffrey Satinover, who served as moderator. These analysts' presentations and interactions with the academic community will help us all, ultimately, better to understand Jung the man and how his psychology and ideas can shed light on a very complicated issue.

For me, while presenting a paper for the first time at an international Jungian conference is a moving moment, this particular presentation was not one I was eager to give. It requires facing a topic that I did not want to deal with, regarding a man whose ideas about psychology have played a most important part in my life. I come from a strong Orthodox Jewish background and to this day Jewish history, culture and tradition are a paramount aspect of my world. Jung's psychology helped me to reconnect with my Jewish roots, making me a better Jew – thanks to Rivkah Kluger, a one-time Zurich analyst who was close to Jung. Thus, to confront publicly this negative aspect of Jung's life is not an easy task. Nevertheless, both personally and professionally, I see this problem as one that must be brought to the light of consciousness or we shall suffer the consequences of denial and repression. It is in this spirit that I present some of the material from our conference.

I cannot do justice to the many fine papers with their varied nuances and psychological subtleties. A few examples must suffice.

Andrew Samuels identified parallels between Jung's attitude that Freud and Adler advocated a Jewish, leveling psychology which undermined national psychological differences, and Hitler's negative view of Jews as denationalizing their host nations. Samuels' paper elsewhere in this chapter spells out these parallels.

Challenging the image of a passive and uninterested political Jung, Samuels suggested that we acknowledge Jung's power ambitions both in his break with Freud and in his assumption in the 1930s of the presidency of the General Medical Society for Psychotherapy.

Ann Ulanov developed the theme of the "double cross" as a metaphor that can be used in understanding Jung's psyche as well as the phenomenon of scapegoating, the primary mover in anti-Semitism. Jung's strengths, she concluded, did not prevent him from getting caught in his own shadow. However, this fact can alert us to the necessity of withdrawing projections of evil that we have made on those around us, culturally as well as individually.

Micha Neumann – son of Erich Neumann as well as President of the Israel Psychiatric Association and a leading Freudian analyst – brought letters never before available between his father and Jung; the letters made clear that Jung's "silence" was a disappointment to Erich Neumann (an Israeli Jungian analyst).

Micha Neumann concluded that, while his father never stopped loving Jung personally, the feeling persisted that Jung himself – as well as his followers – never dealt adequately with this "Jewish question," and by any objective definition today would be considered anti-Semitic.

From my own "sensate" approach in researching this conference, several conclusions emerged:

1. Overall, Jung was neither a Nazi sympathizer nor a rabid, overtly anti-Semitic person. Such accusations are false and either unknowingly ignorant or maliciously slanderous.

2. Jung, as a consequence of accepting the Presidency of the General Medical Society for Psychotherapy, was able to reorganize that predominately German group and, in theory, to enable Jewish German psychotherapists to join a newly formed international organization – of which, also, he was President. The number of Jewish psychotherapists who actually joined the new international organization is not known; it is a question that calls for investigation.

3. Jung gave help to many Jewish people – both personally and professionally – throughout his life, including the period in question. For example, when Aniela Jaffé was ill, Jung insisted on paying personally her medical and hotel bills. Consider also his close relationships with Jewish Jungians Rivkah Kluger, Siegmund Hurwitz, James and Hilde Kirsch, Gerhard Adler, and many others.

4. However, Jung was genuinely impressed, for a time, with the resurgence of German nationalism, as embodied in the Nazi movement of the early 1930s.

5. Jung had his own opportunistic agenda of promoting his ideas and himself. The time has come to acknowledge this. From international activity to the formation of Jungian institutes Jung was interested, understandably, in seeing his work brought to a greater audience and recognized more widely. At times, especially in the 1930s, his own shadow may have prevailed in his quest for influence and recognition.

6. Finally, as Jung himself said: "The greater the light, the greater the shadow." Jung, being indeed a "great light," had a

large shadow. Some of it concerned his negative attitude toward Jews – on a cultural more than a personal level – unconscious perhaps, but real. As a result, he aroused animosity from many people by picking an unfortunate moment in history to discuss the Jewish psyche. He himself knew very little about Jewish history, tradition, mysticism, or even as he put it, "cultural form." Undoubtedly, as has been mentioned often, his multi-faceted and ambivalent attitude toward Jews was connected to his personal experience with Freud and his followers. Nevertheless, Jung shared the prejudices of many Christian Europeans, quite apart from Freud and the psychoanalytic movement.

There is nothing startling in such conclusions. Even the most loyal Jungians must acknowledge and accept them if they examine Jung's writings and secondary source material. Jung's coming from a culture where anti-Semitism flourished, combined with his personal, highly emotional and complex – in all senses of the word – broken connection with Freud, helped lay the groundwork for Jung's difficulty with Jews on a collective level. No amount of explaining can condone some of his culturally stereotypical, negative pronouncements about Jews. Psychologically and symbolically we must accept the fact that, as Hans Dieckmann of Berlin put it so aptly, it is particularly dark at the base of a lighthouse. Jung, while resembling a lighthouse in the scope of his psychology, had a shadow commensurate with this light.

What has obscured the issue for many of us has been Jung's own significant, warm connection to many individuals who were of Jewish origin. For, notwithstanding Jung's private, personal connections, he exhibited a negative attitude, if not outright prejudice, toward Jews on a collective level.

This prejudice was borne out by an additional discovery that emerged through Martin's and my research, a discovery that is most difficult to ignore or to explain away: a secret appendix to the By-Laws of the Analytical Psychology Club of Zurich, limiting the number of Jews who could be accepted as members of the Club. With a membership of some 50 analysands of Jung and those active in Jung's circle, the Club was a group that met regularly to hear lectures, discuss topics of Jungian interest – and to socialize. Jung had no official capacity in the Club but he did attend meetings; it is safe to assume that policy decisions had his acceptance if not blessing.

The document was dated very late in the Hitler era: December 1944. It stated that, when possible, members of the Jewish faith should not exceed 10 percent and limited "guests" (a separate category of membership which bestowed attendance but not voting privileges) to a 25 percent figure. This appendix was signed by members of the Executive Committee and apparently not circulated to the Club members. The President of the Club at that time and for many years was Toni Wolff who, along with Linda Fierz-David, appears to have been the prime mover behind this restriction. (Wolff and Fierz-David were analysts and close associates of Jung.) Naturally, the question that must be answered was whether Jung knew about this restriction. It is clear that he did.

To us, with the admitted perspective and safety of 45 years' time-lapse, none of the explanations put forth are acceptable, though they do provide some psychological insight into the thought processes of the signatories. It is important to put some perspective on our findings, specifically the additional research that is needed before drawing definitive conclusions.

Nevertheless, foremost is not the question of whether Jung knew, but to what extent he was culpable. The fact that he knew seems indisputable. Almost every person interviewed acknowledged that Jung was aware of the quota then in effect. Indeed, the elimination of the Jewish quota took place only in 1950, five years after the end of the Second World War. Thus, although the nuances – as is usual with understanding a man as complex as Jung – are not simple, the facts still speak for themselves. Given Jung's history with the "Jewish issue," and coming after his 1946 meeting with Rabbi Leo Baeck (a leading Jewish scholar) where he acknowledged "slipping up," one would have expected him to be more conscious by that time.

Where do we go from here? For me, personally, the very act of raising this issue to the light of day within our own international community is a healthy one and has begun an important process.

Wounds covered up and buried do not heal; those that are uncovered and exposed to the light of day have a chance for healing. I trust and hope that the publications from the conference in New York and this workshop will contribute a great deal toward dispersing the lingering shadows surrounding Jung and his attitude toward the Jewish people.

[The full eight hours of conference proceedings – together with conference handouts and bibliography – can be obtained on either audio or video tape through the C. G. Jung Foundation of New York. A book is planned, using this material and reflecting some of the several years of preparation and discussions that preceded it. Interviews conducted during the course of researching this topic will be made available for archival and scholarly purposes.]

Jung and Anti-Semitism

Marga Speicher
New York, New York, USA
New York Association for Analytical Psychology

Why am I a panelist in a workshop that explores Jung's relation to anti-Semitism? One of the major struggles in my life has centered around the issue of Germany in World War II, of Nazism, and of the anti-Semitism that exploded so virulently and led to holocaust and genocide. Fate put me in the middle of this thorny issue. Thus, I bring a personal dimension to the topic: what coming to terms with Nazism and anti-Semitism, with the collective shadow, has meant for me as a person and as a Jungian analyst.

I was born in Germany in 1934 and grew up in a Catholic family in a small industrial town. In my family I was told of the Nazis as a godless regime and of their opposition to religious practice. My father was censured for being a practicing Catholic. I experienced the police state directly. As a Catholic, I prayed during the Good Friday liturgy "for the conversion of the unbelieving Jews," as all Catholics did until the reforms of Vatican II. I knew of Jews only in an abstract sense, not as individual persons.

Immediately after the war, in 1945, we were inundated with news of the horrible occurrences of the holocaust. The textbooks issued by the Allied Army of Occupation had stories of concentration camps and death camps; these stories profoundly marked my 11-year-old psyche. Nevertheless, the subsequent years of my schooling were notable for the lack of study of Nazism, anti-

Semitism, and the holocaust. From what I understand now, typical in German education in the late 1940s and early 1950s was the silence on then-recent history. The focus was on events of the postwar period: the establishment and workings of democracy and the movement toward European unity.

I went to the United States in 1956 and spent the next 15 years in South Texas acquiring a professional education and working as a psychotherapist. After I moved to New York City in 1972, life forced me to confront squarely my German background, anti-Semitism, the holocaust – issues of collective shadow and collective guilt that I had managed to avoid, contents that I had split off and had let sink into the unconscious where they were wreaking havoc with my life.

A concern for dealing at a deeper level with blockages in my life led me at that point into another analytic exploration. New York City, with its large Jewish population, where the annual Holocaust Remembrance Week is observed in synagogues but also enters public consciousness, provided the outer stimulus for the confrontation that I had avoided for so long.

Jung's 1945, essay "After the Catastrophe" (CW10), was profoundly meaningful to me. He wrote at length about collective guilt: German collective guilt and European collective guilt. And he called for acknowledgment of the psychic participation in the fall into shadow, lest a person "compound his collective guilt by the sin of unconsciousness" (CW10, par. 404). He spoke of the need for "a proper *rite de sortie*, a solemn admission of guilt" so that we can "escape the contaminating touch of evil" (CW10, par. 411).

In my inner confrontation, it became essential for me: (a) on a personal level, to recall as much as I could of the years I spent in Germany during and after the war; (b) on a wider level, to know as much as I could of Nazism, anti-Semitism, holocaust and genocide; (c) most importantly, to come to a personal stance in relation to collective issues.

My personal confrontation with Nazism, anti-Semitism, holocaust and genocide occurred about 30 years after the war's end, when I was about 40 years old. It was a late confrontation and I have asked myself: where was I, psychically, during those 30 years? Details to that answer are not relevant here today but the fact of the delay needs to be noted. A few years after this confrontation, I married a Jewish man. Within that important relationship, life thrust me closer to the experience of the Jewish minority in Western civilization.

When I look at the topic, "Jung and anti-Semitism," I see an odd similarity between the course that awareness of collective shadow issues took in my life and the course that our communal awareness of Jung's shadow issues has taken thus far and where it is today: a long period of silence; an awakening to the issue at meetings in Jerusalem and Berlin where outer environments contributed to the raising of questions; the conference in New York this year, aptly called "Lingering Shadows," (see paper by Maidenbaum in this chapter) and today's workshop.

What was Jung's position in regard to anti-Semitism and the Nazi regime? I have reviewed much of the available material in his *Collected Works* and his *Letters* as well as preparatory material for the New York conference. It is my belief at present that Jung shared in the anti-Semitism that was rampant throughout Europe and that his position toward Nazism in its early years was naively apolitical and fed by overly-optimistic views of the archetypal energies that he saw activated.

We can consider Jung's anti-Semitism in relation to his family history, to the culture of his time, and especially to the intellectual environment at the turn of the century. We can see also how the conflicts with Freud and the disappointment, hurt, and anger after their parting contributed to his ethnocentric emphasis on the differentiation between Jewish and Germanic psychology which pervaded his statements of the 1920s and early 1930s. We can see, further, how Jung, in the 1930s, seized the opportunity to focus on his contributions to psychotherapy that were acceptable in the Germany of that decade when Freudian views had fallen into political disfavor, irrespective of their merit.

I do not believe that Jung was anti-Semitic on a person-to-person basis nor that he held conscious anti-Semitic views. Jung's orientation was firmly German-Swiss and Protestant Christian.

In the underground waters of that orientation there flowed ethnocentrism and anti-Semitism which remained unconscious, in shadow, but which influenced his views and actions. The ethnocentrism and anti-Semitism in Jung form a background attitude similar to the racism and ethnocentrism of many people today who are consciously neither racist nor ethnocentric.

Looking at Germany in the early 1930s Jung focused on the archetypal dynamic of Wotan as underlying the nationalistic stirrings. He valued this awakening and held hopes that it would yield long-term positive contributions. It is easy for any of us at any time not to see clearly the earthly reality, when we focus on archetypal energies.

Thus, in the 1930s, Jung fell into the shadow, into the anti-Semitism lurking in the psychic underground waters, and into the fascination with the potential of an archetypal awakening in Germany. He also fell into the shadow of being apolitical. He said repeatedly he was a physician and not a political man. He overlooked or ignored the fact that he lived in a body politic, like it or not, and that every action or non-action makes a political statement, overtly or covertly. This is especially evident in the life of a prominent person, and Jung was a prominent person.

I know that there was censorship and fear in Switzerland, especially in the 1940s, as the Swiss tried to stay uninvolved in the European conflicts. Nonetheless, I wish that Jung had spoken out strongly against anti-Semitism. I wish Pius XII had spoken out. I wish leaders in the United States had spoken out and had acted firmly and directly to aid persecuted groups in Germany and under German occupation. I am grateful for each person, prominent or unknown, who did speak out, as well as for each person in the underground and the Resistance who stood against the tide. Jung did not speak out clearly and publicly against anti-Semitism, because he fell into shadow. That is the painful human fact.

Jung defended himself vigorously against charges of anti-Semitism and acquiescence. In 1946, he published a long list of excerpts (CW10, pars. 458-87) out of his earlier writings to show how he had foreseen and warned against the eruptions in Europe.

He had seen and named the archetypal dynamics in their positive and negative aspects but he had not attended actively and publicly to the horrible human manifestations. It has been said: "Too much psychology, not enough political action." But we are all involved in the political world, by action or omission. Omission is also a political act.

Jung wrestled with the events of Nazism and of the holocaust. In 1945, he wrote: "While I was working on this article I noticed how churned up one still is in one's own psyche.... I must confess that no article has ever given me so much trouble, from a moral as well as a human point of view. I had not realized how much I myself was affected.... This inner identity or *participation mystique* with events in Germany has caused me to experience afresh how painfully wide is the scope of the psychological concept of *collective guilt*" (CW10, par. 402). One can read this essay as his way of acknowledging collective shadow and collective guilt that touched him also.

I do not know whether Jung ever wrestled with the anti-Semitism in his shadow. I have not seen an indication of such a struggle in anything I have read or heard. Rather, I have seen denial in his writings. What I miss in Jung is a clear acknowledgment that he had fallen into the shadow of anti-Semitism, of fascination with archetypal energies, of the apolitical stance. I wish he could have come to a clear, open acknowledgment of the fall into shadow. (We do not know what his private acknowledgment may have been.)

What is my relation as a Jungian analyst to Jung's shadow issues? The very same as for all shadow issues: to see them, know them, and name them; to acknowledge them as human and let them be what they are – shadow – without condoning or whitewashing or denying. That is the stance we take toward shadow: know it, name it, be with it, and then ask: How do I live with it? What does it require?

Jung died in 1961. World War II had ended 16 years earlier. The most questionable period in Jung's life was the early and mid-1930's, 10 years still earlier. The time has come when we as a Jungian community can see and name Jung's shadow issues of anti-Semitism, fascination with archetypal energies, the apolitical stance; the time also in which we can seek to understand the dynamics; and the time in which we can grow through this process. Why have we as a community – as distinguished from individuals, many of whom have struggled with these issues – stayed away from this process for so long? Where have we been, psychically, in the interim? Shadow issues claim to be recognized. When we block them out, a price has to be paid.

We must ask ourselves continually: (a) Where do the underground waters of ethnocentrism, anti-Semitism, racism flow at the present time? (b) When and where does our recognition of archetypal energies turn into fascination and cause us to lose sight of earthly reality? (c) Where do we claim an apolitical stance in a rather routine manner without due consideration of the impact of that position?

It is important that an exploration of Jung's fall into shadow lead us, on the one hand, to a better understanding of shadow, personal and archetypal, individual and collective and, on the other hand, to a better understanding of the ever-present pitfalls inherent in personal and communal life as well as of those inherent in the theoretical and philosophical positions we hold.

I close with Jung's words from "After the Catastrophe": "We must all open our eyes to the shadow who looms behind contemporary man.... It is indeed no small matter to know of one's own guilt and one's own evil, and there is certainly nothing to be gained by losing sight of one's shadow.... Anything that remains in the unconscious is incorrigible; psychological corrections can be made only in consciousness" (CW10, par. 440).

Jung and Anti-Semitism

Andrew Samuels
London, England Society of
Analytical Psychology

I begin with a few words about what I am not covering in this paper, so that it is clear what approaches to this subject I find less than satisfying. I do not make much use of psychobiography: the facts of Jung's inner and outer life, his dreams, his father complex, the scars of the break with Freud, his ambition, his shadow problem, his Swiss bourgeois mentality. Nor do I pay much attention to personal testimonies, designed to show that Jung could not have been anti-Semitic or, to the contrary, that he had a positive attitude to Jews and helped many Jews to develop a relationship with their Jewishness.

For a time, I worried that these omissions added up to a failure of feeling on my part. And even now I think we should not ignore Jung's experiences and others' experiences of Jung. But I have come to see that a true failure of feeling occurs when the personal dimension is given too much weight or used to close an awkward issue. There is a pressing need for feeling. *It is for us to get on with the work of mourning for Jung and with taking a critical and reflective psychological attitude to the theme of Jung and anti-Semitism.* If we do that job well, new possibilities will open for Analytical Psychology, both in its internal processes and in its relations with other groups.

In this paper I ask whether something in the heart or essence of Jung's thought made it inevitable that he would develop a kind of anti-Semitism. When Jung wrote about the Jews and Jewish psychology, was there something in his way of thinking that had to lead to anti-Semitism? If so, is this something to worry about?

My brief answer is "yes" to both. By exploring the matter deeply I hope that a form of reparation will ensue. This exploration of a bit of our past can provide ideas for our present renewal and future contribution. Many strengths and subtleties of Analytical Psychology could be lost because of the alleged Nazi collaboration and anti-Semitism, and because of the evident inability of many Jungians to react to such charges in an intelligent, humane way. This loss permits the Freudian establishment, and the rest of the civilized world, to continue to ignore Jung's pioneering contributions, and hence the work of post-Jungian Analytical Psychologists.

I turn my attention to the central matter, Adolf Hitler and his ideas about Jews. It is far too general and facile to see Hitler's theorizing about the Jews solely as racist. It is hard to disentangle his racial from his political ideas. The political dogma employs a racial perspective but Hitler's racism also had a political format, which used a nationalistic vocabulary and focused on the idea of the nation.

Hitler regarded all history as consisting of struggles between competing nations for living space and, eventually, for world domination. The Jews, according to Hitler, are a nation and participate in these struggles, but their first and only goal is world domination. They do not possess living space, an identifiable, geographical locality; they must have the world or nothing. Indeed, for Hitler the nationalism of the Jews is really "de-nationalism, the bastardization of other nations" (quoted in Graham, 1984). The Jewish nation achieves its goal of world domination by de-nationalizing existing states from within and imposing a homogeneous "Jewish" character on them – by "its" international capitalism and "its" equally international communism. Consequently, in Hitler's thinking, there is a struggle between wholesome nationhood and its corrupting enemy, the Jews.

Jung, too, was interested in the idea of the nation; he made innumerable references to "the psychology of the nation" and to the influence of a person's national background. He wrote that "the soil of every country holds (a) mystery ... there is a relationship of body to earth" (CW10, par. 19). For example, in 1918 Jung asserted that the skull and pelvis measurements of second generation American immigrants were becoming "Indianized" (CW10, par. 18). Thus, Jung was not thinking along racial lines, for the immigrants from Europe and the indigenous Indians come from different races. No. Living on American soil, being part of the American nation – these experiences exert profound physiological and psychological effects. "The foreign land ... has assimilated the conqueror," wrote Jung (CW10, par. 103). His argument is based not on race but on earth and culture as the matrix from which we evolve. Earth plus culture equals nation.

However, at the moment we introduce the idea of nation, depth psychology cannot remain uncontaminated by economic, social, political and historical factors. "Nation" is a construct of these factors, and a relatively modern one at that. For example, the German nation, as a recognizable cultural and political phenomenon, did not exist before the rise of Prussia at the end of the 18th century. If we analyze any nationalism, we find that there is much more involved than emphasis on the geographical unit. We find some kind of ethical expression, usually couched in comparative – and self-congratulatory – terms: our soldiers are the bravest, our family life is the finest, we have special rights, we have special responsibilities, we have a unique relationship to higher forces, our apple pie is the greatest, our upper lips the stiffest. In short, nationalism involves a form of psychological expression and self-characterization; therefore nationalism requires the services of psychologists.

It is my contention that, in Jung, nationalism found its psychologist. But in his role as a psychologist of nationhood, a psychologist who lent his authority to nationalism, Jung's pan-psychism (his phrase) ran riot. I refer to the tendency to see all outer events in terms of inner dynamics. Pan-psychism led Jung to claim that the nation is a "personified concept that corresponds in reality only to a specific nuance of the individual psyche.... [The nation] is nothing but an inborn character" (CW10, par. 921). There is no evidence that Jung's concept of nation is metaphorical.

It is certainly not my intention to make a straightforward identification of Hitler's ideas and Jung's. But if we go on to explore the place of the Jews in Jung's mental ecology, to find out where they are situated in his view of the world, then the juxtaposition of the two points of view takes on a profound significance. For my aim is to see whether there is anything in the underlying structure and assumptions of Jung's thought that must lead him into the kind of anti-Semitism that we should be concerned about.

My perception is that the ideas of nation and of national difference form a fulcrum between the Hitlerian phenomenon and Jung's Analytical Psychology. For, as a psychologist of nations, Jung, too, would feel threatened by the Jews, this strange so-called nation without a land, without cultural forms – that is, without national cultural forms – of its own and hence, in Jung's words of 1933, requiring a "host nation" (CW10, par. 353).

What threatened Jung can be illuminated by inquiring closely into what he meant when he wrote, as he often did, of "Jewish psychology." His use of the term was dramatically inconsistent. There is Jewish psychology meaning the typical psychological characteristics of a typical Jewish person. Jung argued that we are all affected by our backgrounds: we have all kinds of prejudices and assumptions; "every child knows that differences exist" (CW10, par. 1029).

One can agree or disagree with Jung's various statements about typical Jews, but there is a second use by Jung of this term "Jewish psychology;" it has another and more provocative implication. He was referring to systems of psychology developed by Jews such as Freud and Adler, systems which claim universal applicability and truth. Such a psychology is a "levelling psychology" (CW10, par. 1029) in that it undermines the idea that there are psychological differences between groups of people such as nations. Such a psychology is wrong to apply "Jewish categories ... indiscriminately" (CW10, par. 354) and we are tempted to make this unpardonable mistake [of] accepting the conclusions of a Jewish psychology as generally valid" (CW7, par. 240n).

Jung was saying that Jewish Psychoanalysis attacks the idea of psychological differences between nations. Jewish Psychoanalysis therefore occupies a place in Jung's mind, analogous to the place occupied in Hitler's mind by Jewish international capitalism and Jewish international communism. The great fears are, respectively, "levelling" and "de-nationalizing." Jung and Hitler did not say the same things about the Jews, of course, but the leveling aim of Jewish psychology and the de-nationalizing aim of Jewish political and economic activity represent a similar kind of threat. Thus Jung and Hitler developed similar obsessions.

For Hitler, the form was an obsession with Jewish "spirit," functioning as a pestilential bacillus, undermining the very idea of nation. For Jung, the form was an obsession with a Jewish psychology, capable of being imposed on all other ethnic and national psychologies, bringing them all down to the same level.

I hope that all of us in Analytical Psychology can work together on the meaning of these reflections for our common humanity, our intellectual integrity, and our identity as Jungian analysts. For the future, it would help if we were to cease expanding the national boundaries of the psychological kingdom and try to work cooperatively with our colleagues in the social sciences. This means stopping the abuse of our authority in advancing definitions of the typical innate psychology of this or that group – Jews, Germans, African-Americans, homosexuals, women. We should think seriously of abandoning Jung's method here. What he did was to assemble lists of characteristics, taken as inborn, and use the lists to make a definition: of Jew, of German the same method that he used to define the psychological attributes of the sexes. Jung's emphasis is upon what a Jew is, not upon what being a Jew is like. The emphasis is on defining or pre-defining difference, not on the experience or living out of difference. Just as with the sexes, we find Jung applying his ethos of complementarity so that any two opposite lists combined produce a wonderful-sounding "wholeness." In Jung's writing, Jew and German seem to constitute two halves of a whole: rational, sophisticated, erudite city-dweller complementing irrational, energetic, earthy peasant-warrior.

If we were to abandon Jung's method, we might be able to revalue what he was trying to do. For, alongside the many problems with Jung's ideas about nation, race and religion, there are the seeds of a marvelously useful approach to difference. Even if Jung's method and ideology are suspect, his intuition of the importance of exploring differences remains intact. We can preserve a connection to Jung's intuition of the importance of difference – but unhindered by dependence on complementarity.

By abandoning complementarity we could ally ourselves to marginal or minority groups, contributing our limited but profound expertise to the achievement of their goals. Analysts are good at helping people to experience consciously what they implicitly know but have not yet thought or felt. We could employ our analytic skills and our capacity to work with the inexpressible in an exploration of the psychological experience of being Jew, German, African-American, homosexual, woman, man. We could assist in getting behind the defensive stereotypes imposed by a threatened dominant culture as we probe the nature of difference itself. It is truly subversive work, breaking the modern taboo on the discussion of national and racial difference. But it has to be done.

Differences among nations, races, classes or between sexes must not be pre-defined. The analyst is not an authority or teacher who has *a priori* knowledge of the psychological implications of the analysand's ethnic and cultural background. Rather, the analyst is a mediator who enables the analysand to experience and express his or her own characteristics. Such an analyst can revalue and support Jung's impassioned rejection of the imposition of the psychology of one group on another. We Jungians have reparations to make and we have much to offer.

POSTSCRIPT

On the second day of this workshop, I expressed some thoughts about how Analytical Psychology might proceed in the future, and was asked to append them to my paper:

1. We must come to terms with the limits of psychology as an explanatory tool when considering complicated social and cultural phenomena.
2. We Jungians must be very careful before we label characteristics as innate: whether gender, race, or nation.
3. Nevertheless, Jung's insights into the importance of difference are important.
4. We must beware of the seductive power of romantic language: words like mystery, blood, earth.
5. We need to cooperate actively with colleagues in the social sciences: economics, political science, sociology.
6. We need to engage politically as individuals as well as under the rubric of "analysts." Why should we have a privileged position? Let the groups we join find out that we are analysts and, if they can see a special use for analytic skills, utilize those skills. "On-high" attitudes cause difficulty when analysts trot out the nostrums of the consulting room, derived from work with individuals, as panaceas for social ills.

REFERENCE

Graham, S. (1984). *Hitler, Germans, and the "Jewish Question."* Princeton, NJ: Princeton University Press.

Opening Remarks for Day Two

Jerome Bernstein

The focus of today's session is: how do we deal with our wound and where do we go from here? Aryeh Maidenbaum and Marga Speicher described in different ways the wound we have experienced as a result of Jung's anti-Semitism. Andrew Samuels pointed to a direction, beyond Jung the man, for Jungians to make a greater commitment to working with "minority" groups. Now I have some personal comments.

We cannot move beyond Jung the man – although we can make some of the other commitments Samuels would like us to make – before we process our wound. These commitments include conscious mourning and forgiving, or refusing to forgive what we cannot forgive. For Jung has been a father figure to us all. How would we react if any of us were to discover, after his death, that our personal father was anti-Semitic or had made statements that indicated even a brief enchantment with Nazism? What would we say to a client in our consulting room who had such a problem?

It takes time to absorb the shock of profound betrayal. Marga Speicher testified that it took her at least 40 years to come to terms with anti-Semitism in her own country. It has taken Jungians collectively over 50 years to begin that process in earnest.

There is danger in moving too quickly from this process. The next generation of Jungians will be removed considerably from the history, the emotions surrounding it, and from Jung the man. It will be easier for them to depart from the work that this issue calls on all of us to do on ourselves – individually and collectively – in favor of dry chapters in biographies of Jung.

Most of us call ourselves Jungian analysts; we carry the name of our intellectual and, yes, our spiritual father, in our very identities as professionals. When someone alludes to Jung's anti-Semitism and to his alleged Nazism, it wounds me personally, as it might if that person were talking about my personal father.

And what do we do when an outsider charges that Jung was anti-Semitic and pro-Nazi and, as a result, discredits the entire body of Analytical Psychology? I have never known how to deal with that problem in a way that feels fully satisfactory to me. I have seen others rush to Jung's defense, or argue the details of how anti-Semitic he was or he wasn't or how he could have sounded pro-Nazi, but really wasn't. Or perhaps we could ignore the question altogether and just press forward with the development of our craft and let the issue recede into the background.

Ignoring the question is neither possible nor desirable. Non-Jungians will not let the issue recede and will continue to reject the body of Analytical Psychology, as they continue to appropriate as their own its most fundamental and penetrating concepts and ideas.

But there is a bigger question here. We are all, in one sense or another, healers. And there is something to be healed here. Guggenbühl-Craig, in his important book, *Power in the Helping Professions*, cautioned Jungians about becoming inflated with the symbol of the wounded healer. He was right. That symbol suggests a healing empathy that derives from personal woundedness. Paradoxically, it suggests a psyche and a soul that wounds out of its own deprivation and woundedness. Jung was a wounded healer who sometimes wounded those he healed, just as each of us has wounded someone we were trying to heal. I believe that until we address this wounding we will carry a collective depression and guilt in relation to it.

At the same time, we are here because we feel more healed by Jung than wounded by him. If I were confronted today by one of Jung's detractors, I would say, "Yes, it does appear that Jung was anti-Semitic in some respects. He was wrong in that. It wounded him and it has wounded me. I have come to be able to forgive him for that, as I have some others, and I continue to mourn its truth.

But I must tell you too that he has given to me – and I think to the world – much more than he has wounded us. And I would reflect back to you your own narrowness on this issue and your investment in throwing out the body of Analytical Psychology because its founder was a human being with an ugly shadow – like many other great human beings."

There is another fact that is worth mentioning. Within a family, a wound to the family by one of the parents often has the effect of drawing the rest of the family together into a closer union and bond. I felt that emerging in the room yesterday.

These comments are some of my personal reflections on yesterday's workshop session. They are not intended to serve as guidelines for today's session.

Jung and Anti-Semitism

Thomas Kirsch
San Francisco, California, USA
Society of Jungian Analysts
of Northern California

A charge of anti-Semitism has been leveled at Jung since the rise of Nazism in the 1930s. This charge is used by his detractors to discount his theories of the psyche. His followers have defended him, saying that there is nothing to these rumors. Every time the subject seems to have died, a new generation resurrects it with the idea of getting to the truth of the matter. This is the first time that the subject has been discussed at an IAAP Congress, and it is good that we are doing it. However, I caution us not to become obsessed with the topic.

I am asked often to speak on this topic; I am Jewish and both my parents were in analysis with Jung during the time that Jung was allegedly anti-Semitic. My parents left Germany in 1933, going to Palestine, England, and finally to Los Angeles. They had contact with Jung from 1929 until his death in 1961. I must say that my parents never felt a trace of anti-Semitism in their personal dealings with him. They always felt that, because of their experience of the unconscious and Jung, they were able to understand what was going on in Nazi Germany and to leave. They had many Jewish colleagues during that period who had similar experiences. I do not believe that friends and colleagues such as Erich Neumann, Aniela Jaffé and Gerhard Adler would have stayed with Jung had they experienced him as being anti-Jewish.

But Jung's attitude toward Jews was not simple. On the one hand he held the typical collective European prejudice of the time, seeing the Jew as the scapegoat. This prejudice was endemic. On the other hand, he had been an early champion of Freud and Psychoanalysis at a time when it was unpopular to be so. He also had a strong erotic countertransference to Sabina Spielrein – a Russian Jew – preceding his relationship with Toni Wolff. Also, Jung seemed never able to work out satisfactorily his relationship to Freud. In a recent interview (Boe, 1989) John Freeman, the journalist who interviewed Jung in the film "Face to Face," stated that, in subsequent visits, Jung would always talk further about his relationship with Freud. It remained unresolved for Jung all his life.

But how does the issue of Jung's alleged anti-Semitism affect us today? How is it when I am with an analysand? Does it make me feel that I am less a Jungian because Jung had some complicated, perhaps terribly negative feelings towards Jews? No. It makes absolutely no difference and the thought never crosses my mind. On the other hand, I am often reminded in a session that I am Jewish; there is a debt of gratitude that through Jung and my analysis – by which I mean the understanding of complexes in a transpersonal archetypal sense – I have come to a deeper understanding of my Jewish roots and my relationship to other cultures and religions.

Let me give you two examples. The first was from early in my practice. A man came to me as a general psychiatrist, not as a Jungian. At the end of the first hour he asked me if I was Christian. I thought for a moment and then answered: No, I was not a Christian, but I did have a respectful attitude toward religion and religious phenomena. Analysis had prepared me to manage this conflict; although I was uncomfortable saying it at the time, what I had said also felt all right. The man seemed satisfied with my response.

The second example, which was more difficult, occurred with a long-term analytic case. He was non-Jewish and his parents had been anti-Semitic during his youth. As part of his rage in the transference, he expressed how he hated to pay me because he hated to have his money supporting Zionist causes. He knew that I was Jewish and imagined me to be a heavy supporter of Israel.

He identified unconsciously with his own father and saw me as the stereotypic Zionist Jew. I did not want to answer him directly because it seemed important to hear out his fantasy about me. At the time I felt deeply wounded by his remarks, but they also helped me to see the level of the wound in his relationship to his father who, similarly, had attacked him in his childhood. We were able to work analytically on this issue, and I am grateful that we both could stand the tension. Again, my own Jungian analysis and Jung's attitude toward the psyche, as I had learned it, helped me to remain analytic under this kind of pressure.

Another consideration is that a Jew may have an expression of the transference different from many others, having to do with a difference in the relationship to the land. The Jews have a long history of being uprooted from the land. As a compensation they have developed a tendency to focus on relations in the family. This tendency makes the transference more intense, personal, and long-lasting. Such a marginality was completely alien to Jung, a Swiss, who was thoroughly rooted in the land of his ancestors.

Obviously, there are other aspects to this multi-level issue but, with respect to the differences between Freud and Jung, this observation can contribute some understanding. Although both men realized the critical nature of the transference, the relative amount of time spent on it during analysis was quite different. For Freud, it was the fulcrum of the work, whereas Jung wanted to discuss and interpret it as little as possible.

Where Jung's alleged anti-Semitism does become an issue for me is in teaching and other public situations. The question often arises: what about Jung and his anti-Semitism? We cannot change a long history of bitterness between Psychoanalysts and Analytical Psychologists. What to do with this question? First, one can offer the personal fact that there were many Jewish people who worked with Jung during those difficult times of the 1930s and 1940s. Second, Jung's concepts of archetypes and the collective unconscious are not racially or nationalistically bound; Jung was talking about universals in humankind. Third, The attacks on Jung and his alleged anti-Semitism are a way to discount his theories so that one does not have to read him. Fourth, Analytical

Psychology is no longer the work of only one person; one should study the field and not the personalities.

There are cycles about this issue; every generation needs to work it through anew. There is no one piece of incontrovertible evidence that is going to settle the matter once and for all. It is almost all hearsay evidence. The Analytical Psychology Club in Zurich had a quota in 1944, but so did many other institutions at that time. The quota limited Jews, but it did not exclude them. Also, we do not know exactly what Jung's own role in this provision was. We are left with hints that Jung did not exhibit exemplary behavior toward Jews. I do not think he liked the law-giving aspect of Judaism, and he only became aware of its mystical traditions late in his life.

In any case, we are left with this shadowy aspect of Jung's life and, as time goes on, it becomes harder to ascertain what is fact and what is fiction. We should only worry if there is some reason to believe that Jung's theories and practice had some racist leanings. That is not the case. In the meantime we are left with the legacy of Jung the man.

REFERENCE

Boe, John (1989). Pleasing and agreeable: An interview with John Freeman. *San Francisco Jung Institute Library Journal*, *8*-4, 75-84.

Jung and Anti-Semitism

Adolf Guggenbühl-Craig
Zurich, Switzerland
Schweizerische Gesellschaft für
Analytische Psychologie

The foci of our discussion about Jung and anti-Semitism seem to be the credibility of Jungian ideas and the injuries that we have suffered from Jung's darker side. I may be the wrong person to talk about this topic, because Jung never injured me nor did he disappoint me.

Why was that? In 1943, when I was 20 years old, I started to read Jung. My father challenged me: "Why are you interested in that man? Don't you know he is an anti-Semite? At that time I had the same political ideas as my father. For us both anti-Semitism was *the* crime. We knew that the Germans had begun to exterminate the Jews. This fact was so shocking to me that I started to learn Yiddish – a feeble attempt to honor the threatened Jewish people. But I continued, in spite of my father, to read Jung.

The opinions of my father about Jung were not original. He never read Jung; his psychological hero was Freud. The ideas he had about Jung were shared by a large number of Swiss who saw in Hitler's Germany a deadly danger for Switzerland and the whole liberal democratic world.

Later when, as a psychiatrist, I joined the Jungians, my father was very disappointed. He could never understand how I could betray my family and myself in joining this, for him, half-fascistic crowd. Hence, to use James Hillman's language (p. 77ff of these Proceedings), I was never a white – innocent – Jungian; I was "yellow" from the beginning.

Nevertheless, the topic interests me. How do the dark sides of Jung affect us, as Christians and as Jews – or whatever? The dark sides of Jung should not affect us at all. For us – the second generation Jungians – the dark side of Jung is a pseudo-issue, a non-event. If it affects us nevertheless, then there is something wrong with us. We must examine ourselves to find out what.

But first, let us turn to Jung. As far as I can see, Jung was certainly anti-Semitic, but in a less ideological, conscious, yet deeper way than Andrew Samuels explained in his foregoing paper. Every country in Europe, with the exception of Italy, was anti-Semitic in the last century – and in the centuries before that, and in this century. Anti-Semitism was and is part of the collective mythology, originating from the Christian religion; the Jews were considered to be the killers of Jesus Christ.

Jung was a psychological genius. He was also an average "middle class" man, a bourgeois, with all the mythological beliefs, images and ideas this class had. Anti-Semitism was – and partially still is – the darker side of this mythology. There are many bright sides too: ideas of freedom, justice, decency, honesty, social justice, and democracy. The anti-Semitism of Jung was a sheer banality of the collective he belonged to.

Jung was an ordinary middle-class man in other ways, positive and negative. He was, for instance, an appeaser: don't make the beast angry; don't anger Hitler. Again, this was a collective attitude. Until 1939 Europe was dominated by appeasers. Remember British Prime Minister Neville Chamberlain's "Peace in our time" after the Munich conference with Hitler, at which Chamberlain agreed to the partition of Czechoslovakia? Appeasing is not always a mistake; it is one way to deal with the dark forces around us and within us. Heroes have done as much damage – and as much good – as appeasers. In the collective psyche sometimes the appeaser is stronger and sometimes the hero is.

Jung was intellectual, again in a very collective way. Intellectuals are inclined to admire power. Hundreds of European intellectuals paid homage to Stalin, while he was walking knee-deep in the blood of Russian peasants. The intellectuals admired even his macabre purges. While Mao was killing millions of Chinese farmers, many intellectuals praised him as a creator of a new and better world. Intellectuals' admiration of power probably is a compensation for their fascination with the spirit. Not all intellectuals are blinded by power; there are always a few individuals who can resist it. But the bulk of them, insofar as they are part of the intellectual collective, are inclined to be attracted by power.

Jung, as a collective intellectual, was fascinated by Hitler and Mussolini. This is not very original. But even the greatest genius can be original only in a small part of the psyche; the bigger part belongs to the collective psyche. And Jung, after the Second World War at least, did not follow the collective craze for the mass-murderers Stalin and Mao.

If we are chagrined, however, by the contradictions in Jung, we are missing some points of Jungian psychology. Jung taught us that human beings are multi-faceted: composed of many archetypes, psychoids, complexes. The different sides may have little to do with each other.

In dealing with my wife, my children, my friends, I have to take all sides into account; with Jung I do not. Jung was not my friend. His contradictory sides may have been a problem for his analysands, but his aura was so overpowering that often their critical faculties melted away and slipped into an eternal happy glorification of the master. We Jungians today have to listen to his genius; the rest should be of no interest to us.

But we still have to ask: Why is this disappointment so widespread among us Jungians? We all have a deep need for a perfect leader, a saint, someone who guides us, a guru. Even though we are psychologists and know about archetypes, we still are not conscious of that longing for the messiah or for the second coming of Christ. We are disappointed, then, when Jesus Christ the second appears and, apart from being a genius, proves to be a very average collective human being.

I must confess that I was very disturbed a few years ago, when it came to be known that, during the War, the statutes of the Jungian Club in Zurich were changed, to limit the number of Jewish members. This action of the Club – whoever the Club was at that time – is very difficult to understand. It is similar to kicking a dying man in the face. But who wants to throw the first stone?

Thus we can see Jung as the psychological genius on one side, the collective man on the other. But Andrew Samuels raised an important issue in his paper: Is there something inherent in Jungian ideas that could lead to anti-Semitism or to Nazism? That is, in my opinion, the only issue we have to worry about. Yet it has limits. Although Christianity has inherent ideas which led to the burning of thousands of women and men as witches and to pogroms, some of us are still Christians.

Samuels mentioned Jung's fascination with nations, and opined that this fascination is suspicious. Here I have to defend Jung, in view of his psychological genius. Nations are a very impressive psychological phenomenon. It makes no difference if Germany existed officially only after 1871, if the Italians became a nation only in the 19th century, if the British nation is really four nations – England, Scotland, Wales, Northern Ireland. The fact is that in past centuries, millions of people died in Europe and elsewhere for their nation, often voluntarily. And just now the last cohesive colonial empire – the Soviet Union – is being threatened by nationalism. Nations constitute a powerful phenomenon and, like all important psychological phenomena, they cannot be explained; they can only be approached by mythological images.

We all talk about the characteristics of different nations: Italians are emotional, French are rational, Swiss are sober, the English are gentlemen and ladies. This is all pure mythology. I hope that Jung realized this when he talked about Germans, Jews and other peoples. Talk about the characters of nations and peoples is all fantasy. Perhaps Jung was inclined at times to take such fantasies too literally. In Jungian psychology, however, we deal with pure mythological images.

The problem of the different characteristics of groups – nations, women, men – is not whether they are inborn or acquired, but that they are powerful collective phenomena, mysterious, to be understood as mythology. Jung tried to do just that, to understand these powerful phenomena by the collective fantasies and the mythologies behind them.

The collective fantasies of some nations became ill during this century, as we saw in German Nazism. Our job as analysts is to treat psychotics and neurotics, with the help of the insight Analytical Psychology gives us. Our job is not only to talk to analysands about their fancy dreams, or to train candidates to become training analysts for future candidates. When we have analysands with delusions, hallucinations, and horrible perversions, there is no use pointing to reality. First we must "join" the psychopathology of the analysand, accept it, go with the psychopathology. We even must do this half unconsciously, and only when we join and are fascinated can we go further and eventually help the analysand.

Jung, the genius, did exactly that. He let himself be drawn into the collective madness; he was fascinated, but then formulated what happened. His little booklet "Wotan" (CW10) is even today the best, most frightening mythological description of Nazism. All the other explanations, based on economics and sociology, look impoverished compared with the tremendous mythological images by which Jung approached National Socialism.

Jung was in many ways a very average man, but once he was caught by a psychological phenomenon his genius surfaced.

But now you may ask: What can we do when we are attacked from all sides because of the dark side of Jung? To that question I can only answer: If you are afraid of being attacked, don't become analysts or psychotherapists.

We can forget the average man Jung, the collective appeaser, anti-Semite and admirer of power. We have mainly to be inspired by Jung's passion for psychology. I say passion, not detached observation but burning, even self-damaging passion for the human psyche in all its manifestations.

Postlogue

Jerome Bernstein

Responses of participants in the two-day workshop varied widely. There was general acceptance that Jung was at some level anti-Semitic. Although Jung's assistance to specific individual Jewish friends and colleagues was acknowledged, workshop participants accepted as fact that Jung knew about and condoned a quota imposed in 1944 on the number of Jewish members who would be admitted to the Analytical Psychology Club of Zurich.

The continuing controversy within the Jungian community centers on whether Jung's position on anti-Semitism is significant on grounds other than historical interest. Responses ranged widely, on the part of presenters and workshop participants.

Andrew Samuels took the position that, as a community, we must move beyond Jung the man and focus on what we as Analytical Psychologists can do to prevent such bigotry. Guggenbühl-Craig's presentation did much to accomplish Samuels' purpose by grounding Jung in his *petit bourgeois* humanity and in his human shadow.

However, Guggenbühl's position was troubling for a number of participants. Is silence on the part of a great healer of no import, when an individual looks him in the eye and says, "Your actions hurt me," as did Erich Neumann repeatedly in his correspondence with Jung? Is it inconsequential that the world's view of Jung's work is affected because many people cannot get beyond Jung's shadow to his body of thought? Is moral consciousness an essential ingredient in healing a wounded psyche and in the development of human thought, particularly as it regards Jungian thought and approaches to healing?

The workshop concluded on a theme of "opposites." The very last response in the meeting was that of John Beebe of San Francisco. He stated his conviction that seeking some act of atonement from the Analytical Psychology Club of Zurich, regarding the quota put on Jewish membership in the Club during the period ending in 1950, is essential for moving forward and for healing. Beebe's position suggests that not only the integrity of Jung, but our own integrity as a community of Jungian analysts, makes a difference. His suggestion was met with approbation.

It was decided that the chairman of the workshop would write to Alfred Ribi, a Zurich analyst who is current President of the Analytical Psychology Club there, for a clarification and any appropriate gesture of atonement. This correspondence is to be reported in the IAAP annual newsletter.

Closing Address: Reflections on Relationships within the IAAP

Hans Dieckmann
Berlin, Germany
President, IAAP

My first contact with the IAAP was in 1962 at its Second International Congress, in Zurich. The IAAP was still a very small group; all the members knew each other personally. There were already some tensions and conflicts in the group but in general the atmosphere was relaxed and agreeable. This atmosphere contrasted with some neo-Freudian associations that I had come to know. That Congress was the first time that I felt familiar with the Jungian colleagues and the world of ideas that they personified; this feeling has not left me.

I am the first president who was not among the founders of the IAAP, but I am the last president who participated in this uroboric-incestuous spirit of pioneers, in which groups in different countries each emerged around a single personality – a great mother or father figure. These groups were then gradually developing from *prima materia* to *nigredo, albedo* and, when everything worked out well, even to *rubedo*.

It is 18 years now that I have been an IAAP officer. When I began I was still relatively young and had given only two Congress lectures. Therefore I was quite surprised when I was elected to take an office. I won over Tom Kirsch, who will now succeed me. During these years I have learned a great deal. I have also found many good friends throughout the world; this has been the most precious experience for me. I have made enemies too; that goes with the job. Today I speak about the enormous changes in our Association that are still taking place. These changes concern the nature of the international and national groups but also the relationships among all the members – as fits the subject of our Congress.

Whenever a new field of science develops, those who are interested in it form groups. They come together to exchange ideas, beginning with those of a spiritual founder such as C. G. Jung. At first the group is small. Its members may live in the same city or they can be scattered all over the world. All the members are highly motivated and fascinated by the new ideas. They become steeped in this new field of science and discover a great deal. Just think of the first generation that gathered around the two great founders, Freud and Jung.

Now one is tempted to say with resignation, "Everything of importance in the field of the unconscious has already been discovered and all that is left for us is to review their great discoveries and to rework them. It is only now and then that one of us can succeed in finding a pearl that has been overlooked or forgotten by the founders." Yet we continue to make discoveries.

In the initial group the members are connected by Eros, along with some tensions of power and competition. If they are dealing with an important discovery that may change the consciousness of humankind, a larger group will develop. This process leads to the formation of groups in various localities. They emphasize different aspects of the work and have different goals.

In our case it became apparent quite quickly that to occupy oneself with the human psyche one needs a careful training, as had been done in medicine and psychology. This need was proven by many failures that occurred in the beginning, some of them even tragic ones. Today, with our greater knowledge, we can avoid most such failures, many of which were due to countertransference problems. For this and other reasons Jung, very early, insisted that a thorough personal analysis is absolutely necessary for each analyst. The personal analysis has remained the basis of our training.

But every training has both a positive side and a shadow side.

Training tends to become more and more specialized. At the 1983 Congress in Jerusalem it became apparent that we have two great schools of thinking: the "symbolists" and the "clinicians." Although the two groups were doing many of the same things, they had different emphases. As a result the training programs diverged. Someone who wishes to become a member of another group or to continue training in another country has to deal not only with getting acquainted with another mentality and a foreign country but also to go through a complicated initiation.

Thus far our training requirements, as laid down in the constitution of our International Association, are relatively flexible. Of course we require a profound knowledge of C. G. Jung's Analytical Psychology. But in the number of hours of personal analysis, hours of practical work with analysands, and hours with control analysts, we are at the lower limit compared to other analytic schools.

Although we have become a big organization we have not developed a rigid administration. We do not even have strict basic positions, as other organizations have, by which one must be sworn in order to be accepted as a Jungian Analyst. At one of the very first international congresses we tried to find some such definitions. After long and heated debates an overwhelming majority turned down the proposal to establish such guidelines for our members. I hope that such guidelines will never be adopted.

Over the years I have been involved in a large number of associations, organizations, institutions, and projects during their establishment. Time and again I have seen that two principles conflict with each other after a short time. According to the subject of our Congress I call these the "principle of relationship" and the "principle of structure." Both are useful and necessary when people come together for a certain purpose. But sooner or later these principles conflict with each other. We, as Jungians, tend to see the first principle as related to the archetype of the mother and the second to the archetype of the father. One represents the creativity of the eternal transformation and creation, the other the eternal and stable order and structure. Chaos and anarchy develop if the first principle negates the other. But if the second one prevails, the organization becomes rigid and turns into dictatorship.

Throughout these decades I have had the impression that we as Jungians are much more attracted by the first principle. We seem to have a certain preference for the fertility of the chaos; in our system of thought there are still many gaps. And instead of filling them ourselves – which would be better for us – we far too often borrow from the Freudians.

Jung pointed to these very gaps in a lecture he gave at the inaugural meeting of the C. G. Jung Institute in Zurich on the 24th of April, 1948. He said: "In the medical and clinical field there is a dearth of fully-elaborated case histories" (CW18, par. 1138). I suggest that this work should be based on a general and specific theory of neurosis. Jung continued: "In normal psychology, the most important subjects for research would be the psychic structure of the family in relation to heredity, the compensatory character of marriage and of emotional relationships in general. A particularly pressing problem is the behavior of the individual in the mass and the unconscious compensation to which this gives rise" (CW18, par. 1139).

We still hold in relatively low esteem some of the matters Jung mentioned in that lecture, especially experimental and statistical work. But some of the other gaps have been filled: research on dreams, the analyses of the paranoid – which today we call borderline – and the collection of dreams in emotionally-charged situations.

I like the relationship approach better than the structural because I have experienced much too often the suffocation of creativity in compulsory structures. Hence, I do not like the fear of setting certain precedents in our organization. We must go on admitting to our Association especially talented, productive and creative persons who may not fulfill our strict and severe requirements of training to the last detail. If we stop admitting such persons we will become petrified in mediocrity. We need to risk sometimes admitting disturbed and non-conformist people. As Lao-tzu said, high belongs to low and you cannot get one without the other. I am aware of the fact that today there are many groups which need to get legal recognition. These groups need detailed and elaborate guidelines for training, which must be fulfilled in detail. But we must keep in mind also that we profit by maintaining a certain independence. I quote again Jung's 1948 lecture: "It is the prerogative of an institution with limited means, and not run by the State, to produce work of high quality in order to survive" (CW18, par. 1141).

Our Congress has been dealing with the subject of relationships. It is a truism that one talks about the matters that cause problems. When arranging the program for the Congress I noticed with pleasure that we escaped the prevalent craze over borderlines. Also, narcissism is mentioned in only one lecture title. Most of the topics refer to general, deeper problems of transference and countertransference.

There may be three reasons that today there is so much talk about relationships and the difficulties in having relationships as well as about this border area between neurosis and psychosis that we call borderline. On the one hand it may be caused by the fact that our world hardly permits significant relationships. The population has increased enormously, especially during this last century. People have become more mobile and less settled. We change not only our residence, jobs and vacation plans, but also our friends, mates and spouses more often and more rapidly than the generations before us. But relationships have something in common with trust; both are plants that grow slowly and need continuous care to be genuine and strong enough for survival in difficult times. Unfortunately this necessary care is something for which most of us have neither time nor opportunity. Perhaps we try to establish relationships artificially with our often very long analyses and group activities. And some people really do travel from one of these group activities to another because they have hardly any private relationships.

A second reason can be seen in the power of fashion or – to use a more refined word – trends, which do not spare science. During the many years in which I have been active as an analyst there has always been some form of psychic disease that was the center of attention for a particular time, and formed the subject of our congresses and publications. At different times we dealt with compulsion neuroses, depressions, addictions, psychosomatic diseases and psychoses. Now, it is the turn of the deep disorders which derive from early childhood and cause problems in the capacity to have significant relationships.

The third reason for the emphasis on relationships may be found in a genuine enlargement of our knowledge. In the course of almost 100 years we have collected a great deal of analytic experience and improved our theoretical knowledge. We are gaining more and more knowledge about the human psyche. As we work on different symptoms and phenomena of transference and countertransference and observe the course the different therapies take, we reach deeper levels that had been ignored because they were not known. Even though Jung's approach to the collective unconscious and the psychoid reached into the deepest levels of the human soul, it was like a drill-hole that went through all layers of the psyche. It is our task to uncover and explore the layers in all their particularities.

Another problem is that all vital sciences venture into new fields that are not yet explored. In doing so one runs the risk of putting forward some unproven but provocative hypotheses. It is of no use to confine ourselves to verifying, interpreting and working on the system of the founder. We would be in danger of coming to resemble a religion, with its truths of revelation or mummy-worship. It is of greatest importance that we take seriously attempts of our members to explore new fields, even though other members might be very opposed to each innovation. We must try to integrate new ideas into the vital process of the individuation of Analytical Psychology – unless of course we face a real charlatanism. I am thinking especially of the work of Erich Neumann, Michael Fordham and, more recently, James Hillman with his Archetypal Psychology. I remember very well the conflict between Zurich and London about Fordham's concepts, which are now generally accepted. There is always much that one may not like in the theoretical system of another person; for me this is the case with Archetypal Psychology. But I must admit that I have learned a great deal from this theory and from my friend James Hillman. And I will always lend my support to maintaining this world of ideas in our society.

But I also think of all those colleagues who – in spite of Jung's disapproval – introduced group therapy, family therapy and therapy with persons from the poorer classes into Analytical Psychology. In 1946 Jung wrote in a letter to UNESCO that his psychology could only be understood by a relatively small group of very educated persons and could be applied only to them. Those persons had to convey the insight they had gained to the stupid masses and become their leaders. I find this to be a very dangerous and elitist remark which he should not have made. And it is just not true. Many German colleagues treat patients who are less educated, and have had a valuable experience. I have published some such cases. We cannot just follow Jung in everything even though he would turn in his grave if he knew about some of the changes Analytical Psychology has made since his time. But he would be in good company; Newton would do the same if he knew that today we consider his beautiful laws of falling bodies only as a high statistical probability.

In his farewell speech in Jerusalem my predecessor, Adolf Guggenbühl, very rightly pointed out that the splits in our group have to be understood symbolically. He said that in each group a number of persons are seized by the archetype of the "Holy Saints;" they must be the custodians of truth. He also described, in a convincing manner, how we separate from one another more and more when we use a purely clinical method. It is much easier to understand each other and the archetypal background on the symbolic level.

The Jerusalem Congress (1983) focused on symbols and clinics and the Berlin Congress (1986) was about shadow and shadow projections, including those onto each other. Evidently they taught us something; the second part of my presidency was much less characterized by conflicts among the different groups. We were much more occupied with the constructive work of helping the many new groups to form a stable basis.

Our present Congress has dealt with the subject of relationship. I prefer to understand the problems of the International

Association – which I have been discussing – as a more or less successful interaction of two great archetypal constellations of which the Holy Saints are only a very small part. One of these constellations is the mother archetype with its positive elementary and transformation character in which the archetypal "child," Analytical Psychology, can flourish, grow and prosper under the care of the Eros principle. The other is the father archetype which can provide us with the necessary structure to survive in this world and to help in making it a little better. In view of our ecological situation – a cause for great concern – it is obvious that a new consciousness is needed for this world to survive. Perhaps we can help to turn the power principle, which forms the background of the exploitation of Nature, into a relationship principle, Eros.

To conclude I emphasize that in spite of all the time, money and nerves I invested in this work for the International Association I have truly enjoyed the work. When I now pass it over to my successor I have mixed feelings of relief and regret. With all my heart I wish for him and our whole organization that the work will be as satisfactory and enjoyable for him as it was for me.

Index

THE PREVIOUS CONGRESS PROCEEDINGS:

JERUSALEM 1983

Symbolic and Clinical Approaches
in Theory and Practice
edited by Luigi Zoja
and Robert Hinshaw
375 pgs, hardbound, illustrations
ISBN 3-85630-504-1

This handsome volume, drawn from the Ninth International Congress of Analytical Psychology in Jerusalem, contains contributions from 25 prominent Jungian analysts from around the world. Among the authors are Alfred Ziegler and Adolph Guggenbühl-Craig from Zurich, Rafael López-Pedraza from Caracas, and Aldo Carotenuto from Rome. The essays reflect on the meaning and significance of contemporary analytical work.

BERLIN 1986

The Archetype of Shadow
in a Split World
edited by Mary Ann Mattoon
456 pgs., paper and hardbound,
numerous pictures and diagrams
ISBN (Paperback) 3-85630-506-8
ISBN (Hardbound) 3-85630-514-9

The Tenth International Congress of Analytical Psychology was held in West Berlin September 2-9, 1986. Its theme, **The Archetype of Shadow in a Split World,** was the focus of 25 major papers, with prepared responses to 14 of them. Congress participants were several hundred Jungian analysts.

The papers comprising these proceedings are available not only as a whole in bound volumes, but also as separate offprints. For further information please write to Daimon Press in Switzerland

Heinrich Karl Fierz

JUNGIAN PSYCHIATRY

Foreword by C.T. Frey-Wehrlin
Preface by Joseph Wheelwright
illustrations and index
430 pages; paper
ISBN 3-85630-521-1

This newly translated book is the life work of the well-known psychiatrist and co-founder of the renowned Jungian "Klinik am Zürichberg" in Switzerland. From the contents: Meaning in Madness / The Attitude of the Doctor in Psychotherapy / Psychological-Psychiatric Diagnosis and Therapy / Psychotherapy in the Treatment of Depression.

Verena Kast

SISYPHUS

The old Stone, a new Way
A Jungian Approach to Midlife Crisis
ca. 130 pages, paper,
ISBN 3-85630-527-0

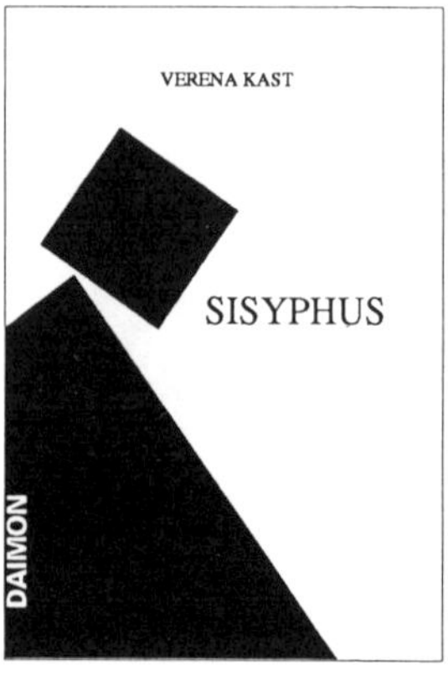

Verena Kast refers to Sisyphus as the "myth of the forty-year-olds," who often experience their lot in life to be a Sisyphus task. Are our human efforts all in vain, or is there some meaning to be found? In the end it is a struggle with death itself.

Verena Kast deals with a problem that also fascinated Nietzsche and Freud. ... This book is packed with down-to-earth experience, clinical anecdotes, wit and insight.

Murray Stein

Susan Bach – *Life Paints its Own Span*

E.A. Bennet – *Meetings with Jung*

George Czuczka – *Imprints of the Future*

Heinrich Karl Fierz – *Jungian Psychiatry*

von Franz / Frey-Rohn / Jaffé – *What is Death?*

Liliane Frey-Rohn – *Friedrich Nietzsche*

Aniela Jaffé – *The Myth of Meaning*
– *Was C.G. Jung a Mystic?*
– *From the Life und Work of C.G. Jung*
– *Death Dreams and Ghosts*

Siegmund Hurwitz – *Lilith – The First Eve*

Verena Kast – *A Time to Mourn*
– *Sisyphus*

James Kirsch – *The Reluctant Prophet*

Rivkah Schärf Kluger – *The Gilgamesh Epic*

Rafael López-Pedraza – *Hermes and his Children*
– *Cultural Anxiety*

Alan McGlashan – *The Savage and Beautiful Country*

Gitta Mallasz (Transcription) – *Talking with Angels*

C.A. Meier – *Healing Dream and Ritual*
– *A Testament to the Wilderness*

Laurens van der Post – *A «Festschrift»*

Available from your bookstore or from our distributors:

In the United States:
The Great Tradition
11270 Clayton Creek Road
Lower Lake, CA 95457
Tel. (707) 995-3906
Fax: (707) 995-1814

Chiron Publications
400 Linden Avenue
Wilmette, IL 60091
Tel. (708) 256-7551
Fax: (708) 256-2202

In Great Britain:
Element Books Ltd.
Longmead, Shaftesbury
Dorset SP7 8PL, England
Tel. (747) 51339
Fax: (747) 51394

Worldwide:
Daimon Verlag
Hauptstrasse 85
CH-8840 Einsiedeln Switzerland
Tel. (41)(55) 532266
Fax (41)(55) 532231